THE PAPERS
OF
JOHN MARSHALL

Sponsored by
The College of William and Mary
and
The Institute of Early American History and Culture
under the auspices of
The National Historical Publications and Records
Commission

The Great Seal Die of the United States,
engraved by Robert Scot in 1782.
Courtesy of the National Archives.

THE PAPERS

OF

JOHN MARSHALL

Volume IV

Correspondence and Papers, January 1799—October 1800

CHARLES T. CULLEN, *Editor*

LESLIE TOBIAS, *Assistant Editor*

The University of North Carolina Press, Chapel Hill
in association with the
Institute of Early American History and Culture
Williamsburg, Virginia

The Institute of Early American History and Culture
is sponsored jointly by The College of William and Mary in Virginia
and The Colonial Williamsburg Foundation

© *1984 The University of North Carolina Press*
All rights reserved
Manufactured in the United States of America
Set in Monophoto Baskerville by Oliver Burridge and Company Ltd.
ISBN 0–8078–1586–1
Library of Congress Catalog Card Number 74–9575

The ornament on the title page is based upon John Marshall's personal seal, as it appears on a gold watch fob that also bears the seal of his wife, Mary Willis Marshall. It was drawn by Richard J. Stinely of Williamsburg, Virginia, from the original, now owned by the Association for the Preservation of Virginia Antiquities, Richmond, Virginia, and is published with the owner's permission.

Library of Congress Cataloging in Publication Data

Marshall, John, 1755–1835.
  The papers of John Marshall.
  Vol. 2 edited by C. T. Cullen and H. A. Johnson.
  "Sponsored by the College of William and Mary and the Institute of Early American History and Culture under the auspices of the National Historical Publications Commission."
  Includes bibliographical references and indexes.
  CONTENTS: v. 1. Correspondence and papers, November 10, 1775–June 23, 1788. Account book, September 1783–June 1788.—v. 2. Correspondence and papers, July 1788–December 1795. Account book, July 1788–December 1795.—[etc.]—v. 4. Correspondence and papers, January 1799–October 1800.
  1. Marshall, John, 1755–1835. 2. Statesmen—United States—Correspondence. 3. Judges—United States—Correspondence. 4. United States—Politics and government—Revolution, 1775–1783. 5. United States—Politics and government—1783–1865. I. Johnson, Herbert Alan, ed. II. Cullen, Charles T., 1940–   ed. III. Institute of Early American History and Culture (Williamsburg, Va.)
E302.M365   347.73'2634 [347.3073534]   74–9575
ISBN 0–8078–1233–1 (v. 1)
ISBN 0–8078–1302–8 (v. 2)
ISBN 0–8078–1337–0 (v. 3)
ISBN 0–8078–1586–1 (v. 4)

Dedicated to
MARY DOUTHAT HIGGINS,
whose friendship and support has enriched
The Papers of John Marshall

The publication of this volume has been assisted by special grants from the Association for the Preservation of Virginia Antiquities, the William Branch Cabell Foundation, the National Endowment for the Humanities, the John Ben Snow Foundation, and the Windsor Foundation.

CONTENTS

January 1799—October 1800

1799

FOREWORD

This is the first volume of John Marshall's papers in which a majority of the documents presented were generated as a direct result of political offices Marshall held in the nation's capital. Government paperwork, even in the eighteenth century, was relatively voluminous. The large number of documents from Marshall's term in the Sixth Congress indicates that he held a pivotal position in the first session and was involved in and contributed to most of the important business to come before the House of Representatives. Much of this material has never been identified as Marshall's, and for that reason the editors have presented it as fully as documents from earlier, more obscure, periods of Marshall's life.

Documents from Marshall's tenure as secretary of state are quite different in nature from those produced during his service in Congress. Many of the State Department documents received little attention from him, even though he signed them or they arrived addressed to him. The number of documents that can be identified as Marshall's from May 1800 when he became secretary of state to March 1801 when he left that office to join the Supreme Court alone constitute approximately one-third of the entire corpus of his papers. Printing or summarizing all of these papers would give readers a comprehensive view of the affairs of the State Department in 1800, but this wealth of material would not tell the reader much about John Marshall as secretary. The editors have therefore decided to print only selected documents. A reading of all of the materials passing through that office from the time Marshall was appointed until he turned it over to James Madison shows that Marshall was closely involved in only a few public issues: negotiations with the British over article six of the Jay Treaty; the Barbary pirates; the negotiation with the French for a new treaty; impressments; and implementation of the Pinckney Treaty with Spain. These were the foreign affairs with which he concerned himself; to most of the routine consular dispatches Marshall gave little personal attention. The editors have therefore economized on space by excluding from the volume most consular dispatches. However, a list of all that have been identified is printed as an appendix in order to provide a reference for those who want to make a more detailed study of Marshall's tenure than this text will allow.

Another small problem presented by the documents in this volume concerns the incongruity created in the sequence of letters when strict chronological order is followed. Near the end of the group of documents that relate to the first session of the Sixth Congress readers will encounter correspondence to Marshall from Rufus King in London or from John Quincy Adams in Berlin. These letters were addressed to the secretary of state, and although the writers believed they were writing to Timothy Pickering, John Marshall held the office when the letters arrived, in some cases months after they were written, and it was he who read and responded to them. Printing them in strict chronological order interrupts the sequence of letters related to activities in Congress, but the problem did not seem to the editors to be great enough to justify a deviation from the general policy of following chronological order.

The responsibilities of the State Department for domestic affairs were numerous in 1800. In addition to granting patents, copyrights, and passports, the secretary of state conducted the census, recorded land patents, distributed the laws of the United States, supervised the territories, prepared and delivered all commissions and appointments, and administered the federal judicial system. During the 1790s the secretary also helped coordinate the work of the commissioners of the District of Columbia as they prepared the new capital for the government's move from Philadelphia. The editors have included samples of documents to illustrate the variety of duties that the secretary handled, but we have made no attempt to be comprehensive. Strictly routine requests from Marshall to the secretary of the Treasury for the issuance of bank drafts have been omitted, as have other relatively inconsequential documents of an official nature. Our goal has been to print those documents that show Marshall's effect on the office and its effect on him. Marshall's brief tenure as secretary of state was historically important, as the material presented here will establish. The documents from the Sixth Congress together with those from Marshall's tenure as secretary of state illuminate the national role being played by this former regional figure and make more understandable John Adams's selection of him to lead the judicial branch of government in the wake of the elections of 1800.

For special assistance in editing the documents in this volume, the editors wish to thank Mr. Paul Gay of the University of Pennsylvania

Law School Library, who provided generous access to that institution's rare book collection. Trudi M. Heyer assisted in proofreading many of the transcripts of documents and typed all of the annotation and calendar entries. Her cheerful and excellent work has contributed greatly to the completion of this volume. Finally, the editors wish to express their appreciation to the Association for the Preservation of Virginia Antiquities, the William Branch Cabell Foundation, the National Endowment for the Humanities, the John Ben Snow Foundation, and the Windsor Foundation for special grants in support of this editorial project. The editors wish also to express special thanks to the project's two sponsoring institutions, The College of William and Mary and the Institute of Early American History and Culture, for their continuing support, and to the National Historical Publications and Records Commission for its constant encouragement.

EDITORIAL APPARATUS

In accordance with modern editorial standards, the editors have attempted to render the text of documents as faithfully as possible. However, the editors have established and consistently applied certain guidelines in transcribing the documents. Each sentence begins with a capital letter and ends with a period, a question mark, or an exclamation point. All dashes at the end of sentences and paragraphs have been silently omitted except for those that appear on previously printed documents that are reproduced here. In all cases superscript letters have been lowered to the line. The ampersand (&) has been retained, and the tailed p (ꝑ) has been rendered as either "pro" or "per," depending on the context in which it appears in the original.

The format and typography of each letter and document have been standardized. The dateline, which indicates the place and date of composition, has been set at the top of the document flush with the right margin. Should a letter bear a dispatch number or the designation "private," or both, these have been placed at the left margin above the salutation. The salutation has been set flush with the left margin on the same line as the dateline and has been rendered in capital and lowercase letters, except in the case of previously printed documents, where the original typography has been followed. The complimentary close has been run in with the text of the letter, with commas marking the end of a line. The signatures to letters have been set flush with the right margin and have been rendered in large and small capital letters. However, where the editors have not examined the original signature or have no reason to believe that the signature on a previously edited document was copied from an original signature, the signature has been rendered as it appears in the text being copied. This usually occurs in the case of printed documents for which the original manuscript copy and all contemporary copies and later transcripts from the original manuscript have been lost. Acknowledgments or jurats to documents have been brought to the left margin, as have the signatures of witnesses or notaries. Postscripts have also been placed flush with the left margin, regardless of their position on the original.

For each document and calendared synopsis the editors have composed a heading that provides a brief key to the nature of the document. These headings are designed solely to assist the reader in identifying particular classes of documents. Letters are identified by the name of the individual who wrote to John Marshall or by the name of the person to whom Marshall wrote. Documents other than letters, both printed and calendared, are usually identified by the category of the document, such as "Petition," "Speech," or "Legislative Bill." For printed or calendared legal documents the heading includes not only the category of the document but also the title of the case.

Where interpolation has become necessary, the editors have been sparing and cautious in their exercise of imagination. Omitted letters have been inserted only when necessary to preserve the meaning of a word. If the meaning of a word was clear, although some letters may have been illegible or missing because of mutilation, up to four missing letters have been supplied without the use of brackets; more than four missing letters in a word have been inserted in roman type within square brackets ([ ]) and, if necessary, the editors have explained the insertion in a footnote. Where more than one word was missing, or the text was supplied conjecturally, this material has been inserted in italic type within square brackets. Where material in a manuscript text appears to have been inserted through a slip of the author's pen, the editors have followed the text and explained the error in a footnote. Obvious typographical errors in printed matter that are more likely the compositor's rather than the author's mistakes have been silently corrected.

Matter deleted by the writer has usually been omitted from the text as printed in this edition except when the editors believe that the deletion is sufficiently significant to justify an exception to this policy. In such cases the canceled word or passage has been placed *before* the material that replaced it and enclosed in angle brackets (⟨ ⟩). A deletion within a deletion has been indicated by double angle brackets (⟪ ⟫), and the preceding rule concerning its placement in the text has been followed.

Coded material has been deciphered and rendered in italic type. The editors have silently corrected obvious coding errors and have explained special problems in footnotes. Words supplied conjecturally within decoded material have been printed in italics within brackets.

ANNOTATION OF DOCUMENTS

While the editors prefer a policy of sparse annotation, they have attempted to give the reader some guidance in interpreting Marshall's papers, including essential explanations and a reasonably complete identification of individuals upon their first mention in the text of the papers. (The volume index facilitates cross-reference to the first mention of a given name or individual.) Biographical references to well-known individuals who are listed in the *Dictionary of American Biography* or the *Dictionary of National Biography* are intentionally brief, and the editors similarly have not expansively discussed individuals of slight importance to Marshall's career or those whose identity is not material to an understanding of the text of the document. Whenever possible, book-length biographies have been cited at the first mention of an individual. When the editors have been unsuccessful in identifying a person mentioned in the text, they upon occasion have advanced a supposition based upon knowledge of Marshall's activities and associations, but in most cases they have chosen to leave it to the reader to speculate upon the identity of an unknown person.

The source of each document is identified in full in the line immediately below its heading. In cases where this description is not adequate, the first footnote gives further information and also identifies the writer or recipient if he has not been previously identified. In the case of a particularly delicate problem of documentary analysis, there is, of course, no substitute for seeing the original document, but the editors believe that their annotation policy reduces to a minimum the researcher's need to consult the original documents.

In preparing calendared synopses of documents the editors have tried to summarize concisely the contents of the manuscript or printed source. The synopsis generally includes a notation concerning John Marshall's connection with the document, and an attempt has been made to identify individuals mentioned in the synopsis. Additional details, if available, have been given in footnotes, but these have been kept to a minimum. Synopses dealing with Marshall's law practice include, if possible, sufficient information for the reader to identify the case involved, the nature of the litigation, and the court that heard the case.

Many routine government documents, such as consular dispatches to the secretary of state, have been listed in an appendix to the volume. In addition, routine legal documents written or signed by John Marshall are listed at the end of each month, with a description of the document and its present location.

When a document or group of documents has required more extended discussion than could be conveniently included in a footnote, an editorial note has been added immediately preceding the document to which it pertains. Although these notes frequently are extensive discussions, they obviously are limited in scope to a consideration of the basic document and the situation that gave rise to the documentary material. The notes also contain editorial commentary about interpretive difficulties that have arisen concerning the paper or papers being edited.

ABBREVIATIONS AND SHORT TITLES

The editors have tried to avoid ambiguous abbreviations and have made short titles in citations sufficiently complete to permit ease in bibliographic reference. The following lists contain, first, explanations of abbreviations that may not be readily understood and that have a special meaning in this series and, second, full citations for short titles that are used frequently throughout this volume. Generally accepted abbreviations, such as months of the year, have not been listed, nor have short titles that occur in a limited section of the volume. The latter can easily be expanded by going to the first reference to a work in each document or editorial note, where a full citation is provided.

ABBREVIATIONS

AD   Autograph Document
ADS   Autograph Document Signed
AL   Autograph Letter
ALS   Autograph Letter Signed
DS   Document Signed
LS   Letter Signed

SHORT TITLES

Amer. State Papers   Walter Lowrie *et al.*, eds., *American State Papers. Documents, Legislative and Executive, of the Congress of the United States* . . . , 38 vols. (Washington, D.C., 1832–1861). This short title will be followed by a subtitle describing the category of document and the volume number.

Annals of Congress	[*Annals of the Congress of the United States.*] *Debates and Proceedings in the Congress of the United States, 1789– 1824 . . .* , 42 vols. (Washington, D.C., 1834–1856)
Barbary War Docs., I	(United States. Office of Naval Records and Library.) *Naval Documents Related to the United States Wars with the Barbary Powers: Naval Operations Including Diplomatic Background from 1785 through 1801*, I (Washington, D.C., 1939)
Carter, ed., *Terr. Papers*	Clarence Edwin Carter, ed., *The Territorial Papers of the United States*, 28 vols. (Washington, D.C., 1934– 1975). This short title will be followed by the name of the territory.
King, ed., *Life and Corres. of Rufus King*, III	Charles R. King, ed., *The Life and Correspondence of Rufus King . . .* , III (New York, 1896)
Miller, ed., *Treaties*, II	Hunter Miller, ed., *Treaties and Other International Acts of the United States of America*, II (Washington, D.C., 1931)
Quasi-War with France Docs.	(United States. Office of Naval Records and Library.) *Naval Documents Related to the Quasi-War between the United States and France: Naval Operations from February 1797 to December 1801*, 7 vols. (Washington, D.C., 1935–1938)
WMQ	*William and Mary Quarterly*

In addition to the foregoing abbreviations and short titles, the editors have followed the policy of using legal form citations when discussing or citing the reports of cases in courts and statutes passed by legislative bodies in England or the United States. These generally conform to *A Uniform System of Citation*, 11th ed. (Cambridge, Mass.,

1967), adopted for use by several law reviews. All other legal citations follow the Institute of Early American History and Culture's *Style Sheet for Authors*, with the following exception:

Stat.   *Statutes at Large of the United States of America, 1789–1873* (Boston, 1845–1873)

MARSHALL CHRONOLOGY

January 1799–October 1800

ca. April 21, 1799	Elected to Sixth Congress.
July–August 1799	Visited parents in Kentucky.
October 9, 1799	Admitted to practice in Winchester District Court.
December 1799–May 8, 1800	Attended Sixth Congress.
May 7, 1800	Nominated secretary of war.
May 9, 1800	Senate approved appointment as secretary of war.
May 12, 1800	Nominated secretary of state.
May 13, 1800	Senate approved appointment as secretary of state.
June 5–8, 1800	Traveled to Washington to assume office.
ca. July 3–15, 1800	Visited Richmond.
ca. September 27– *ca.* October 22, 1800	Visited Richmond.

CORRESPONDENCE AND PAPERS

January 1799—October 1800

To George Washington

ALS, Sparks Papers, Harvard University

Dear Sir   Richmond, January 8, 1799

I had the pleasure of receiving your letter of the 30th. of Decr. while Genl. Pinckney was at this place & of delivering to him the packet it inclos'd.[1] He left us with the ladies of his family on the 4th. in health & spirits.

I thank you for the charge of Judge Addison;[2] 'tis certainly well written & I wish that as well as some other publications on the same subject coud be more generally read I beleive that no argument can moderate the leaders of the opposition—but it may be possible to make some impression on the mass of the people. For this purpose the charge of Judge Addison seems well calculated. I shall forward it to Mr. Washington.[3]

However I may regret the passage of one of the acts complaind of, I am firmly persuaded that the tempest has not been raised by them. Its cause lies much deeper & is not easily to be removed. Had they never pass'd, other measures woud have been selected which woud have been attackd with equal virulence. The misfortune is that an act operating on the press in any manner, affords to its opposers arguments which so captivate the public ear, which so mislead the public mind that the efforts of reason to correct false impressions will often fail of success.

Two very interesting subjects have during the present session peculiarly engag'd the attention of the legislature. The first was a paper produc'd by Colo. Taylor of Caroline, & which you must have seen, containing resolutions which take advantage of the irritation excited by the alien & sedition laws, to criminate the whole conduct of our administration & charge it with the design of introducing monarchy;[4] the other was a proposition from Mr. George K. Taylor

1. See George Washington to JM, Vol. III, 530–531.

2. Alexander Addison, of Washington County, Pa., a U.S. District Court judge, had published a defense of the Alien and Sedition Acts entitled *Liberty of Speech and of the Press. A charge to the grand juries of the county courts of the Fifth circuit of the state of Pennsylvania* (Washington, Pa., 1798). See Vol. III, 531 n. 2.

3. Bushrod Washington.

4. The resolutions introduced by John Taylor of Caroline were written by James Madison and debated in the Virginia House of Delegates from Dec. 14 to Dec. 21, 1798. See Ralph Ketcham, *James Madison: A Biography* (New York, 1971). For the debates in the Virginia legislature, see *The Virginia Report of 1799–1800, Touching the Alien and Sedition Laws: Together with the Virginia Resolutions of December 21, 1798, The Debates and Proceedings Thereon in the House of Delegates of Virginia . . .* (Richmond, 1850).

of Prince George expressive of sentiments similar to those which have been declard by other legislatures of the union on our controversy with France, in the place of which was substituted by a majority of twenty nine a counter proposition termd an amendment which was offerd by Colo. Nicholas⁵ of Albemarle & which seems calculated to evince to France & to the world that Virginia is very far from harmonizing with the American government or her sister States.

The debates on these subjects were long & animated. In the course of them sentiments were declard & (in my judgement) views were developed of a very serious & alarming extent. To me it seems that there are men who will hold power by any means rather than not hold it; & who woud prefer a dissolution of the union to the continuance of an administration not of their own party. They will risk all the ills which may result from the most dangerous experiments rather than permit that happiness to be enjoy'd which is dispensd by other hands than their own. It is more than ever essential to make great exertions at the next election, & I am persuaded that by making [*them*]⁶ we obtain a legislature if not foederal, so divided as to be moderate.

I am by no means certain who will be elected for this district. Whatever the issue of the election may be I shall neither reproach my self nor those at whose instance I have become a candidate, for the step I have taken. I feel with increasd force the obligations of duty to make sacrafices & exertions for the preservation of American union & independence, as I am more convinc'd of the reality of the danger which threatens them. The exertions made against me by particular characters throughout this state & even from other States have an activity & a malignancy which no personal considerations woud excite. If I fail I shall regret the failure more on account of the evidence it will afford of the prevalence of a temper hostile to our government & indiscriminately so to all who will not join in that hostility, than of the personal mortification which woud be sustaind. With the most respectful attachment, I remain Sir your obedt.

J MARSHALL

5. Wilson Cary Nicholas.
6. This word was inserted on the manuscript by Jared Sparks, first editor of Washington's papers.

Deeds

Deed Book Copies, Office of the Clerk of Hardy County, Moorefield, W.Va.

[*January 12, 1799* (*Hardy County, Va.*). JM conveys parcels of land in the South Branch Manor to Phoebe Couchman, 81 acres for £20 5s., and to Robert Porter, 86 acres for £30 15s. Both deeds were recorded in the District Court at Hardy County on Feb. 14, 1799.]

To Thomas Posey

ALS, Indiana Historical Society

My dear Sir[7]   Richmond, January 30, 1799

I have to apologize for not having given an earlier answer to your letter by Mr. Dandridge.[8] The truth is that its delivery was postpond for a considerable time first by my absence & afterwards by his attendence on a dying & now a dead brother. Since it was deliverd I have been so occupried as to let two or three posts slip me.

The political conversation to which you allude is this: I had stated that America ought to view all foreign nations with an equal eye. That we ought to assure ourselves that no nation ever had or ever woud have any regard for us—that they woud regulate themselves entirely by their own interest & that we ought to think so. That we were in the habit of expressing immense affection & gratitude for France & unlimited hate for Britain. Yet at a very critical period the conduct of those two nations towards us had been such as ought to induce to consider them as exactly equal—without favor to either. That while France was our friend, our ally, & united with us in a common war the use she made of her influence was to endeavor to deprive us of our western country & of the navigation of the mississipi in support of which I read the journals of Congress. That Britain on the other hand the instant she ceasd to be our foe ceded to us the western country & the mississipi. I added on other documents which I have seen but did not then produce that France our friend had endeavord to induce us to negotiate as a dependent nation & had sought to deprive us of all share in the fisheries—that Britain our foe, the instant she determind on peace acknowledgd our independence & ceded to us a share in the fisheries. That this was not producd by

7. JM addressed the letter to "Genl. Thomas Posey, Near Fredericksburg."
8. The letter from Posey has not been found.

the friendship of Britain or the hostility of France but by a political regard on the part of each to its own interest. That France had reason to beleive & did beleive that our weakness woud produce a dependence on her & a consequent sacrafice of our interest to hers while Britain beleivd that the stronger & the more independent we were of France the more certainly we shoud pursue our own interest which from her superiority in commerce & manufactures woud promote her interests also. That therefore each nation acted with a view only to herself with this difference. France erected her interest on our weakness, Britain on our attaining precisely that degree of strength which woud make us independent of France. We ought to regard neither as our friend further than particular interests shoud make them so.[9]

I was a good deal surpriz'd at your postscript altho I rejoice at having receivd it. The circumstance which gave you umbrage has pass'd so many years that I do not precisely recollect the state of the fact. Of this I am sure—I did not neglect nor was I capable of neglecting the business you allude to. My feelings for the officers & their interests were as warm as if I had at that instant been one of them, [it][1] was not possible to carry what measure I pleasd nor was it possible to introduce any measure precisely when I pleasd to introduce it. I recollect that I had the papers & I recollect also that I returnd them & that I was wounded by the person who gave them to me but I do not recollect the particulars. If the fault had been mine some other person woud have corrected & have effected what you wish'd but I beleive the fault was not mine & that I could not succeed in obtaining what you wish'd. I am dear Sir with real esteem, your

J MARSHALL

Law Papers, January 1799

U.S. Circuit Court, Va.

Gist v. Hill, replication, AD, U.S. Circuit Court, Va., Ended Cases (Unrestored), Virginia State Library.

9. JM's argument about the role of France in the peace negotiations in 1782 was a standard charge made by Americans since 1783. See Richard B. Morris, *The Peacemakers: The Great Powers and American Independence* (New York, 1965), 324–327; William C. Stinchcombe, *The American Revolution and the French Alliance* (Syracuse, N.Y., 1969), 181, 191–194.

1. Torn by seal.

To Thomas Posey

ALS, Indiana Historical Society

Dear Sir   [Richmond], February 1, 1799
    In the letter of yesterday I omited to answer some of your enquiries.
The paper I read was a statement of the propositions of the minister
of France made to Congress during our revolution war.[2] I am dear
Sir yours truely

[J MARSHALL][3]

Deed

Deed Book Copy, Office of the Clerk of Hardy County, Moorefield, W.Va.

[*February 4, 1799* (*Hardy County, Va.*). John Ashby and his wife convey 61
acres on the North Branch of the Potomac River in Hampshire County to
JM for £120. The deed was recorded in the District Court at Hardy County
on May 6, 1799.]

To Timothy Pickering

ALS, Pickering Papers, Massachusetts Historical Society

Dear Sir   Richmond, February 19, 1799
    An occasional absence from Richmond suspended for some time
my acknowlegement of the receit of your very correct analysis of &
able commentary on the late negotiation with France.[4] I wish it coud
be read more generally than I fear it will be.
    I am griev'd rather than surpriz'd at Mr. Gerry's letter.[5] To my
comprehension the evidence on which his judgement is formd positively contradicts the opinion he has given us. From what facts he

2. See Gaillard Hunt, ed., *Journals of the Continental Congress 1774–1789*, XVI (Washington, D.C., 1910), 106–109, 114–116. The French minister to the United States from
1778 to 1779 was Conrad Alexandre Gérard (1729–1790). For information on Gérard
and on the French negotiations with the new nation, see John J. Meng, ed., *Despatches
and Instructions of Conrad Alexandre Gérard, 1778–1780: Correspondence of the First French
Minister to the United States with the Comte de Vergennes* . . . (Baltimore, 1939).
    3. Most of JM's signature has been cut from the document.
    4. Pickering's report of the transactions relating to the United States and France,
dated Jan. 18, 1799, was submitted to Congress on Jan. 21, 1799. *Annals of Congress*, IX,
3531–3558.
    5. See Elbridge Gerry to John Adams, Oct. 20, 1798, Pickering Papers, Massachu-
setts Historical Society, and Timothy Pickering to JM, Nov. 5, 1798, Vol. III, 521–522.

infers the pacific temper of the french government I am unable to conjecture. That France is not desirous of immediate war with America is obvious—that is of reciprocal war, for she has been long making it on us; but that any indications appear of a disposition for a solid accomodation, on terms such as America can accede to, is by no means to be admited.

It is strange that Mr. Gerry shoud state the negotiation to have been in a fair train when inteligence of the publication of the dispatches[6] arriv'd in Paris; while he represents Mr. Talleyrand as having declind entering on the proposd treaty, until he coud know the temper of our government on the communications that had been made, which communications related chiefly to money; & while also he states Mr. Talleyrand to declare that he had never approvd of sending a minister to the United States. With very much respect & esteem, I remain Sir your obedt.

J MARSHALL

The federalists seem determind to exert themselves every where in the state elections. Mr. Henry has become a candidate for the state legislature.[7]

Deeds

Deed Book Copies, Office of the Clerk of Hardy County, Moorefield, W.Va.

[*March 13, 1799* (*Hardy County, Va.*). By his attorney, Rawleigh Colston, JM conveys parcels of land in the South Branch Manor to Jesse Welton, 35 acres for £8 15s., and to Job Welton, 56 acres for £35 5d. Both deeds were recorded in the District Court at Hardy County on May 7, 1799.]

Deed

Deed Book Copy, Office of the Clerk of Hardy County, Moorefield, W.Va.

[*March 14, 1799* (*Hardy County, Va.*). By his attorney, Rawleigh Colston, JM conveys 15.5 acres in the South Branch Manor to David Welton for £3 18s. The deed was recorded in the District Court at Hardy County on May 6, 1799.]

6. JM originally wrote, "when the inteligence of the public dispatches."
7. For information on Patrick Henry's campaign for the state legislature, see Congressional Election Campaign: Editorial Note, Vol. III, 500.

Deed

Deed Book Copy, Office of the Clerk of Hardy County, Moorefield, W.Va.

[*March 15, 1799 (Hardy County, Va.).* By his attorney, Rawleigh Colston, JM conveys 57 acres in the South Branch Manor to David Welton for £14 5s. The deed was recorded in the District Court at Hardy County on May 6, 1799.]

To James Markham Marshall

ALS, Marshall Papers, Library of Congress

My dear brother   [Richmond], April 3, 1799

I have receivd your letters by Mr. Smith & by the post.[8] I approve entirely of the ejectment in the winchester case & shoud never have suggested the distress but on your informing me that the lott holders woud not abide by the decision of one case. There has been no express decision of a court stating Lord Fairfax to have been siezed in fee of the northern neck, the Judges have expressd that opinion but not formally. There can therefore be no objection to finding the title of Lord Fairfax. In the district court of Winchester you will perceive the case agreed between Hunter & Fairfax in which his title is found & which you may translate into your present case with the necessary alterations fitted to your being plaintiff instead of defendent.[9] I will endeavor to send you by Mr. Smith so much of the case agreed in the Fedl. court in which Fairfax was plaintiff as relates to his title.[1] If however I shoud not do so you may form one very readily from that

8. This letter is addressed to J. M. Marshall in Winchester. His letters to JM have not been found.

9. At the district court meeting on Apr. 22, 1799, in Winchester, James Markham Marshall brought actions of ejectment against Henry Bush and Daniel Conrad, occupants of lots 152 and 139 in that city. In 1798 Marshall had demanded rent, unpaid for 18 years, and when payment was refused he tried to distrain goods owned by the tenants. He filed these actions when nothing was found upon which distress could be made. See Superior Court Order Book, 1797–1800, 413–414, 511–515, Frederick County, Virginia State Library.

Evidence suggests that JM hoped to handle this case personally. He was admitted to practice in the District Court at Winchester on Oct. 9, 1799, but apparently his subsequent career in Philadelphia and Washington intervened. *Ibid.,* 452.

1. The case to which JM refers was heard in Apr. 1794. See Vol. II, 141–143 and n. 9. James Markham Marshall incorporated the case agreed into his ejectment action against Conrad. See Superior Court Order Book, 1797–1800, 511–515, Frederick County, Va. State Lib.

which you will find in Peytons office. The alteration in the finding relative to the old town is not I think essential tho perhaps it may be proper & necessary to alter it so as to show that the particular lot in question was sold.[2]

I shall bring in chancery the suit against Pendleton & others.[3] I have no doubt myself of the jurisdiction of the court but I think our court of appeals very ill instructed on that subject & I fear its decisions.

I had wish'd to encourage Davies after his loss of the place of public printer & took two papers.[4] As one answerd all my purposes I subscrib'd for the other in your name. I will examine the sum I receivd for you at the treasury & inform you of its amount. I wish you not to mention to Mr. Marshall the money lent to him as I am confident he is not in a situation to repay it.

I never suspected Doctor Conrod of having stated any thing as coming from me which was not strictly true nor shoud I have written to him on the subject had it not been absolutely necessary to do so in order to show that the authority I was told Mr Hite woud resort to woud not support him. I have no right to object to any thing the Doctor might have stated as his conjecture of my opinion since it was unconnected with any evidence proceeding from myself & only founded on his own opinions of the conduct of Mr. Gerry himself. I have always thought highly of Doctor Conrod nor is my good opinion of him in any degree diminish'd.

The fate of my election is extremely uncertain. The means used to defeat it are despicable in the extreme & yet they succeed. Nothing I believe more debases or pollutes the human mind than faction.

I shall not prevent the ejectment you deem necessary to secure the payment of rent [arrear] on any of the property.

I regret very sincerely the situation of Genl. Morgan & wish you

2. Apparently the finding necessitated an alteration in Marshall's case. On Apr. 30, 1800, he withdrew the original case agreed and replaced it with another. See *ibid.*, 30–34. For the earlier federal case, see U.S. Circuit Court, Va., Record Book, III, 346–357, Va. State Lib.

On Apr. 30, 1800, the District Court at Winchester found for Conrad, and Marshall appealed the decision. In Oct. 1805 the Court of Appeals reversed the district court's judgment. Superior Court Order Book, 1803–1807, 30–34, Frederick County, Va. State Lib., and 9 Va. (5 Call) 364–406.

3. Case not found.

4. Augustine Davis published the *Virginia Gazette, and General Advertiser* (Richmond), which had changed on Jan. 1, 1799, from a weekly to a semiweekly. He had been public printer from 1791 to 1797 and was replaced by Meriwether Jones and John Dixon in 1798. Earl G. Swem, *A Bibliography of Virginia, Part II*, in Virginia State Library, *Bulletin*, X (1917), 1082.

shoud you see him to present me respectfully & affectionately to him.[5]

I understand that my sister Jane while here was addressd by Major Taylor & that his addresses were encouraged by her. I am not by any means certain of the fact nor did I suspect it until we had separated the night preceeding her departure & consequently I coud have no conversation with her concerning it. I beleive that tho Major Taylor was attachd to her it woud probably have had no serious result if Jane had not manifested some partiality for him. This affair embarasses me a good deal. Major Taylor is a young gentleman of talents & integrity for whom I profess & feel a real friendship. There is no person with whom I shoud be better pleasd if there were not other considerations which ought not to be overlookd. Major Taylor possesses but little if any fortune [&] is encumberd with a family & does not like his profession. Of course he will be so eminent in it as from his talents he ought to be. These are facts now unknown to my sister but which ought to be known to her. Had I conjecturd that Mr. Taylor was contemplated in the character of a lover I shoud certainly have made to her all the proper communications. I regret that it was conceald from me. I have a sincere & real affection & esteem for Major Taylor but I think it right in affairs of this sort that the real situation of the parties shoud be mutually understood.[6] Present affectionately to my sister, Your

J MARSHALL

Since writing the above I have receivd your letter with the certificates.[7] I regret much that they do not state the truth more fairly.

To George Washington

ALS, Washington Papers, Library of Congress

Dear Sir   Richmond, May 1, 1799
    You may possibly have seen a paragraph in a late publication,[8]

5. Daniel Morgan, major general of the Virginia troops that helped suppress the Whiskey Rebellion in 1795, served as a Federalist in the House of Representatives from 1797 to 1799. He left Congress at the end of February because of illness. Don Higginbotham, *Daniel Morgan: Revolutionary Rifleman* (Chapel Hill, N.C., 1961), 208.
    6. Jane Marshall and George Keith Taylor were married on Dec. 22, 1799.
    7. Letter not found.
    8. JM referred to a letter printed in the *Virginia Gazette, and General Advertiser* (Richmond), Apr. 19, 1799, 3.

stating that several important offices in the gift of the Executive, &
among others that of secretary of State, had been attainable by me.
Few of the unpleasant occurrences produc'd by my declaration as a
candidate for congress (& they have been very abundant) have given
me more real chagrin than this. To make a parade of profferd offices
is a vanity which I trust I do not possess, but to boast of one never in
my power woud argue a littleness of mind at which I ought to blush.

I know not how the author may have acquird his information, but
I beg leave to assure you that he never receivd it directly nor in-
directly from me. I had no previous knowledge that such a publication was designd, or I woud certainly have suppressd so much of it
as relates to this subject. The writer was unquestionably actuated by
a wish to serve me & by resentment at the various malignant calumnies which have been so profusely bestowd on me. One of these was
that I only wish'd a seat in Congress for the purpose of obtaining
some office which my devotion to the administration might procure.
To repel this was obviously the motive of the indiscreet publication
I so much regret.

A wish to rescue myself in your opinion from the imputation of an
idle vanity which forms, if I know myself, no part of my character,
will I trust apologize for the trouble this explanation may give you.

Messrs. Goode & Gray who are the successors of Messrs. Claiborne
& Harrison are both foederalists.[9] Mr. Hancock who opposd Mr.
Trig will, to our general disappointment not succeed.[1] At least such
is our present information. Shoud Haymond or Preston[2] be elected
the Virginia delegation will stand ten in opposition to the government—nine in support of it. Parties, I fear will not be so nearly
balancd in our state legislature. With the most respectful attachment, I remain Sir your obedt. Servt.

J. MARSHALL

9. Samuel Goode (1756–1822), a lawyer in Chesterfield County, Va., was defeated
after serving only one term in Congress, from 1799 to 1801. Edwin Gray (1743–*ca.* 1813),
of Southampton County, Va., was elected in 1799 and served in the six succeeding Con-
gresses until Mar. 3, 1813. Thomas Claiborne and Carter Basset Harrison were defeated.

1. George Hancock (1754–1820), of Chesterfield County, Va., served in Congress
from 1793 to 1797. John Johns Trigg (1748–1804) defeated Hancock in the congressional
election of 1799.

2. This was probably William Haymond (1740–1821), a major in the Virginia Line
during the Revolution. Abram Trigg (1750–1809), brother of John Johns Trigg, defeated
William Preston in 1799. Abram Trigg served in Congress from 1797 to 1809.

The delegation elected in 1799 consisted of 11 Republicans and 8 Federalists. See
Daniel Porter Jordan, Jr., "Virginia Congressmen, 1801–1825" (Ph.D. diss., University
of Virginia, 1970), 359, and Myron F. Wehtje, "The Congressional Elections of 1799 in
Virginia," *West Virginia History*, XXIX (1968), 251–273.

Deeds

Deed Book Copies, Office of the Clerk of Hardy County, Moorefield, W.Va.

[*May 4, 1799 (Hardy County, Va.)*. By his attorney, Rawleigh Colston, JM conveys parcels of land in the South Branch Manor to: William Bullit, 20 acres for £5; Robert Darling, 33 acres for £8 5s.; Jonathan Hutton, 5 acres for £13 12s. and 193.5 acres for £36; James Snodgrass, 74 acres for £19 4s. 9d. All the deeds were recorded in the District Court at Hardy County on May 7, 1799.]

From George Washington

ALS, Collection of Charles B. Coleman, Chattanooga, Tenn.

Dear Sir,   Mount Vernon, May 5, 1799

With infinite pleasure I received the news of your Election. For the honor of the District, I wish the Majority had been greater; but let us be content; and hope, as the tide is [turning, the cu]rrent[3] will soon run strong in our favor.

[I am] sorry to find that the publication [you allude to, s]hould have given you a moments [disquietude.] I can assure you, it made no im[pression on my] mind, of the tendency apprehen[ded by you.][4]

[The] doubt you have expressed of Mr. [Handcock's Ele]ction, is as unexpected as it is painf[ul. In these] parts, we had set it down as cer[tain; and ou]r calculations went to eleven instead of nine. A few days now, will give us the result of *all* the Elections, to Congress and the Legislature of the State; and as you are at the fountain of information respecting the politics of the members, give me, I pray you, the amount of the parties on each side, if you have leisure & can ascertain them. With very sincere esteem & regard, I am, Dear Sir, Yr. Obedt & Affect Servt.

Go: Washington

3. A large portion of the letter is torn away. Missing words were taken from a letter-press copy in Washington Papers, Ser. 4, Library of Congress (microfilm ed., reel 114).
On JM's election to Congress, see Congressional Election Campaign: Editorial Note, Vol. III, 494–502.
4. See JM to Washington, May 1, 1799.

From George Washington

Presscopy, Washington Papers, Library of Congress

[*May 12, 1799, Mount Vernon.* Writing jointly to JM, Edward Carrington, and William Heth, Washington asks for recommendations of officers for Virginia regiments of the Provisional Army. Enclosures from Secretary of War James McHenry and the inspector general outline the method of selection of officers and the division of the state into districts. Washington adds a list of the Virginia quota of officers for the 12 regiments assigned the state. None of the enclosures in this letter has been found, although the original of McHenry to Washington, Apr. 10, 1799, is in Washington Papers, Ser. 4, Library of Congress (microfilm ed., reel 114).]

From Timothy Pickering

Presscopy, Pickering Papers, Massachusetts Historical Society

Dear Sir,   Philadelphia, May 16, 1799
   I have received your letter of the 9th.[5] We have but one consul in Scotland—Mr. Hary Grant, at Leith. He has not long since manifested an inclination to be the Consul for Glasgow. That port and all others in Scotland are, according to custom, under his consular jurisdiction, & will so remain until another consul shall be appointed at or nearer to any of them than these are to Leith.
   Consuls ought to be men of upright characters. They give certificates to entitle our merchants to drawbacks on goods exported from the U.States. A defect of honesty might occasion many frauds on our revenues. When Mr. Pendleton mentions Mr. Dunlop as a "sensible, respectable man," I presume he speaks from his own knowledge; and that in the character of "respectable" he comprehends *unblemished integrity.* Your information concerning Mr. Pendleton will induce me to attend with pleasure to what he shall say further in regard to Mr. Dunlop; and as soon as an appointment can be made to lay his recommendations before the President. It is doubtful whether as there has not yet been any consul for Glasgow, an appointment can be made until the Senate meets next December.[6]

   5. Not found.
   6. Dunlop did not receive the appointment. The post was tendered to John J. Murray (d. 1805), a judge in Richmond County, N.Y. He was the first U.S. consul appointed to Glasgow and was confirmed Jan. 26, 1802.

The elections in Virginia, though not equal to our late hopes, surpass former expectations, and with those in New-York, give joy to all the real friends of the U States. I am with great respect & esteem Dr. Sir, Your obt. servant.

TIMOTHY PICKERING

To George Washington

ALS, Washington Papers, Library of Congress

Dear Sir   Richmond, May 16, 1799

Neither Colo. Carrington nor Colo. Heth are now in town. So soon as they arrive your letter of the 12th. inst. with its inclosures, will be communicated to them. I wish it may be in our power to furnish any useful information on the subjects inquird into.

Returns of all the elections have been receivd. The failure of Colo. Hancock & of Major Haymond[7] was unexpected & has reducd us to eight in the legislature of the Union. In the state elections very considerable changes have been made. There are from fifty to sixty new members. Unfortunately the strength of parties is not materially varied. The opposition maintains its majority in the house of Delegates. The consequence must be an antifoederal Senator & Governor.[8] In addition to this the baneful influence of a legislature hostile perhaps to the Union—or if not so—to all its measures, will yet be kept up.

If it be true that France has declard war against Austria, it will be now apparent that it woud have been wise to have attempted the releif of Ehrenbreightstein & the preservation of Naples & Sardinia.[9] Even this instructive lesson will probably make no impression on the nations of Europe or the people of America. With the utmost respect & attachment, I am Sir your Obedt. Servt.

J MARSHALL

7. See JM to George Washington, May 1, 1799.
8. Wilson Cary Nicholas was elected to finish the U.S. Senate term of Henry Tazewell, who had died on Jan. 24, 1799. Republicans elected James Monroe governor over James Breckinridge, the Federalist candidate. The straight party vote was 116–66. Harry Ammon, *James Monroe: The Quest for National Identity* (New York, 1971), 172–173.
9. Ehrenbreightstein was a fortress at Koblenz on the Rhine where the Austrian and French armies were fighting for the spoils of the Holy Roman Empire. Italy, Austria, Russia, and Great Britain combined to drive the French out of southern Italy. See C. T. Atkinson, *A History of Germany 1715–1815* (Westport, Conn., 1971 [orig. publ. London, 1908]), 426–439.

From André Toussaint Delarüe

Draft, Private Collection

Dear Sir: Paris, May 31, 1799
    What words shall I find to express to you the extreme grief we feel by my father-in-law's unfortunate and sudden death in the night of the 18 of this month, occasioned by an apoplexy.[1] He did not in the least Suffer, he fell asleep, the next morning the Servant going to wake him found him dead in his bed. I wish to be the first in letting you know this fatal event. You were reckoned, Sir, among the number of his friends, considered by him as one of the eminent men of this Age, and whose talents and virtues he admired and esteemed.
    I hope Sir, you will still interest yourself in the lawsuit which you have so well conducted,[2] and that the concern you shewed us for our Welfare will not be in the least diminished, but rather Redouble your Ardour in favour of his unhappy Daughter, plunged into the deepest distress, deprived of almost all her fortune, unless alas! you deign to assure her of your protection.
    As for me Sir I enter into the most Solemn engagement to confirm all those contracted by My father in-law, Mr. Beaumarchais, and even to go beyond them, if they were not proportioned to the care and attention which might have been taken; in short I shall approve of every expence you shall think necessary.
    I have the honor of being with the hightest Sentiments of Esteem and the most inviolable attachment, Dear Sir, Your very obed. Servt.

Law Papers, May 1799

U.S. Circuit Court, Va.

    Hatton v. Kerr, declaration, ADS, U.S. Circuit Court, Va., Ended Cases (Restored), Virginia State Library.

    1. Delarüe (1768–1864) married Caron de Beaumarchais's daughter, Amélie Eugénie, in 1796.
    2. See Vol. II, 126 n. 8, for a description of the case in which JM represented Beaumarchais. For a further description of the case and for the outcome, see Court of Appeals Order Book, IV, 114–115, 274, Virginia State Library, and *The Memorial and Claim of Amélie Eugénie Caron de Beaumarchais, Wife of André Toussaint de la Rüe . . . by Her Agent John Augustus Chevallié for a Balance Due His Estate . . .* (Richmond, 1801).

From George Washington

LS, Washington Papers, Library of Congress

[*June 6, 1799, Mount Vernon.* Washington writes in reply to JM's letter of May 16 that he will accept the inspector general's plan to divide Virginia into four districts, each commanded by a prominent figure who should furnish the president with recommendations of officers to fill the lower grades. He includes a letter intended for John Cropper of the Eastern Shore of Virginia,[3] which he asks JM, Edward Carrington, and William Heth to peruse and to forward if it meets with their approval. In addition, if they approve, Washington intends to offer one of the regimental commands to Callohill Minnis. He asks their help in choosing two men to command the remaining two regiments, suggesting Robert Porterfield of Frederick County for their consideration.]

To Thomas Bayly

ALS, Virginia Historical Society

Dear Sir[4]   Richmond, June 12, 1799

I have just receivd yours of the 4th. inst.[5] inclosing a record in the case of Watson & Powell. This case is not like Kennon & McRoberts[6] in the circumstances of the family but it bears a strong analogy to it in the expression of the will. I am therefore rather inclind to the opinion that it will follow the fate of that case. I shoud however have applied for a supersedeas had you sent me a complete record but as you have only sent the special verdict I cannot present it to a Judge of appeals. If you wish the opinion of that court it will be adviseable to send up a complete record by october next when it can be offerd to the court in session with a declaration that a supersedeas is not

3. Washington requested Cropper to furnish the names of persons "to fill the Offices of Two Majors, ten Captains, ten first and ten second Lieutenants." Washington to John Cropper, June 6, 1799, Washington Papers, Ser. 4, Library of Congress (microfilm ed., reel 114).

4. Thomas Monteagle Bayly (1775–1834), of Accomack County, Va., served in the House of Delegates from 1797 to 1801, in the state Senate from 1801 to 1809, and in the U.S. House of Representatives from 1813 to 1815. This is item no. Mss2M3567a14 in the society's collections.

5. Not found.

6. See Vol. II, 427 n. 18, and 1 Va. (1 Wash.) 96–114 (1792), for a report of this case.

wishd if it be considerd as governd by the case of Kennon & McRoberts. This will give us the opinion of the court at a less expense than it coud be obtaind by an application to a single Judge. I am dear Sir very respectfully, Your Obedt.

J MARSHALL

To George Washington

ALS, Washington Papers, Library of Congress

[*June 12, 1799, Richmond.* JM writes in reply to Washington's letter of June 6 that Edward Carrington has seen his previous letter although William Heth has still not been reached. JM agrees that John Cropper would be a fit person for the post Washington suggests but points out that if Cropper were offered the position he would be serving under such men as William Bentley and Josiah Parker whom he previously would have commanded. Carrington has suggested that if the army is called into service, brigadier generals will necessarily be appointed from Virginia, and Cropper, George Rogers Clark, or Thomas Posey would be eminently eligible for those positions. For this reason JM and Carrington will detain the letter to Cropper awaiting further instructions. JM recommends Callohill Minnis but cautions that those who know him suppose him best fitted for command of a battalion rather than a regiment, although he might be willing to serve under a man such as James Breckinridge, a Virginia legislator. He further recommends Robert Porterfield, Joseph Blackwell, and Joseph Swearingean.[7]

JM closes by writing, "Virginia has sustaind a very serious loss which all good men will long lament, in the death of Mr. Henry. He is said to have expird on thursday last. The inteligence is not absolutely certain, but scarcely a hope is entertaind of its untruth."[8]]

From George Washington

Copy, Washington Papers, Library of Congress

[*June 16, 1799, Mount Vernon.* Washington thanks JM for not sending the letter to Cropper and indicates that he was aware of the problems JM men-

7. Joseph Swearingean (1754–*ca.* 1821). Washington was not satisfied with the recommendations he received from JM, Heth, and Carrington and believed that the three men had not devoted enough time to the task of composing lists of men eligible for appointment. See Washington to James McHenry, Aug. 12, 1799, Washington Papers, Ser. 4, Library of Congress (microfilm ed., reel 114).

8. Patrick Henry died June 6, 1799.

tioned. He now intends to write to Cropper in such a way that will lead to Cropper's offering his services. This letter will be first forwarded to JM for his inspection. Washington thanks JM for the recommendations he sent.

"In the Death of Mr. Henry (of which I fear there is little doubt) not only Virginia, but our Country at large has sustained a very serious loss. I sincerely lament his death as a friend; and the loss of his eminent talents as a Patriot I consider as peculiarly unfortunate at this critical juncture of our affairs."]

From George Washington

LS, Henry E. Huntington Library

[*June 17, 1799, Mount Vernon.* Washington sends the revised letter for John Cropper, which he wishes JM, Edward Carrington, and William Heth to read and approve before forwarding it to Cropper.]

To George Washington

ALS, Washington Papers, Library of Congress

[*June 21, 1799, Richmond.* JM apologizes for not immediately replying to Washington's letter; an "accidental absence from town" had prevented him from doing so. He acknowledges receipt and conveyance of Washington's second letter to John Cropper and herein returns Washington's first letter to Cropper. See Washington to Cropper, June 17, 1799, Washington Papers, Ser. 4, Library of Congress (microfilm ed., reel 114).]

Law Papers, June 1799

U.S. Circuit Court, Va.

Swift v. Ross (debt), declaration, ADS, U.S. Circuit Court, Va., Ended Cases (Unrestored), Virginia State Library.

Swift v. Ross (case), declaration, ADS, U.S. Circuit Court, Va., Ended Cases (Unrestored), Va. State Lib.

From George Washington

Copy, Washington Papers, Library of Congress

[*July 1, 1799, Mount Vernon.* Washington acknowledges receipt of JM's letter of June 21 and thanks JM for his assistance.]

Address and Reply

Printed, *Virginia Gazette, and General Advertiser* (Richmond), September 10, 1799, 3

[*August 23, 1799, New London, Va.* The citizens of the town of New London thank JM for having supported the honor and dignity of the United States while acting as "Ambassador to France."[1] They declare that "peace, in our judgment, next to liberty, is one of the greatest blessings that a nation can enjoy; yet, we prefer war with all its horrors and calamities, to a dishonorable peace." JM replies by asserting, "a sincere and ardent wish to obtain peace and to procure the honor and independence of our common country guided the American ministers throughout their arduous mission, and while I regret that the first was unattainable, I am proud to know that my fellow citizens would disdain to purchase it by a surrender of the latter."]

To Timothy Pickering

ALS, Pickering Papers, Massachusetts Historical Society

Dear Sir   Richmond, August 25, 1799

A visit to an aged & rever'd Father from which I have only returnd to day, prevented my receiving earlier & giving an earlier answer to your letter of the 5th. inst.[2]

1. New London was the county seat of Bedford County. The town, which no longer exists, was situated west of Lynchburg on the Otter River. JM passed through New London on his return from Kentucky.

2. JM had gone to Kentucky late in June or early in July. See George Washington to James McHenry, July 7, 1799, John C. Fitzpatrick, ed., *The Writings of George Washington from the Original Manuscript Sources, 1745–1799*, XXXVII (Washington, D.C., 1940), 272.

Pickering's letter has not been found. Pickering was interested in a passage in JM's Paris Journal in which JM had stated his opposition to recognizing any French claims, even those of Beaumarchais, without a corresponding recognition of American claims. Pickering wanted to know why JM held this position and thought his reasons would be helpful to the next set of envoys about to embark for Paris. When he learned JM was in Kentucky, he wrote Pinckney for an explanation of the journal entry. See Vol. III, 191, for the pertinent portion of the Paris Journal, and Timothy Pickering to Charles Cotesworth Pinckney, Aug. 8, 1799, Pickering Papers, Massachusetts Historical Society.

It is impossible to state in such a manner as to make on others the impression I feel myself, the various circumstances which have led to my conviction that leaving the question of the role d'equipage unsettled in a negotiation with France is, at best, leaving it to chance. I will however mention some considerations which on my mind were most operative.

That construction of the treaty which requird a role d'equipage from American vessels is obviously & for many reasons a favorite construction with the french government.

1st. It was maintaind officially by Merlin[3] while minister of justice. He is now a very influential member of the Directory.

2dly. It woud secure to the owners of privatiers who are a powerful body of men in the councils, the wealth of which they have plunderd us.

3dly. Under whatever pretexts vessels may have been condemnd few if any of them have been furnishd with a role d'equipage in the forms requird by the resolutions & orders of France. Consequently the want of this paper will justify almost every condemnation which has been made. The result is that by establishing this construction France will save a great deal in point of interest—she will save a great deal too in point of reputation as she will thereby in a considerable degree free herself from the disgrace in which her lawless & shameless piracies have involvd her. This is not all. It will be an object with France to revive & preserve her influence in the United States. Nothing can contribute more effectually to this than the opinion that her conduct has not been particularly hostile to us— that her unauthoriz'd depredations have not been considerable. This will enable her party in America to attack from very advantageous ground the government of the United States & consequently to strengthen itself by giving some color to the charge of having wishd to provoke a war with France by causeless military preparations & operations by sea. This important result will be effected by establishing that construction which requires the role d'equipage since it is a fact that few vessels were furnishd with that instrument in such form as woud defy a rigid scrutiny. With a government wanting principle the existence of additional motives cannot be necessary to induce the establishment of any particular construction however erroneous provided its establishment be practicable.

If the whole subject of depredations be left at large to commis-

3. Philippe-Antoine Merlin de Douai.

sioners chance will decide whether the majority shall be French or American. If they be French their construction will conform to the will of their government. I do not think this can be doubted because on a point so important & which has been so much discussd (for it has been argued in all the tribunals of France) the government woud not appoint a man whose opinion did not conform to its own. There are some additional reasons for beleiving this woud be the decision of the french commissioners formd on their national character. It appears to me that in a contest with another nation a Frenchman can never see wrong in his own government. Frenchmen too seem not to have the same ideas of judicial purity with Americans. It is usual for the parties openly to sollicit the Judges & if the court of commissioners was even not to be a political court I shoud despair of a decision against France for any considerable sum shoud the majority of commissioners be Frenchmen.

I am sensible that some of these opinions are unfit for any but your own eye—they are however my real opinions. With much respect & esteem, I am dear Sir your obedt

J MARSHALL

Law Papers, August 1799

U.S. Circuit Court, Va.

Carry v. Watson, declaration, copy, U.S. Circuit Court, Va., Ended Cases (Unrestored), Virginia State Library.

Deed

Deed Book Copy, Office of the Clerk of Hardy County, Moorefield, W.Va.

[*September 2, 1799* (*Hardy County, Va.*). By his attorney, Rawleigh Colston, JM conveys 92 acres in the South Branch Manor to David Welton for $85. The deed was recorded in the District Court at Hardy County on May 5, 1800.]

Communication

Printed, *Virginia Federalist* (Richmond), September 7, 1799, 3

[Richmond, *ca.* September 7, 1799]

I observe in a late paper of the *Examiner* several strictures on the case of Robbins, who was lately delivered to the British Consul at Charleston, under the 27th article of the Treaty of Amity and Commerce between Great Britain and America, censuring the measure in general, but reprobating the conduct of the President in a particular manner.[4] These strictures calculated to exasperate the public mind, would probably lose their effect upon a fair explanation of the nature of the business, and therefore I have thought it worth while for the sake of removing unjust impressions, and satisfying the minds of those, who really wish for information relative to the necessary mode of proceeding in cases of that kind, to endeavour to make a just representation of the matter as far as I am able to understand the case from the mutilated publications which we have seen of it.

As to the opinion of the learned Judge upon the case, I shall not enter into any arguments in support of it; because they would be useless and unnecessary, as the reasoning contained in his own excellent speech upon the subject is perfectly correct, and must be convincing to every unprejudiced mind.[5]

I shall therefore confine myself to that part of the case which respects the President's letter only:[6] which I am induced to do, not because I think it needs any justification with candid men, who know the nature of such proceedings, but because I wish to prevent the effects which are intended to be produced from it, upon the minds of those who do not possess the kind of information necessary to enable them to judge impartially on the subject.

4. This communication was attributed to JM when it was reprinted in 1821 in John E. Hall, *The Journal of Jurisprudence: A New Series of the American Law Journal*, I (Philadelphia, 1821), 28–32. In 1849, Francis Wharton said that the attacks in the Richmond *Examiner* had been written by James Madison and were "answered in the Virginia 'Federalist' by Mr. Marshall." Francis Wharton, *State Trials of the United States during the Administrations of Washington and Adams . . .* (Philadelphia, 1849), 404. The issues of the *Examiner* in which the attacks appeared have not been found. Benjamin Moodie was the British consul at Charleston, S.C. For more information on the Robbins affair, see Larry D. Cress, "The Jonathan Robbins Incident: Extradition and the Separation of Powers in the Adams Administration," *Essex Institute Historical Collections*, CXI (1975), 110.

For JM's defense of the administration's actions, see Speech, Mar. 7, 1800.

5. Wharton, *State Trials*, 401–404.

6. "The President's letter" was actually the opinion of President Adams as conveyed to Judge Thomas Bee (1725–1812) by Timothy Pickering. See *ibid.*, 416.

The case from the publication, which I have seen, I suppose to be this. The British government having discovered that Robbins was in Charlestown applied to the Judge for a warrant to secure him until application could be made to Government for him. The warrant was granted, and an application, with the evidences of the charge, were laid before the President—who being satisfied that it was a case within the treaty, directed the Judge, as he was arrested under his warrant, to deliver him up, and the single question is, whether this proceeding in the President was regular.

By the Treaty of Amity made when the two nations neither did or could contemplate this, or the case of any other individual, it is mutually stipulated that fugitives from justice who have been guilty of murder or forgery in one of the nations, and have taken shelter in the territories of the other, shall be delivered up to the injured government. These stipulations are reciprocal, and America, whenever a case shall happen, will have the same right to demand a fugitive of Great Britain, that the latter had to demand Robbins of the United States. Nor can either nation refuse, for the words are positive. They are, "*It is further agreed, that his Majesty and the United States on mutual requisition, by them, or by their respective ministers or officers authorized to make the same, will deliver up to justice all persons, who, being charged with murder or forgery, committed within the jurisdiction of either, shall seek an asylum within any of the countries of the other, provided that this shall only be done on such evidence of criminality as, according to the laws of the place, where the fugitive or persons charged shall be found, would justify his apprehension and commitment for trial, if the offence had there been committed. The expense of such apprehension and delivery shall be borne and defrayed by those who make the requisition and receive the fugitive.*"[7] Which words contain an absolute engagement to deliver such characters up, and neither nation can refuse or neglect it without a violation of the Treaty.

It is therefore a certain fact, that Great Britain, by the express words of the Treaty, had a right to demand Robbins in the present case; who was accused of murder, one of the enumerated offences for which fugitives were to be delivered up.

There must therefore have been some mode of carrying the provision of the treaty in this respect into execution, or else the articles would be nugatory; and it would be absurd to suppose the parties meant to stipulate for a thing which could not be performed.

7. This slightly inaccurate quotation is from art. 27 of the Jay Treaty. See Miller, ed., *Treaties*, II, 263.

The question then is, what mode should be pursued when a requisition of this kind is made, and what proceedings should take place in order to comply with it.

The treaty has not pointed out any mode, and therefore we must recur to principles and the nature of things in order to discover it.

As nations do not communicate with each other, but through the channel of their governments, the natural, and obvious and the proper mode is an application on the part of the government (requiring the fugitive) to the executive of the nation to which he has fled, to secure and cause him to be delivered up.

1. Because the governments being the only channel of communication between the nations, the British government in cases of this kind has nothing to do with the detail and internal regulations of ours, nor we with theirs. For as the governments have respectively undertaken to do the thing which is required, the injured nation is not concerned any further with the business than merely to exhibit the proofs and call on the other for the performance of the treaty; and the nation called on, must attend to the details and internal regulations themselves.

2. Because the government to which the fugitive has fled ought to be informed, why an inhabitant is forced away from its territories; and therefore a removal of any person therefrom without an application to the chief magistrate would not only be dangerous to the personal safety of individuals, but would be an indignity and affront which ought not to be offered.

3. Because without such an application, the injured nation could not complain of an infraction of the treaty on the part of the other government in not delivering up the fugitive. For it would be an irresistible argument to such a complaint that no application was ever made to the government itself. Nor would it strengthen the complaint, that an application was made to some inferior authority; Because an application to subordinate officers who do not represent the general national concerns would not only be improper on account of the inconvenient practices it might introduce (for by that means a man might be carried off, without governments having an opportunity of protecting him), but, in case the requisition were not complied with, could not be a just ground of reproach to the government itself, which was never informed of the application.

4. Because it is manifest from what has been said, as well as from the very nature of things, that government must have a right to decide whether a fugitive should be delivered up or not. For it is a

mere question of state, and all questions relative to the affairs of the nation emphatically belong to the government to decide upon.

Therefore in case of a requisition for a fugitive by the United States from Great Britain, the application would be to the executive and not to the judiciary, or any other inferior department of the government.

It follows therefore that an application to the government itself is essential; and accordingly in the case under consideration such an application was actually made.

But surely the business was not to rest there. Some further steps were necessary or else the application would have been to no purpose.

The government, as we have already seen, was bound by its engagement, to cause delivery to be made; and therefore the president was under a necessity of taking some order in the business, which might produce the object of the application. For having been informed, that the man was under confinement, upon the charge on which the application was made, until the determination of government upon the subject could be known; he was bound to give some directions in the business, so that the prisoner might either be liberated or delivered up; and those directions could only be given in writing.

If the President had said to the British ambassador, you must apply to the Judge under whose warrant he was arrested, and he will deliver the prisoner to you, the obvious answer would have been, "Sir, I cannot do so without your warrant. If I apply to your Judge, I shall certainly be told again as I was told before, that he cannot interfere in a business of State, without the knowledge of Government; and it will be in vain for me to tell him that I have your instructions upon the subject, unless I am able to produce some evidence of them."

It follows, therefore, that the President was bound to give some written instructions upon the subject; because no other would, or ought to have been credited by the Judge.

The only question then is, whether the letter of the Secretary of State contained the proper instructions or not?

If I am right in my position, that the application in all such cases should be made to the Executive, and that the Executive has a right to decide whether the requisition should be complied with or not; it follows necessarily, that when information was given to the Judge, that application had been made, it ought to have been accompanied with some expression of the will of Government upon the subject. For it would have been ridiculous in the President to have ordered a letter to be written to the Judge, informing him that such an application had been made, without informing him also what Government had resolved to do in the business; because that would have left the Judge exactly where he was; and he would have been at liberty to have considered it as a mere private letter from one gentleman to another, and not as an official document, on which he was bound to act. So, that if under that impression he had resolved to have taken no steps in the business, he not only would have stood excused himself, but the British government would have had just cause to complain that our conduct was illusory, and that the stipulations of the treaty were evaded.

But, if it be admitted that any declaration of the President was necessary upon the subject, more eligible terms than those used by the Secretary of State, even according to the garbled publication which we have of them, could not have been chosen. For they are the usual phrases all over the United States, from the Governor down to the County Court Magistrate. There is not a mandate of any kind in use amongst us, which does not contain the word *require*; and it will surely be admitted that the word "*advise*" is at least as harmless as the words "command" and "*at your peril*," which are to be found in the warrant of every superior to his inferior officer throughout the United States.

Let me now then ask any candid man, if the inference drawn by the Examiner from this letter, namely, that the President had endeavoured to influence the opinion of a Judge in a matter depending before him, be a correct one?

On the contrary, it is manifest from what has been said, that the matter never was, nor could be regularly before the Judge, until he had received this letter, which was the ground and foundation on which he was to proceed. 'Till then he had no authority to act definitely upon the question; and so the Judge evidently appears to have considered it himself. For it was handed to the counsel on both sides, plainly as the authority on which he proceeded. Otherwise he would not have shown it at all, or else he would have done it in a very different manner.

It was therefore a mere official paper, and not a letter which was intended to be intruded upon the Judge, in order to influence his determination in a matter depending before him. It was itself the very process, if I may use the expression, which brought the case before the Judge.

Perhaps it will be said that the Judge himself had denied the authority of the Executive; and there is a passage in his speech which looks that way.

But this is a part of the opinion of the Judge, which seems liable to be questioned; and I strongly suspect it is not truly stated in the public prints, or else it comes to this, that the Judge was of opinion that every thing relative to treaties was to be transacted by the Judges, and not by the Executive. A position which he certainly did not mean to maintain; and therefore the passage alluded to, ought to be understood with some qualification.

Perhaps the following solution may reconcile his opinion with the doctrine I have been contending for.

The Judge probably meant to say, that he once thought it a question which exclusively belonged to the Executive, and therefore, that he, as a Judge, could not in any manner be required to aid in the execution of the treaty. But finding, by recurrence to the Constitution, that the Judicial power extended to Treaties, he was then satisfied that the Judges might be called on where circumstances rendered it proper, to take the necessary steps, in order to have the Treaty carried into effect, as by issuing a warrant to secure the fugitive, until the determination of government could be known, and after that was promulgated, giving the necessary orders for carrying the determination into effect.

With this qualification, the opinion of the Judge was correct, and therefore I incline to think that he ought to be so understood in the passage under consideration.

Upon the whole, the President appears to have done no more than his duty.

For suppose it had been said that the British government had applied to the president for a fugitive from justice under the treaty, and that the latter instead of ordering him to be delivered up, had refused or neglected to do it without assigning any reason for it. How could the president have justified his conduct in that case? and might it not then have been said with propriety, that he had neglected his duty and omitted to execute one of the supreme laws of the land, which he was bound to observe and have carried into effect.

In short, if some men would use but half the industry in examining into the real motives of the president's conduct upon any occasion that they do in finding out reasons to reproach him, they would soon be convinced that in no instance of his administration has he either encroached upon the duty of others, or omitted to perform his own.

Deeds

Deed Book Copies, Office of the Clerk of Hardy County, Moorefield, W.Va.

[*September 9, 1799 (Hardy County, Va.).* By his attorney, Rawleigh Colston, JM conveys parcels of land in the South Branch Manor to: Andrew and Morgan Byrns, 244 acres for £73; Conrad Carr, 28 acres for £11; James Parsons, 251 acres for £99; Abraham Shobe, 126 acres for £31 10s.; Rudolph Shobe, 302 acres for £75 10s. All the deeds were recorded in the District Court at Hardy County on May 5, 1800.]

Deeds

Deed Book Copies, Office of the Clerk of Hardy County, Moorefield, W.Va.

[*September 10, 1799 (Hardy County, Va.).* By his attorney, Rawleigh Colston, JM conveys parcels of land in the South Branch Manor to George Harness, Jr., 420 acres for £146, and to John Harness, Sr., 283 acres for £70 17s. 6d. Both deeds were recorded in the District Court at Hardy County on May 5, 1800.]

To Abel Catlin

Printed extract, Charles Hamilton Autographs, Inc., Catalog No. 41 (New York, April 23, 1970), 61

[*September 25, 1799, Richmond.* "I have enquired for Asa Morgan but have heard nothing of him. He may with much care pass through this place unknown. Should I have any knowledge of his being here, the suit you request shall be instituted. . . ." Catlin lived in Litchfield, Conn.]

Power of Attorney

AD, Roberts Collection, Haverford College

[*October 11, 1799, Richmond.* John Cox of Essex County, Va., authorizes JM to receive dividends payable at the Treasury of the United States.]

To Thomas W. Griffith

ALS, Maryland Historical Society

Dear Sir   Richmond, November 14, 1799
    I had the pleasure of receiving a few days past your letter inclosing one from Mrs. Curtine & thank you for the information you give relative to the affairs of that lady.[8] I will write to her from Philadelphia.
    I receivd your letter from Paris expressing your wish to be appointed Consul for the United States at that place. It was then certain that no such appointment woud immediately be necessary & was understood that Major Mountflorence had been contemplated & indeed actually namd for the office. I mentiond you however to the Secretary of State.[9]
    Shoud it be in my power I shall feel much pleasure in being serviceable to you in the manner you mention. I am Sir very respectfully, Your Obedt.

                                            J MARSHALL

Land Bounty Certificate

ADS, Bounty Warrants, Virginia State Library

                            [Richmond], November 19, 1799
    The bearer Joseph Garner was enlisted in Capt. William Blackwells company in the 11th. Virginia Regt. to serve for three years or during the war I am now uncertain which, but I beleive for three years.[1] He was appointed a serjeant & did his duty faithfully for more than two years when he was dischargd as being unfit for service. His unfitness was producd by a wound in his arm. I was originally first

8. Letters not found. Griffith (1767–1838), a Baltimore merchant, had been appointed U.S. consul at Le Havre by George Washington. See Vol. III, 465–466.
    9. See *ibid.*, 162 n. 13.
    1. Garner had enlisted for three years. See Vol. I, 5 n. 3.
    At the bottom of the certificate is written, 'I have examined the Register. The above name is not on it. JW" The handwriting may be that of Jacob Wagner (1772–1825), chief clerk of the State Department. See David Hackett Fischer, *The Revolution of American Conservatism: The Federalist Party in the Era of Jeffersonian Democracy* (New York, 1965), 369.

Lieut. & afterwards Captain of the company in which he was enlisted.

J MARSHALL

late Capt. in 11th. Virga. Regt.

Law Papers, November 1799

U.S. Circuit Court, Va.

Livesay v. Trouin, declaration, copy, U.S. Circuit Court, Va., Ended Cases (Unrestored), Virginia State Library.

Congressional Career

EDITORIAL NOTE

When John Marshall arrived in Philadelphia for the convening of the Sixth Congress early in December 1799, it was assured that he would begin his congressional career as one of the leading members of the Federalist wing in the House of Representatives. His important role in the XYZ affair and the impact of foreign policy on domestic political affairs generally made it certain that he would immediately assume a position of leadership in Congress.

American political sentiment was predominantly anti-French following the return of the envoys from Paris in 1798, and the repercussions of the diplomatic struggle with France had the effect of replacing a number of incumbent Republicans with Federalists in the elections of 1799. This occurred more widely in the South, where in many cases Federalists, including Marshall himself, were for the first time elected to Congress. The elections secured a Federalist majority in the upcoming congress, but they also stimulated a drive by the Republicans for consolidation of their party as they looked ahead to the presidential election of 1800.[2]

Although the Federalists held the majority, they were far from united. John Adams's decision to pursue a second negotiation with the French unsettled Federalist ranks. In October 1799 he had ordered Oliver Ellsworth and William R. Davie to sail for France, where they were to join William Vans Murray in opening a new series of talks with French officials that might produce a peaceful solution to the Quasi-War. Many Federalists believed that Adams's decision was a fundamental mistake. Some of these men, particularly those from Adams's own region, began to consider ways of replacing him with someone they found more acceptable.[3]

2. See Vol. III, 494–502, and Noble E. Cunningham, Jr., *The Jeffersonian Republicans: The Formation of Party Organization, 1789–1801* (Chapel Hill, N.C., 1957), 134–140, 144–210.

3. Stephen G. Kurtz, *The Presidency of John Adams: The Collapse of Federalism, 1795–1800* (Philadelphia, 1957), 374–378, 384–389; Ralph Adams Brown, *The Presidency of John Adams* (Lawrence, Kans., 1975), 167–168.

Most of the newly elected Federalists, including John Marshall, came into office unallied with either side of the intraparty battle. This independence from party factions enabled them to cast deciding votes on key issues. John Marshall was immediately recognized as the leader of this group. His past support of the party during debates over neutrality and the Jay Treaty, as well as his well-known role in the XYZ mission, gave him credence with both the so-called High Federalists and the moderate Federalists, and he was also respected by a number of Republicans.[4]

The first session of the Sixth Congress was not one of great accomplishment, however. The intraparty strife created by Adams's foreign policy and by the Federalist attempt to implement the attendant domestic policy vied with Republican efforts to seize every opportunity to show the nation the mistake of allowing the Federalists to remain in power.[5] At the opening of the session Adams had delivered a short speech that was more a report on affairs than a call for legislation, and his comments on the mission to France were listened to with great interest by both parties. Because Federalists were badly divided over the mission, Adams merely reflected upon his "duty" to send the envoys in order to persevere "in the pacific and humane policy which had been invariably professed and sincerely pursued" by him in the past few years.[6] Republicans hoped, on the one hand, that the mission would succeed so that the Quasi-War could end and Federalists would lose support for many of their measures; but they also worried that success would reinforce Adams. The southern Federalists generally supported Adams's decision to send envoys to Paris. The Speaker of the House, Theodore Sedgwick, who considered the mission unwise, appointed Marshall chairman of a committee to prepare an official response because he thought he "could perfectly rely, that General Marshall entertained the same opinion of the mission" as himself, an opinion he later discovered was inaccurate.[7]

When the draft response came before the Committee of the Whole on December 9, few were inclined to criticize it. Marshall had succeeded in writing the letter to the president in sufficiently innocuous terms. Although no one, perhaps, felt entirely satisfied with the result, the members were unwilling, so early in the session, to risk the dangers inherent in a heated debate. The Federalists generally thought it best to take notice of the mission but to downgrade its importance, although some— about thirty eastern members—favored omitting any direct reference to it at all, just as the Senate had done. The Republicans considered inserting a strong statement of approval of the mission, but they backed away from this approach for fear of increasing Adams's popularity. "The address passed with silent dissent," reported Oliver Wolcott.[8]

4. For a description of JM's tenure in Congress and his standing among his colleagues, see Albert J. Beveridge, *The Life of John Marshall*, II (Boston, 1916), 432–484.

5. Brown, *Adams*, 166–167.

6. *Annals of Congress*, X, 187–191.

7. Quote from John Dawson to James Madison, Mar. 30, 1800, Madison Papers, Library of Congress. See Oliver Wolcott to Fisher Ames, Dec. 29, 1799, in George Gibbs, ed., *Memoirs of the Administrations of Washington and John Adams . . .* , II (New York, 1846), 314; Sedgwick to Peter Van Schaack, Dec. 9, 1799, Sedgwick Papers, Massachusetts Historical Society; see also Address, *ca.* Dec. 6, 1799. Sedgwick (1746–1813), a Federalist, served as Speaker for the Sixth Congress only.

8. Leven Powell to Burr Powell, Dec. 11, 1799, in "Correspondence of Leven Powell," *The John P. Branch Historical Papers of Randolph-Macon College*, I (1903), 232; John Dawson

Before the session was fully under way, news arrived on December 18 that George Washington had died. Marshall obtained the floor and moved an immediate adjournment. Afterward he took an active role in planning proper expressions of mourning. Partisanship did not appear until the period of mourning was well along, but throughout this period Republicans worried about the political capital Federalists were gleaning from Washington's death. Thomas Jefferson avoided the official memorial ceremonies, as did Aaron Burr.[9]

Very little substantive business took place on the floor of the House during December. One member complained that Congress, having finished with the president's speech, "appear at a loss what to take up next."[1] It is clear that the political rivalry and the presence of several new members from the South meant that the Federalist leadership needed more time to chart a course and prepare a legislative program. Theodore Sedgwick attributed the difficulty of organizing his party at this session to the mission to France, and he was aware of the Republicans' plans to capitalize on this situation. At the same time, as Sedgwick warned the Federalists, "In all our measures, we must never lose sight, of the next election of President."[2]

The opposition party opened its attack by supporting steps to disband the army. On New Year's Day, John Nicholas of Virginia moved that the acts to augment the army be repealed. Marshall spoke and voted against the motion, and after several days of debate it was defeated.[3] A few days later, a committee that had prepared resolutions on the army recommended what was in effect a compromise position. Their proposal embraced the Federalist policy, which recommended the retention of soldiers already recruited but a suspension of all further recruiting. This suspension was ostensibly an economy measure and a concession to the Republicans. A bill was drawn, and on the first day of debate John Randolph moved an amendment, similar to Nicholas's earlier motion, that would have sent many soldiers home. John Marshall also opposed this amendment, as he had Nicholas's resolution, and it was defeated. After additional motions and debate, the committee's bill finally passed unmodified on January 24, suspending additional recruitments unless war broke out with France.[4]

---

to James Madison, Dec. 12, 1799, Madison Papers; *Annals of Congress*, X, 193–196; *Journal of the House of Representatives . . . first session of the Sixth Congress*, III (Washington, D.C., 1826), 530–533; quote from Wolcott to Ames, Dec. 29, 1799, in Gibbs, ed., *Memoirs*, II, 314. Only one minor suggestion for revision was made, and this failed to win approval. See Address, *ca.* Dec. 6, 1799.

9. *Annals of Congress*, X, 203–204, 207–223, 708; *Journal of the House*, III, 540, 542–547, 702. See also Robert Troup to Rufus King, Jan. 1, 1800, in King, ed., *Life and Corres. of Rufus King*, III, 171; Motion, Dec. 18, 1799; Speech, Dec. 19, 1799; and Resolutions, Dec. 23 and 30, 1799.

1. Dawson to Madison, Dec. 12, 1799, Madison Papers.

2. Sedgwick to King, Dec. 12, 1799, in King, ed., *Life and Corres. of Rufus King*, III, 154–155.

3. The previous congress had authorized the recruiting of 12 additional regiments to augment the army. 1 Stat. 604 (1798); *Annals of Congress*, X, 227–228, 251–369; *Journal of the House*, III, 556. See also Kurtz, *Adams*, 366–371, and Speech, Jan. 7, 1800.

4. *Annals of Congress*, X, 370, 389–404. See Speech, Jan. 22, 1800.

By the end of April attitudes had changed. Republican Stevens Thomson Mason (1760–1803) introduced a supplemental bill in the Senate that revived the militia issue by authorizing a permanent suspension of enlistments. This measure passed the Senate, but when the House debated it, Federalists, led by Robert Goodloe Harper, inserted

Just prior to the opening debate on the first army bill, a select committee introduced a bankruptcy bill in the House. Marshall had been appointed to this committee on December 5 in an apparent effort to win support for this controversial measure, which had failed by narrow margins since 1789. Marshall added to the bill novel provisions requiring that a jury decide the question of bankruptcy and the amount of the debt. Sedgwick thought that putting these questions to jurors would prove to be "infinitely" perplexing, but he acknowledged that Marshall's standing made acceptance of this provision necessary in order to save the bill.[5] When the final vote was taken on February 21, a tie resulted and the bill passed only with the vote of the Speaker. Federalists were jubilant, seeing in the bill opportunities for national unity. Republicans complained of the "out of doors" efforts exerted by the bill's supporters and noted that the bill would have been killed in either house had votes not come when strategic members were absent. Attempts to weaken the bill in the Senate failed.[6]

From the time the committee on the bankruptcy bill was first appointed, members of Congress associated the measure with recent attempts to expand the judicial system in the United States. In fact, the committees appointed to draft bills on these two subjects were composed of the same five Federalists: Robert Goodloe Harper, Chauncey Goodrich, Samuel Sewall, James A. Bayard, and John Marshall. The proposals for the judiciary system, like the bankruptcy bill, were clearly intended to aid Federalist plans for further consolidation of the Union; one Republican labeled the judiciary bill "the eldest child of the bankrupt system."[7] Opposition to the judiciary bill was formidable, and its enemies succeeded in striking its key sections. A motion to postpone consideration of a revised version until the following session carried by two votes. To help defeat the bill, opponents capitalized on the poor financial condition of the country, insisting that the revised system would add $100,000 to the budget.[8]

---

amendments that would in effect have reduced the size of the army by allowing the president to discharge soldiers as soon as he thought negotiations with France warranted it. This bill was finally approved on May 14, the day Congress adjourned. *Annals of Congress*, X, 148–150, 166–167, 169, 180, 182, 691–692, 713–716; 2 Stat. 85–86.

5. *Annals of Congress*, X, 191, 247; IX, 2441, 2488, 2676; *Journal of the House*, III, 121, 164, 405, 409. See also Legislative Bill, calendared at Jan. 6, 1800.

6. *Annals of Congress*, X, 110–111, 115–116, 125–126, 534; Bayard to Richard Bassett, Feb. 1, 1800, in Elizabeth Donnan, ed., *Papers of James A. Bayard, 1796–1815* (American Historical Association, *Annual Report, 1913*, II (Washington, D.C., 1915), 95; Stevens Thomson Mason to James Madison, Mar. 7, 1800, Madison Papers; Sedgwick to King, in King, ed., *Life and Corres. of Rufus King*, III, 189–190. See also Robert Goodloe Harper to Constituents, May 15, 1800, in Noble E. Cunningham, Jr., ed., *Circular Letters of Congressmen to Their Constituents, 1789–1829*, I (Chapel Hill, N.C., 1978), 216; and Legislative Bill, calendared at Jan. 6, 1800.

7. Leven Powell to Burr Powell, Dec. 11, 1799, *Branch Papers*, I, 233; Dawson to Madison, Mar. 30, 1800, Madison Papers; Wolcott to John Adams and to Fisher Ames, Dec. 29, 1799, in Gibbs, ed., *Memoirs*, II, 299, 316; and Anthony New to Constituents, in Cunningham, ed., *Circular Letters*, I, 196. For observations on the similarity in committee membership and a cogent examination of this legislation, see Kathryn Turner, "Federalist Policy and the Judiciary Act of 1801," *WMQ*, 3d Ser., XXII (1965), 3–14.

8. *Annals of Congress*, X, 643–649, 665–666; *Journal of the House*, III, 642, 645, 663. See Committee Reports, Mar. 11 and *ca.* May 1, 1800; Legislative Bills, calendared at Mar. 11 and 31, 1800; and Speech, calendared at Mar. 27, 1800.

Much of the time at this session was spent in lengthy partisan debate. Political issues were seized upon by Republicans as a way to embarrass Federalist congressmen and the administration, which caused delays in the consideration of more serious legislative issues. Attention, as always, was given to public opinion and the upcoming presidential election.[9] Each month the House of Representatives lost at least a week of productive legislative work while it concentrated on political issues. The first one involved the question of a citizen's breach of Republican John Randolph's privileges as a congressman.[1] The most controversial political skirmish to occur during this session, however, came when Republicans brought the case of Jonathan Robbins before the House. Robbins had been released from the custody of a South Carolina court the previous summer, at which time he was taken by the British authorities and subsequently executed for mutiny and murder. At the time he was turned over to the British, charges were made that the Adams administration had interfered improperly, but the controversy over Robbins's extradition had subsided. On February 4 the Republicans attempted to revive the matter as a campaign issue.[2] Edward Livingston presented resolutions calling for legislation on article 27 of the Jay Treaty, the article dealing with extradition, and requesting from the State Department documents relating to Adams's conduct in the extradition of Robbins. Both resolutions were adopted, and on February 7 the secretary of state sent a collection of materials indicating that Robbins was actually Thomas Nash, that he was not an American citizen, and that he had been delivered to the British "in compliance with the request of the President of the United States." Livingston insisted that these documents be considered by the Committee of the Whole, and James A. Bayard answered with a resolution approving the president's conduct in the affair. After Livingston introduced a resolution condemning Adams on February 20, the members began a series of lengthy speeches that had little purpose beyond partisanship.[3]

After getting all the charges out in the open, the Republicans recognized that they could not prove Robbins had been a United States citizen, and they became locked in a debate over presidential conduct. They next tried to cut off further discussion, hoping Federalists would welcome the move, but the Federalists insisted that the issue be thoroughly examined and the president vindicated. Republicans then began calling for additional documents, realizing they could not be obtained and examined before Congress adjourned.[4] Following Livingston's and Albert Gallatin's extended speeches on the issue, John Marshall took the floor and delivered what some consider his most impressive speech. Afterward, debate fizzled, Livingston's resolution

---

9. Brown, *Adams*, 166–168.

1. *Annals of Congress*, X, 298, 367, 378–388, 426–507; Stevens Thomson Mason to James Monroe, Jan. [7], 1800, Monroe Papers, Lib. Cong. See also William Cabell Bruce, *John Randolph of Roanoke, 1773–1833* . . . , I (New York, 1922), 158–165.

2. For the best account of the affair, which concludes that Robbins was a U.S. citizen, see Larry D. Cress, "The Jonathan Robbins Incident: Extradition and the Separation of Powers in the Adams Administration," *Essex Institute Historical Collections*, CXI (1975), 99–121.

3. Livingston's (1764–1836) resolutions are printed in *Annals of Congress*, X, 511–512. See also *ibid.*, 515–518, 526, 532–533, 541–578, 584–620.

4. See Speech, calendared at Feb. 27, 1800, and JM to James Markham Marshall, Feb. 28, 1800.

was soundly defeated, and Bayard's resolution was as strongly adopted.[5] Marshall's speech and the tired disgust that emerged after so fruitless a debate put an end to this topic as a campaign issue in the 1800 elections.

The related question of article 27 of the Jay Treaty was now less important, although John Nicholas tried diligently to make an issue out of the bill when it was first debated, well after discussion of the Robbins affair was exhausted. Nicholas's objections were met by counter-arguments and proposals from Marshall. In the end, both sides allowed this measure to die quietly.[6]

The issue of the upcoming presidential election came directly before Congress when Federalist senator James Ross introduced a bill that proposed the establishment of a joint committee to make the final determination on the election for president and vice-president.[7] This seemed to some, including Marshall, contrary to Article II of the Constitution, which assigned to the House of Representatives the responsibility for choosing a president if none of the candidates received a majority of electoral votes cast. The Ross bill attempted to give the Senate an equal role in this procedure, and opponents of the measure hoped this alone might kill it.[8]

When the measure came up for debate in the House, many Republicans as well as some Federalists, such as Marshall, considered the entire bill unconstitutional. Theodore Sedgwick claimed to have changed Marshall's mind, but Marshall argued ultimately that the authority for choosing a president was "too delicate to be delegated, untill experience had demonstrated that great inconveniences would attend its exercise by the Legislature."[9] Marshall proposed amendments to the Ross bill, but before a vote was taken the House decided to submit the bill to a select committee for redrafting. Marshall was named chairman of a select committee of seven, only one other member of which, John Nicholas, was an opponent of the measure.[1]

The select committee reported a new bill, referred to as "John Marshall's amendment," that withheld from the proposed joint committee any power of decision, giving it the responsibility only of reporting the facts relating to the votes cast. Surprisingly, the Senate accepted this alteration after it passed the House. The upper house did try, however, to include in the new bill a modification that would permit one or two members to require specific action by Congress before accepting any

5. *Annals of Congress*, X, 621; Leven Powell to Burr Powell, Mar. 5 and 26, 1800, *Branch Papers*, I, 238–240. JM's speech is printed at Mar. 7, 1800. See also JM to Reuben George, Mar. 16, 1800.

6. *Annals of Congress*, X, 537, 654–655, 691. See Amendment, Apr. 2, 1800.

7. James Morton Smith, *Freedom's Fetters: The Alien and Sedition Laws and American Civil Liberties* (Ithaca, N.Y., 1956), 288–289; G. S. Rowe, *Thomas McKean: The Shaping of an American Republicanism* (Boulder, Colo., 1978), 307–317. See also JM to Reuben George, Mar. 16, 1800.

8. Stevens Thomson Mason to Madison, Mar. 7, 1800, Madison Papers; Thomas Jefferson to Madison, Mar. 4, 1800, *ibid.*; Mason to Monroe, Apr. 29, 1800, Monroe Papers. Attempts to involve the Senate more fully in the process of counting electoral votes and deciding disputes culminated in a provision of the 11th Amendment that allowed the Senate to choose the vice-president in case the electors failed to elect a candidate by majority vote.

9. Sedgwick to King, May 11, 1800, in King, ed., *Life and Corres. of Rufus King*, III, 237–238; JM to James Markham Marshall, Apr. 4, 1800.

1. See Amendment, *ca.* Apr. 16, 1800, and *Journal of the House*, III, 675.

challenged votes. When the House refused this change and the Senate would not give it up, the bill was lost.[2]

Marshall had a significant influence on other pieces of legislation brought before the House. As chairman of the committee to consider whether Connecticut's offer to cede the Western Reserve was acceptable, he pushed through a bill that finally brought that perplexing problem to a resolution.[3] He adhered to his moderate and sometimes independent Federalism by carrying out his pledge to his constituents to oppose the Sedition Act, and he voted for its repeal. When it was moved that the offenses specified by the law should remain punishable at common law, however, Marshall voted against the motion. Because this amendment passed in the House, Marshall then turned around and voted against the resolution to repeal the Sedition Act, joining with the Republicans in a decision that carried by only two votes.[4] The issue at stake was the introduction of a federal common law, and opposition to that was widespread. Some members apparently voted for the common law provision with the knowledge that it would render the measure unacceptable to the House. The bill to repeal the Sedition Act, therefore, was defeated, and the law expired as scheduled on March 1, 1801.[5]

Marshall served on some minor select committees during this session. In the dispute over defining the limits of Georgia and establishing a government for the Mississippi Territory, he voted with the minority against restricting the powers of the governor. When the Senate amended the House's bill, taking out the restrictions, Marshall served on a select committee to consider the Senate's action. This committee, perhaps at Marshall's urging, reported that the bill now should be accepted, but the House rejected their report and refused the amendment.[6]

Marshall was also closely involved in an effort by the House to authorize the incorporation of a company that would provide sheet copper for the nation's military needs. The House appointed Samuel Smith, Marshall, and Robert Waln, three supporters of the idea, to prepare a more acceptable draft of the copper bill after it had been narrowly defeated. The improved version, which called for incorporation of the Passaick Copper Company, was adopted by the House, but the measure was later defeated in the Senate.[7]

2. Thomas Jefferson to Edward Livingston, Apr. 30, 1800, and Jefferson to Madison, May 12, 1800, Jefferson Papers, Lib. Cong.; *Annals of Congress*, X, 175–176, 710, 713. See Committee Report, Apr. 25, 1800.

3. *Annals of Congress*, X, 658, 661. See Committee Report, calendared at Mar. 21, 1800, Legislative Bill, calendared at *ca.* Mar. 21, 1800, and Speeches, calendared at Apr. 7 and 8, 1800.

4. *Annals of Congress*, X, 404–410, 419, 424. As first printed in the *Annals*, it appears that the common law amendment was part of the original resolution introduced by Nathaniel Macon (1757–1837). Actually, the clause was suggested by James A. Bayard after debate began.

5. Sedgwick to King, May 11, 1800, in King, ed., *Life and Corres. of Rufus King*, III, 237; Mason to Monroe, Jan. [7], 1800, Monroe Papers. The Federalists had little more than political position at stake in this vote; the Sedition Act was already scheduled to expire on Mar. 3, 1801.

6. *Annals of Congress*, X, 632, 680, 682, 685; *Journal of the House*, III, 632, 670, 680, 682.

7. *Annals of Congress*, X, 651, 664, 678–679, 681–682, 684, 688, 691; *Journal of the House*, III, 679, 682, 685, 687, 714.

About a week before Congress adjourned and without any consultation or warning, President Adams nominated Marshall to succeed James McHenry as secretary of war. Marshall was on the verge of leaving for Richmond to prepare for the term of the U.S. Circuit Court that convened on May 22,[8] and declined the offer. He had obtained permission on May 8 to be absent for the remainder of the congressional session.[9]

Marshall and his colleagues had often been hindered in their attempts to obtain passage of certain bills by the nature of the bills themselves. Many of the important bills that came before Congress during this session—the judiciary bill and the Bankruptcy Act, in particular—were deeply controversial and were tainted by having failed of passage in earlier sessions. Marshall's role in modifying the bankruptcy bill by providing for jury participation probably brought enough votes to obtain the tie that Sedgwick broke to enact the bill. Marshall's efforts in committee and on the floor might have brought the judiciary bill closer to adoption, but it remained too radical and expensive to secure passage in this session despite its close association with the bankruptcy bill. The standing army issue could have resulted in a bitter partisan battle that would have helped the Republicans regardless of what action was taken on the bill. Marshall suggested the compromise that enabled the Federalists to claim popular favor when a bill authorizing the president to disband portions of the army passed the day before adjournment. "On the approach of an election," Vice President Jefferson complained, the Federalists were "trying to court a little popularity, that they may be afterwards allowed to go on 4 years longer in defiance of it."[1]

The Federalists themselves were not pleased with their position as the session drew to a close. Theodore Sedgwick characterized the session as "long tedious and unproductive." He described a "feebleness of character" in the House and blamed Marshall for contributing to the weakening of Federalist principles.[2]

Marshall's effectiveness in the House was not unseen or unappreciated by John Adams, however. His demonstrated loyalty and ability would lead to another offer to join the administration, an offer Marshall found too attractive to decline after he reviewed his opportunities in Richmond.[3] Once again, his able conduct in public service led to a higher and more responsible position, a pattern that ended only when he was given the highest judicial office in the nation.

---

8. See JM to John Adams, May 8, 1800. See also *Journal of the House*, III, 702; U.S. Circuit Court, Va., Order Book, II, 342, Virginia State Library; and *Virginia Federalist* (Richmond), June 7, 1800, 3.

9. *Journal of the House*, III, 702.

1. Jefferson to Thomas Mann Randolph, May 14, 1800, Jefferson Papers.

2. Sedgwick to King, May 11, 1800, in King, ed., *Life and Corres. of Rufus King*, III, 237.

3. See Brown, *Adams*, 167, and Secretary of State: Editorial Note, June 6, 1800.

Resolution

Printed, *Annals of Congress*, X, 191

Philadelphia, December 4, 1799

Resolved,   That it is the opinion of this Committee, that a respectful Address ought to be presented by the House of Representatives to the President of the United States, in answer to his Speech to both Houses of Congress, on the opening of the present session, containing assurances that this House will duly attend to the important objects recommended by him to their consideration.[4]

Address

Printed, [U.S. Congress, House], *Report of the Committee Appointed to Prepare an Address to Both Houses of Congress* (Philadelphia, 1800)

[Philadelphia, *ca.* December 6, 1799]

To the PRESIDENT *of the* UNITED STATES.

SIR,[5]

WHILE the House of Representatives contemplate the flattering prospects of abundance from the labors of the people by land and by sea, the prosperity of our extended commerce, notwithstanding interruptions occasioned by the belligerent state of a great part of the world; the return of health, industry and trade to those cities which

4. On the day the session opened, JM was appointed chairman of the committee to inform John Adams that the House was prepared to receive his annual address. The president spoke to a joint session of Congress the next day, Dec. 3. When the Committee of the Whole met to consider the speech, JM introduced this resolution. The motion carried, and JM was named chairman of a committee to prepare a response for the House. *Annals of Congress,* X, 188–191.

5. JM reported this address on behalf of the committee appointed to draft it. According to Oliver Wolcott, the political climate in the House made it "necessary and proper that the answer to the speech should be prepared by Mr. Marshall." Wolcott added that JM had the difficult task of preparing a response that would unite the Federalists, and while the reply had to appear to approve of the mission to France, it had to do so in terms that all factions could agree on. Wolcott to Fisher Ames, Dec. 29, 1799, in George Gibbs, ed., *Memoirs of the Administrations of Washington and John Adams . . .*, II (New York, 1846), 314.

After the House approved the letter, JM, John Rutledge, Jr. (1766–1819), of South Carolina, and Samuel Sewall (1757–1814), of Massachusetts, were asked to call on Adams to learn when he would be willing to have the Speaker of the House deliver the message. *Annals of Congress,* X, 193, 196.

have lately been afflicted with disease, and the various and inestimable advantages, civil and religious, which, secured under our happy frame of government, are continued to us unimpaired, we cannot fail to offer up to a benevolent Deity, our sincere thanks, for these, the merciful dispensations of his protecting providence.

That any portion of the people of America should permit themselves, amidst such numerous blessings, to be seduced by the arts and misrepresentations of designing men into an[6] open resistance of a law of the United States, cannot be heard without deep and serious regret. Under a constitution where the public burthens can only be imposed by the people themselves, for their own benefit, and to promote their own objects, a hope might well have been indulged that the general interest would have been too well understood, and the general welfare too highly prized, to have produced in any of our citizens, a disposition to hazard so much felicity, by the criminal effort of a part, to oppose with lawless violence the will of the whole. While we lament that depravity which could produce a defiance of the civil authority, and render indispensible the aid of the military force of the nation, real consolation is to be derived from the promptness and fidelity with which that aid was afforded. That zealous and active co-operation with the judicial power, of the volunteers and militia called into service, which has restored order and submission to the laws, is a pleasing evidence of the attachment of our fellow citizens to their own free government, and of the truly patriotic alacrity with which they will support it.

To give due effect to the civil administration of government, and to ensure a just execution of the laws, are objects of such real magnitude as to secure a proper attention to your recommendation of a revision and amendment of the judiciary system.[7]

Highly approving, as we do, the pacific and humane policy which has been invariably professed, and sincerely pursued by the Executive Authority of the United States, a policy which our best interests enjoined, and of which honor has permitted the observance, we consider as the most unequivocal proof of your inflexible perseverance in the same well chosen system, your preparation to meet the first indications on the part of the French Republic, of a disposition to

6. Andrew Gregg (1755–1835), of Pennsylvania, moved on Dec. 9 that the words "be seduced by the arts and misrepresentations of designing men, into an" be replaced by "act in," but this motion was defeated. The draft was then approved as submitted. *Annals of Congress*, X, 194. *Claypoole's American Daily Advertiser* (Philadelphia), Dec. 10, 1799, the *Aurora* (Philadelphia), Dec. 12, 1799, and the *Annals* printed the original words in italics.

7. See Committee Report, Mar. 11, 1800, and Speech, calendared at Mar. 27, 1800.

accommodate the existing differences between the two countries, by a nomination of Ministers on certain conditions, which the honor of our country unquestionably dictated, and which its moderation had certainly given it a right to prescribe.[8] When the assurances thus required of the French government, previous to the departure of our Envoys, had been given through their Minister of foreign relations, the direction that they should proceed on their mission, was, on your part, a completion of the measure, and manifests the sincerity with which it was commenced. We offer up our fervent prayers to the Supreme Ruler of the universe for the success of their embassy, and that it may be productive of peace and happiness to our common country. The uniform tenure of your conduct through a life useful to your fellow-citizens, and honorable to yourself, gives a sure pledge of the sincerity with which the avowed objects of the negotiation will be pursued on your part, and we earnestly pray that similar dispositions may be displayed on the part of France. The differences which unfortunately subsist between the two nations cannot fail, in that event, to be happily terminated. To produce this end, to all so desirable, firmness, moderation, and union at home, constitute, we are persuaded, the surest means. The character of the gentlemen you have deputed, and still more, the character of the government which deputes them, are safe pledges to their country, that nothing incompatible with its honor or interest, nothing inconsistent with our obligations of good faith or friendship to any other nation, will be stipulated.

We learn, with pleasure, that our citizens with their property trading to those ports of St. Domingo with which commercial intercourse has been renewed, have been duly respected, and that privateering from those ports has ceased.

With you we sincerely regret that the execution of the VIth article of the treaty of amity, commerce, and navigation with Great-Britain, an article produced by a mutual spirit of amity and justice, should have been unavoidably interrupted. We doubt not that the same spirit of amity, and the same sense of justice in which it originated, will lead to satisfactory explanations; and we hear with approbation,

---

8. Adams had nominated William Vans Murray as envoy to Paris on Feb. 18, 1799, upon receiving indications of French willingness to negotiate. Oliver Ellsworth (1745–1807) and William R. Davie were later appointed envoys to join Murray in Europe, and they departed on Nov. 3. Stephen G. Kurtz, *The Presidency of John Adams: The Collapse of Federalism, 1795–1800* (Philadelphia, 1957), 348, 388; Ralph Adams Brown, *The Presidency of John Adams* (Lawrence, Kans., 1975), 95–113, 162. See JM to James Markham Marshall, Dec. 16, 1799, for JM's comments on the nomination of envoys to France.

that our Minister at London will be immediately instructed to obtain them.[9] While the engagements which America has contracted by her treaty with Great-Britain, ought to be fulfilled with that scrupulous punctuality and good faith to which our government has ever so tenaciously adhered; yet no motive exists to induce, and every principle forbids us to adopt a construction which might extend them beyond the instrument by which they are created. We cherish the hope that the government of Great-Britain will disclaim such extension, and by cordially uniting with that of the United States, for the removal of all difficulties, will soon enable the boards appointed under the VIth and VIIth[1] articles of our treaty with that nation, to proceed, and bring the business committed to them respectively, to a satisfactory conclusion.

The buildings for the accommodation of Congress, and of the President, and for the public offices of the government at its permanent seat, being in such a state as to admit of a removal to that district by the time prescribed by the act of Congress, no obstacle, it is presumed, will exist to a compliance with the law.

With you, sir, we deem the present period critical and momentous. The important changes which are occurring, the new and great events which are every hour preparing in the political world, the spirit of war which is prevalent in almost every nation with whose affairs the interests of the United States have any connection, demonstrate how unsafe and precarious would be our situation, should we neglect the means of maintaining our just rights. Respecting, as we have ever done, the rights of others, America estimates too correctly

9. Art. 6 of the Jay Treaty called for the convening in Philadelphia of a joint Anglo-American commission to discuss the questions of debts owed British creditors by Americans. Miller, ed., *Treaties*, II, 249–251.

In the summer of 1799 the meeting collapsed in disagreement. Secretary of State Timothy Pickering sent instructions to Rufus King, U.S. ambassador in London, outlining procedures for resuming discussions. The British rejected the suggested procedures but, in Apr. 1800, hinted that a lump-sum settlement might be acceptable. By the time that issue was considered, JM had become secretary of state and was fully involved in policy making. Bradford Perkins, *The First Rapprochement: England and the United States, 1795–1805* (Berkeley, Calif., 1967), 117–120; Robert Ernst, *Rufus King: American Federalist* (Chapel Hill, N.C., 1968), 247–248; Pickering to King, Dec. 31, 1799, Pickering Papers, Massachusetts Historical Society; King to [JM], Apr. 7, 22 (2 letters), and 26 (calendared), 1800; JM to John Adams, July 21, Aug. 12, 16, and 23, 1800; Adams to JM, Aug. 1 and 22, 1800; JM to King, Aug. 23, 1800 (2 letters).

1. Art. 7 of the Jay Treaty dealt with American claims of British spoliations during the war. Miller, ed., *Treaties*, II, 252–253. A commission, similar to the debt commission, that was meeting in London ceased deliberations upon learning of the collapse of the Philadelphia meeting. Perkins, *First Rapprochement*, 119.

the value of her own and has received evidence too complete, that they are only to be preserved by her own vigilance, ever to permit herself to be seduced by a love of ease or by other considerations, into that deadly disregard of the means of self defence, which could only result from a carelessness as criminal as it would be fatal, concerning the future destinies of our growing republic. The result of the mission to France is, indeed sir, uncertain. It depends not on America alone. The most pacific temper will not always insure peace. We should therefore exhibit a system of conduct as indiscreet as it would be new in the history of the world, if we considered the negotiation happily terminated because we have attempted to commence it, and peace restored because we wish its restoration. But, sir, however this mission may terminate, a steady perseverance in a system of national defence, commensurate with our resources, and the situation of our country, is an obvious dictate of duty. Experience, the parent of wisdom, and the great instructor of nations, has established the truth of your position, that, remotely as we are placed from the belligerent nations, and desirous as we are, by doing justice to all, to avoid offence to any, yet nothing short of the power of repelling aggressions will secure to our country a rational prospect of escaping the calamities of war or national degradation.

In the progress of the session, we shall take into our serious consideration the various and important matters recommended to our attention.

A life devoted to the service of your country, talents and integrity which have so justly acquired and so long retained the confidence and affection of your fellow citizens, attest the sincerity of your declaration, that it is your anxious desire so to execute the trust reposed in you as to render the people of the United States prosperous and happy.

Deed

Deed Book Copy, Office of the Clerk of Hardy County, Moorefield, W.Va.

[*December 13, 1799* (*Hardy County, Va.*). By his attorney, Rawleigh Colston, JM conveys 12.25 acres in the South Branch Manor to David Welton for £3 1s. 3d. The deed was recorded in the District Court at Hardy County on May 6, 1799.]

To James Markham Marshall

ALS, Bixby Collection, Washington University Library

My dear brother   Philadelphia, December 16, 1799

I receivd yours of the 7th. inst.[2] Mr. Pleasant has remitted to me a draft on the bank of Pennsylvania for two thousand & thirteen dollars & seventy five cents & has sent me certificates for fourteen shares of bank stock. Inclosd you will receive a blank power of attorney to transfer the stock & one for drawing the dividends. These are to be filld up & executed before a notary public or before the Mayor & attested by two witnesses. The eight per cent stock is without my knowledge transferd to the books in Richmond. It is probable that it may be sold there. I will write to Hopkins[3] on the subject. If I remit the bills on account of this stock I must lay hold of any money to replace it in the event of an unfortunate decision in the court of appeals.[4]

I shoud be perfectly satisfied with the sale to Vanmetre[5] or with any other sale you may wish to make shoud this not be adherd to. I am also well pleas'd with the change of the lease for the swan ponds & wish you to complete the contract. Let him know the hazard of a forfeiture.

I approve too of your determination respecting the manor of Leeds. Woud it not be adviseable to write to Fairfax on the subject & endeavor to obtain a conveyance on reexecuting a mortgage or if that be impracticable a power of attorney to collect the rents?[6]

I will attend to your request concerning the reports.

I can tell you in confidence that the situation of our affairs with respect to domestic quiet is much more critical than I had conjecturd. The eastern people are very much dissatisfied with the President on account of the late mission to France.[7] They are strongly disposd to

2. Not found.

3. John Hopkins was U.S. commissioner of loans in Richmond. JM's blank power of attorney has not been found.

4. JM may have anticipated the adverse ruling of the District Court at Winchester in Marshall v. Conrad that came in Apr. 1800, but he had already decided that his brother should appeal that ruling to the Court of Appeals. See JM to James Markham Marshall, Apr. 3, 1799. The case involved back rents for Fairfax lands purchased by the Marshalls, rents they needed in order to make payments to Denny Martin Fairfax.

5. In 1802 Isaac and Jacob Vanmeter purchased a tract known as the "resurvey" from JM. See Vol. II, 148.

6. For a general discussion of the purchase of the Fairfax lands, see Vol. II, 140–149.

7. See Alexander DeConde, *The Quasi-War: The Politics and Diplomacy of the Un-*

desert him & to push some other candidate. King or Ellsworth with one of the Pinckneys—most probably the general, are thought of. If they are deterd from doing this by the fear that the attempt might elect Jefferson I think not improbable that they will vote generally for Adams & Pinckney so as to give the latter gentleman the best chance if he gets the southern vote to be the President. Perhaps this ill humor may evaporate before the election comes on—but at present it wears a very serious aspect. This circumstance is renderd the more unpleasant by the state of our finances. The impost receivable this year has been less productive than usual & it will be impossible to continue the present armament without another loan. Had the impost producd the sum to which it was calculated a loan woud have been unavoidable.[8] This difficulty ought to have been foreseen when it was determind to execute the law for raising the army. It is now conceivd that we cannot at the present stage of our negotiation with France change the defensive position we have taken without much hazard. In addition to this many influential characters not only contend that the army ought not now to be disbanded but that it ought to be continued so long as the war in europe shall last. I am apprehensive that our people woud receive with very ill temper a system which shoud keep up an army of observation at the expence of the annual addition of five million to our debt.[9] The effect of it woud most probably be that the hands which hold the reins woud be entirely changd. You perceive the perplexities attending our situation. In addition to this there are such different views with respect to the future, such a rancarous malignity of temper among the democrats, such an apparent disposition—(if the aurora be the index of the [*views*] of those who support it) to propel us to a war with Br[*itain*] & to infold us within the embrace of France such a detestation & fear of France among others [*that*] I look forward with more apprehension than I have ever done to the future political events of our country.

Mr. Morris & the family are all well. My wife is in good health &

---

declared War with France, 1797–1801 (New York, 1966), 223, and Ralph Adams Brown, *The Presidency of John Adams* (Lawrence, Kans., 1975), 162.

8. Oliver Wolcott's February report to Adams on financial matters indicated a Treasury deficit of approximately $5 million for the fiscal year ending in 1799. George Gibbs, ed., *Memoirs of the Administrations of Washington and John Adams . . .*, II (New York, 1846), 300.

9. See Speech, Jan. 7 and 22, 1800.

joins me in best wishes for the happiness of you & yours. You will perceive that this letter is in absolute confidence. Your affectionate

J MARSHALL

We are just informed of the total defeat of the English in Holland.[1]

Motion

Printed, *Claypoole's American Daily Advertiser* (Philadelphia), December 19, 1799, 3

Philadelphia, December 18, 1799

MR. SPEAKER,

Information has just been received, that our Illustrious Fellow Citizen, the COMMANDER IN CHIEF *of the* AMERICAN ARMY, *and the late President of the United States, is no more.*[2]

Tho' this distressing intelligence is not certain, there is too much reason to believe its truth. After receiving information of this National calamity, so heavy and so afflicting, the House of Representatives can be but ill fitted for public business. I move you, therefore, they adjourn.

Speech

Printed, *Claypoole's American Daily Advertiser* (Philadelphia), December 20, 1799, 3

Philadelphia, December 19, 1799

MR. SPEAKER,

The melancholy event which was yesterday announced with doubt, has been rendered but too certain. Our Washington is no more! The hero, the sage, and the patriot of America—the man on whom in times of danger every eye was turned and all hopes were

1. In August a combined Anglo-Russian amphibious operation had landed in Holland, and word reached Philadelphia in October that the Dutch fleet had surrendered. On Oct. 10, without a major military engagement, the opposing armies signed the Convention of Alkmaar, and the Anglo-Russian force departed with only a few vessels of the Dutch fleet to claim for their efforts. See R. R. Palmer, *The Age of the Democratic Revolution: A Political History of Europe and America, 1760–1800*, II (Princeton, N.J., 1964), 567–568.

2. George Washington had died at Mt. Vernon during the evening of Dec. 14. Immediately after JM introduced his motion the House adjourned for the remainder of the day. *Annals of Congress*, X, 203.

placed, lives now, only in his own great actions, and in the hearts of an affectionate and afflicted people.

If, sir, it had even not be unusual[3] openly to testify respect for the memory of those whom Heaven had selected as its instruments for dispensing good to men, yet such has been the uncommon worth, and such the extraordinary incidents which have marked the life of him whose loss we all deplore, that the whole American nation, impelled by the same feelings, would call with one voice for public manifestation of that sorrow which is so deep and so universal.

More than any other individual, and as much as to one individual was possible, has he contributed to found this our wide spreading empire, and to give to the western world its independence and its freedom.

Having effected the great object for which he was placed at the head of our armies, we have seen him converting the sword into the plough-share, and voluntarily linking the soldier in the citizen.

When the debility of our federal system had become manifest, and the bonds which connected the parts of this vast continent were dissolving, we have seen him the chief of those patriots who formed for us a constitution, which, by preserving the union, will, I trust, substantiate and perpetuate those blessings our revolution had promised to bestow.

In obedience to the general voice of his country, calling on him to preside over a great people, we have seen him once more quit the retirement he loved, and in a season more stormy and tempestuous than war itself, with calm and wise determination, pursue the true interests of the nation, and contribute more than any other could contribute, to the establishment of that system of policy, which will, I trust, yet preserve our peace, our honor and our independence.

Having been twice unanimously chosen the Chief Magistrate of a free people, we see him, at a time when his re-election with the universal suffrage, could not have been doubted, affording to the world a rare instance of moderation, by withdrawing from his high station to the peaceful walks of private life.

However the public confidence may change, and the public affections fluctuate with respect to others, yet with respect to him they have, in war and in peace, in public and in private life, been as steady as his own firm mind, and as constant as his own exalted virtues.

---

3. In the record of this address, printed in 1851, this sentence reads, "had even not been usual." *Annals of Congress*, X, 203.

Let us then, Mr. Speaker, pay the last tribute of respect and affection to our departed friend—Let the grand council of the nation display those sentiments which the nation feels.

For this purpose I hold in my hand some resolutions which I will take the liberty to offer to the House.

Resolved, That this House will wait on the President of the United States, in condolence of this mournful event.[4]

Resolved, That the Speaker's chair be shrouded with black, and that the Members and Officers of the House wear black during the Session.

Resolved, That a committee, in conjunction with one from the Senate, be appointed to consider on the most suitable manner of paying honour to the memory of the man, first in war, first in peace, and first in the hearts of his country.[5]

Resolved, That this House, when it adjourns, do adjourn to Monday.

Resolutions

Printed, *Claypoole's American Daily Advertiser* (Philadelphia), December 24, 1799, 3

Philadelphia, December 23, 1799

RESOLVED, *By the Senate and House of Representatives of the United States of America, in Congress assembled*, That a Marble Monument be erected by the United States, in the Capitol, in the city of Washington, and that the family of Gen. Washington be requested, to permit his body to be deposited under it; and that the monument be so designed as to commemorate the great events of his military and political life.[6]

4. These resolutions were drafted by Henry Lee, who asked JM to introduce them in his absence. The House adopted them unanimously. JM was appointed with Samuel Smith, of Maryland, to carry out the first resolution, and he was named chairman of a committee to implement the third. *Ibid.*, 204; John Marshall, *The Life of George Washington . . .* , V (Philadelphia, 1807), 765.

5. The identical account of JM's address appeared in the *Aurora* (Philadelphia), Dec. 21, 1799, but see also *Annals of Congress*, X, 204, 708, where "countrymen" was used.

6. These resolutions constituted the first report of the committee appointed on Dec. 19 and were submitted by JM. *Annals of Congress*, X, 207–208.

Congress had approved the idea of an equestrian statue of Washington as early as 1783, but this committee recommended on May 8 that Congress authorize construction of an additional monument in the Capitol. Although Martha Washington gave her consent to having her husband's remains moved to a mausoleum to be incorporated in the monument, the committee's report omitted this recommendation. Robert Goodloe

And be it further resolved, That there be a funeral procession from Congress Hall to the German Lutheran Church, in Honor of the memory of Gen. George Washington, on Thursday the 26th inst. and that an Oration be prepared at the request of Congress, to be delivered before both Houses on that day, and that the President of the Senate and Speaker of the House of Representatives, be desired to request one of the members of Congress, to prepare and deliver the same.[7]

And be it further resolved, That it be recommended to the people of the United States to wear crape on the left arm, as mourning, for thirty days.

And be it further resolved, That the President of the United States be requested to direct a copy of these resolutions to be transmitted to Mrs. Washington, assuring her of the profound respect Congress will ever bear to her person and character; of their condolence on the late afflicting dispensation of Providence; and entreating her assent to the interment of the remains of General George Washington, in the manner expressed in the first resolution.

And be it further resolved, That the President of the United States be requested to issue a Proclamation, notifying to the people throughout the United States, the recommendation contained in the third resolution.[8]

To John Ambler

Printed, John Edward Oster, ed., *The Political and Economic Doctrines of John Marshall* . . . (New York, 1914), 183–184

DEAR SIR.   Philadelphia, December 29, 1799
Receive our sincere congratulations on your marriage & our

Harper (1765–1825) moved an amendment to the report that in effect substituted the mausoleum plan for the equestrian statue and the marble monument. Harper's motion carried, and subsequent discussion focused on the kind of mausoleum to be erected. *Ibid.*, 285, 708, 711–712; Charles E. Brownell, ed., *The Architectural Drawings of Benjamin Henry Latrobe* (New Haven, Conn., forthcoming). See also Resolutions, Dec. 30, 1799; William Thornton to JM, calendared at Jan. 2, 1800; and St. George Tucker to JM, calendared at Jan. 15, 1800.

7. Henry Lee delivered the oration at the German Lutheran Church on the designated day. *Annals of Congress*, X, 210, 1305–1311.

8. The resolutions were approved unanimously after Henry Lee urged that differences of opinion be suppressed on this occasion. *Ibid.*, 208, 209.

wishes for the happiness of Mrs. Ambler and yourself.[9] We have at this place no news but what is contained in the public papers. They will show you the manner in which we have manifested our deep affection for the loss of Genl Washington. Never was mourning more universal or so generally sincere.

Nothing of very serious importance has yet come before Congress. The material business of the session is preparing in the committees. I hope a mutual spirit of toleration and forbearance will succeed to the violence which seemed in too great a degree to govern last year. As far as I can judge from present appearances this will be a temperate session & I wish most devoutly that the prevalence of moderation here may diffuse the same spirit among our fellow citizens at large.

In the State of Pennsylvania there appears to be a considerable degree of exasperation among parties. The new Governor has, it is said, greatly increased it by turning or threatening to turn out of office every man however respectable & well qualified, who voted against him.[1] I am told that every clerk in the state is removed. The clerks here, who are [not clear],[2] hold their offices during the pleasure of the Governor. This is a very irritating measure & will koop[3] up in a considerable degree that party use for which this state has been long so remarkable. Molly[4] joins me in compliments to Mr. Ambler. I am dear Sir with much regard, Your Obedt

J. MARSHALL.

Resolutions

Printed, *Aurora* (Philadelphia), January 3, 1800, 3

Philadelphia, December 30, 1799

Resolved, by the Senate and House of Representatives of the United States, in Congress assembled, That it be recommended to the people of the United States, to assemble on the 22d day of Feb-

9. John Ambler, after the death of his wife Lucy Marshall Ambler in 1795, married Catherine Bush Norton, widow of John H. Norton and daughter of Philip Bush of Winchester, Va.

1. Thomas McKean (1734–1817) was elected governor of Pennsylvania over the Federalist candidate, James Ross (1762–1847), in 1799.

2. The brackets and the words within are Oster's insertions.

3. The original letter probably read "keep."

4. J. E. Oster, in transcribing this letter for publication, undoubtedly misread "Polly."

ruary next, in such numbers and manner as may be convenient, publicly to testify their grief for the death of Gen. George Washington, by suitable eulogies, orations and discourses; or by public prayers.

And be it further resolved, That the President of the United States be requested to recommend the same, by a proclamation for that purpose.[5]

Speech

Printed, *Aurora* (Philadelphia), January 7, 1800, 3

[*December 31, 1799, Philadelphia*. JM speaks in favor of a motion to resubmit section 8 of the census bill to committee in order to amend it. In previous debate Abraham Nott had voted against altering section 8 because he understood a motion to amend that section was forthcoming. The bill was ordered engrossed, however, and Nott then argued that he had been misled during committee consideration. JM avers that this was sufficient reason to vote for reconsideration and that members should ignore warnings that new issues might be raised during reconsideration.[6]]

Law Papers, December 1799

U.S. Circuit Court, Va.

Swift v. Ross (debt), computation of judgment amount, AD, U.S. Circuit Court, Va., Ended Cases (Unrestored), Virginia State Library.

Swift v. Ross (case), computation of judgment amount, AD, U.S. Circuit Court, Va., Ended Cases (Unrestored), Va. State Lib.

Warrick v. Kennedy, declaration, AD, Robert Morton Hughes Papers, Swem Library, College of William and Mary.

5. JM introduced these additional recommendations of the committee appointed to suggest appropriate measures for honoring the memory of Washington. The resolutions were unanimously agreed to by the House. *Annals of Congress*, X, 223. Services were held in Philadelphia on Feb. 22 at Catholic and Protestant churches. *Ibid.*, 536.

6. Sec. 8 of the bill required the secretary of state to issue regulations for conducting the census. Some feared this provided too much latitude, and they wanted to amend the section to specify the kind of regulations the secretary could impose. The motion to resubmit this section was defeated by a 43–41 vote. *Annals of Congress*, X, 227.

Nott (1768–1830) was a Federalist representative from South Carolina.

Deeds

Deed Book Copies, Office of the Clerk of Hardy County, Moorefield, W.Va.

[*ca. 1799 (Hardy County, Va.*). By his attorney, Rawleigh Colston, JM conveys parcels of land in the South Branch Manor to Peter Horse, 50 acres for £30, and to Jacob Vanmeter, 291 acres for £139 4d. Both deeds were recorded in the District Court at Hardy County on Sept. 9, 1800.]

From William Thornton

Copy, Thornton Papers, Library of Congress

[*January 2, 1800, Washington.* Thornton[7] responds to the resolution of Congress to erect a monument to George Washington. He recommends placing Washington's body "in the Center of that National Temple which he approved of for a Capitol." This action will honor the man and "will be a very great inducement to the completion of the whole Building, which has been thought by some contracted Minds, unacquainted with grand works to be upon too great a Scale." Thornton also wishes that Congress pass a resolution granting Martha Washington a place in the tomb, recommending that the House take a secret vote and divulge the result only to the widow or friends, to be publicly declared after her death.]

Legislative Bill

Printed, [U.S. Congress, House], *A Bill to Establish an Uniform System of Bankruptcy throughout the United States* (Philadelphia, 1800)

[*January 6, 1800 (Philadelphia).* A bill providing for a uniform system of bankruptcy based on British statutes is introduced. The bill contains 59 sections and is identical to the one proposed and debated at the previous session of Congress.[8]]

---

7. Thornton (1761–1828) was the chief architect of the Capitol and later became superintendent of the Patent Office.

8. JM had been appointed to the committee to prepare this bill on Dec. 5, 1799. The committee—James A. Bayard (1767–1815), Chauncey Goodrich (1759–1815), Samuel Sewall, Robert Goodloe Harper, and JM—was composed of the same members who were appointed to prepare a judiciary bill. *Annals of Congress,* X, 191; Committee Report, Mar. 11, 1800; and Kathryn Turner, "Federalist Policy and the Judiciary Act of 1801," *WMQ,* 3d Ser., XXII (1965), 10. See also Congressional Career: Editorial Note, Dec. 4, .

Speech

Printed, *Aurora* (Philadelphia), January 17, 1800, 2

Philadelphia, January 7, 1800

Mr. MARSHAL said that if[9] it was true that America commencing her negociation with her present military force, would appear in the armour which she could only wear for a day, the situation of our country was lamentable indeed. If our debility was really such, that the troops sought to be disbanded, could not be kept up but for a day, or for a very short period, our situation was truly desperate. No cheaper mode of self defence had been or could be devised, and it amounted to a declaration that we were unable to defend ourselves. He thought differently from the honorable gentleman who moved the resolution.[1] He thought America could maintain if it should be necessary, a much larger force, for a much longer time, than was contemplated with respect to the troops to which the resolution under consideration related.

1799.

Attempts to enact a bankruptcy act began at the first session of Congress in 1789, but serious efforts, led by Harper and Bayard, did not begin until 1797. The bill that was introduced late that year was reintroduced in 1798 and received extended debate before it was defeated by three votes. *Annals of Congress*, IX, 2441, 2676. For general information on bankruptcy legislation, see F. Regis Noel, *A History of the Bankruptcy Law* (Washington, D.C., 1919), and Charles Warren, *Bankruptcy in United States History* (Cambridge, Mass., 1935).

The present bill differed little, if any, from the 1797–1798 draft. The House debated the issue on several occasions and added provisions that would, among other things, limit the duration of the system to five years. JM successfully opposed an amendment that would restrict the application of the statute to debts contracted after its passage, an argument related to his later opinions in Sturgis v. Crowninshield and Ogden v. Saunders. The bill, enlarged to 64 sections, finally passed the House on Feb. 21 after the Speaker, Theodore Sedgwick, voted to break a 48–48 tie. The Senate gave its approval on Mar. 28. *Annals of Congress*, X, 126, 376, 388, 507, 508–509, 519–520, 533–534, and 1452–1471; [U.S. Congress, House], *A Bill to Establish an Uniform System of Bankruptcy throughout the United States* (Philadelphia, 1800).

This bill was so controversial and political that it was repealed before its five-year term had expired. In Dec. 1803, Congress ended the bankruptcy system by votes of 99–13 in the House and 17–12 in the Senate. *Annals of Congress*, XIII, 215, 631, 1249.

9. The word "if" was omitted from this account and has been supplied from *Annals of Congress*, X, 251.

1. On Jan. 1, John Nicholas of Virginia moved that the July 1798 and Mar. 1799 acts to enlarge the U.S. Army be repealed—an action that would in effect disband the standing army. Nicholas spoke at length on Jan. 7, relying upon a report from the secretary of the Treasury that anticipated a $5 million deficit in the 1800 budget. Nicholas argued that disbanding the army should have no effect on the negotiations under way in France

It was also to be observed that the hon. gentlemen had predicted all his arguments on the idea, that the troops must be immediately disbanded, or that the original law, unmodified, must have its full effect—That no middle ground might be taken. He was of a very different opinion, he thought middle ground might be taken, and that the law might be modified, so as to diminish the estimated expence, without dismissing the troops already in actual service.

The resolution proposed, he said, occupied such broad ground, as necessarily to unite against it, a considerable variety of opinions respecting the future disposition of the army. Not only those who thought the original law ought to have its full course and effect, but those also who thought it ought to receive certain modifications, and even those who thought that in the event of the failure of the present negotiation, the army ought, under certain circumstances, to be disbanded, but that this was not the time for disbanding it must unite against the motion now under consideration. It could only be supported by those who, like the mover of the resolution, thought that in the present moment, uninformed as we were concerning all those circumstances which should govern our decision, we ought to retrace the steps we had taken, and very materially to change the ground on which we found ourselves placed. This being the opinion on which alone it could be maintained, it became necessary to examine the arguments urged in support of this opinion.

It had been urged that the army ought to be disbanded because it was totally useless, because the United States was unable to bear the expence, and on some other suggestions which should be considered in the course of the argument.

Its inutility has been maintained on the impossibility of invading our country in the present state of things, on the difficulty of invading it at any time, and on the total indisposition to invasion, arising from the inadequacy of the object to the difficulty of attaining it.

---

and that borrowing money to support the army would in fact expose the weakness of the United States. *Ibid.*, 227–228, 247–251.

JM spoke in favor of a compromise position, outlined by Theodore Sedgwick and others, that would suspend new enlistments while retaining the standing army until news from the U.S. ministers in Paris indicated a peace agreement was likely. See *ibid.*, 251–255; Sedgwick to Rufus King, Dec. 29, 1799, in King, ed., *Life and Corres. of Rufus King*, III, 162–163; Richard H. Kohn, *Eagle and Sword: The Federalists and the Creation of the Military Establishment in America, 1783–1802* (New York, 1975), 260–263; JM to Charles Dabney, Jan. 20, 1800; and Speech, Jan. 22, 1800. See also a lengthy reply to this address in Manlius to JM, *ca.* Jan. 18, 1800.

After considerable debate, Nicholas's resolution was defeated on Jan. 10. *Annals of Congress*, X, 257–369.

But what assurance have gentlemen that invasion is now impracticable! The present state of Europe is totally unknown to us. The effects of the late decisive victories of France have not reached us. It is by no means certain that these victories may not have produced a negociation with some of the continental powers, which may liberate a considerable portion of her force, which she may send across the Atlantic. By the opening of the next campaign we shall be informed on this subject, and shall be able to act with proper knowlege of it— at present we are uninformed and are urged to act without the requisite knowlege.

On this point it was necessary to enquire into the relative situation of two nations. All commercial and friendly intercourse between us was suspended. Whenever we met, the stronger party attacked and captured the weaker. The property of the captured was confiscated and their persons imprisoned. This was war in fact though not in form. We are in fact, at war with France, though it is not declared in form. What security then is there that no dispositions will exist to invade us? The unimportance of the object forms no such security.

Neither is there any security that there exists no disposition to invade us. On this subject he differed, essentially from the honorable gentleman, who supported the resolution. He thought America of vast importance to France. Whatever might be the views of France, whether they were merely to humble her great rival or were still more extensive, it was impossible to consider the effect which a controul over American affairs must have in promoting, those views, without being satisfied on this subject. Independent of the effective force which might be used, the great advantage which the monopoly of our commerce would give in time of peace for the formation of a naval power, was of importance to France or England. The result of the two last wars between those two nations, in one of which the force of America was added to that of Britain, and in the other to that of France evinces the importance of America, even at that time in either scale. Unquestionably that importance cannot be diminished.

With respect to the difficulty of attaining the object, Mr. Marshall said that France could not be so much governed by the difficulty which might actually exist, as by the opinion she would previously entertain of that difficulty. Before the real difficulty could be ascertained, the invasion must take place. Of consequence her opinion on this subject would regulate her conduct, and her opinion would depend on the measures which might be adopted, and the disposition which might be manifested by America.

But it has been urged, not only that the army is useless, but that there is in the United States a positive inability to maintain it. To prove this our revenue and expenditure has been stated. Suppose this had been the language of '75—Suppose at the commencement of our revolution, a gentleman had risen on the floor of congress, to compare our revenues with our expences—what would have been the result of the calculation? Would not the same system of reasoning which the gentleman from Virginia has adopted, have proved that our resources were totally inadequate to the prosecution of the war? Yet it was prosecuted, and with success. If vast exertions were then made to acquire independence, will not the same exertions be now made to maintain it? The question now is—whether self-government and national liberty be worth the money which must be expended to preserve them.

The mover of the resolution, Mr. Marshall said, had urged as his strongest reason for the measure, the saving of public money which it would produce. Any argument of which the object was economy, came home to the feelings of every member of the community, and came home to the feelings of every member of the house.—Such arguments would, and ought to have great weight, but it should never be forgotten; that true economy did not content itself with enquiring into the mere saving of the present moment, a true and wise economy would take an enlarged view of the subject, and determine, on correct calculation, whether the consequence of a present saving might not be a much more considerable future expenditure. The reduction of the army would certainly diminish the expences of the present year; but if it should have any operation on the existing negociation with France, the present saving it would produce, would bear no proportion to the immense waste of blood as well as treasure, which it might occasion us. To determine in what manner this measure might, and probably would bear on the existing negociation; it became indispensable to take into our view what had preceded the actual state of things between the United States and France. In doing this it could not be necessary to enumerate the various injuries our country had sustained. They rested in the memory of every American and need not be recited. It must, however, be particularly observed, that while prayers for peace were returned for indignities of every sort, while America was humbly supplicating for peace, and that her complaints might be heard—France spurned her contemptuously & refused to enter on a discussion of differences, unless that discussion was preceded by a substantial surrender of the essential attributes of independence. America was at length goaded into resistance, and resolved on that system of defence, of which the army now sought to be disbanded, forms a part. Immediately the tone of France was changed, and she consented to treat us as an independent nation. Her depredations indeed did not cease. She continued still to bring war upon us. But although peace was not granted, the door to peace was opened.

What could have produced this change. Every member of the house is called upon to put this question to himself and to weigh it according to his best judgment. To supplicating America even discussion was denied. America armed and immediately a different language was used, and the rights of an independent nation were allowed her. What, he repeated, could have produced this change? Can any other motive be assigned, than the defensive system which America had adopted. If in the mind of any gentleman, any other motive did exist, he is called upon to assign that motive. If no other did exist, is it wise immediately to change the system which has alone been effectual? Is it not to be apprehended that this change may revive those sentiments which existed before the system was adopted?

This subject, he said, was also to be considered in another point of view, which had been foreseen by the mover of the resolutions, and declared to be intimately connected with that which had been already stated.

It was this. The policy of this measure depends entirely on the state of things when the negociation shall be determined.

Will gentlemen say that, under any state of things, the army ought to be disbanded; Will they say that if peace should be made with the continental powers of Europe, and a French army should be crossing the Atlantic to invade our territory, that yet our military force ought to be diminished? He believed no gentleman would say so. He was certain the mover of the resolution would not. Is it then wise to precipitate a measure, the policy of which depends entirely on an event which is not yet, but will soon be ascertained.

In a few months the fate of the present negociation will be decided. Should it terminate favourably, the army expires by the law which gave it being, and the additional expence to be incurred, will be very inconsiderable. Should it fail, we shall then know the disposition of France and the situation of Europe. We shall be able to form a just estimate of the danger of invasion, and consequently to decide with much better information than we can now possess, on the question under discussion. If such a state of things should then exist as would justify disbanding the army, the loss produced by the delay of that measure, would be very inconsiderable. If the then state of things should require even an augmentation of the existing force, the injury occasioned by our precipitation might be very considerable. We should certainly throw away all the expence incurred in recruiting men, all the discipline the present army had acquired and be in a state as unprepared, as if the expence for those objects had never been sustained.

He concluded with observing that this was not the time for diminishing the force of the nation and therefore he was opposed to the resolution.

Bill of Exchange

ADS, Stauffer Collection, New York Public Library

[*January 8, 1800 (Richmond)*. John Hopkins, U.S. commissioner of loans for Virginia, transmits a bill of exchange to JM for $375.00, one-fourth of Hopkins's annual salary, and for two accounts, totaling $572.83, transmitted to the Treasury for settlement. The bill is addressed to George Simpson, cashier of the Bank of the United States.]

Deed

Deed Book Copy, Clerk of the Office of Hardy County, Moorefield, W.Va.

[*January 8, 1800 (Hardy County, Va.)*. James Markham Marshall relinquishes two parcels of land in Hampshire County to John Marshall for 5s. and in exchange for other land purchased from Denny Martin Fairfax. The deed was recorded in the District Court at Hardy County on Sept. 7, 1802.]

From John Quincy Adams

LS, RG 59, National Archives

No. 160
Sir,[2]   Berlin, January 14, 1800
    I have the honor to enclose the copy of a Note, which I received

2. This dispatch, addressed to the secretary of state, arrived at the State Department on June 25, 1800, after JM assumed the duties of that office. See JM to John Adams, June 30, 1800; John Adams to JM, July 11, 1800; and JM to John Quincy Adams, July 24, 1800.

a few days ago from Baron Engeström, the Swedish Minister at this court;[3] containing a proposal for the employment of a number of frigates in the Mediterranean in concert between the United States, Sweden & Denmarc, an object which he assured me the king of Sweden had peculiarly at heart. As all the security, which our navigation can enjoy in the Mediterranean by virtue of any Treaty with the Barbary powers must be precarious & as even to obtain that Security we have submitted to an expence so much more considerable, than had ever before been applied to that purpose by any european power, this proposal appears to deserve the peculiar attention of the Government.

The Swedish minister enquired at the same time whether I had received any answer to another proposal, which I transmitted about a year ago, relative to the island of St. Bartholomew.[4] I told them, that I had not, but that I presumed the answer would be such as I anticipated at the time when the proposal was communicated.

On the 3d: instt: died here very suddenly, at the age of eighty five Count Finckenstein, first minister in the department of foreign affairs, a station which he had held upwards of half a century. He was undoubtedly the oldest diplomatic character in Europe, having entered the career in the year 1735, when he was sent as minister to Sweden by the predecessors of Frederic the great. He had signed several dispatches to the Ministers abroad on the day of his death. There will probably be for the future only two Ministers in the Department, at the head of which will be the late Baron Alvenslaben,[5] whom the king has now made a Count. I have the honor to be, Sir, with great respect your humble Servant.

JOHN Q ADAMS

3. The note from Lars von Engeström is enclosed in JM to John Adams, June 30, 1800.

4. The Swedish government had offered to sell the island of St. Bartholomew to the United States. John Quincy Adams had informed the Swedish minister that the possession of colonies was contrary to the political system of the United States. See John Quincy Adams to Timothy Pickering, Dec. 24, 1798, printed in Worthington Chauncey Ford, ed., *Writings of John Quincy Adams*, II (New York, 1913), 381.

5. Karl Wilhelm von Finkenstein (1714–1800) and Philipp Karl von Alvensleben (1745–1802).

From St. George Tucker

Copy, Tucker-Coleman Papers, Swem Library, College of William and Mary

[*January 15, 1800, Williamsburg*. Tucker writes that although his "former unbounded veneration for the character" of George Washington was somewhat reduced by a few "circumstances in his administration," he nevertheless wants to suggest the erection of a monument to the memory of the late general and president. He encloses a detailed description of an inscribed obelisk to be 100 feet tall with events from Washington's life represented in bas-relief around the base.[6]]

To Samuel Bayard

ALS, Gratz Collection, Historical Society of Pennsylvania

Sir   Philadelphia, January 16, 1800

Accept my sincere thanks for a copy of the oration deliverd at New Rochelle on the 1st. of Jany. which has reachd me to day.[7]

I have read it with that melancholy pleasure which is inspird by well merited & well executed eulogies on those whose death we greatly lament, & whose memory is most dear to us.

To the friends of the departed patriot whose talents & virtues you have so elegantly & so justly celebrated, & to the friends of the American character, the deep & universal grief which has been every where manifested, & the impressive orations which have flowd from that grief, constitute some consolation for the irreparable loss our country has sustaind. With very much respect, I am Sir your obedt. Servt.

J MARSHALL

6. See Speech, Dec. 19, and Resolutions, Dec. 23, 1799.

7. Samuel Bayard (1765–1840) was U.S. commissioner of claims in London from 1794 to 1798. When he returned to the United States, he served as editor of the New York City *Daily Advertiser*. For a copy of the oration, see Samuel Bayard, *A Funeral Oration, Occasioned by the Death of Gen. George Washington and Delivered on the First of January, 1800. In the Episcopal Church at New Rochelle, in the State of New-York* (New Brunswick, N.J., 1800).

JM addressed this letter to Bayard at New Rochelle, N.Y., although the letter was forwarded to Philadelphia.

From Manlius

Printed, Anonymous, *A Letter from Manlius, to John Marshall, Esq. Member of Congress* (Richmond, 1800)

[Richmond, *ca.* January 18, 1800]

HOWEVER[8] true the maxim may be, that the splendid talents of the statesman too often meet with the censure of criticism as well as the lashes of invidious malice, yet it is also one of which he as promptly avails himself to bar the door of vindication, & to clothe his political conduct with the mantle of contemptuous silence.—As my principal objects are the investigation of truth, on one of the most interesting subjects to America, the expediency of our present military establishment, I shall neither be mortified by your silence, nor consider such silence as resulting from an unequivocal conviction of your own political rectitude. You state, sir, that there can be no cheaper mode of defence than the present one, and that, if America could not maintain a much larger army, and for a much longer time, her situation would be lamentable indeed. If for a moment a standing army shall be necessary to defend us from foreign invasion, I ask if we ought to cling to the shadow of a military defence? Is the present military establishment sufficient to defend the whole of our coasts from invasion? Upon the principles of *political economy*, we ought to consider whether the means be equal to the accomplishment of the end proposed; if they be not sufficient, we become prodigals of the public money, and render ourselves weak at home as well as contemptible abroad. If we make the means equal to the accomplishment of the end, we ought then to consider whether the accomplishment of that end be the most economical and salutary for the general welfare. Attached as you seem to be, to an economy founded on the present military arrangement, I ask, of whom are your present soldiery composed, but of victims to dissipation and every abandoned profligacy; who have fled from the vortex of debt, and disgraceful laziness, to your military banners, as the last asylum for their wretched existence—ignorant and debauched, without property, without reputation, true patriotism is a stranger to their bosoms. From such men, their

8. On the verso of the title page, the printer, Samuel Pleasants, Jr., wrote that this letter "was received at the Office of the Printer on the 18th of January last, but from other pressing engagements, he has been reluctantly compelled to postpone the publication thereof." The letter was printed in Feb. 1800 and is a specific response to the speech JM delivered in Congress opposing John Nicholas's motion to disband the standing army. See Speech, Jan. 7, 1800.

officers however respectable, can have but little to hope, and a foreign power much less to fear.

France is now taking the most effectual remedy to revenge herself upon you—she finds that upon the possibility of invasion, you are establishing a standing army, as the cheapest mode of defence—she finds the people of America, groaning under the present governmental incumbrances, and jealously suspective of your increased army—she finds that with the terrors of warfare, she can load you with that horrible scourge which always arises from war, a great national debt. When France sees you at war with yourselves, at war with your political economy, spending many millions per annum, to lull the fear of warfare with her, she must enjoy the political pantomime considerably more, than she can possess the disposition to invade you. But why this army as the cheapest mode of defence? Virginia alone has in her arsenal at present 18,000 stand of arms, besides a great many other implements of war. Can it be supposed that if any state in the union was invaded, she would not shew a timely resistance, at a crisis when every thing sacred to freedom and happiness was at stake? Can it be supposed that any state in the union would be tardy in the repulsion of invasion, when under our present system of government, such an invasion must equally strike home to every member of the union? How do you conjure up this great magic of power in a few thousand of the very dregs of the American creation, in preference to an organized militia throughout the union, who have every thing to fight for, most dear, most sacred to humanity. Twice have the embers of civil war been kindling in the very bosom of your country, the most serious, the most tremendous of all military conflicts, and as often have your now despised militia, asswaged and suppressed the dreadful monster. When the imperious necessity of the times, shall rouse your citizens with patriotic ardor to point their bayonets at a refractory brother's breast, can *they* be useless, can *they* shrink away from the most bloody, the most desolative designs of an invading enemy? If the perilous times require a ready watchfulness, why not make your militia organization adequately strict and severe? They have been the defence of all free governments—they raised the American colonies from the most abject oppression, upon a basis, which characterises them to be a great, free and independent nation, and why not that the same means shall protect and secure it? I grant that America could maintain a larger army and for a much longer time, but our enquiries ought to be, not what America by her extremest exertions might do, but what she ought to do. A great and free people upon emergencies can perform wonderful things—but we ought to pause and solemnly consider whether those great emergencies do now exist. Does war ravage our country? Are there strong assurances of invasion? Have the American government reason to believe that the state militia would become traitors to them, and of consequence, traitors to their own lives, liberties and fortunes? No. We have only the apprehensions of invasion, to quiet which the people are to be loaded in time of peace, with the very curses of actual war. The principle does not end here—it does not end with one or two years—it is a boundless one. For when the people with an anxious eye look towards a probable amelioration of their difficulties, hope sickens, and they see nothing but that dreaded harbinger of revolutions, a political bankruptcy; in as much as the rising greatness of the American world will doubtlessly cause us too often to have a coldness or misunderstanding with some one of the European powers. What is the result? Upon *this precedent* of dreaded invasion, an additional army must be raised, the number of which must be apportionate to the fear or designs of government; and thus we find, by the pretexts for the present military establishment, that a standing army and an overgrown debt must be the inevitable result. But this is not all; exclusive of the alarming apprehensions which seize upon the minds of the citizens at the very idea of a standing army (a monster which the times past as well as present, invariably proclaim to be the relentless destroyer of the republican system) the Apalachian country particularly will not be enabled to discharge this monstrous accession of the public debt. I am well acquainted with the country from the Atlantic states west of the Allegehany mountains. Remote from navigation, they depend upon the bosom of the Mississippi as the only resource for a circulating medium—they necessarily feel the burthens of taxation in a ten fold degree—for some years past, deluded with the navigation of that river, they fell in debt for four times the amount of their annually received circulating medium; hence have they been so embarrassed, that almost every dollar has disappeared from among them. The consequence has been that in Kentucky particularly, a great proportion of the people have it not in their power to pay the debts which they owe to the state government. The Apalachian people have been heretofore prey to a speculative junto at Orleans, from not having it in their power to go to any other port, so that the avenue to commerce clogged and impeded, can claim but slender resources from that quarter.

The federal requisitions of 1799, alarmed them in an awful manner, but when they shall find that they cannot even enjoy "hope deferred," as to a diminution of expenses, but rather that they are rapidly growing, on the never-ceasing wheel of continual accumulation, upon principles too which may be destructive of our political salvation, and, giving the most benevolent construction, which are not of that *high imperious nature*, that alone ought to justify government in wringing from the people their last circulating pittance! we ought to be highly interested at the consequences—For whilst you talk by *your kind of economy*, of preserving *our blood* and our *treasure*, relatively to a foreign power, an event upon all grounds problematic, it is an *economy* which holds out positively an extortion upon the poverty of a great many of our citizens, or it is an *economy* probably which either prostrates our rights or invites the horrors of a civil war. If two internal convulsions have already from lesser causes, marked the progress of our government, it is not chimerical to suppose that a commotion should now seriously arise under the present unpopular exactions from, and the high dominations over, the people. It is not chimerical to suppose, that the formidable phalanx of the whole western world should attempt to rescue itself from what they conceive to be an unnecessary as well as an intolerant burthen. You, sir, ought to view these things with a more scrutinizing eye than you appear to have done. The misfortune is, that some of the political gentlemen in the present day, supplied by their great abilities or hereditary estates, feel not the burthens and exactions of government; they are not charitable enough to examine into the situations of the numerous people, when in fact such an investigation is the great palladium of political justice, and the highest science of a government founded upon republicanism.

You say that the American people *can* raise money enough to support a much larger army and for a much longer time, but alas! your conscience must tell you, when you will candidly lower your eyes, towards the humble millions of society, that this fear of government, this apparent political hyppo, ought not to be gratified, by such dangerous, such oppressive, such alarming means. It would appear from your doctrines, that the states had no alarms or fears for themselves, or if they had, that their stupid lethargy is such, as to require your kind of military guardians; and when they come to view whom those guardians are, they are a few thousand profligate mercenaries,[9] with

9. The following note is inserted at this point in Manlius's account: "This characteristic of the common soldier now in the service of the United States, experience justifies almost every day."

whom to associate the most simple yeoman would feel himself disgraced. You make each state government a political non compos mentis against their most serious wishes, against their most solemn avowals, against the most obvious reasons for the soundness of their minds and the virtue of their hearts; and you set over them these *guardians*, who are to be rewarded even by the last eventual shilling of their fortunes. Was this imposition upon the free people of America to terminate only with the relief of governmental horrors as to France, without bringing worse upon ourselves, I should feel more tranquilized. But let not precipitation say that the internal evils arising from the present proceedings of the general government are chimerical. If the dreaded invasion from France is not chimerical, how very distant from a chimera is the alarm of the people, first excited by aggresions upon the constitution, and now agitated by the establishment of an army, the necessity of which is at least doubtful, the principles dreadful to the people, and the expenses griping if not fatally extortive from them. When the minds of the American people have been so agitated by various conflicting causes, when the honest indignation of some states has been so firmly exhibited, at the continued arrogations of the general government, when a political ferment caused by that government, appears almost ready to burst itself, is it chimerical to suppose that additional evils, actually goading the people in the most severe and terrifying manner, by this established armament, may not hasten us to mingle kindred blood, to mingle the blood of Americans, which should be dear and inviolate, upon the fields of civil war? Thus then in our attempting to avert a contemplated evil from abroad, we shall certainly bring on an increased dissatisfaction against the general government, an increased national debt, and probably an effusion of human blood, more fatal to our internal repose, than the combined warfare of Europe against us. Can this be "*the cheapest mode of defence?*" Can this be the way "*to prevent the situation of America from being lamentable?*"[1] Unfortunately for the great mass of mankind, they never see oppression at a distance. The Americans have been astonishingly acquiescent under the alien, sedition laws, &c. more alarming to political refinement than your army; but as they will *feel* more sorely your military arrangement; if tyranny raising its frightful head from the clouds of mystery, does not strike the fatal panic of submission, they

1. See Vol. III, 22–24, 74. Since JM's comments were made in the Virginia House of Delegates and in public meetings in 1796, Manlius must have heard them there or received detailed reports of JM's remarks.

must struggle for some ameliorating change.—Can this, sir, be your middle ground? You instance the important era of 1775, & ask if the language now used should have been then exhibited, the expenses must have been wholly inadequate for the war. Can you, sir, with the present crisis, seriously compare the time, when Great Britain denied to America not only a reciprocation of privileges under the same government; but attempted to destroy the most sacred and imprescriptible rights of human nature? When under these doctrines, both the property and the persons of the colonies were liable to be sacrificed to the absolute dominion of the English government, they had no other election but of hazarding for themselves the lesser evil of devoting every active resource to the establishment of their independence. Their resort then was either to surrender tamely both, or by the destruction even of the one to preserve the other. The question then was, whether they should secure liberty at the entire hazard of their property, or whether they should miserably deplore the loss of both. The impulse of nature's self defence, then called them not to scrutinize the means of a political *economy*, but to defend their jeopardized rights. Who were the men that commenced the revolution? Not a standing army. They were, sir, citizens who fought and conquered against that very kind of army upon which you seem so confidently to rely. You have brought the question then to this point, whether from a contemplated invasion from France, it should not only be expedient, that we should be regardless of our finances as in '75, but that those little to be regarded finances should be extended to (what was then unknown) a standing army among us. Our *national independence* has received no shock from any foreign power. The people of America must be as much alive to protect their rights from foreign invasion, as in '75. Why then the strange doctrine, that national liberty and self government *must* be protected by a standing army, the converse of which principle both the spirit of '75, and the avowed republican declarations have been, that self government and national liberty, should be *particularly* protected without it. I agree with you that self government and national liberty, are always worth the money which *must* be expended to preserve them. Can you, sir, without the hectic of confusion, venture to assert, that this army, *must* be the talisman of our governmental salvation? Can you vainly hope from a confidence in your talents and popularity, that the free constituents of your district, could be so humbled to the degraded ebb of servile credulity, as to be deluded with the notion that a great national debt *must* be increasing upon the people to preserve their liberties, not upon that fair, pleasant and undreaded structure, which would afford some consolation for the heavy claims upon their purses, but upon grounds precarious, if not subversive of their liberties by this army; as if it were our only refuge, as if in no other view and important tract, money could be as beneficially expended, for the preservation of government and our national liberty!—Remember, sir, the severe, the lawless, and unprovoked spoliations of England —Where then were your military preparations? Altho' England was the great monster of the ocean, altho' the countervailing navy of France could not have prevented an invasion from England; you heard no loud buz of an expected invasion. Government then did not think it expedient to *frighten* England from invasion, or *alarm* her into a *negociation*, by your *beloved defensive system*. But France, whose naval powers are weak, is dreaded lest in despite of the British thunder, she should not only invade but conquer America, if this army be not established. The principle then, which better would have applied to England, as she was more powerful, as the general situation of the people was more prosperous, and as our national debt had not so greatly progressed, is at this late period brought forward against France. To prove that it ought to exist, you say that as vast exertions are now necessary to acquire our independence, the same exertions are now necessary to maintain it, against France. Had you proven, sir, that those exertions were now necessary, every voice would now have been responsive to you. If the terrible features of '75 do exist, why not that the same means should still be applied, as were then applied, your militia. If the features of '75 do exist, I charge it home upon you, to reply whether they are not rather those same features which caused disunion from England? governmental hauteur, violations upon their constitutional rights, and remorseless exactions from the people. However you may attempt to display a disposition "for your middle ground," however desirous you may appear to save "our blood and treasure," however solicitous you may appear for the preservation of "national liberty," these appearances are not satisfactory to your constituents. If they are uncharitable enough to suspect you, they claim as a palliation that they have grounds for suspicion. When a difference with England existed, our situation was as gloomy as the most sombre pencil of your ingenuity could pourtray; pacific measures were then strongly urged by you. You stated that the imbecility of our situation was so tottering and resourceless, that an attempt at warfare with England, would be a precipitate rashness, which could only terminate in the ruin of your country. All

America were then too feeble to withstand the monarchy of England. You went further, you hurried yourself on to the extremest apprehensions. You solemnly stated, after an embellished eulogium upon the advantages of the British treaty, that if the treaty did not hold out all the benefits which might be expected, yet that its adoption at all hazards should be made, for its rejection, would in your opinion, bring on the horrors of a British war.

Could you, sir, without the pangs of an apostate republican, have made such a declaration? or could you really have supposed, if the treaty was fraught with the advantages which you enumerated, that Great Britain would scourge us like improvident children, because we would not accept of her favors? Where was then that manliness, that patriotism, that high indignation, which you have of late days exhibited at foreign contempt or injury? You then exchanged the indignant frown of the insulted republican for the mildness of the christian philosopher, and the expensive unweildy apparatus of war, for the humble garb of the peace-maker. Four years have only glided away, and you pretend that a few thousand mercenary troops are indispensably necessary to defend us from a French invasion, to defend us against that nation whose successful arms have made all Europe tremble. Your continued and uniform exertions for the most substantial amity with England, under every insult and every outrage, which could be devolved upon a free people, and your never ceasing opposition, your deep rooted aversion against a powerful nation, whose greatest sin has been in humbly pursuing the conduct of your darling England, have assigned you a situation, at which that bosom must recoil, which feels with honest indignation, insults or aggressions from every indiscriminate power.

France proposed the renewal of her treaty with us on ampler grounds, and it was rejected on the strict determination of neutrality. England, without ostensible causes, carried your vessels with triumphant insolence to their ports of rapine and plunder, and with England a treaty was supplicated. France alone pursued, what England had done for the accomplishment of accommodation? Yet your continued theme is "that France has offered us every injury," France only "by her contemptuous treatment could goad us into resistance." When your decided position previous to your mission to France had proclaimed you to be the undissembled friend of England, when your political determinations made you no less obnoxious to France, and they shewed you to be, by no means, assuming the character of a friend. Could you have considered yourself as a proper subject for accommodation? You, sir, the strongest avowed friend of her most inveterate enemy; you, who then exhibited the lowering features of prejudice and disdain towards her. To conclude a treaty with England, your chief justice was taken from the sacred banners of the constitution, which we all know were intended to confine him from the power of treaty-making, and dispatched in the very capacity to England. It was alledged, to smoothe the alarms of the people, that Mr. Jay's superior popularity there would more effectually promote our general interest; but in the proposed accommodation with France, the very reverse of this principle was pursued, and you, sir, were one of the three persons selected to bring about an accommodation. When France discovered this barefaced deviation from those friendly, accommodating and conciliatory measures, which had been so invariably pursued towards England, she fathomed the pretence to accommodation, she beheld with indignation the apparent duplicity, and treated you with insult and disdain. Could they have forgotten the recal of the amiable, the independent, the much beloved Monroe by them, and the substitution of Pinckney, who had been dandled in the lap of England? The ungenerous recal of the only minister who had candor and virtue enough to establish some kind of confidence between the two nations, is still recent upon the minds of the people. The refusal to satisfy his agitated bosom with the causes of his dismission, causes which he knew not, but which he conceived necessary to be related, as surmises and dark conjectures hovered over his honest fame, pourtrayed an ingratitude, if not an unfeeling despotism of the administration, which oblivion can only destroy.— The people are not so hood-winked to prejudice, nor are they such dupes to the purity of government, as not to entertain some strong suspicions as to her objects with France. They begin to think, from a collected arrangement of your political manoeuvres, that a negociation with France was never bona fide sought after. A successless return must have the effect of uniting the public mind in the most resentful opposition against them. Your mission was successless, and they now find that their conclusion was in a great measure realized. Disgusts have been consequently multiplied against them, and a connection with England has been astonishingly substantialized. This is, sir, an awful crisis for America, and he who disguises apprehensions which he conceives to be founded on a rational probability, becomes an accessary to that political murder, which I fear is meditated against the rights and liberties of the people. I most seriously apprehend the consequences of this army, more than I do invasion.

The promptitude which the administration have discovered to bear down every trivial opposition with a *numerous* and expensive army, is alarming. But when it is united with a more fatal promptitude to destroy the sacred *Constitution*, when to be responsive to the administration, the federal judiciary have exhibited a surprizing alacrity, a promptitude so glaringly manifested by the execrated Bee and detested Elsworth, to mark this new pioneered way through the vitals of the constitution, by the blood of the unfortunate Robbins, and the imprisonment of the persecuted Williams;[2] I turn a fearful eye to '75, and I almost become an involuntary proselyte to your fatal sentiment, "that the same exertions are now as necessary to protect, as those exertions which were necessary to acquire our independence."[3]

It is a melancholy fact, that when designing men contemplate the change of the republican system, external war has been the fatal resort.—The whole souls and minds of the people are aroused at the approaching calamity. One single battle stamps the most deep rooted hatred upon the contending parties, and thirsting for a mutual revenge, governmental aggressions are neglected or forgotten. Then come on the halcyon days for a standing army—then come on the British blessings of a national debt, and then follow those dreadful changes which terminate in despotism. Whilst invasion was expected from France, government could not with honorable policy, have continued to sow the seeds of jealousy among the people, by particular laws, the impolicy of which, and the unconstitutionality of a part, I am told you have the credit of avowing. If you did deem any one act of the administration to have been unconstitutional, it ought to have been a primary object with you to have protected that "national liberty" which should be positively invaded at home, before you should have so sternly, so vindictively, put yourself in battle array against a bare contemplated injury of "national liberty," from abroad.

Like America, every nation, in every age, under every clime, have set out with the soundest principles of a social compact, by which their lives, liberties and fortunes, should be equally and reciprocally

2. On Jonathan Robbins, Judge Thomas Bee, and Oliver Ellsworth, see Congressional Career: Editorial Note, Dec. 4, 1799. For information on Isaac Williams, see John Adams to JM, Aug. 7, 1800 (second letter).

3. According to the account in the Philadelphia *Aurora* of Jan. 17, JM actually said, "If vast exertions were then made to acquire independence, will not the same exertions be now made to maintain it?" The use of slightly different phraseology suggests that perhaps Manlius had a Richmond newspaper's account of JM's address.

secured; but as they journied along the road of time, by the slumber-ings of the unsuspicious people, and by the active vigilance of the ambitious and designing, as often have Gogs and Magogs risen up among them, until not only the virtue, but the name of liberty have been scouted from their records. The object of our constitution was the most pure reciprocation of privileges—at the period of its adop-tion by the different states, it never was suspected that government should view it as a book of riddles, or rather as a monster which they exulted in assailing whenever they should find it pregnable. With the corruption of the times, the first great patrons of that constitution have become alarmed; they have shrunk away from the adminis-tration's pampered arrogance, and have firmly raised up their defen-sive fortifications within the state governments. When we find that some of the most illumined and positive supporters of the federal con-stitution, the goodness of whose hearts never could have dreamed of the present administrative degeneracy, compelled to rally under the banners of the states, as the last resort for the protection of our liber-ties, danger is to be apprehended. Such a scene must not only be alarming, but it is a fatal prognostic that we are verging to that degradation of government, which despises every tie, every barrier necessary to controul it. Only twelve months ago, I saw good men blush at being told they were *no governmental men*. Your Neroes, your Tarquins, your Louis's of France, had all their governmental men; & if those same good men had retrospected the truths of history, they would have found millions and millions of the human race struggling amidst the ruins of persecution and oppression, occasioned by these same governmental men. They would have discovered that often in revolving centuries, humanity has shuddered at the sound of govern-mental men. The free people of America have been compelled by the administration to discover that altho' a constitution cannot exist without government, that government may exist without a consti-tution. They have been compelled by the daring innovations of your favorite administration, to treasure up this important republican principle, that for freemen to rest on a permanent structure, they ought to watch over their constitutional rights with the eyes of Argus, and if they suffer themselves to be lulled to sleep by *designing Mer-curies*, they lean against those shifting quicksands which are con-tinually heaped up and overturned, by every gust of governmental passion.

You speak, and attempt to act, as if America was already con-vulsed in all the dreadfulness of a Gallic war. The great and decisive victories of France, say you, will probably now authorize her to send a considerable portion of her force across the Atlantic. France, in such an attempt, must unquestionably contemplate the subjugation of America, or a partial injury. If a subjugation should be her object, it follows, that against such a preparation, your present military establishment would be a forlorn hope indeed. If to harrass you be the extent of her expectations, she must despoil you on the ocean, as she has heretofore done. For consequences she will wait, until the political feuds and animosities which now burn internally, shall break forth into an unfortunate flame. Whilst you apprehend those dreaded evils from France, you still think that "middle ground" might be pursued, that the present estimated expense might be diminished without diminishing the troops now in the actual service. This can only be effected by putting a stop to the enlistments. A group of officers then, without soldiers to command, would be dependent on the public treasury. This would be a most extraordinary *middle ground*. With your alarms and apprehensions, I never should have thought of this *middle ground*; instead of arresting enlistments, you ought at least to have had the additional regiments completed. You seem to admit by *your middle ground*, that the present number of soldiery are sufficiently propitious for our views to France. If they will answer, it follows that the danger to be apprehended cannot be formidable; because it is well known, that the efficacy of an army can only be beneficial in case of an invasion, and because in case of an invasion, it is well known that such an army as we now possess could not be efficacious.

Say you, France denied to America the rights of an independent nation; America armed herself, and the rights of an independent nation were allowed her. You seem exultingly to enquire whence could this arise, but from our defensive system? Suppose that France never had, and never should acknowledge your rights, as a great, free and independent nation, you can injure her in no way but denying her your commerce; the denial of which she must have expected, when she did not treat us, as a great, free and independent nation. The denial of which she must have expected, when acknowledging us to be a great, free and independent nation, "she still continued to commit spoliations upon us."[4] If then the loss of our commerce was the only evil which France could dread, and that evil did still exist

---

4. In the account of JM's speech in the *Aurora*, JM said: "She continued still to bring war upon us."

from her continued depredations, how, and in what manner could our system of defence constrain them into an acknowledgment of our sovereign rights? The unhappy fact must have been, that France discovered the system of defence, as you term it, to be the internal poison which has been seriously apprehended. She found it to be a burthen which would alarm and agitate the people; she found that with "the waste of her blood and treasure," she could make our situation but very little more deplorable, than in leaving us to ourselves. Was France to invade America, she would be giving the political balsam, which government will never apply. Her invasion would tranquilize our internal jarring, & make the long divided people of America, consolidate themselves into the most strong and effective opposition. This is the influential reason why France will not now invade us. The reasons why invasion appears to be wished for by you, as well as by government, have already been suggested.

View the deep agitations which have arisen with respect to governmental aggressions. View the most solemn protests of the state powers, made against the depredations of the general government, upon the sacred charter of its political existence. View the accression of taxes, under which the people declare, with a solemn deliberation and uplifted hands, they unnecessarily groan. View the jarring interests which arise in an union so vast as that of America, and those jarring interests aggravated by the administration, and say, whether the very delusive means which are attempted to be exercised, for the aversion of foreign evils, may not in a short period, bring about the most opportune crisis for invasion?—As the most refined reason, the most independent mind, cannot be shielded from the shades of prejudice, I am the more emboldened to declare, united with other circumstances, that you have your ample share. Your delegation to France, & the reception of that delegation are well known; but however impressive on your mind your treatment there may be, you ought to consider that by idly conjuring up retortion upon France, you only wound the bosom of your own country, and by aspiring at Gallic homicide, you eventually perpetrate a fatal suicide.

The person who shall dare to censure the conduct of administration, enters upon a pilgrimage of the most gloomy and hazardous nature. When it is obvious that among those men only who chaunt the hallelujahs of adulation to the ears of government, all its favors are profusely squandered. When it is notorious that every feeble voice of opposition, is not only attempted to be crushed, by the hissing refinement of degradation, but by holding up the terrible beacons of poverty and disgraceful confinement, the persecuted martyr to the constitution from that quarter, has not the feintest ray to cheer him. Spurned as a reptile, from her angry, inflated bosom, he has nothing to receive but despair, when even mercy, the attribute of the savage wanderer, flies her hated presence to promulge a most horrid deed! I mean the case of Jonathan Robbins, than which, a blacker outrage could not have been perpetrated on the rights of humanity.—It has been reported that Robbins has ultimately been discovered to have been a foreigner. Admitting the report to be true, it neither patronizes or changes the principles upon which Judge Bee acted, previous to the developement.

Impressed with my present sentiments, I know that I shall never be hovered under the wings of the administrative patronage. Considering the executive warfare against the constitution, with the repeated, the reiterated lacerations of its most dear and important virtues, to be so glaring as to dazzle away the shade of controversy, I do most solemnly believe that I should not be received as a welcome companion, were I even the august personage of omnipotent truth. Truth, sir, may be assailed—it may be obscured by sophistry, whose smooth blandishments often deceive the ears of unsuspective credulity: but it is not to be destroyed; it is eternal, like freedom, it is "that hardy plant which will strike an everlasting root in the most unfavorable soil," and although the changes of nature may blight its luxuriance, in progressive time it must reanimate, wax strong, and spread forth its mighty branches.—Considering both as the most refined essences of all terrestrial attributes, adoring both as the nearest models to divine perfection, to both I shall cling, amidst every difficulty, every surrounding danger; and whilst I am shielded by the armour of my own conscience, I shall consider the shafts of enmity or malice, as impotently vain!

MANLIUS.

To Charles Dabney

ALS, Southern Historical Collection, University of North Carolina Library, Chapel Hill

My dear Sir[5]   [Philadelphia], January 20, 1800

I inclose you a report lately made by our secretary of war.[6] It contains much matter which in some better state of our finances will well deserve the attention of the government. At present it is perhaps unsuited to our situation. Our revenues fall short of expenses actually incurd & a loan has become absolutely unavoidable. This is much to be regreted but we have really no option. We must endeavor to provide for the future but for the present there [is] to be no ⟨option⟩ choice. We ought not therefore even for useful institutions to incur expence. Yet attention must be paid to our defence. The whole world is in arms & no rights are respected but those which are maintaind by force. In such a state of things we dare not be totally unmindful of ourselves or totally neglectful of that military position to which in spite of the prudence & pacific disposition of our government we may be driven for the preservation of our liberty & national independence.

Altho we ought never to make a loan if it be avoidable yet when forced to it much real consolation is to be derivd from the future resources of America. These resources, if we do not throw them away by dissolving the union, are infallible. It is not to be doubted that in twenty years from this time the United States woud be less burthend by a revenue of twenty millions than now by a revenue of ten. It is the plain & certain consequence of our increasing population & our increasing wealth. The fund afforded too by our back lands will in that time have a powerful operation. I do not mention these things as inducements to expense but as facts which brighten our prospect & afford consolation under expense which is unavoidable.

5. JM addressed this letter to Dabney in Hanover, Va., "by way of Richmond." Dabney was an ardent Federalist who served in 1800 as an elector for Hanover, Caroline, and Louisa counties. He was noted for his efforts to secure grants of land for veterans of the Revolution. See Charles William Dabney, "Colonel Charles Dabney of the Revolution: His Service as Soldier and Citizen," *Virginia Magazine of History and Biography*, LV (1943), 186–199.

6. Secretary of War James McHenry sent John Adams a report dated Jan. 5, 1800, in which he discussed his views of the status of the military. He proposed the establishment of a military academy to train officers and a general plan for the reorganization of the army. Adams submitted this report to Congress on Jan. 13, and it was referred to the committee appointed to consider the military portions of the president's Dec. 3, 1799, address to Congress. This committee reported the compromise military bill that JM mentions later in this letter. See *Amer. State Papers, Claims*, I, 133–139, and *Annals of Congress*, X, 370, 374–375.

The system of defence which has renderd this measure necessary was not only essential to our character as an independent nation but it has actually savd more money to the body of the people than has been expended & has very probably prevented either open war or such national degradation as woud make us the object of general contempt & injury.

A bill to stop recruiting in the twelve additional regiments has been brought in & will pass without opposition. An attempt was made absolutely to disband them but [*it*] was negativd by a great majority.[7] It has been so plainly provd to us that french aggression has been greatly increasd, & that their contemptuous refusal even to treat with us as an independent nation, has been entirely occasiond, by a beleif that we woud not resist them; & it is [*so clear*] that their present willingness to treat is occasiond by perceiving our determination to defend ourselves, that it was thought unwise to change materially our system, at the commencement of negotiation. In addition to this it had much weight, that we shoud know in a few months the fate of our negotiation, & shoud then be able to judge whether the situa[*tion &*] temper of France renderd an invasion pro[*bable*]. Then woud be the time to decide on demini[*shing or*] augmenting our military force.

A French 64 has it is said arrivd in the west indies & three frigates are expected.

My respectful compliments to your circle. I am dear Sir with much esteem, your

J MARSHALL

Speech

Printed, *Claypoole's American Daily Advertiser* (Philadelphia), February 12, 1800, 3

Philadelphia, January 22, 1800

Mr. Marshall said this was precisely the same question as had taken up so much time in the House, and had been maturely dis-

---

7. On Jan. 15, the House of Representatives adopted a resolution to suspend further recruitments and ordered a bill drawn. The bill was introduced the following day, but debate was delayed until Jan. 17. The attempt to disband the army, led by John Nicholas, had been defeated on Jan. 10. JM's optimism over easy passage of the new bill proved unfounded. John Randolph moved on Jan. 22 an amendment to the bill that would release most of the officers in the army; long debate ensued. See Speech, Jan. 22, 1800.

cussed, and on which a majority of the House had expressed an opinion by rejecting the motion to disband the army.[8]

He would call the attention of the House to the particular principle upon which that decision was grounded. It was this. The state of the country at the present moment was such as to leave it absolutely uncertain whether the twelve regiments would or would not be necessary for our defence, but that the period would soon arrive when that uncertainty would be removed. On these grounds it was the determination of the House not to recede from any measure they had ordered, nor to progress, and agreeable to that principle, a bill was reported to suspend the enlistments.

Mr. M. called to the recollection of the House some of the arguments which were used against the motion to disband the army, and applied them to the present amendment. A large majority he said then decided in favor of maintaining exactly the same ground as present, and he presumed no circumstance had appeared to change the opinions of the House on that point. The adoption of the motion would certainly very materially derange the system. Gentlemen supposed the President could re-create the officers. He could not do it without a law to enable him. The original law would have been fully executed, and nothing would remain to do in it, the executive could not therefore create an officer. Besides there would be a great inconsistency: the bill pointed to an event when recruiting must recommence, but the amendment removed that power by taking away the officers who were to execute that service, besides leaving the men recruited (if it were possible) without officers! Thus, though the time was appointed, the means were taken away until at a future meeting of Congress an act should be passed to enable him to appoint officers.

If the number of men were never to be increased, then indeed the arguments in favor of discharging the officers would be unanswerable, but in the prospect of such an event as an increase, those arguments must fall. It was and with propriety, thought prudent to retain the skeleton of an army to enable the President in case of invasion, or actual war, to recommence the recruiting service.

8. While the House of Representatives was considering a measure that would suspend additional recruitment of soldiers and officers in order to save money, John Randolph proposed an amendment that would partially disband the existing army. A motion to this effect, which had been debated earlier in the month, was soundly defeated on Jan. 10. Randolph's amendment was also defeated on the day it was introduced, and the militia bill finally passed two days later on Jan. 24. See Speech, Jan. 7, 1800; JM to Charles Dabney, Jan. 20, 1800; and Congressional Career: Editorial Note, Dec. 4, 1799. See also *Annals of Congress*, X, 370, 374–375, 389–401, 425, and 2 Stat. 7.

It was observed that the same patriotism which called forth the spirit of our citizens to accept of Commissions would excite them again to enter the service. Mr. Marshall believed it to be a fact; he believed they would again enter the public service if required: no doubt but they did estimate love of country sufficient to obey the orders of their country, at any time, or in any way, but would it be right and proper to call gentlemen from their occupations and families, and dismiss them before the service was performed, for which their patriotism called them out merely because their zeal could be depended on? He hoped the national spirit would never yield to that false policy. He hoped the now existing station would be maintained, and no measure at present be receded from, on which the country had placed their confidence for defence.

Legislative Bill

Printed, *Annals of Congress*, X, 527

[*ca. February 18, 1800, Philadelphia.* JM, as chairman of a select committee, introduces a bill "for removing any military force of the United States from the places of holding elections."[9]]

To James McDowell

ALS, Marshall Papers, Swem Library, College of William and Mary

Dear Sir   Philadelphia, February 19, 1800
    Since receiving your letter of the 29th. of Jany.[1] I have had a conversation with the secretary of the treasury relative to the organization of the law for collecting the internal revenue of the United States in Virginia.[2] He says that the change you mention is not now

9. No copy of the bill has been found.
    Largely because of the efforts of Michael Leib (1760–1822), of Pennsylvania, the House on Feb. 13 appointed a committee composed of JM, Leib, and Harrison Gray Otis (1765–1848) to prepare the bill. After debate and amendments, the measure was adopted on Mar. 14. The Senate, however, defeated it by a vote of 17–12 on Apr. 4. *Annals of Congress*, X, 109, 151, 522–523, 625, 626, 656.
    1. Not found. McDowell (1770–1836), of Rockbridge County, Va., was the first cousin of Mary McDowell (1772–1823), who married JM's brother Alexander Keith Marshall, and the father of James McDowell (1796–1851), governor of Virginia from 1842 to 1846.
    2. Oliver Wolcott was serving as secretary of the Treasury. The law for collecting internal revenue in the United States was changed in 1802. See 2 Stat. 148.

contemplated. The present system will continue at least for a time. Shoud it be changd the present inspectors will indubitably be supervisors if there shoud be as many supervisor districts as there are inspection districts. The secretary assurd me that there was no probability at present that the condition of the inspectors woud be alterd for the worse.

We have been employd several days on the non intercourse law with France & there will be a final question on the bill tomorrow.[3] I beleive the state of our affairs with that nation will remain as at present until some arrangements shall be made between the governments. There is however a strong effort to impress on the public mind an opinion that the non intercourse with France has producd the present low price of tobacco. It is impossible that the untruth of any proposition can be demonstrated more certainly than this & yet it is persisted in with unremitting perseverance. I am dear Sir with much esteem, Your obedt.

J MARSHALL

Speech

Printed, *Annals of Congress*, X, 531

[*February 20, 1800, Philadelphia.* JM speaks in support of a bill "to suspend the commercial intercourse between the United States and France." The bill passed following debate. Speech not found.]

Speech

Printed, *Annals of Congress*, X, 564–565

[*February 27, 1800, Philadelphia.* JM speaks against a resolution proposed by Thomas T. Davis, of Kentucky, requesting that John Adams order the court records pertaining to the case of Jonathan Robbins sent to the House.[4] JM states that the records would have to be obtained from South Carolina

---

3. "An act further to suspend the commercial intercourse between the United States and France" passed on Feb. 20 after a long debate during which JM spoke in favor of its adoption. See *Annals of Congress*, X, 529–532, and 2 Stat. 7–11.

4. Davis's (d. 1807) motion followed one of the previous day that would have discharged the Committee of the Whole from further deliberation of the resolutions regarding the Jonathan Robbins affair. That motion had been soundly defeated, and apparently JM thought Davis was attempting to obtain the same results with a different resolution.

and that the effect of adopting this resolution would be to delay consideration of the issue until the next session. Too much time already has been
spent debating such matters, making it impossible to treat properly the
primary question of the constitutional legality of the president's action in
the Robbins case. To permit this accusation to lie unresolved until the next
session of Congress would be unfair to the president and to the country. JM
urges the House to examine the evidence it has before it and not to ask the
president to obtain more information from the federal judiciary. Moreover,
the House could properly request the records from the South Carolina court
without asking the executive branch to intercede. Edward Livingston
accused Timothy Pickering of withholding some of the evidence in this
affair, JM asserts, in particular the court records, which are not in the
possession of the executive branch. "The House could as well despatch a
messenger [to South Carolina] as the Executive could. How was the President, then, to consider those papers asked for of him? Was he to be a *menial*
to the House in a business wherein himself was seriously charged? Certainly
not."

Later in the day, JM again speaks in opposition to what he considers
dilatory tactics by the president's enemies.[5]]

To James Markham Marshall

ALS, Collection of Ellen Morris Manganaro, Westtown, Pa.

My dear brother   [Philadelphia], February 28, 1800
    Mr. Bell requests that I will allow as a deduction from the bill
drawn on him in your favor a balance which he says you owe him on
a note as appears by the inclosd statement. I told him I woud write
to you for instructions on the subject. If the money be really due I

After JM's speech, John Nicholas moved a substitute motion to have the Speaker of the
House obtain the South Carolina court records directly, whereupon Davis withdrew his
motion. Robert Goodloe Harper then moved postponement of the new motion for one
week. *Annals of Congress*, X, 548–569. See also Congressional Career: Editorial Note,
Dec. 4, 1799.

5. After John Nicholas spoke against Harper's motion to postpone consideration of
Nicholas's motion, JM said the House should not "indulge a few gentlemen in their
objections. Was the gentleman [Nicholas] confident that there would be a majority of
his opinion? A few, it must be remembered, could make a decision, and, if so, the result
of the opinion of those few might guide the question. Much had been said about the
introduction of the motion, and the motives ascribed to the supporters of it, as though it
was a planned object." *Annals of Congress*, X, 570.

After Harper's motion to postpone was defeated, JM spoke a third time "at length"
against the resolution to call for the South Carolina court records. The resolution was
defeated by a 57–44 vote. *Ibid.*, 577–578.

For JM's major address on this subject, see Speech, Mar. 7, 1800.

think you had better allow the discount. I know your unwillingness to mingle you private accounts with those of the company but this small sum you may easily replace. The interest on your stock will go far towards it. I wrote you sometime past that it was yet on the books here but you have not sent me a power of attorney to draw the interest or given me any directions concerning it.[6]

We have been three days on the preliminaries to the case of Thomas Nash & I am not sure that we shall be able to get any further today. Every stratagem seems to be usd to give to this business an undue impression. On the motion to send for the evidence from the records of South Carolina altho it was stated & provd that this woud amount to an abandonment of the enquiry during the present session & to an abandonment under circumstances which woud impress the public mind with the opinion that we really beleivd Mr. Livingstons resolutions maintainable; & that the record coud furnish no satisfaction since it coud not contain the parol testimony offerd to the Judge & further that it coud not be material to the President but only to the reputation of the Judge what the amount of the testimony was, yet the debate took a turn as if we were precipitating a decision without enquiry & without evidence.

I have just receivd your letter inclosing your power of attorney. I send you a power to convey the land you sold.[7] Your affectionate

J MARSHALL

To Samuel Overton, Jr.

ALS, Overton Papers, Swem Library, College of William and Mary

Dear Sir   [Philadelphia, *ca.* February 1800]

I receivd your letter inclosing a recommendation from some gentlemen of Fredericksburg of you for the office of postmaster at that place which I deliverd at the office of the postmaster general & at the same time stated my perfect conviction of your fitness for the office.[8] I coud not however sollicit your appointment because I had before at the

6. Neither the enclosed statement nor letters on this subject between JM and his brother have been found.

7. The documents have not been found.

8. For additional information on Overton's (1768–1823) interest in the appointment, see William Austin to Overton, Feb. 14, 1800, Overton Papers, Swem Library, College of William and Mary. Timothy Green was deputy postmaster of Fredericksburg, Va., in 1802. See *Amer. State Papers, Miscellaneous*, I, 292.

request of Mr. Rootes recommended Mr. Green. That gentleman was appointed immediately on the death of Mr. Wyatt & I am sure woud have been appointed had I not mentiond him because he was recommended by almost the whole town of Fredericksburg. My acquaintance with you however woud have left no doubt on my mind respecting a particular application for you on my part had I not previously applied for another.

I shall set out for Virginia so as to be in Richmond by the 12th. of May & am dear Sir, Your Obedt.

J MARSHALL

Deed

Deed Book Copy, Office of the Clerk of Hardy County, Moorefield, W.Va.

[*March 5, 1800 (Hardy County, Va.*). By his attorney, Rawleigh Colston, JM conveys 32 acres in the South Branch Manor to John Fisher for £9. The deed was recorded in the District Court at Hardy County on May 9, 1800.]

Speech

Printed, *Speech of the Hon. John Marshall, Delivered in the House of Representatives, of the United States, on the Resolutions of the Hon. Edward Livingston, Relative to Thomas Nash, Alias Jonathan Robbins* (Philadelphia, 1800)

[Washington, March 7, 1800]

MR. MARSHALL said, believing, as he did most seriously—that in a government constituted like that of the United States, much of the public happiness depended, not only on its being rightly administered, but on the measures of administration being rightly understood:—On rescuing public opinion from those numerous prejudices with which so many causes might combine to surround it:—he could not but have been highly gratified with the very eloquent,—and what was still more valuable, the very able, and very correct argument, which had been delivered by the gentleman from Delaware (Mr. Bayard) against the resolutions now under consideration.[9] He

9. Edward Livingston of New York on Feb. 20 had introduced resolutions criticizing President Adams for his handling of the Robbins affair. *Annals of Congress*, X, 532–533. See also Congressional Career: Editorial Note, Dec. 4, 1799. James A. Bayard's principal argument, a three-hour speech, was delivered on Mar. 5 but was not recorded. *Annals of Congress*, X, 595.

had not expected that the effect of this argument would have been universal, but he had cherished the hope, and in this he had not been disappointed, that it would be very extensive. He did not flatter himself with being able to shed much new light on the subject, but, as the argument in opposition to the resolutions had been assailed, with considerable ability, by gentlemen of great talents, he trusted the house would not think the time misapplied, which would be devoted to the re-establishment of the principles contained in that argument, and to the refutation of those advanced in opposition to it. In endeavouring to do this, he should notice the observations in support of the resolutions, not in the precise order in which they were made, but as they applied to the different points he deemed it necessary to maintain, in order to demonstrate, that the conduct of the executive of the United States, could not justly be charged with the errors imputed to it by the resolutions.

His first proposition, he said, was that the case of Thomas Nash, as stated to the President, was completely within the 27th article of the treaty of amity, commerce, and navigation, entered into between the United States of America and Great Britain.[1]

He read the article and then observed—The casus foederis of this article occurs, when a person, having committed murder or forgery within the jurisdiction of one of the contracting parties, and having sought an asylum in the country of the other, is charged with the crime, and his delivery demanded, on such proof of his guilt as according to the laws of the place where he shall be found, would justify his apprehension and commitment for trial, if the offence had there been committed.

The case stated is, that Thomas Nash, having committed a murder on board a British Frigate, navigating the high seas under a commission from his Britannic Majesty, had sought an asylum within the United States, and on this case his delivery was demanded by the minister of the King of Great Britain.

It is manifest that the case stated, if supported by proof, is within the letter of the article, provided a murder committed in a British frigate, on the high seas, be committed within the jurisdiction of that nation.

1. JM and other Federalists insisted on using the name Thomas Nash, refusing to recognize the claim that he might be Jonathan Robbins and an American citizen. On art. 27, the clause in the Jay Treaty providing for extradition of persons charged with murder or forgery, see Amendments, Apr. 2 and 29, 1800, and Miller, ed., *Treaties*, II, 236.

That such a murder is within their jurisdiction, has been fully shown by the gentleman from Delaware. The principle is, that the jurisdiction of a nation extends to the whole of its territory, and to its own citizens in every part of the world. The laws of a nation are rightfully obligatory on its own citizens in every situation, where those laws are really extended to them. This principle is founded on the nature of civil union. It is supported every where by public opinion, and is recognized by writers on the law of nations. Rutherforth in his second volume page 180 says, "The jurisdiction which a civil society has over the persons of its members, affects them immediately, whether they are within its territories or not."[2]

This general principle is especially true, and is particularly recognized, with respect to the fleets of a nation on the high seas. To punish offences committed in its fleet, is the practice of every nation in the universe; and consequently the opinion of the world is, that a fleet at sea, is within the jurisdiction of the nation to which it belongs. Rutherforth 2 vol. page 491, says, "There can be no doubt about the jurisdiction of a nation over the persons, which compose its fleets, when they are out at sea, whether they are sailing upon it, or are stationed in any particular part of it."[3]

The gentleman from Pennsylvania, (Mr. Gallatin) tho' he has not directly controverted this doctrine, has sought to weaken it, by observing, that the jurisdiction of a nation at sea could not be compleat even in its own vessels;—and in support of this position he urged the admitted practice, of submitting to search for contraband—a practice not tolerated on land, within the territory of a neutral power.[4] The rule is as stated; but is founded on a principle which does not affect the jurisdiction of a nation over its citizens or subjects in its ships. The principle is, that in the sea, itself, no nation has any jurisdiction. All may equally exercise their rights, and consequently the right of a belligerent power to prevent aid being given to his enemy, is not restrained by any superior right of a neutral in the place. But if this argument possessed any force, it would not apply to national ships of war, since the usage of nations does not permit them to be searched.

2. T[homas] Rutherforth, *Institutes of Natural Law, Being the substance of a Course of Lectures on Grotius de Jure Belli et Pacis . . .* , II (Cambridge, 1756).

3. *Ibid.*

4. Albert Gallatin spoke at length on Mar. 6. *Annals of Congress*, X, 596. No copy of his speech has been found, but see "Observations on Robbins's case," Feb. 7–Mar. 7, 1800, Carl E. Prince and Helene H. Fineman, eds., The Papers of Albert Gallatin, microfilm ed. (Philadelphia, 1969), reel 3.

According to the practice of the world then, and the opinions of writers on the law of nations, the murder committed on board a British frigate navigating the high seas, was a murder committed within the jurisdiction of the British nation.

Altho such a murder is plainly within the letter of the article, it has been contended not to be within its just construction, because at sea, all nations have a common jurisdiction, and the article correctly construed, will not embrace a case of concurrent jurisdiction.

It is deemed unnecessary to controvert this construction, because the proposition—*that the United States had no jurisdiction over the murder committed by Thomas Nash,* is believed to be completely demonstrable.

It is not true that all nations have jurisdiction over all offences committed at sea. On the contrary no nation has any jurisdiction at sea, but over its own citizens or vessels, or offences against itself. This principle is laid down in 2d. Ruth. 488, and 491.[5]

The American government has on a very solemn occasion, avowed the same principle. The first minister of the French republic asserted and exercised powers of so extraordinary a nature, as unavoidably to produce a controversy with the United States. The situation in which the government then found itself was such, as necessarily to occasion a very serious and mature consideration of the opinions it should adopt. Of consequence, the opinions then declared, deserve great respect. In the case alluded to, Mr. Genet had asserted the right of fitting out privateers in the American ports, and of manning them with American citizens, in order to cruize against nations with whom America was at peace. In reasoning against this extravagant claim, the then secretary of state, in his letter of the 17th of June, 1793, says "For our citizens then to commit murders and depredations on the members of nations at peace with us, or to combine to do it, appeared to the executive and to those whom they consulted, as much against the laws of the land, as to murder or rob, or combine to murder or rob, its own citizens; and as much to require punishment, if done, within their limits, where they have a territorial jurisdiction, or on

---

5. See also Rutherforth, who wrote, "Whatever does not admit of full property or absolute ownership, cannot be a part of the territory or under the jurisdiction of a nation: because all jurisdiction or right of territory presupposes full property or absolute ownership. . . . There can be no doubt about the jurisdiction of a nation over the persons, which compose its fleet, when they are out at sea; whether they are sailing upon it, or are stationed in any particular part of it. But when they are thus stationed, this jurisdiction of the nation is merely a jurisdiction over their persons, and not over that part of the ocean, where those persons are." *Institutes of Natural Law,* II, 491.

the high seas, where they have a *personal jurisdiction*, that is to say, one which reaches *their own citizens only*; this being an *appropriate part* of each nation, on an element where all have a common jurisdiction."[6]

The well considered opinion then of the American government on this subject is, that the jurisdiction of a nation at sea is "*personal*," reaching its "*own citizens only*," and that this is "*the appropriate part* of each nation" on that element.

This is precisely the opinion maintained by the opposers of the resolutions. If the jurisdiction of America at sea be personal—reaching its own citizens only, if this be its appropriate part, then the jurisdiction of the nation cannot extend to a murder committed by a British sailor, on board a British frigate navigating the high seas under a commission from his Britannic majesty.

As a further illustration of the principle contended for, suppose a contract made at sea, and a suit instituted for the recovery of money which might be due thereon. By the laws of what nation would the contract be governed? The principle is general, that a personal contract follows the person, but is governed by the law of the place where it is formed. By what law then would such a contract be governed! If all nations had jurisdiction over the place, then the laws of all nations would equally influence the contract but certainly no man will hesitate to admit, that such a contract ought to be decided according to the laws of that nation, to which the vessel or contracting parties might belong.

Suppose a duel attended with death, in the fleet of a foreign nation, or in any vessel which returned safe to port, could it be pretended that any government on earth, other than that to which the fleet or vessel belonged, had jurisdiction in the case; or that the offender could be tried by the laws, or tribunals, of any other nation whatever.

Suppose a private theft by one mariner from another and the vessel to perform its voyage and return in safety, would it be contended that all nations have equal cognizance of the crime; and are equally authorized to punish it?

If there be this common jurisdiction at sea, why not punish desertion from one belligerent power to another, or correspondence with the enemy, or any other crime which may be perpetrated? A common jurisdiction over all offences at sea, in whatever vessel committed, would involve the power of punishing the offences which have been

6. Thomas Jefferson to Edmond Charles Genet, June 17, 1793, Jefferson Papers, Library of Congress.

stated. Yet all gentlemen will disclaim this power. It follows then that no such common jurisdiction exists.

In truth the right of every nation to punish, is limited, in its nature, to offences against the nation inflicting the punishment. This principle is believed to be universally true.

It comprehends every possible violation of its laws on its own territory, and it extends to violations committed elsewhere by persons it has a right to bind. It extends also to general piracy.

A pirate under the law of nations, is an enemy of the human race. Being the enemy of all he is liable to be punished by all. Any act which denotes this universal hostility, is an act of piracy. Not only an actual robbery therefore, but cruizing on the high seas without commission, and with intent to rob, is piracy. This is an offence against all and every nation and is therefore alike punishable by all. But an offence which in its nature affects only a particular nation, is only punishable by that nation.

It is by confounding general piracy with piracy by statute, that indistinct ideas have been produced, respecting the power to punish offences committed on the high seas.

A statute may make any offence piracy, committed within the jurisdiction of the nation passing the statute, and such offence will be punishable by that nation. But piracy under the law of nations, which alone is punishable by all nations, can only consist in an act which is an offence against all. No particular nation can increase or diminish the list of offences thus punishable.

It had been observed by his colleague (Mr. Nicholas) for the purpose of showing that the distinction taken on this subject by the gentleman from Delaware, (Mr. Bayard) was inaccurate, that any vessel robbed on the high seas, could be the property only of a single nation, and being only an offence against that nation could be, on the principle taken by the opposers of the resolutions no offence against the law of nations:[7] But in this his colleague had not accurately considered the principle. As a man, who turns out to rob on the high way, and forces from a stranger his purse with a pistol at his bosom, is not the particular enemy of that stranger, but alike the enemy of every man who carries a purse, so those, who, without a commission, rob on the high seas, manifest a temper hostile to all

---

7. John Nicholas made this point during a long speech to the Committee of the Whole in support of Livingston's resolutions. *Annals of Congress*, X, 595. No copy of his speech has been found.

nations, and therefore become the enemies of all. The same inducements which occasion the robbery of one vessel, exist to occasion the
robbery of others, and therefore the single offence is an offence
against the whole community of nations, manifests a temper hostile
to all, is the commencement of an attack on all, and is consequently,
of right, punishable by all.

His colleague had also contended that all the offences at sea, punishable by the British Statutes from which the act of Congress was in
a great degree copied, were piracies at common law, or by the law of
nations, and as murder is among these, consequently murder was an
act of piracy by the law of nations, and therefore punishable by every
nation. In support of this position he had cited 1. Hawk. P. C. 267
and 271.[8] 3d Inst. 112 and 1st Woodison 140.

The amount of these cases is, that no new offence is made piracy
by the statutes; but that a different tribunal is created for their trial,
which is guided by a different rule, from that which governed, previous to those Statutes. Therefore, on an indictment for piracy, it is
still necessary to prove an offence which was piracy before the
Statutes. He drew from these authorities a very different conclusion
from that which had been drawn by his colleague. To show the correctness of his conclusion, it was necessary to observe, that Statute
did not indeed change the nature of piracy since it only transferred
the trial of the crime to a different tribunal, where different rules of
decision prevailed, but having done this, other crimes committed on
the high seas, which were not piracy, were made punishable by the
same tribunal, but certainly this municipal regulation could not be
considered as proving, that those offences were before, piracy by the
law of nations. Mr. Nicholas insisted that the law was not correctly
stated, whereupon Mr. Marshall called for 3d inst. and read the
statute. "All treasons, felonies robberies, murders, and confederacies
committed in or upon the seas, &c. shall be enquired, tried, heard,
determined and judged in such shires, &c. in like form and condition
as if any such offence had been committed on the land, &c."

8. Hawkins states that piracy was changed from treason to felony by the statute of
treason (25 Edw. 3, c. 2), and that "the statute 28 Hen. 8. c. 15 does not alter the nature
of the offence so as to make that which was before a felony only by the civil law, now
become a felony by the common law; for the offence must still be alledged as done upon
the sea, and is no way cognizable by the common law but only by virtue of this statute,
which, by ordaining that in some respects it shall have the like trial and punishment as
are used for felony at common law, shall not be carried so far as to make it also agree
with it in other particulars which are not mentioned." William Hawkins, *A Treatise of
the Pleas of the Crown* . . . , 7th ed., I (London, 1795), 267, 270–271.

"And such as shall be convicted &c. shall have and suffer such pains of death, &c. as if they had been attainted of any treason, felony, robbery, or other the said offences done upon the land."[9]

This statute it is certain, does not change the nature of piracy, but all treasons, felonies, robberies, murders and confederacies committed in or upon the sea, are not declared to have been, nor are they, piracies. If a man be indicted as a pirate, the offence must be shown to have been piracy before the statute, but if he be indicted for treason, felony, robbery, murder, or confederacy committed at sea, whether such offence was or was not a piracy, he shall be punished in like manner as if he had committed the same offence at land. The passage cited from 1. Woodison 140, is a full authority to this point. Having stated that offences committed at sea were formerly triable before the Lord high Admiral, according to the course of the Roman civil law, Woodison says but by the Statutes 27. H. 8th. C 4. and 28. H. 8. C. 15. all treasons, felonies, piracies and other crimes committed on the sea or where the Admiral has jurisdiction, shall be tried in the realm as if done on land." But the Statutes referred to affect only the manner of the trial *so far as respects piracy*. The nature of the offence is not changed. Whether a charge amounts to piracy or not, must still depend on the law of nations, except where, *in the case of British subjects*, express acts of Parliament have declared that the crimes therein specified shall be adjudged piracy, or shall be liable to the same mode of trial and degree of punishment."[1]

This passage proves not only that all offences at sea are not piracies by the law of nations, but also that all indictments for piracy must depend on the law of nations, "except where, *in the case of British subjects, express acts of Parliament*" have changed the law. Why do not these "express acts of Parliament" change the law as to others than "British subjects"? The words are general—"All treasons, felonies &c." Why are they confined in construction to British subjects? The answer is a plain one. The jurisdiction of the nation is confined to its territory and to its subjects.

The gentleman from Pennsylvania (Mr. Gallatin) abandons, and very properly abandons, this untenable ground. He admits that no nation has a right to punish offences against another nation, and that

9. Edward Coke, *The Third Part of the Institutes of the Laws of England* . . . (London, 1797), 111, 112.

1. The quotation is preceded by "offences committed on the sea were antiently tried before the lord high admiral, according to the course of the Roman civil law." Richard Wooddeson, *A Systematical View of the Laws of England* . . . , I (Dublin, 1792), 139–140.

the United States can only punish offences against their own laws, and the laws of nations. He admits too, that if there had only been a mutiny (and consequently if there had only been a murder) on board the Hermoine, that the American courts could have taken no cognizance of the crime. Yet mutiny is punishable as piracy by the law of both nations. That gentleman contends that the act commited by Nash was piracy according to the law of nations. He supports his position by insisting, that the offence may be constituted by the commission of a single act, that unauthorized robbery on the high seas is this act, and that the crew having seized the vessel and being out of the protection of any nation, were pirates.[2]

It is true that the offence may be complete by a single act—but it depends on the nature of that act. If it be such as manifests general hostility against the world, an intention to rob generally, then it is piracy; but if it be merely a mutiny and murder in a vessel, for the purpose of delivering it up to the enemy, it seems to be an offence against a single nation, and not to be piracy. The sole object of the crew might be to go over to the enemy, or to free themselves from the tyranny experienced on board a ship of war, and not to rob generally.

But should it even be true, that running away with the vessel to deliver her up to an enemy, was an act of general piracy, punishable by all nations, yet the mutiny and murder was a distinct offence.— Had the attempt to seize the vessel failed, after the commission of the murder, then, according to the argument of the gentleman from Pennsylvania, the American courts could have taken no cognizance of the crime. Whatever then might have been the law respecting the piracy, of the murder there was no jurisdiction. For the murder, not the piracy, Nash was delivered up. Murder, and not piracy, is comprehended in the 27th article of the treaty between the two nations. Had he been tried then, and acquitted on an indictment for the piracy, he must still have been delivered up for the murder, of which the court could have no jurisdiction. It is certain that an acquittal of the piracy, would not have discharged the murder; and therefore in the so much relied on trials at Trenton,[3] a separate indictment for

2. Gallatin's speech has not been found, but see "Observations on Robbins's case," filed under Mar. 7, 1800, Papers of Albert Gallatin.

3. JM referred to the trial of William Brigstock, John Evans, and Joannes Williams in the U.S. Circuit Court of New Jersey, which was called to the attention of the House of Representatives by Edward Livingston on Mar. 3. The following day Albert Gallatin introduced a resolution calling for the president to submit to the House any papers he

murder was filed, after an indictment for piracy. Since then, if acquitted for piracy, he must have been delivered to the British government on the charge of murder, the President of the United States might, very properly, without prosecuting for the piracy, direct him to be delivered up on the murder.

All the gentlemen who have spoken in support of the resolutions, have contended that the case of Thomas Nash is within the purview of the act of Congress, which relates to this subject, and is, by that act, made punishable in the American courts. That is, that the act of Congress designed to punish crimes committed on board a British frigate.

Nothing can be more completely demonstrable than the untruth of this proposition.

It has already been shewn, that the legislative jurisdiction of a nation, extends only to its own territory, and to its own citizens, wherever they may be. Any general expression in a legislative act, must, necessarily be restrained to objects within the jurisdiction of the legislature passing the act. Of consequence, an act of Congress can only be construed to apply to the territory of the United States, comprehending every person within it, and to the citizens of the United States.

But independent of this undeniable truth, the act itself affords complete testimony of its intention and extent. (See Laws of the U. S. vol. 1. P. 100.)[4]

The title is, "An act for the punishment of certain crimes against the United States." Not against Britain—France—or the World;—but singly "against the United States."

The first section relates to treason, and its objects are "any person or persons owing allegiance to the United States." This description comprehends only the citizens of the United States, and such others as may be on its territory, or in its service.

The second section relates to mis-prison of treason, and declares, without limitation, that any person or persons, having knowledge of any treason, and not communicating the same, shall be guilty of that crime. Here then is an instance of that limited description of persons in one section, and of that general description in another, which has

---

might have on the subject. Consideration of the resolution produced a long debate, and its defeat came only when the Speaker voted to break a tie vote. *Annals of Congress*, X, 583–595.

4. 1 Stat. 112–119 (1790).

been relied on to support the construction contended for by the friends of the resolutions. But will it be pretended that a person can commit mis-prison of treason, who cannot commit treason itself? That he would be punishable for concealing a treason, who could not be punished for plotting it? Or can it be supposed that the act designed to punish an Englishman or a Frenchman, who, residing in his own country, should have knowledge of treasons against the United States, and should not cross the Atlantic to reveal them?

The same observations apply to the 6th section which makes "any person or persons" guilty of mis-prison of felony, who having knowledge of murder or other offences enumerated in that section, should conceal them. It is impossible to apply this to a foreigner, in a foreign land, or to any person not owing allegiance to the United States.

The 8th section, which is supposed to comprehend the case, after declaring that if any person or persons shall commit murder on the high seas, he shall be punishable with death, proceeds to say, that if any captain or mariner shall piratically run away with a ship or vessel, or yield her up voluntarily to a pirate, or if any seaman shall lay violent hands on his commander, to prevent his fighting, or shall make a revolt in the ship, every such offender shall be adjudged a pirate, and a felon.

The persons who are the objects of this section of the act, are all described in general terms, which might embrace the subjects of all nations. But it is to be supposed, that if, in an engagement between an English and a French ship of war, the crew of the one or the other, should lay violent hands on the captain, and force him to strike, that this would be an offence against the act of Congress punishable in the courts of the United States? On this extended construction of the general terms of the section, not only the crew of one foreign vessel forcing their captain to surrender to another, would incur the penalties of the act, but if in the late action between the gallant Truxton and a French frigate,[5] the crew of that frigate had compelled the captain to surrender, while he was unwilling to do so, they would have been indictable as felons in the courts of the United States. But

5. Thomas Truxtun (1755–1822) commanded the U.S.S. *Constellation* and had defeated the French frigate *La Vengeance* in a five-hour battle the night of Feb. 1, 1800, in the waters near Puerto Rico. The House voted to ask the president to present Truxton with a gold medal commemorating his gallantry in the action. *Annals of Congress*, X, 629–632, 640–642. For a biographical sketch, see Eugene S. Ferguson, *Commodore Thomas Truxtun, 1755–1822: A Description of the Truxtun-Biddle Letters in the Collections of The Library Company of Philadelphia* (Philadelphia, 1947).

surely the act of Congress admits of no such extravagant construction.

His colleague, Mr. Marshal said, had cited, and particularly relied on the 9th section of the act. That section declares, that if a citizen shall commit any of the enumerated piracies, or any act of hostility on the high seas, against the United States, under color of a commission from any foreign Prince or State, he shall be adjudged a pirate, felon and robber, and shall suffer death.

This section is only a positive extension of the act to a case, which might otherwise have escaped punishment. It takes away the protection of a foreign commission, from an American citizen who, on the high seas robs his countrymen. This is no exception from any preceding part of the law, because there is no part which relates to the conduct of vessels commissioned by a foreign power; it only proves that, in the opinion of the legislature, the penalties of the act could not, without this express provision, have been incurred by a citizen holding a foreign commission.

It is then most certain, that the act of Congress does not comprehend the case of a murder committed on board a foreign ship of war.

The gentleman from New-York has cited 2d Woodison 428, to show that the courts of England extend their jurisdiction to piracies committed by the subjects of foreign nations.

This has not been doubted. The case from Woodison is a case of robberies committed on the high seas by a vessel without authority. There are ordinary acts of piracy, which, as has been already stated, being offences against all nations, are punishable by all. The case from 2d Woodison, and the note cited from the same book by the gentleman from Delaware, are strong authorities against the doctrines contended for by the friends of the resolutions.[6]

It has also been contended that the question of jurisdiction was decided at Trenton, by receiving indictments against persons there arraigned for the same offence, and by retaining them for trial after the return of the habeas corpus.

Every person in the slightest degree acquainted with judicial proceedings, knows, that an indictment is no evidence of jurisdiction; and that in criminal cases, the question of jurisdiction will seldom be made, but by arrest of judgement after conviction.

6. The case involved a French ship, the captain of which upon arriving in an Irish port was accused of robbery on the seas. The king claimed jurisdiction, "as every man by the usage of our European nations is *justiciable* in the place, where the crime is committed, so are pirates, being reputed out of the protection of all laws and privileges, and to be tried in what ports soever they are taken." 2 Sir L. Jenk. 714, in Wooddeson, *Laws of England*, II, 428.

The proceedings after the return of the habeas corpus, only prove, that the case was not such a case as to induce the Judge immediately to decide against his jurisdiction. The question was not free from doubt, and therefore might very properly be postponed until its decision should become necessary.

It has been argued by the gentleman from New-York, that tne form of the indictment is, itself, evidence of a power in the court to try the case. Every word of that indictment said the gentleman, gives the lie, to a denial of the jurisdiction of the court.[7]

It would be assuming a very extraordinary principle indeed to say, that words inserted in an indictment for the express purpose of assuming the jurisdiction of a court, should be admitted to prove that jurisdiction. The question certainly depended on the nature of the fact, and not on the description of the fact. But as an indictment must necessarily contain formal words in order to be supported, and as forms often denote what a case must substantially be, to authorize a court to take cognizance of it, some words in the indictments at Trenton, ought to be noticed. The indictments charge the persons to have been within the peace, and the murder to have been committed against the peace of the United States. These are necessary averments, and, to give the court jurisdiction, the fact ought to have accorded with them. But who will say that the crew of a British frigate on the high seas, are within the peace of the United States, or a murder committed on board such a frigate, against the peace of any other than the British government.

It is then demonstrated that the murder with which Thomas Nash was charged, was not committed within the jurisdiction of the United States, and, consequently, that the case stated was completely within the letter, and the spirit, of the 27th article of the treaty between the two nations. If the necessary evidence was produced, he ought to have been delivered up to justice. It was an act to which the American Nation was bound by a most solemn compact. To have tried him for the murder would have been mere mockery. To have condemned and executed him, the court having no jurisdiction, would have been murder:—to have acquitted and discharged him, would have been a breach of faith and a violation of national duty.

But it has been contended that altho' Thomas Nash ought to have been delivered up to the British Minister, on the requisition made by him in the name of his government, yet the interference of the President was improper.

7. Speech not found.

This Mr. Marshall said led to his second proposition, which was— That the case was a case for executive and not judicial decision. He admitted implicitly the division of powers stated by the gentleman from New York, and that it was the duty of each department to resist the encroachments of the others.

This being established, the enquiry was, to what department was the power in question allotted?

The gentleman from New-York had relied on the 2d section of the 3d article of the constitution, which enumerates the cases to which the judicial power of the United States extends,—as expressly including that now under consideration. Before he examined that section, it would not be improper to notice a very material mis-statement of it, made in the resolutions offered by the gentleman from New York. By the constitution, the judicial power of the United States is extended to all *cases in law and equity* arising under the constitution, laws and treaties of the United States; but the resolutions declare the judicial power to extend to *all questions* arising under the constitution, treaties and laws of the United States. The difference between the constitution and the resolutions was material and apparent. A case in law or equity was a term well understood, and of limited signification. It was a controversy between parties which had taken a shape for judicial decision. If the judicial power extended to every *question* under the constitution it would involve almost every subject proper for legislative discussion and decision; if to every *question* under the laws and treaties of the United States it would involve almost every subject on which the executive could act. The division of power which the gentleman had stated, could exist no longer, and the other departments would be swallowed up by the judiciary. But it was apparent that the resolutions had essentially misrepresented the constitution. He did not charge the gentleman from New-York, with intentional misrepresentation; he would not attribute to him such an artifice in any case, much less in a case where detection was so easy and so certain. Yet this substantial departure from the constitution, in resolutions affecting substantially to unite it, was not the less worthy of remark for being unintentional. It manifested the course of reasoning by which the gentleman had himself been misled, and his judgement betrayed into the opinions those resolutions expressed.

By extending the judicial power to all *cases in law and equity*, the constitution had never been understood, to confer on that department, any political power whatever. To come within this description, a question must assume a legal form, for forensic litigation, and judicial decision. There must be parties to come into court, who can be reached by its process, and bound by its power; whose rights admit of ultimate decision by a tribunal to which they are bound to submit.

A case in law or equity proper for judicial decision, may arise under a treaty, where the rights of individuals acquired or secured by a treaty, are to be asserted or defended in court. As under the 4th or 6th article of the treaty of peace with Great Britain, or under those articles of our late treaties with France, Prussia and other nations, which secure to the subjects of those nations, their property within the United States: or as would be an article which, instead of stipulating to deliver up an offender, should stipulate his punishment, provided the case was punishable by the laws, and in the courts of the United States. But the judicial power cannot extend to political compacts—as the establishment of the boundary line between the American and British dominions; the case of the late guarantee in our treaty with France; or the case of the delivery of a murderer under the 27th article of our present treaty with Britain.

The gentleman from New-York has asked, triumphantly asked, what power exists in our courts to deliver up an individual to a foreign government? Permit me, said Mr. Marshal, but not triumphantly, to retort the question.—By what authority can any court render such a judgement? What power does a court possess to seize any individual, and determine that he shall be adjudged by a foreign tribunal? Surely our courts possess no such power, yet they must possess it, if this article of the treaty is to be executed by the courts.

Gentlemen have cited and relied on that clause in the constitution, which enables Congress to define and punish piracies, and felonies; committed on the high seas, and offences against the law of nations; together with the act of Congress declaring the punishment of those offences; as transferring the whole subject to the courts. But that clause can never be construed to make to the government a grant of power, which the people making it, did not themselves possess. It has already been shown that the people of the United States have no jurisdiction over offences, commited on board a foreign ship, against a foreign nation. Of consequence, in framing a government for themselves, they cannot have passed this jurisdiction to that government. The law therefore cannot act upon the case. But this clause of the constitution cannot be considered and need not be considered, as affecting acts which are piracy under the law of nations. As the judicial power of the United States extends to all cases of admiralty and maritime jurisdiction, and piracy under the law of nations is of admiralty and maritime jurisdiction, punishable by every nation, the judicial power of the United States of course extends to it. On this principle the courts of admiralty under the Confederation, took cognizance of piracy, altho' there was no express power in Congress to define and punish the offence.

But the extension of the judicial power of the United States to all cases of admiralty and maritime jurisdiction, must necessarily be understood with some limitation. All cases of admiralty and maritime jurisdiction which, from their nature, are triable in the United States, are submitted to the jurisdiction of the courts of the United States. There are, cases of piracy by the law of nations, and cases within the legislative jurisdiction of the nation. The people of America possessed no other power over the subject, and could consequently transfer no other to their courts, and it has already been proved that a murder committed on board a foreign ship of war, is not comprehended within this description.

The consular convention with France has also been relied on, as proving, the act of delivering up an individual to a foreign power, to be in its nature judicial and not executive.

The 9th article of that convention authorizes the consuls and vice consuls of either nation, to cause to be arrested all deserters from their vessels, "for which purpose the said consuls and vice consuls shall address themselves to the courts, judges and officers competent."[8]

This article of the convention does not, like the 27th article of the treaty with Britain, stipulate a national act, to be performed on the demand of a nation; it only authorizes a foreign minister to cause an act to be done, and prescribes the course he is to pursue. The contract itself is, that the act shall be performed by the agency of the foreign consul, through the medium of the courts; but this affords no evidence that a contract of a very different nature, is to be performed in the same manner.

It is said that the then President of the United States declared the incompetency of the courts, judges and officers to execute this contract without an act of the legislature. But the then President made no such declaration. He has said that some legislative provision is requisite, to carry the stipulations of the convention into *full* effect. This however is by no means declaring the incompetency of a department to perform an act stipulated by treaty, until the legislative authority shall direct its performance.

8. Miller, ed., *Treaties*, II, 237.

It has been contended that the conduct of the executive on former occasions, similar to this in principle, has been such, as to evince an opinion even in that department, that the case in question is proper for the decision of the courts.

The fact adduced to support this argument is, the determination of the late President, on the case of prizes made within the jurisdiction of the United States, or by privateers fitted out in their ports.

The nation was bound to deliver up those prizes in like manner as the nation is now bound to deliver up an individual demanded under the 27th article of the treaty with Britain. The duty was the same, and devolved on the same department.

In quoting the decision of the executive on that case, the gentleman from New-York has taken occasion to bestow high encomium on the late President, and to consider his conduct as furnishing an example worthy the imitation of his successor.[9]

It must be cause of much delight to the real friends of that great man,—to those who supported his administration while in office, from a conviction of its wisdom and its virtue, to hear the unqualified praise which is now bestowed on it, by those who had been supposed to possess different opinions. If the measure now under consideration, shall be found, on examination, to be the same in principle, with that which has been cited, by its opponents, as a fit precedent for it, then may the friends of the gentleman now in office indulge the hope, that when he, like his predecessor, shall be no more, his conduct too may be quoted as an example for the government of his successors.

The evidence relied on to prove the opinion of the then executive on the case, consists of two letters from the Secretary of State, the one of the 29th of June 1793 to Mr. Genet, and the other of the 16th of August 1793 to Mr. Morris.[1]

In the letter to Mr. Genet, the Secretary says, that the claimant having filed his libel against the ship William, in the court of Admiralty, there was no power which could take the vessel out of court, until it had decided against its own jurisdiction, that having so decided, the complaint is lodged with the executive, and he asks for evidence to enable that department to consider and decide finally on the subject.

It will be difficult to find in this letter an executive opinion, that

9. Speech not found.
1. Thomas Jefferson to Edmond Charles Genet, June 29, 1793, and Jefferson to Gouverneur Morris, Aug. 16, 1793, Jefferson Papers.

the case was not a case for executive decision. The contrary is clearly avowed. It is true that when an individual claiming the property as his, had asserted that claim in a court, the executive acknowledges in itself a want of power, to dismiss or decide upon the claim thus pending in court. But this argues no opinion of a want of power in itself to decide upon the case, if instead of being carried before a court as an individual claim, it is brought before the executive as a national demand. A private suit instituted by an individual, asserting his claim to property, can only be controled by that individual. The executive can give no direction concerning it. But a public prosecution carried on in the name of the United States, can without impropriety be dismissed at the will of the government. The opinion therefore given in this letter is unquestionably correct, but it is certainly misunderstood when it is considered as being an opinion that the question was not, in its nature, a question for executive decision.

In the letter to Mr. Morris the secretary asserts the principle, that vessels taken within our jurisdiction ought to be restored; but says it is yet unsettled whether the act of restoration is to be performed by the executive or judicial department.

The principle then according to this letter is not submitted to the courts, whether a vessel captured within a given distance of the American coast was or was not captured within the jurisdiction of the United States, was a question not to be determined by the courts, but by the executive. The doubt expressed is, not what tribunal shall settle the principle, but what tribunal shall settle the fact. In this respect a doubt might exist in the case of prizes, which could not exist in the case of a man. Individuals on each side claimed the property, and therefore their rights could be brought into court, and there contested as a case in law or equity. The demand of a man made by a nation stands on different principles.

Having noticed the particular letters cited by the gentleman from New-York, permit me now said Mr. Marshall to ask the attention of the house to the whole course of executive conduct on this interesting subject.

It is first mentioned in a letter from the secretary of state to Mr. Genet of the 25th of June 1793.[2] In that letter, the secretary states a consultation between himself and the secretaries of the treasury and war, (the President being absent) in which (so well were they assured of the President's way of thinking in those cases) it was determined,

2. Jefferson to Genet, June 25, 1793, *ibid.*

that the vessels should be detained in the custody of the consuls in the ports, "until the government of the United States shall be able to *enquire into and decide on the fact.*"

In his letter of the 12th of July 1793 the secretary writes that the President has determined to *refer* the questions concerning prizes "to *persons learned in the laws.*" And he requests that certain vessels enumerated in the letter should not depart "until *his* ultimate determination shall be made known."[3]

In his letter of the 7th of August 1793, the Secretary informs Mr. Genet that the President considers the U. States as bound to "*to effectuate the restoration of,* or to make compensation for, prizes which shall have been made of any of the parties at war with France, subsequent to the 5th day of June last, by privateers fitted out of our ports." That it is consequently expected that Mr. Genet will cause restitution of such prizes, to be made. And that the United States "will cause restitution" to be made "of all such prizes as shall be hereafter brought within their ports by any of the said privateers."[4]

In his letter of the 10th of November 1793 the Secretary informs Mr. Genet, that, for the purpose of obtaining testimony to ascertain the fact of capture within the jurisdiction of the United States, the Governors of the several states were requested on receiving any such claim, immediately to notify thereof the Attornies of their several districts; whose duty it would be to give notice "to the principal agent of both parties and also to the consuls of the nations interested, and to recommend to them, to appoint by mutual consent, arbiters to decide whether the capture was made within the jurisdiction of the United States as stated in my letter of the 8th. inst. according to whose award the Governor may proceed to deliver the vessel to the one or the other party." If either party refuses to name arbiters then the attorney is to take depositions on notice, which "he is to transmit for the *information and decision of the President.*" "This prompt procedure is the more to be insisted on, as it will enable the President, *by an immediate delivery* of the vessel and cargo to the party having title, to prevent the injuries consequent on long delay."[5]

In his letter of the twenty-second of Nov. 1793 the Secretary repeats, in substance, his letter of the 12th of July and 7th of August, and says that the determination to deliver up certain vessels, involved the brig Jane of Dublin, the brig Lovley Lass, and the brig

3. Jefferson to Genet, July 12, 1793, *ibid.*
4. Jefferson to Genet, Aug. 7, 1793, *ibid.*
5. Jefferson to Genet, Nov. 10, 1793, *ibid.*

Prince William Henry. He concludes with saying, "I have it in charge to enquire of you, sir, whether these three brigs have been given up, according to the *determination of the President*, and if they have not to repeat the requisition that they be given up to their former owners."[6]

Ultimately it was settled that the fact should be investigated in the courts, but the decision was regulated by the principles established by the executive department.

The decision then on the case of vessels captured within the American jurisdiction, by privateers fitted out of the American ports, which the gentleman from New-York has cited with such merited approbation; and which he has declared to stand on the same principles, with those which ought to have governed, in the case of Thomas Nash; which deserves the more respect, because the government of the United States was then so circumstanced as to assure us, that no opinion was lightly taken up, and no resolution formed but on mature consideration. This decision quoted as a precedent and pronounced to be right, is found, on fair and full examination, to be precisely and unequivocally the same, with that which was made in the case under consideration. It is a full authority to show, that, in the opinion always held by the American government, a case like that of Thomas Nash, is a case for Executive and not judicial decision.

The clause in the constitution which declares that "the trial of all crimes, except in cases of impeachment, shall be by jury," has also been relied on as operating on the case, and transferring the decision on a demand for the delivery of an individual, from the executive to the judicial department.

But certainly this clause in the constitution of the United States cannot be thought obligatory on, and for the benefit of, the whole world. It is not designed to secure the rights of the people of Europe and Asia, or to direct and controul proceedings against criminals throughout the universe. It, can then, be designed only, to guide the proceedings of our own courts, and to prescribe the mode of punishing offences committed against the government of the United States, and to which the jurisdiction of the nation may rightfully extend.

It has already been shown that the courts of the United States were incapable of trying the crime for which Thomas Nash was delivered up to justice, the question to be determined was not how his crime should be tried and punished but whether he should be delivered up to a foreign tribunal which was alone capable of trying

6. Jefferson to Genet, Nov. 22, 1793, *ibid.*

and punishing him. A provision for the trial of crimes in the courts of the United States is clearly not a provision for the performance of a national compact, for the surrender to a foreign government of an offender against that government.

The clause of the constitution declaring that the trial of all crimes shall be by jury, has never even been construed to extend to the trial of crimes committed in the land and naval forces of the United States. Had such a construction prevailed, it would most probably have prostrated the constitution itself, with the liberties and the independence of the nation, before the first disciplined invader who should approach our shores. Necessity would have imperiously demanded the review and amendment of so unwise a provision. If then this clause does not extend to offences committed in the fleets and armies of the United States, how can it be construed to extend to offences committed in the fleets and armies of Britain or of France, of the Ottoman or Russian empires?

The same argument applies to the observations on the 7th article of the amendments to the constitution. That article relates only to trials in the courts of the United States, and not to the performance of a contract for the delivery of a murderer not triable in those courts.

In this part of the argument, the gentleman from New-York has presented a dilemma of a very wonderful structure indeed. He says that the offence of Thomas Nash was either a crime or not a crime. If it was a crime, the constitutional mode of punishment ought to have been observed—if it was not a crime, he ought not to have been delivered up to a foreign government, where his punishment was inevitable.[7]

It had escaped the observation of that gentleman, that if the murder committed by Thomas Nash was a crime, yet it was not a crime provided for by the constitution, or triable in the courts of the United States: And that if it was not a crime, yet it is the precise case in which his surrender was stipulated by treaty. Of this extraordinary dilemma then, the gentleman from New-York is, himself, perfectly at liberty, to retain either form.

He has chosen to consider it as a crime, and says it has been made a crime by treaty, and is punished by sending the offender out of the country.

The gentleman is incorrect in every part of his statement. Murder on board a British frigate, is not a crime created by treaty. It would

7. Speech not found.

have been a crime of precisely the same magnitude, had the treaty never been formed. It is not punished by sending the offender out of the United States. The experience of this unfortunate criminal, who was hung and gibbeted, evinced to him, that the punishment of his crime was of a much more serious nature, than mere banishment from the United States.

The gentleman from Pennsylvania and the gentleman from Virginia have both contended, that this was a case proper for the decision of the courts, because points of law occurred, and points of law must have been decided, in its determination.[8]

The points of law which must have been decided, are stated by the Gentleman from Pennsylvania to be, first, a question whether the offence was committed within the British jurisdiction; and, secondly, whether the crime charged was comprehended within the treaty.

It is true, sir, these points of law must have occurred, and must have been decided: but it by no means follows that they could only have been decided in court. A variety of legal questions must present themselves in the performance of every part of executive duty, but these questions are not therefore to be decided in court. Whether a patent for land shall issue or not, is always a question of law, but not a question which must necessarily be carried into court. The gentleman from Pennsylvania seems to have permitted himself to have been misled, by the misrepresentation of the constitution, made in the resolutions of the gentleman from New York: and, in consequence of being so misled, his observations have the appearance of endeavouring to fit the constitution to his arguments, instead of adapting his argument to the constitution.

When the gentleman has proved that these are questions of law, and that they must have been decided by the President, he has not advanced a single step towards proving, that they were improper for executive decision. The question whether vessels captured within three miles of the American coast, or by privateers fitted out in the American ports, were legally captured or not, and whether the American government was bound to restore them if in its power, were questions of law, but they were questions of political law, proper to be decided and they were decided by the executive and not by the courts.

The casus foederis of the guaranty was a question of law but no man would have hazarded the opinion; that such a question must be

8. Speeches not found.

carried into court, and can only be there decided. So the casus foederis under the 27th article of the treaty with Britain is a question of law, but of political law. The question to be decided is whether the particular case proposed be one, in which the nation has bound itself to act, and this is a question depending on principles never submitted to courts.

If a murder should be committed within the United States, and the murderer should seek an asylum in Britain, the question whether the casus foederis of the 27th article had occurred, so that his delivery ought to be demanded, would be a question of law, but no man would say it was a question which ought to be decided in the courts.

When therefore the gentleman from Pennsylvania has established, that in delivering up Thomas Nash, points of law were decided by the President, he has established a position, which in no degree whatever, aids his argument.

The case was in its nature a national demand made upon the nation. The parties were the two nations. They cannot come into court to litigate their claims, nor can a court decide on them. Of consequence the demand is not a case for judicial cognizance.

The President is the sole organ of the nation in its external relations, and its sole representative with foreign nations. Of consequence the demand of a foreign nation can only be made on him.

He possesses the whole executive power. He holds and directs the force of the nation. Of consequence any act to be performed by the force of a nation, is to be performed through him.

He is charged to execute the laws. A treaty is declared to be a law. He must then execute a treaty, where he and he alone possesses the means of executing it.

The treaty which is a law enjoins the performance of a particular object. The person who is to perform this object is marked out by the constitution, since the person is named who conducts the foreign intercourse, and is to take care that the laws be faithfully executed. The means by which it is to be performed—the force of the nation, are in the hands of this person. Ought not the person to perform the object, altho' the particular mode of using the means, has not been prescribed? Congress unquestionably may prescribe the mode; and Congress may devolve on others the whole execution of the contract: but till this be done, it seems the duty of the executive department to execute the contract, by any means it possesses.

The gentleman from Pennsylvania contends that, altho' this should be properly an executive duty, yet it cannot be performed until Congress shall direct the mode of performance. He says that altho' the jurisdiction of the courts is extended by the Constitution, to all cases of admiralty and maritime jurisdiction, yet if the courts had been created without any express assignment of jurisdiction, they could not have taken cognizance of causes expressly allotted to them by the constitution. The executive he says can no more than courts,—supply a legislative omission.

It is not admitted that in the case, stated courts could not have taken jurisdiction. The contrary is believed to be the correct opinion. And, altho' the executive cannot supply a total legislative omission, yet it is not admitted or believed that there is such a total omission in this case.

The treaty stipulating that a murderer shall be delivered up to justice, is as obligatory as an act of Congress making the same declaration. If then there was an act of Congress in the words of the treaty, declaring that a person who had committed murder within the jurisdiction of Britain, and sought an assylum within the territory of the United States, should be delivered up by the United States, on the demand of his Britannic Majesty, and such evidence of his criminalty, as would have justified his commitment for trial, had the offence been here committed; could the President who is bound to execute the laws have justified a refusal to deliver up the criminal, by saying that the legislature had totally omitted to provide for the case?

The executive is not only the constitutional department, but seems to be the proper department, to which the power in question may most wisely and most safely be confided.

The department which is entrusted with the whole foreign intercourse of the nation, with the negotiation of all its treaties, with the power of demanding a reciprocal performance of the article, which is accountable to the nation for the violation of its engagements, with foreign nations, and for the consequences resulting from such violation, seems the proper department, to be entrusted with the execution of a national contract, like that under consideration.

If at any time policy may temper the strict execution of the contract, where may that political discretion be placed so safely, as in the department, whose duty it is to understand precisely, the state of the political intercourse and connection between the United States and foreign nations; to understand the manner in which the particular stipulation is explained and performed by foreign nations; and to understand completely the state of the union?

This department too, independent of judicial aid which may, perhaps, in some instances be called in, is furnished with a great law officer, whose duty it is to understand and to advise, when the casus foederis occurs. And if the President should cause to be arrested under the treaty, an individual who was so circumstanced, as not to be properly the object of such an arrest, he may perhaps bring the question of the legality of his arrest, before a Judge by a writ of habeas corpus.

It is then demonstrated, that according to the practice, and according to the principles of the American government, the question whether the nation has or has not bound itself to deliver up any individual, charged with having committed murder or forgery within the jurisdiction of Britain, is a question the power to decide which, rests alone with the executive department.

It remains to enquire, whether in exercising this power, and in performing the duty it enjoins, the President has committed an unauthorized and dangerous interference with judicial decisions.

That Thomas Nash was committed originally, at the instance of the British consul at Charleston, not for trial in the American courts, but for the purpose of being delivered up to justice in conformity with the treaty, between the two nations, has been already so ably argued by the gentleman from Delaware, that nothing further can be added to that point. He would therefore, Mr. Marshall said, consider the case as if Nash, instead of having been committed for the purposes of the treaty, had been committed for trial. Admitting even this to have been the fact, the conclusions which have been drawn from it were by no means warranted.

Gentlemen had considered it as an offence against judicial authority, and a violation of judicial rights, to withdraw from their sentence a criminal against whom a prosecution had been commenced. They had treated the subject, as if it was the privilege of courts, to condemn to death, the guilty wretch arraigned at their bar, and that to intercept the judgement was to violate the privilege. Nothing can be more incorrect than this view of the case. It is not the privilege, it is the sad duty of courts to administer criminal justice. It is a duty to be performed at the demand of the nation, and with which the nation has a right to dispense. If judgment of death is to be pronounced, it must be at the prosecution of the nation, and the nation may at will stop that prosecution. In this respect the President expresses constitutionally the will of the nation, and may rightfully as was done in the case at Trenton, enter a nolle prosequi, or direct that the criminal be prosecuted no further. This is no interference with judicial decisions, nor any invasion of the province of a court. It is the exercise of an indubitable and a constitutional power. Had the President directed the judge at Charleston to decide for or against his own jurisdiction—to condemn or acquit the prisoner—this would have been a dangerous interference with judicial decisions and ought to have been resisted.

But no such direction has been given, nor any such decision been required. If the President determined that Thomas Nash ought to have been delivered up to the British government, for a murder committed on board a British frigate, provided evidence of the fact was adduced; it was a question which duty obliged him to determine, and which he determined rightly. If in consequence of this determination he arrested the proceedings of a court on a national prosecution, he had a right to arrest and to stop them, and the exercise of this right was a necessary consequence of the determination of the principal question. In conforming to this decision, the court has left open the question of its jurisdiction. Should another prosecution of the same sort be commenced, which should not be suspended but continued by the executive, the case of Thomas Nash would not bind as a precedent against the jurisdiction of the court. If it should even prove that, in the opinion of the executive, a murder committed on board a foreign fleet was not within the jurisdiction of the court, it would prove nothing more: and though this opinion might rightfully induce the executive to exercise its power over the prosecution, yet if the prosecution was continued, it could have no influence with the court in deciding on its jurisdiction.

Taking the fact then even to be, as the gentlemen in support of the resolutions would state it, the fact cannot avail them.

It is to be remembered too, that in the case stated to the President, the judge himself appears to have considered it as proper for executive decision, and to have wished that decision. The President and judge seem to have entertained, on this subject, the same opinion: and in consequence of the opinion of the judge, the application was made to the President.

It has then been demonstrated.

1st. That the case of Thomas Nash, as stated to the President, was compleatly within the 27th article of the treaty between the United States of America and Great Britain.

2ly That this question was proper for executive and not for judicial decision, and

3dly   That, in deciding it, the President is not chargeable with an interference with judicial decisions.

After trespassing so long Mr. Marshall said on the patience of the house, in arguing what had appeared to him to be the material points growing out of the resolutions, he regretted the necessity of detaining them still longer, for the purpose of noticing an observation, which appeared not to be considered, by the gentleman who made it, as belonging to the argument.

The subject introduced by this observation however was so calculated to interest the public feelings, that he must be excused for stating his opinion on it.

The gentleman from Pennsylvania had said, that an impressed American seaman, who should commit homicide for the purpose of liberating himself from the vessel in which he was confined, ought not to be given up as a murderer.[9] In this, Mr. Marshall said, he concurred entirely with that gentleman. He believed the opinion to be unquestionably correct,—as were the reasons that gentleman had given in support of it. He had never heard any American avow a contrary sentiment, nor did he believe a contrary sentiment could find a place in the bosom of any American. He could not pretend, and did not pretend, to know the opinions of the executive on the subject, because he had never heard the opinions of that department, but he felt the most perfect conviction, founded on the general conduct of the government, that it could never surrender an impressed American to the nation, which, in making the impressment, had committed a national injury.

This belief was in no degree shaken, by the conduct of the executive in this particular case.

In his own mind it was a sufficient defence of the President, from an imputation of this kind, that the fact of Thomas Nash being an impressed American, was obviously not contemplated by him in the decision he made on the principles of the case. Consequently if a new circumstance occured, which would essentially change the case decided by the President, the judge ought not to have acted under that decision, but the new circumstance ought to have been stated. Satisfactory as this defence might appear, he should not resort to it, because to some it might seem a subterfuge. He defended the conduct of the President on other, and still stronger ground.

The President had decided that a *murder* committed on board a

9. Speech not found.

British frigate on the high seas, was within the jurisdiction of that nation, and consequently within the 27th. article of its treaty with the United States. He therefore directed Thomas Nash to be delivered to the British minister, if satisfactory evidence of the *murder* should be adduced. The sufficiency of the evidence was submitted entirely to the judge. If Thomas Nash had committed a murder, the decision was that he should be surrendered to the British minister, if he had not committed a murder, he was not to be surrendered.

Had Thomas Nash been an impressed American, the homicide on board the Hermoine, would, most certainly, not have been murder.

The act of impressing an American is an act of lawless violence. The confinement on board a vessel is a continuation of that violence, and an additional outrage. Death committed within the United States, in resisting such violence, would not have been murder, and the person giving the wound could not have been treated as a murderer. Thomas Nash was only to have been delivered up to justice on such evidence as, had the fact been committed within the United States, would have been sufficient to have induced his commitment and trial for murder. Of consequence the decision of the President was so expressed, as to exclude the case of an impressed American liberating himself by homicide.[1]

He concluded with observing that he had already too long availed himself of the indulgence of the House, to venture further on that indulgence, by recapitulating, or reinforcing the arguments which had already been urged.

Deed

Deed Book Copy, Office of the Clerk of Hardy County, Moorefield, W.Va.

[*March 7, 1800 (Hardy County, Va.*). By his attorney, Rawleigh Colston, JM conveys 440 acres in the South Branch Manor to Edward Williams for £2. The deed was recorded in the District Court at Hardy County on Sept. 9, 1800.]

1. Thomas Jefferson remained unconvinced. On the verso of the last page of the printed speech, Jefferson wrote: "1. It was Pyracy by the law of nations, & therefore cognisable by our courts. 2. if alleged to be a murder also, then whether he was an impressed American was an essential enquiry. 3. tho' the President as a party subordinate to the court might enter a Nolle pros, ⟨he could not controul the court as⟩ a requisition in the style of a Superior ⟨by requisition⟩ was a violation of the Constitutional independancy of the Judiciary." Political Pamphlets, I, no. 7, Virginia Historical Society.

From John Quincy Adams

Copy, RG 59, National Archives

[*March 8, 1800, Berlin*. Adams writes a letter to Pickering that was received by JM on June 29.[2] He informs JM of the arrival of Oliver Ellsworth and William R. Davie in Portugal and of their journey to Paris.[3] Adams is hopeful about the outcome of the mission. He reports on the "real and important change in the system of administration in France; and a circumstance deserving special consideration is, that for the first time since the fall of the monarchy, the Government of that country has an evident interest in seeking peace. This is perhaps one of the reasons why the English Government have so coldly rejected the advances repeatedly made by France for pacific negotiations." Adams continues by discussing the unfavorable prospects of the English campaign in Europe. He concludes with news of French military prowess and the general European acquiescence to it.

Adams also gives an account of the tribute given to the memory of George Washington by the French. Napoleon Bonaparte "has ordered black crapes to be suspended to the flags and colours of the french armies throughout the whole Republic for ten days and that the bust of Washington shall be placed in the Thuileries with those of many other illustrious military characters of antient and modern times—and a funeral eulogium,[4] at his desire was delivered at the hotel des Invalides, in honour of our great patriot and statesman."]

Deed

Deed Book Copy, Office of the Clerk of Hardy County, Moorefield, W.Va.

[*March 8, 1800 (Hardy County, Va.*). Edward Smith and his wife, Elizabeth, convey 900 acres in Hampshire County to John Marshall and James Markham Marshall for $1. The deed was recorded in the District Court at Hardy County on Mar. 13, 1800.]

2. See John Adams to JM, July 11, 1800, and JM to John Quincy Adams, July 24, 1800.

3. See Ralph Adams Brown, *The Presidency of John Adams* (Lawrence, Kans., 1975), 162–163.

4. See "Washington's Funeral Eulogy Delivered in the Temple of Mars," in Gilbert Chinard, ed. and trans., *George Washington as the French Knew Him: A Collection of Texts* (Princeton, N.J., 1940), 129–138.

Deeds

Deed Book Copies, Office of the Clerk of Hardy County, Moorefield, W.Va.

[*March 8, 1800 (Hardy County, Va.*). By his attorney, Rawleigh Colston, JM conveys parcels of land in the South Branch Manor to: Benjamin Beene, 46 acres for £11 16s.; Robert Cunningham and Robert Porter, 104 acres for £28 12s.; Robert Daring, 59 acres for £15 19s. 9d.; Jacob Fisher, 6 acres for £4 13s.; Leonard Shoab, 31 acres for £8 19s.; James Snodgrass, 34 acres for £7 10s. All the deeds were recorded in the District Court at Hardy County on May 5, 1800.]

Deeds

Deed Book Copies, Office of the Clerk of Hardy County, Moorefield, W.Va.

[*March 10, 1800 (Hardy County, Va.*). By his attorney, Rawleigh Colston, JM conveys parcels of land in the South Branch Manor to: John Hay, 59 acres for £12 5s.; Moses Hutton, 140 acres for £24; James Parsons, 105 acres for £21 10s. All the deeds were recorded in the District Court at Hardy County on May 5, 1800.]

Committee Report

Printed, *Report . . . on so much of the President's Speech, As relates to "a Revision and Amendment of the Judiciary System"* (Philadelphia, 1800)

[Philadelphia], March 11, 1800

[The committee[5]] FIND, THAT from its great extent and importance, it ought to be treated under several distinct heads. The first and most important of these relates to the organization, powers, and jurisdiction of the courts; for which objects the Committee have proposed, and herewith report, a bill in part, reserving to themselves the power of making a further report, on the other branches of the subject referred to them.[6]

5. The committee was appointed on Dec. 9, 1799, six days after John Adams's speech, and consisted of Robert Goodloe Harper, James A. Bayard, Samuel Sewall, Chauncey Goodrich, and JM. Harper offered this report for the committee. *Annals of Congress*, X, 188–190, 197, 623. See also Kathryn Turner, "Federalist Policy and the Judiciary Act of 1801," *WMQ*, 3d Ser., XXII (1965), 10, where the identical composition of this committee and the one that drafted the bankruptcy bill is noted.

6. The second part of the committee's work was devoted to drafting a bill on the "administration of justice in the courts." See Committee Report, calendared at *ca.* May 1, 1800.

Legislative Bill

Printed, [U.S. Congress, House], *A Bill to Provide for the Better Establishment & Regulation of the Courts of the United States* (Philadelphia, 1800)

[*March 11, 1800, Philadelphia.* The committee preparing the bill to revise the federal judiciary submits a bill of 52 sections.[7] The key jurisdictional alteration was contained in sections 5 and 6,[8] but the heart of the measure was section 7,[9] which provided for the creation of 29 judicial districts, and section 10, which classed those districts into 9 circuits, some of which crossed state lines.[1] Other sections provided that these new territorial divisions were to be presided over by a specific bench of judges, thus omitting the need for Supreme Court justices to ride circuit, and that the old district courts were to be turned into admiralty courts.]

Legislative Petition

ADS, RG 233, National Archives

[Philadelphia], March 13, 1800

To the Honble. the Speaker & members of the house of representa-

7. Immediately after the committee presented its report, this bill was introduced, read twice, and submitted to the Committee of the Whole for subsequent debate. *Annals of Congress*, X, 623. For a summary of the bill and its significance, see Kathryn Turner, "Federalist Policy and the Judiciary Act of 1801," *WMQ*, 3d Ser., XXII (1965), 3–32.

On Mar. 24, the first day of debate, the House voted to cease consideration of the bill, an apparent victory for its opponents. The following day, however, proponents argued that the bill should be further debated, and a motion to recommit the measure to the Committee of the Whole then passed. Subsequent debate began on Mar. 25. *Annals of Congress*, X, 643–645.

8. Albert Gallatin moved to strike these sections on Mar. 25. On the next day, supporters agreed to their removal from the bill when it became clear that opposition to them was widespread. *Annals of Congress*, X, 645–646. See also Turner, "Federalist Policy," *WMQ*, 3d Ser., XXII (1965), 11 n. 43.

9. After John Nicholas moved to strike sec. 7 on Mar. 26, JM offered "a lengthy defense of the new system," but the motion carried. On Mar. 28, Robert Goodloe Harper, in an effort to save the bill, moved that it be recommitted for modification by the drafting committee since sec. 7 had "contained the essential principle of the bill, by which almost all the subsequent sections were guided." The House agreed to recommit the measure. *Annals of Congress*, X, 646–649, and Robert Goodloe Harper to Constituents, May 15, 1800, in Noble E. Cunningham, Jr., ed., *Circular Letters of Congressmen to Their Constituents, 1789–1829*, I (Chapel Hill, N.C., 1978), 216–217. See also the revised bill, calendared at Mar. 31, 1800.

1. The committee had named districts after bodies of water and regions rather than after states, a system that met with disfavor in the House. The revised bill contained such designations as North Virginia and Jersey. One Republican reported happily, "The ancient dominion will yet for a while be known as Virginia" instead of Potomac, Fluvanna, and Kanawha. Anthony New to Constituents, Apr. 8, 1800, in Cunningham, ed., *Circular Letters*, I, 196.

tives of the United States the petition of William Tazewell humbly showeth

That your petitioner was the secretary of Mr. Gerry one of the late Envoys extraordinary from the United States of America to the french republic.[2] When the diplomatic character of that gentleman had terminated he directed your petitioner to remain in Paris for the purpose of superintending the publication of his letters to Mr. Talleyrand the minister of exterior relations. He further directed your petitioner to proceed to Holland & from thence to London for the purpose of conveying to Mr. Murry & Mr. King information of the state in which ⟨Mr. Gerry's⟩ his departure from France had left the political relations between the United States & that country. This duty was undertaken in the confidence that in addition to the proper compensation your petitioners expences until his return to Philadelphia woud be allowd. In this expectation he gave up his passage in a national vessel & engagd in the new service to which he was appointed. Having performd the duty assignd to him he was detaind a considerable time for a passage & after embarking was capturd on his way to the United States & carried into Spain. From thence he was under the necessity of travelling by land to Lisbon at which place he again embarkd for the United States. When capturd he was rob'd of his cloaths to a considerable value. On presenting to the secretary of State his account for settlement that Gentleman did not think himself authorizd to allow your petitioner for his losses & extraordinary expences nor for the time he was detaind in consequence of his capture. This your petitioner conceives to be unjust in as much as all his expences losses & capture were entirely occasiond by his being employd by the minister of the United States on an extra service. Your petitioner therefore prays that the secretary of state may be authorizd to settle his accounts & to allow him for his extra expences & loss as well for the detention occasiond by his capture & your petitioner will ever pray &c.

WILLIAM TAZEWELL

2. The entire petition, including the signature, is in JM's hand. It was introduced in the House of Representatives the day it was written and was immediately referred to a committee consisting of JM, William Gordon (1763–1802), of New Hampshire, and Thomas Pinckney. This select committee recommended on Apr. 9 that Tazewell be allowed his expenses. *Annals of Congress*, X, 625, and *Journal of the House of Representatives . . . first session of the Sixth Congress*, III (Washington, D.C., 1826), 624. The membership of the committee is listed on the document. See also Timothy Pickering to JM, Apr. 1, 1800, and Committee Report, Apr. 9, 1800.

To Reuben George

ALS, Virginia State Library

Dear Sir[3]   Philadelphia, March 16, 1800

I receivd a few days past yours of the 28th. of Feby.[4]

I took the deposition of Doctor Rush & inclosd it to Mr. Wickham.[5] If you will call on him you will see it. It is not what I expected. In conversation with him sometime before I had been led to expect that his testimony woud have been much more favorable to you than it turnd out to be. I really am doubtful whether it will be of use or not.

When I have sent only parts of news papers to my friends the reason has been that there was nothing else in the papers of any consequence & I have not supposd it to be worth while to send a sheet of advertizements. However I shall take the hint.

We have had a great deal of debate in Congress about the case of Thomas Nash who took the name of Jonathan Robins.[6] A violent effort was made to suppo[rt] some [*resolutions crimi*]nating the Presidents conduct in this respect but they were so manifestly improper that several of the antis voted against them. The case really was that he was an irishman who had committed a horrid murder on board a british frigate for which he was given up. After he had been several months in prison he was inducd to declare himself an American seaman in the hope that this untruth woud save him. The debate was for the purpose principally of affecting the next election of President, but I beleive it has completely faild of its object.

The legislature of Pennsylvania will rise without passing any law for the purpose of enabling the state to vote at the next election of President & vice President.[7] In consequence of this the state will lose

3. This letter is addressed to George "near Richmond, Virginia."

4. Letter not found.

5. Benjamin Rush, the Philadelphia physician, had served earlier by appointment of George Wythe, chancellor of the High Court of Chancery in Virginia, as a commissioner in a suit for annulment of a marriage. It is possible that a similar situation existed and that John Wickham was representing Reuben George or the other party. The nature of JM's argument in McHaney v. George's Executor might also suggest an appeal by George in that case, although JM had represented Cornelius McHaney in the lower court. See Vol. II, 91 and n. 6, 123.

6. See Speech, Mar. 7, 1800.

7. The Pennsylvania legislature, dominated in the lower house by Republicans while Federalists held a slim majority in the senate, had divided over the question of how presidential electors should be chosen. A conference committee failed to reach agreement,

its vote unless the Governor will call the legislature together in time to chuse electors in the fall. Whether he will do this or not will probably depend on the political temper of the next assembly. If they suit the governor they will, it is most likely, be calld together, if they do not suit him, the state will lose its vote.

The parties are on both [*sides sanguine*] with respect to the President but in my opinion the chances are more than two to one in favor of the re-election of Mr. Adams.

We have as yet no news from our Envoys.[8] I hope they will be succesful—but we must not be too confident of their success. I am dear Sir your obedt

J MARSHALL

Committee Report

Printed, *American State Papers, Public Lands,* I, 94–98

[*March 21, 1800, Philadelphia.* JM, as chairman, reports for the committee appointed to consider whether Congress should accept Connecticut's cession of the territory west of Pennsylvania commonly called the Western Reserve. The report consists of consecutive summaries of charters, royal proclamations, acts of Parliament, and steps taken by the colonies involved in the tangled claim to lands from 1606 to 1784. At that time Congress renewed its request that every state surrender its western lands, or claims to those lands. JM's committee called attention to Connecticut's cession of its lands in 1786, noting that the state had excepted a small portion lying west of Pennsylvania, thus creating her western reserve. Furthermore, the report attempts to summarize the history of the Susquehannah Company and its complicated relationship with Connecticut and Pennsylvania and the associated involvement of New York, Massachusetts, and Virginia. The report concludes: "As the purchasers of the land commonly called the Connecticut Reserve hold their title under the State of Connecticut, they cannot submit

---

and the session ended with no provision for the fall presidential election. Gov. Thomas McKean first intended to convene a special session, but later he decided to wait until after the general elections in October, when the political composition of the body would be known. After a Republican victory in October, McKean called a special session of the legislature, and a deadlock over procedure threatened to deny Pennsylvania a voice in the election of the president. Harry Marlin Tinkcom, *The Republicans and Federalists in Pennsylvania, 1790–1801: A Study in National Stimulus and Local Response* (Harrisburg, Pa., 1950), 243–253, and G. S. Rowe, *Thomas McKean: The Shaping of an American Republicanism* (Boulder, Colo., 1978), 314–317. See also Congressional Career: Editorial Note, Dec. 4, 1799, and Committee Report, Apr. 25, 1800.

8. William Vans Murray, Oliver Ellsworth, and William R. Davie. See Address, *ca.* Dec. 6, 1799.

to the Government established by the United States in the Northwestern territory, without endangering their titles, and the jurisdiction of Connecticut could not be extended over them without much inconvenience. Finding themselves in this situation, they have applied to the Legislature of Connecticut to cede the jurisdiction of the said territory to the United States. In pursuance of such application, the Legislature of Connecticut, in the month of October, 1797, passed an act authorizing the Senators of the said State in Congress to execute a deed of release in behalf of said State to the United States of the jurisdiction of said territory.[9]

"The committee are of opinion that the cession of jurisdiction offered by the State of Connecticut ought to be accepted by the United States, on the terms and conditions specified in the bill which accompanies this report."]

Legislative Bill

Printed, 2 Stat. 56–57

[*ca. March 21, 1800, Philadelphia.* A bill accepting the cession of the territory west of Pennsylvania known as the Western Reserve of Connecticut is submitted by JM's committee appointed to consider the question. The bill, adopted by the House of Representatives on Apr. 10, authorizes the delivery of letters patent to the governor of Connecticut for the benefit of those holding title to land in an area claimed by Pennsylvania "whereby all the right, title, interest, and estate, of the United States to the soil of that tract of land . . . shall be released and conveyed as aforesaid to the said governor of Connecticut, and his successors in said office, forever, for the purpose of quieting the grantees and purchasers under said state of Connecticut, and confirming their titles to the soil of the said tract of land." Provisions in the act require Connecticut to renounce within eight months all "territorial or jurisdictional claims" to land along the New York border, and to transfer by deed that area known as the Western Reserve, "expressly releasing to the United States the jurisdictional claim of the said state of Connecticut, to the said tract of land." Among other provisions is verification of the continuation of the 1782 federal court decree at Trenton regarding a territorial dispute between Pennsylvania and Connecticut[1] and a statement "that nothing herein contained shall be construed, in any manner, to pledge the

9. The act and deed are printed in Carter, ed., *Terr. Papers, NW*, II, 657–658.
1. Albert Gallatin moved this proviso upon the urging of Tench Coxe. See *Annals of Congress*, X, 661; Gallatin to Coxe, Feb. 28, 1800, and Coxe to Gallatin, Mar. 2, 1800, in Robert J. Taylor, ed., *The Susquehannah Company Papers*, X (Ithaca, N.Y., 1971), 499–505.

United States for the extinguishment of the Indian title to the said lands, or further than merely to pass the title of the United States thereto."[2]]

Speech

Printed, *Annals of Congress*, X, 646

[*March 27, 1800, Philadelphia.* JM speaks at length in favor of replacing the existing federal circuit court system with a new system that would end circuit riding by Supreme Court justices upon the creation of new courts with new judges. Specifically, JM argues in favor of retaining section 7 of the bill providing for 29 new circuit courts.[3]]

Legislative Bill

Printed, [U.S. Congress, House], *A Bill to Provide for the More Convenient Organization of the Courts of the United States* (Philadelphia, 1800)

[*March 31, 1800, Philadelphia.* The committee on a judiciary bill reports a revision of the Mar. 11 measure for consideration.[4] The new proposal omits sections 5 and 6, which opponents had voted out of the former bill,[5] but the key sections, numbered 5 and 7 in this revision, only modify the provision for reorganizing the judiciary. Nineteen districts are to be contained in six circuits, and the circuits do not divide any of the states, as the former

2. The act is also printed in full and with annotation in Carter, ed., *Terr. Papers, NW*, II, 84–86. Connecticut adopted an act renouncing its claims to the Western Reserve on May 8. That act is printed in Taylor, ed., *Susquehannah Papers*, X, 514–517. For the background and a general summary of this issue, see Julian Parks Boyd, *The Susquehannah Company: Connecticut's Experiment in Expansion* (New Haven, Conn., 1935).

3. No copy or account of the address has been found. JM had been appointed to a committee to draft a bill revising the judicial system on Dec. 9, 1799. Robert Goodloe Harper introduced "a bill to provide for the better establishment and regulation of the Courts of the United States" on Mar. 11, and debate began on Mar. 24. *Annals of Congress*, X, 197, 623, 643, and Legislative Bill, calendared at Mar. 11, 1800. After considerable partisan debate, the measure was finally deferred on Apr. 14. *Annals of Congress*, X, 666. For a detailed discussion of this measure and its significance, see Kathryn Turner, "Federalist Policy and the Judiciary Act of 1801," *WMQ*, 3d Ser., XXII (1965), 9–14.

4. The bill was not read until the next day, when it was ordered committed to the Committee of the Whole for debate on Apr. 14. On that day, "a warm and lengthy debate was had" on a motion of Aaron Kitchell (1744–1820), of New Jersey, to postpone consideration of the bill until the next session. The motion passed by two votes. *Annals of Congress*, X, 652, 665–666.

5. See Legislative Bill, calendared at Mar. 11, 1800, and notes, for specific changes made by the committee.

measure proposed. Also, districts are named by states rather than by rivers or regions, a sensitive issue in the Mar. 11 proposal. This revised bill also includes in sections 13 and 14 a grant to the circuit courts of jurisdiction over all cases in law and equity arising under the Constitution, laws, and treaties of the United States—an omission in the previous bill.]

From Timothy Pickering

Presscopy, Pickering Papers, Massachusetts Historical Society

Sirs.[6]   [Philadelphia], April 1, 1800

Agreeably to your request I present to you such facts and observations as appear to me proper to elucidate the claim of Doctor William Tazewell, for services and expenses performed and incurred, in the employment of Secretary to Elbridge Gerry, Esqr. one of the Envoys of the United States to France.

In general it is supposed that an American Minister and his Secretary go from their home in the United States on the appointed mission: And when a minister is recalled, it has been the invariable practice to allow him one quarter's salary, and no more, after the day, on which he receives his letter of recall, to compensate for the [probable time][7] and expense of his return. If his passage be short, and the voyage be performed in one month, the salary of the other two months are his gain. If a long passage or other accidents procrastinate his return to any period after the lapse of the quarter, it is his loss. On an average, three month's time and pay may be considered fully adequate to the return of a minister. As to the Secretaries of ministers, altho' I did not find [the like] established usage, yet the reason being the same, I have constantly made them the same allowance of one quarter's salary for their return when the Ministers they attended have resigned or been recalled.

If any exception to this rule were to be made, Doctor Tazewell presents an instance. He did not leave home to attend one of our Ministers to Europe: He was in Paris attending [the lectures] to qualify himself for the medical profession. In this situation, and when it is understood, that having finished his medical education, Dr.

6. The letter is addressed to JM, "Chairman of the Committee on Doctor Tazewell's Claim." See Legislative Petition, Mar. 13, 1800.

7. The words in brackets, illegible on the presscopy, are supplied from a printed report of JM's committee. See Committee Report, Apr. 9, 1800, and *Amer. State Papers, Claims*, I, 240.

Tazewell was about returning to Virginia, Mr. Gerry wanting a Secretary to replace the one who had resigned, engaged Dr. Tazewell. This, as appears by a letter from Mr. Gerry, was on the 30th. of March 1798.

On the 12th: of May following, Mr. Gerry received my letter of the 23d: of March 1798; and as he had no authority to negotiate alone, and as none of the circumstances existed, which, according to the tenor of that letter, if all the Envoys had remained in Paris, would have justified a continuance of negotiations, it was consequently a letter of recall; and from three months after that day I have considered that Mr: Gerry's salary ought to cease; and of course, in ordinary cases, the salary of the secretary would also cease. But viewing the secretary as not responsable for the misconduct, or erroneous judgment, of a Minister, I consented to extend Dr. Tazewell's salary to July [26th:] when Mr. Gerry quitted Paris, thence to August 7th: while the Doctor remained there, pursuant to Mr. Gerry's orders, to get translated and printed his last letter and note to M: Talleyrand; and from August 7th: to the 23d: while he was travelling from Paris to the Hague, and thence to London, to communicate to Mr. Murray & Mr. King the state of things at the conclusion of Mr Gerry's negotiation with M. Talleyrand: and reckoning from the 23d. of August, as you may recollect, during our conversation last autumn, I proposed to allow Dr. Tazewell one quarter's salary for his return. I continue to think that with a settlement on these principles he ought to be well satisfied.

The Doctor says that his detention in England, and his subsequent capture and detention in Spain and Portugal are to be ascribed to his executing Mr. Gerry's orders at Paris, the Hague, and London; and that otherwise he should have come home in the U. States brigantine Sophia, with Mr. Gerry, and thus have lost no time nor incurred any expenses. To which I answer, That, tho' sometimes done, it is not usual for the U. States to provide vessels to convey their ministers to and from European Courts: but they generally provide and pay for their passages themselves; and Dr. Tazewell cannot found a *right* on what is *sometimes* a public *gratuity*. Further, [I remark] agreeably to what has been stated as the general rule, that Dr. Tazewell cannot with any sort of propriety insist that the United States should ensure him against contingences which might occasion his loss, while they were excluded from any benefit of his gain. Decency even required that he should be content, and not persist in urging the violation of a general rule, because its operation chanced in his par-

ticular case to be unfavourable. Perhaps an adjustment not chargeable with rigour might be made, which should exclude Dr. Tazewell
from the quarter's salary for his return: The U. States did not send
him abroad for their service: and I do not know that they were bound
to bring him home. I am with great respect Sir your obedt. Servant,

TIMOTHY PICKERING

Amendment

Printed, [U.S. Congress, House], *A Bill to Provide for the Execution of the Twenty-Seventh Article of the Treaty . . . with Great Britain* (Philadelphia, 1800)

[Philadelphia], April 2, 1800

The testimony[8] upon which such person shall be committed shall
be taken in writing, and transmitted to the Secretary of State, who
shall lay the same before the President of the United States, to enable
him to decide on the requisition made as aforesaid; and if, in the
opinion of the President, the person so committed ought not to be
delivered up, to the person making such demand, the same shall be
signified to the judge or justice by whom he was committed, who
shall proceed in the case according to law; and if it shall be the
opinion of the President, that the person so committed ought to be
delivered up on the requisition so made as aforesaid, he shall signify
his opinion to the Secretary of State: and thereupon it shall be lawful
for the Secretary of State, by warrant under his hand and seal, to
direct the person so committed, to be delivered to such person or
persons, as shall have been authorized on the part of his Britannic
Majesty to receive the person so committed, and convey such person
to the British Dominions, to be tried for the offense with which such
person shall have been so charged.

---

8. The first of Edward Livingston's resolutions on the Jonathan Robbins affair called
for legislation to implement art. 27 of the Jay Treaty. Samuel W. Dana (1760–1830), a
Federalist from Connecticut, Livingston, and James A. Bayard were appointed a committee to prepare a bill. On Feb. 24, during debate over the Robbins affair, Dana introduced a bill "to provide for the execution of the 27th article" of the Jay Treaty. Debate
did not occur until Apr. 2, whereupon John Nicholas expressed reservations about the
role of the secretary of state as described in the bill. JM replied that he had prepared an
amendment dealing with this question. The summary of JM's amendment printed in the
Annals indicates the portion of the bill that he wrote. *Annals of Congress*, X, 511–512, 537,
654.

JM's amendment was immediately accepted by the House. For additional action on
the bill, see Amendments, Apr. 29, 1800.

From Rufus King

ALS, RG 59, National Archives

[*April 3, 1800, London.* In dispatch no. 65,[9] King notifies the government that he has not received any communication from Lord Grenville since giving him a note on Feb. 18. He believes the delay is justified by the "pressure of more urgent concerns" upon the British cabinet.[1]]

To [James Markham Marshall]

ALS, Henry E. Huntington Library

My dear brother   Philadelphia, April 4, 1800

I am entirely pleasd with the contract you have made with Vanmetre & Seymour & will execute it this summer.[2]

Capt. Barry[3] has just arrivd with information that our envoys in attempting to [*go*] from Lisbond to L'Orient encounterd such obstinate head winds as to be under the necessity of puting in to Corunna in Spain where they receivd letters from Talleyrand [*urging*] them to proceed immediately to Paris with assurances of a pacific temper on the part of France.

I think with you that the Senate woud have acted more wisely had they avoided the present controversy with Duane.[4] Questions of

9. This dispatch was received by the State Department on July 13, 1800.

1. See King to [JM], Apr. 22, 1800 (first letter). The Feb. 18 letter to Grenville, containing rules of procedure for the debt commission meeting under the terms of art. 6 of the Jay Treaty, is printed in full in *Amer. State Papers, Foreign Relations*, II, 395–398. See also Bradford Perkins, *The First Rapprochement: England and the United States, 1795–1805* (Berkeley, Calif., 1967), 120.

2. Contract not found, but see JM to James Markham Marshall, Dec. 16, 1799, and Vol. II, 148.

3. John Barry (1745–1803) was the captain of the *United States* (frigate), in which Oliver Ellsworth and William R. Davie sailed to Europe. See Noble E. Cunningham, Jr., ed., *Circular Letters of Congressmen to Their Constituents, 1789–1829*, I (Chapel Hill, N.C., 1978), 188, 190, 198, and Alexander DeConde, *The Quasi-War: The Politics and Diplomacy of the Undeclared War with France, 1797–1801* (New York, 1966), 223–224.

4. The Senate had created a committee of privileges after William Duane (1760–1835), editor of the *Aurora* (Philadelphia), published a report of that body's deliberations on James Ross's election bill. Duane called the measure a Federalist attempt to control the election of 1800. The committee, in a deliberate effort to punish Duane, conducted a private investigation of the *Aurora* and found its editor guilty of a "high breach of the privileges" of the Senate. When Duane failed to appear before the Senate on Mar. 26, a summons for his arrest was issued, and he was forced into hiding until Congress adjourned. For an excellent account of this affair, see James Morton Smith, *Freedom's Fetters: The Alien and Sedition Laws and American Civil Liberties* (Ithaca, N.Y., 1956), 286–306. See also Amendment, *ca.* Apr. 16, 1800.

privilege are delicate in their nature & such as are most apt to interest the public mind against those who exercise the power of punishing for its breach. Yet it is observable that the sense of America seems to have been unequivocally expressd in favor of the existence of the power. The house of Delegates of Virginia exercisd it in the case of Warden.[5] The legislatures of several other states have exercisd it. If it is possessd by the separate branches of the state legislatures, it is also possessd by each house of the national legislature, because any difference producd by the difference in the structure of the Genl. & State Governments, is confind to the acts of the legislature & does not extend to the distinct acts of each branch. The house of representatives exercisd it in the case of Randal & Whitney & the democrats carried it so far as to declare an application made to a member before he set out for congress & before the commencement of the session a breach of privilege.[6] In the case of Mr. Randolph the repetition in his presence of words he had usd in debate was considerd as a breach of privilege & the democrats & the democratic papers with the Aurora in the van have been incessant in their abuse of the house of representatives for not punishing it.[7] If the privilege of members

5. On June 9, 1784, a member of the Virginia House of Delegates charged that John Warden of Hanover County was guilty of "a high contempt and breach of the privileges of this House, in uttering certain expressions derogatory to the honor and justice of the same." The matter was sent to the committee of privileges and elections, and Warden was ordered arrested by the sergeant at arms. Five days later the committee reported that Warden had appeared before it and had testified that "in a mistaken opinion that the House of Delegates had voted against the payment of British debts, agreeable to the treaty of peace . . . , I said, that if it had done so, some of them had voted against paying for the coats on their backs." Warden apologized for his statement, but the House refused to accept the apology, ordering him to be released nonetheless. See *Journal of the House of Delegates of the Commonwealth of Virginia* . . . (Richmond, 1784), 62, 77.

6. On Dec. 28, 1795, William L. Smith, of South Carolina, informed the House that Robert Randall had offered to bribe him and other congressmen to secure authorization to purchase 20 million acres of public land near Detroit. It appeared that Charles Whitney, of Vermont, was an accomplice and that, separately, the two men had spoken to many congressmen. Fearing charges of "a second Georgia business," Congress ordered both men arrested and brought before the House to answer charges that they had committed "a contempt and a breach of privileges of this House, by attempting to corrupt the integrity of its members." *Annals of Congress*, X, 166–170.

After 4 days of debate over whether the charges were within the authority of the House and, if so, how the members should proceed in the matter, the House heard Randall's testimony on Jan. 4. The business of the House was consumed for 4 days by this issue. Randall was found guilty and ordered held in custody; Whitney was judged not guilty and released, having been held in jail for 10 days. Randall was released 6 days later, on Jan. 13. *Ibid.*, 171–244. See also St. George Tucker, ed., *Blackstone's Commentaries* . . . , I, pt. 1 (Philadelphia, 1803), 200–205, and *Amer. State Papers, Miscellaneous*, I, 196–202.

7. During debate on Jan. 9 and 10 on reducing the size of the U.S. Army, John Randolph referred to the troops as "ragamuffins" and "mercenaries." Although he with-

extends beyond the walls of their hall, & such seems to have been the opinion of both parties, it was unquestionably violated by Duane. The paper of each day contain a falsehood & an insult on the members of each branch of the legislature & frequently on the body of the senate. Perhaps it was unwise to notice them; but the power to notice them is loudly questiond by those who on other occasions have most loudly contended for it.

The bill providing for the manner of counting the votes of President & Vice President of the United States which has been sent to us by the Senate, will be very warmly contested.[8] It has excited more feeling than any other subject which has come before us. It is as difficult as it is interesting. In defiance of law & the constitution Governor McKean has declard a determination to hold in Pennsylvania an election by proclamation.[9] If by such an election Mr. Jefferson shoud be President, the choice woud not & ought not to be submitted to. If therefore the power to regulate this subject exists in the govern-

drew the former term as he invoked the latter, two Marine officers, Capt. James McKnight and Lt. Michael Reynolds, insulted Randolph and pulled at his coat as he was leaving the theater the evening following his second speech. Randolph complained to President Adams in a letter the next day, demanding that he take action that would deter others from introducing a "Reign of Terror into our country." Adams sent the complaint to the House, suggesting the encounter was a breach of its privileges. Despite Randolph's insistence that the matter be left to the president as commander in chief, the issue was submitted to a select committee whose subsequent report concluded that the privileges of the House had not been breached. *Annals of Congress*, X, 298, 367, 372–374, 378–388.

The select committee's report prompted four days of discussion, the level of which Randolph's biographer described as "below the dignity of a field debate." Afterward the House thanked President Adams for submitting the issue, but a resolution, expressing the committee's view that the House's privileges had not been breached in this case, was rejected. *Ibid.*, 426–505, and William Cabell Bruce, *John Randolph of Roanoke, 1773–1833* . . . , I (New York, 1922), 163.

At its next session the House of Representatives engaged in yet another debate over its privileges when its sergeant at arms was arrested on the complaint of a man whom the House had ordered apprehended for disorderly conduct in the visitors' gallery. See *Annals of Congress*, X, 865, 880–890.

8. See Congressional Career: Editorial Note, Dec. 4, 1799; Amendment, *ca.* Apr. 16, 1800; and Committee Report, Apr. 25, 1800.

9. Although the Pennsylvania General Assembly had failed to enact an election law, Gov. Thomas McKean had known for some time that it would not succeed in doing so. He had told Thomas Jefferson that he intended to call a special session to meet in August and that if the Assembly again failed to enact a law, he would "direct the manner by a Proclamation." At some point, perhaps prior to the date of this letter, McKean decided not to convene an August session. Rather than naming the electors by proclamation, he called a meeting of the Assembly after fall elections had made it more strongly Republican. McKean to Thomas Jefferson, Mar. 7, 1800, Jefferson Papers, Library of Congress, and Harry Marlin Tinkcom, *The Republicans and Federalists in Pennsylvania, 1790–1801: A Study in National Stimulus and Local Response* (Harrisburg, Pa., 1950), 245. See also JM to Reuben George, Mar. 16, 1800.

ment of the United States it ought to be exercisd. That it does exist is I [*beleive the*] fair construction of the constitution & will I beleive be admitted by any person who will candidly examine the subject. The difficulty is in the manner of con[*struc*]ting the tribunal to judge of the votes. The democrats say the convention of the two houses is that tribunal & to this opinion I at first very much inclind myself— but I have abandond it. The constitution does not speak of the two houses in convention & on the contrary contemplates them in the very act of counting the votes not as a convention but as a senate & house of representatives—& consequently as two unmixd bodies. To a resolution on any vote which is to pass the houses separately there is this insuperable objection. Such a vote according to the constitution must receive the sanction of the President & nothing can be more absurd than the idea of his negativing or affirming a vote for or against himself. Under these difficulties the opinion to which I incline is that the votes may be counted by a committee but must be counted in presence of both houses & must be one continued act. This is the system I now intend to support. I am not sure I may not change it.

Let me do what I will. I am sure the democrats will abuse me & therefore I need only try to satisfy myself.

I have purchasd four bank shares with the money receivd on your bill. Your affectionate brother

J MARSHALL

From Rufus King

ALS, RG 59, National Archives

No. 66.

Dr sir,   London, April 7, 1800

As I may not be able to see Lord Grenville again for some days, he having gone to his Country-House where he will probably remain thro' the Easter Holidays, I think it proper to acquaint you that in a conference I had with his Lordship the day before yesterday, he distinctly informed me, that it was the unanimous opinion of himself and colleagues not to enter into the formal discussion of the explanatory articles which I had proposed to him on the 18th. of February, as they saw no probability that the two governments would be able to agree in any Explanation upon that subject; but that they would consent to the dissolution of the present Board, and to the appointment of a new set of Commissioners, who should be governed by the stipulation already concluded, without regard to the constructive Resolutions of the former Commissioners;[1] the 5th. Commissioner to be named by the King and instead of two Americans being appointed by the President, and two British subjects by the King, that the President should appoint one American and name a British subject to whose appointment the King's consent should be requisite; and that the King should appoint one British subject and name one American to whose appointment the President's consent should be requisite. This modification of the choice of the Commissioners, it was suggested, might diminish the influence of national Prejudice on both sides; but I conclude that it is not thought of sufficient importance to be insisted upon if the former mode of choice should be preferred. I cannot now send you a detail of the Reasons upon which his Lordship placed their refusal to agree to, or to discuss, the explanatory articles that we had proposed. After hearing the few words in which he communicated this decision, I only replied that I would consider of what he had informed me, and take the earliest opportunity of communicating to him the Result of my Reflections.

I accordingly called today at his Lordship's house, but he had left town early in the morning. It was my intention to have represented to him the Reasons why upon the appointment of a new board of Commissioners, it would be necessary that certain Explanatory Rules should be settled for the government of their Proceedings, and to inform him that I was not authorised to agree to a New Commission without such Rules.

We have Paris Papers to the 3d.—the Campaign had not then opened: They state that the french Commissioners appointed to negotiate with those of the U. States met on the 1st. instant, for the purpose of exchanging their powers.[2]

---

1. King's Feb. 18 letter to Grenville was based on a draft written by Pickering and was not acceptable to the British. The collapse of the debt commission meeting in Philadelphia in 1799 and of the spoliation commission meeting in London is discussed in Bradford Perkins, *The First Rapprochement: England and the United States, 1795–1805* (Berkeley, Calif., 1967), 116–120. See also John Bassett Moore, ed., *International Adjudications Ancient and Modern . . .* , III (New York, 1931).

   For more information on these negotiations, see King to [JM], calendared at Apr. 3, 1800, King to [JM], Apr. 22, 1800 (first letter), and JM to John Adams, June 24, 1800. This dispatch was received by the State Department on July 13, 1800.

2. The French commissioners were Joseph Bonaparte (1768–1844), eldest brother of Napoleon Bonaparte; Pierre-Louis, comte Roederer (1754–1835); and Charles-Pierre Claret, comte de Fleurieu (1738–1810). See Alexander DeConde, *The Quasi-War: The Politics and Diplomacy of the Undeclared War with France, 1797–1801* (New York, 1966), 227–228.

The French & Spanish fleets at Brest amounting to more than forty sail of the line, are ready for sea : upwards of 15,000 troops are actually embarked, and here it is fully believed that they will come out; their destination supposed to be Ireland or Portugal, probably the latter. Lord Bridport was on the 31st. ult. off Brest with 28 sail of the Line: five or six ships more may have since joined him. I have the honor to be, with perfect esteem & Respect, Dr Sir, Your obedt & very humble servant

RUFUS KING

Speech

Printed, *Annals of Congress*, X, 658

[*April 7, 1800, Philadelphia.* JM opposes a motion of William Cooper[3] to postpone consideration of the bill on the cession of the Western Reserve until the following term of Congress. The motion was defeated by a 57–30 vote. Speech not found.]

Speech

Printed, *Annals of Congress*, X, 661

[*April 8, 1800, Philadelphia.* JM opposes successfully a motion of William Cooper to amend the Western Reserve bill in such a way as to defeat it.[4] JM then delivered a "lengthy" speech in favor of the bill. Speech not found.]

Committee Report

Printed, [U.S. Congress, House], *Report of the Committee to whom was referred, on the 13th ultimo, the Petition of William Tazewell* (Philadelphia, 1800)

[Philadelphia, April 9, 1800]
[The committee reports[5]] THAT when Mr. Gerry was about to embark for the United States, he requested Mr. Tazewell to remain in Paris, for the purpose of superintending the publication of some

---

3. Cooper (1754–1809), a representative from New York, later wrote to JM about the employment of his son by the government. See Cooper to JM, July 13, 1800, Miscellaneous Letters Received, RG 59, National Archives.

4. See Committee Report, Mar. 21, 1800, and Legislative Bill, *ca.* Mar. 21, 1800.

5. See Legislative Petition, Mar. 13, 1800.

letters from Mr. Gerry to the Minister of Exterior Relations of the French Republic; and employed Mr. Tazewell, after that service should have been performed, to carry dispatches to Mr. Murray, and Mr. King, the Ministers of the United States at the Hague, and at London, informing them of his departure from Paris, and of the existing state of the relations between the United States and France. In consequence of this extra service, Mr. Tazewell was prevented from embarking with Mr. Gerry on board the United States' brig Sophia, and on his return to America, was captured by a French privateer and sent into Corunna, in Spain, from whence he travelled by land to Lisbon, at which place he embarked for the United States. Mr. Tazewell claims a continuance of compensation until his arrival in the United States, and a reimbursement of the expences incurred while on his journey to the Hague, and to London, and afterwards until his arrival in America.—Two letters from Mr. Gerry to Mr. Tazewell, and one from Mr. Tazewell to the Secretary of State,[6] which accompany this Report, shew the nature of Mr. Tazewell's engagement with Mr. Gerry, and of his claim on the United States, with the causes of his situation.

A letter from the Secretary of State to the Chairman of this Committee,[7] and which also accompanies this Report, shews the allowance he is willing to make Mr. Tazewell, and states his view of the claim.

Your Committee is of opinion, that the principles adopted by the Secretary of State, for the settlement of the compensation to be received by Mr. Tazewell, for his services, are reasonable; but that in the settlement of his accounts, his claim for necessary expences incurred by a capture to which he was subjected by being employed in the service of the United States, ought to be admitted. Your Committee, therefore, propose the following resolution:

Resolved, That in settling the accounts of William Tazewell, Secretary of Elbridge Gerry, Esq. one of the late Envoys from the United States of America to the French Republic, the Secretary of State be authorized to allow the expences incurred by him in consequence of his being captured on his return to his country.[8]

6. These letters were printed with the report of the committee and are also in *Amer. State Papers, Claims*, XIX, 239–240.

7. See Timothy Pickering to JM, Apr. 1, 1800. The letter was printed with the committee's report.

8. After JM introduced the resolution, it was approved on Apr. 16. JM then prepared a bill to authorize compensation. The bill was adopted on Apr. 28, but no copy has been found. *Annals of Congress*, X, 661, 673, 675, 683, 688. See William Tazewell to JM, June 8, 1800.

Deeds

Deed Book Copies, Office of the Clerk of Hardy County, Moorefield, W.Va.

[*April 16, 1800 (Hardy County, Va.)*. By his attorney, Rawleigh Colston, JM conveys parcels of land in the South Branch Manor to John Hogbin, 83 acres for £20 15s., and to Alexander McKinley, 7 acres for £1 19s. Both deeds were recorded in the District Court at Hardy County in May 1800.]

Amendment

Printed, [U.S. Congress, House], *Mr. Marshall's Motion* (Philadelphia, 1800)

[Philadelphia, *ca.* April 16, 1800]

STRIKE out, beginning with the 7th. line to the words "United States" inclusive in the 12th. line, and insert,—*Immediately after this choice each House shall nominate by ballot one of its Members, and transmit his name to the other.*[9] *The names of the two Members, thus nominated, shall be communicated by the President of the Senate and the Speaker of the House*

---

9. On Mar. 28, the Senate passed and sent to the House of Representatives a bill "prescribing the mode of deciding disputed elections of President and Vice President of the United States." The bill as adopted by the Senate was printed for the Committee of the Whole, and it was this printed version to which JM referred in proposing amendments. The Senate bill differs significantly from the version printed in the *Aurora* (Philadelphia) on Feb. 19, 1800. See [U.S. Congress, House], *An Act Prescribing the mode of deciding disputed elections of President and Vice-President of the United States* (Philadelphia, 1800), which was first read in the House on Mar. 31, 1800.

On Apr. 16, the Committee of the Whole began consideration of the measure by debating its first section. JM opposed the provision that the Senate would name the chairman of the Grand Committee and that the opinion of that committee would be final. He moved acceptance of these changes. Debate ended without a vote, and on the following day John Randolph moved an amendment to JM's motion, proposing that the Grand Committee be chosen by lot rather than by ballot. John Nicholas expressed his belief that the entire bill was unconstitutional and moved to strike the first section completely. JM spoke against this motion, but again no vote was taken. On Apr. 18, Robert Goodloe Harper, a supporter of the bill, moved that further consideration be postponed until Apr. 21, and after Nicholas tried once more to kill the measure, Harper's motion passed. On Apr. 21, Harper moved that the bill be sent to a select committee. JM supported this motion, which carried, whereupon JM was named chairman of the select committee. After the House adopted a new version of the bill, the Senate insisted on additional alterations that were unacceptable to the House, and the measure failed to pass. See *Annals of Congress*, X, 146, 670, 673, 674, 678, 691, 692, 694–697, 710, 713; Committee Report, Apr. 25, 1800; and *Journal of the House of Representatives . . . first session of the Sixth Congress*, III (Washington, D.C., 1826), 675.

JM discussed his view of the problem in JM to James Markham Marshall, Apr. 4, 1800.

of Representatives, severally to the twelve persons who shall have been chosen as above mentioned. One of them shall be selected by lott in the following manner: The twelve persons, chosen as aforesaid, shall assemble, and then one of the six chosen by the House of Representatives shall write, in the presence of those assembled, on separate and similar pieces of paper the name of each Member nominated as aforesaid, and shall roll them up separately as nearly alike as may be, and shall place them in a ballot box and shake them. One of the six chosen by the Senate shall then draw out one of the papers, and the person whose name shall be found on the paper so drawn out of the box, shall be considered as selected for the purposes of this act. The person so selected, together with the twelve Members chosen as aforesaid, shall form a Grand Committee of which the person selected by lott as aforementioned, shall be the Chairman, and shall have power to examine and decide finally, unless such decision be disapproved by a vote of the Senate and House of Representatives, all disputes relative to the election of President and Vice President of the United States; but the vote of no elector shall be questioned merely on account of the insufficiency of the number of votes by which he was elected.

Strike out the 2d. section.[1]

Strike out the 3d. section to the 6th. line inclusive, and insert— *when the Grand Committee shall be formed, the President of the Senate shall, in the Senate Chamber, administer to the Chairman and other Members the following oath.*[2]

After the word "them," in the 10th. line, insert—*and will fairly take and report the testimony relative thereto.*[3]

In the 14th. line after the word "Committee," strike out to the word "all" in the 16th. line.[4]

Section 4, strike out from the word "directed," in the 2d. line, to the word "they" in the 4th. line.[5]

After the word "if" in the 7th. line, insert—*the Chairman or.*

After "such," in the 11th. line, insert—*the Chairman or.*

1. Sec. 2 provided for tellers from both houses who would record specific information from the certificates of the electors and then read it before both houses of Congress. See [U.S. Congress, House], *Report on "An Act [for] Deciding Disputed Elections."*

2. JM proposed striking a longer preamble to the oath that mentioned the work of the tellers. *Ibid.*

3. The portion of the oath that JM wanted to replace read, "and a true judgment given thereon agreeable to the Constitution and Laws, and according to the evidence." *Ibid.*

4. The words that JM wanted to remove instructed the president of the Senate to send the electors' certificates to the committee. He proposed that the committee receive only the petitions protesting the votes of the electors or the people for whom they had voted. *Ibid.*

5. This portion of sec. 4 clarified the Senate's election of the chairman of the committee. It would have been altered by JM's suggested amendment to sec. 1. *Ibid.*

Strike out from the word Senate, in the 14th. line, to the end of the section.[6]

Legislative Bill

Printed, *Annals of Congress*, X, 1524

[*ca. April 17, 1800, Philadelphia.* JM introduces a bill authorizing the issuance of patents or surveys within the "territory reserved by the State of Virginia, northwest of the river Ohio, and being part of her cession to Congress, on warrants for military services," issued by Virginia to soldiers who had served in the Virginia Line during the Revolution. The total amount of land was limited to 60,000 acres, and the surveys had to be deposited with the secretary of war by Dec. 1, 1803. Furthermore, this act disallows conflicting claims already made, although anyone losing a legal claim on a previous warrant will have the right to patent the same acreage on vacant land within the said territory.[7] Bill not found.]

6. The remaining changes merely simplified the wording of the bill, allowing the omission of 108 words by inserting the 6 that JM suggested.

7. The Committee of Claims of the House had reviewed several petitions sent by Virginia veterans, or their heirs, requesting grants of federal land because the state's territory had been ceded to the United States after the Revolution. The committee recommended on Feb. 25 that the petitions be denied. The House did not consider this report until Apr. 15, at which time JM spoke against accepting the committee's recommendation. It was argued that Virginia had ceded a huge tract of land to the United States and that all of the claims, present and potential, amounted to no more than 100,000 acres. The House then rejected the report and, on Apr. 16, asked JM, Anthony New (1747–1833), and Henry Lee to prepare this bill. *Annals of Congress*, X, 668–672. See also Otway Byrd's Petition, Mar. 31, 1800, Committee on Claims, RG 233, National Archives, and [U.S. Congress, House], *Report of the Committee of Claims, to whom were Referred, the Petitions of Temple Elliot, Simon Sommers, and William Boyce* (Philadelphia, 1800). For JM's earlier involvement with Byrd's petition, see *Journal of the House of Delegates of the Commonwealth of Virginia . . .* , May 1789, 39.

The bill was agreed to on Apr. 25 and formally passed the House the next day. The Senate added amendments, probably limiting the acreage, and approved the bill on May 10, by which time JM had left Philadelphia. The House accepted the amended bill on May 12. *Annals of Congress*, X, 177, 179–180, 684, 685, 715. See also *ibid.*, 519, 520.

From American Envoys

LS, RG 59, National Archives

[*April 18, 1800, Paris*. The envoys report that they have received the State Department dispatches of Jan. 6 and 20, 1800.[8] They enclose papers marked A through V that trace the circumstances connected with their mission.[9] The enclosed documents describe the progress of the mission up to the note

8. This dispatch, the first sent by the Ellsworth mission envoys after their arrival in Paris, was addressed to Timothy Pickering but arrived in Washington after JM had assumed the duties of secretary of state. The italicized words, originally in code, were decoded by JM. See Pickering to American Envoys, Jan. 6 and 20, 1800, Despatches from Diplomatic Officers, France, VII, RG 59, National Archives.

9. Exhibit A: Envoys to Talleyrand, Mar. 3, 1800, asking to be received; and Talleyrand to Envoys, Mar. 4, 1800, asking them to visit him the next day. Exhibit B: Envoys to Talleyrand, Mar. 4, 1800, accepting the invitation. Exhibit C: Talleyrand to Envoys, Mar. 5, 1800, informing them of an appointment with Napoleon on Mar. 17 at the Tuileries. Exhibit D: Envoys to Talleyrand, Mar. 5, 1800, acknowledging invitation to meet with Napoleon. Exhibit E: Talleyrand to Envoys, Mar. 9, 1800, informing them of the appointment of the French ministers who will negotiate with them. Exhibit F: Envoys to Talleyrand, Mar. 9, 1800, acknowledging receipt of his of the 8th, and assuring him of their willingness and eagerness to begin negotiations. Exhibit G: Envoys to French Ministers, Mar. 15, 1800, asking for a meeting to exchange powers and to schedule negotiations on "the strange Phenomenon of a misunderstanding between the" two nations. Exhibit H: Envoys to French Ministers, Mar. 29, 1800, repeating the message of Mar. 15, now that Joseph Bonaparte has recovered. Exhibit J: French Ministers to Envoys, Mar. 29, 1800, inviting them to meet on Apr. 1 or 2. Exhibit K: Envoys to French Ministers, Mar. 30, 1800, agreeing to meet on Apr. 2. Exhibit L: Extract from a decree of Napoleon, Mar. 4, 1800, instructing the French ministers to treat with the envoys. Exhibit M: Envoys to French Ministers, Apr. 3, 1800, requesting clarification of their powers, hoping they may be authorized to make a treaty and therefore have powers equal to theirs. Exhibit N: Talleyrand to French Ministers, Apr. 6, 1800, on the differences perceived in the powers of the negotiating teams. Exhibit O: French Ministers to Envoys, Apr. 7, 1800, transmitting Exhibits N and P. Exhibit P: Extract of a decree of Napoleon, Apr. 5, 1800, giving them broader powers to negotiate with the American envoys. Exhibit Q: Envoys to French Ministers, Apr. 7, 1800, transmitting Exhibit R. Exhibit R: Envoys to French Ministers, Apr. 7, 1800, proposing they first discuss claims of citizens of either nation. Exhibit S: French Ministers to Envoys, Apr. 9, 1800, proposing they first discuss how to estimate and make awards for injuries suffered by citizens of either nation and by the governments, and requesting assurance that the Treaty of 1778 will be executed. Exhibit T: Envoys to French Ministers, Apr. 11, 1800, agreeing to discuss claims of the governments but only after agreeing on details for treating individuals' claims and explaining their desire to write a new treaty, sidestepping references to the voiding of the old one. Exhibit U: French Ministers to Envoys, Apr. 13, 1800, insisting that a new treaty cannot be discussed until claims under the old one are determined and asking for assurances that the United States will abandon its "hostile position" toward France. Exhibit V: Envoys to French Ministers, Apr. 18, 1800, advising them of their willingness to incorporate assurances desired by the French in a new treaty and suggesting that they proceed by proposing articles of such a treaty. Most of these enclosures are printed in *Amer. State Papers, Foreign Relations*, II, 309–316, although in many instances the dates of the French letters are incorrect in translation.

of Apr. 18, which was "accompanied with *six articles covering* the whole ground of *individual claim* and *form'd for a treaty*." There has been no time to prepare a copy of the accompanying articles for this dispatch. The envoys conclude with a postscript: "We shall *be hard pressd to revive the old treaty to save its anteriority.*"[1]]

From Rufus King

LS, RG 59, National Archives

No: 67.

Dear Sir.[2]   London, April 22, 1800

So much impatience had appeared in respect to the delay that happened in the transmission of my Instructions concerning the separation of the Commission at Philadelphia that I judged it expedient to lose no time after their arrival in beginning the negotiation; I accordingly informed Lord Grenville the day after the receit of your No. 71.[3] that I was ready to proceed, and would either write him an official Note, as the commencement of the negotiation, or prepare and deliver to him an informal Paper containing the Propositions we had to offer, and which might become the subject of free discussion in future conferences: his Lordship intimated a preference of the latter course; and I accordingly delivered to him the Paper, mentioned in my No. 65,[4] a copy of which is annexed.[5] In my No. 66.[6] I gave you an account of what passed between Lord Grenville and me in our next Conference; in addition to which I might have added

1. The envoys had been instructed to argue that the Treaty of 1778 established American rights to indemnities for French violations of American commerce even though Congress had declared the treaty now void. The French countered with the argument that voided treaties removed claims under them and left no anterior rights. See Pickering to American Envoys, Oct. 22, 1799, in *Amer. State Papers, Foreign Relations*, II, 301–306, and Alexander DeConde, *The Quasi-War: The Politics and Diplomacy of the Undeclared War with France, 1797–1801* (New York, 1966), 229–237.

2. This dispatch was received by the State Department on July 23, 1800. See JM to John Adams, July 26, 1800, by which JM transmitted this letter. See also JM to Adams, July 21, 1800, and Adams to JM, Aug. 1, 1800.

3. See Timothy Pickering to Rufus King, Dec. 31, 1799, Pickering Papers, Massachusetts Historical Society.

4. King to [JM], calendared at Apr. 3, 1800.

5. In this letter King stated that clarification of art. 6 of the Jay Treaty was necessary in light of the suspension of the Board of Commissioners' meeting in Philadelphia. The letter contains commentary on the American view of the article. King to Lord Grenville, Feb. 18, 1800, enclosed in this letter and printed in *Amer. State Papers, Foreign Relations*, II, 395–398. See also the enclosures in King's private letter to [JM], Apr. 22, 1800.

6. King to [JM], Apr. 7, 1800.

that his Lordship asked if I was authorized to offer any specific sum of money, on the payment of which Great Britain should engage to satisfy the Claims of the whole of the British Creditors?[7] Having no such power my answer was of course in the negative.

On the 19. instant I received his Lordship's written answer to the Proposals I had delivered to him on the 18. of February corresponding, as you will perceive by the subjoined Copy, with the verbal answer that had before been given to me.[8] As this Answer precludes all discussion of the articles we had proposed, on the plan that the whole Subject had been finally settled by the Treaty of Amity, and that the United States are bound by the decision of the majority of the Commissioners whether the matter decided is within or above their Powers, my first thought was to prepare and send to his Lordship a Note exposing the error of a Principle that confounds the distinction between a limited and an unlimited delegation of authority, and which should, at the same time, support, by further arguments the Justice and Expediency of the explanatory Articles that we had offered.

But as the Language of Lord Grenville, in our conference was equally explicit and decided as that of the Paper delivered in answer to our Proposals I on reflection changed my first opinion, from the persuasion that nothing would be gained by that course in favor of the future execution of the article, and as the answer had placed the negotiation in a situation that had not been foreseen that it was my Duty to refer it, in its present stage, to the further consideration of the President.

The written answer of Lord Grenville having intimated a disposition to accede to certain Regulations which it was supposed might facilitate the execution of the Treaty, I yesterday asked a conference with his Lordship for the purpose of obtaining a precise idea of the nature and extent of these Regulations: this was immediately granted, and afforded an opportunity for a free conversation upon the general Topic, as well as respecting the particular Subject that

7. JM had anticipated such a suggestion prior to receipt of this letter. See JM to John Adams, June 24, 1800. Lord Grenville had considered a lump-sum settlement as a possible solution as early as 1794, before the Jay Treaty was signed. See John Bassett Moore, ed., *International Adjudications Ancient and Modern . . . ,* III (New York, 1931), 353.

8. Grenville laid the blame for the debt commission's dissolution on the partiality of the American members' majority. He felt that King's explanation of art. 6 only increased that partiality, and he favored reconstituting the commission with new members or decreasing the size of the old panel. Grenville to King, Apr. 19, 1800, enclosed in this letter and printed in *Amer. State Papers, Foreign Relations,* II, 398–399. See also the enclosures in King's private letter to [JM], Apr. 22, 1800.

brought us together. Many things were said on both sides that it would be useless to repeat: these therefore are omitted in this Report.

His Lordship observed that the object of the delay that took place at London was to allow time to the Court of Appeals to decide the several Prize Cases before their examination by the Commissioners, and that a like arrangement might be made in respect to the Cases before the Commissioners at Philadelphia. With regard to the Questions of impediment, Solvency, insolvency, and Some others of equal importance, Lord Grenville said, their decision must be left to the Provisions of the Treaty, to the particular circumstances of each case, and to the sound discretion of the Commissioners; adding that upon a full investigation of the subject he was convinced that no new and general Rule upon these Points could be made without affecting cases and Claims that ought not to be affected; and that even with respect to an Agreement to delay the Cases before the Commissioners at Philadelphia, in order that the Claimants should have an opportunity first to obtain the decision of our Courts, it would be difficult, not to say impossible, for him to form any satisfactory idea of what would be a convenient time unless he had a more adequate knowledge of our Judiciary Proceedings, and a particular instead of a general acquaintance with the Claims. Upon this Point, as on most others, there seemed to be wanting a discretionary Power always present, and ready to act as occasions arose, and according to the nature, and circumstances of the particular question: that the Persons whom he had thought of as two of the Commissioners to be appointed by the King were men of prudence and discretion, and with whom he thought we should be satisfied: that Mr. Liston having repeatedly asked and lately received leave of absence on account of his health, might not be at Philadelphia; and he saw no preferable course, in case we acceded to the suggestion, to that of sending these two Persons to Philadelphia to concert with us such analagous Regulations, in respect to the Commission there, as were agreed to with regard to the Commission here. We should by this means have an opportunity of knowing the character and dispositions of the Persons sent to prepare and agree to these Regulations, and who would afterwards be appointed to assist in the execution of the Treaty.

Lord Grenville asked me in what time I supposed the Courts would be able to go thro' the whole of the Cases? I answered that this must chiefly depend upon the diligence of the Creditors, and that I could not form any satisfactory Estimate of the Time that might be necessary: on the one hand it should not be so short as, with a disposition in the Courts to avoid delay, would defeat the object of the Regulation; and on the other it should not be so long, as to afford any ground from the Delay to infer that there was a denial of Justice: No precise time was settled here; and perhaps none should be at Philadelphia. His Lordship asked if there could be no means found to accelerate the Trials? I repeated the observation that more would depend on the Diligence of the Creditors than upon the Courts of whose disposition to give the greatest dispatch there could be no doubt: that a Law requiring extraordinary Sessions of the Courts, or prescribing a more summary Proceeding would not only interfere with the established Course of our Judiciary, but give berth to other and still more difficult questions which it would be unwise to agitate.

His Lordship asked Whether the cases before the Board are any of them in a state for the new Commissioners to take up, suggesting that it would be desirable that the new Board should, at their commencement, have something to do. I replied that tho' I could not then answer the question with any degree of accuracy, I was inclined to believe that many Cases were in a situation that, without recourse to the Courts, might soon be prepared for the Commissioners to decide, and that the progress of the Trials would be constantly furnishing additional cases. Lord Grenville expressed his opinion that the new Board ought to proceed in a different manner from their Predecessors, by deciding Cases singly one after another, instead of attempting to decide them by general Resolves, and in classes.

I observed that it was possible that new difficulties might arise in the course of future Proceedings, and should Mr. Liston be absent there would be no one with whom we could confer for the purpose of removing them: Lord Grenville replied that in this case he must endeavour to find out a proper character to supply Mr. Listons Place.

I then asked Lord Grenville if he had formed any idea of the Gross sum on the payment of which they would engage to Compensate the Claims of the British Creditors: his Lordship replied that he had not; adding that he thought the Creditors had not been wise in Levelling, as they had done, their claim to four or five Millions Sterling; tho it might have no influence upon our Government, it would be likely to have some upon the People: that he himself did not like the idea of the payment of a gross Sum; and that he had mentioned it to me in compliance with the opinion of his Colleagues; but that on the supposition that the Debt due to British Creditors did not exceed two Millions, that they might be willing to accept a gross sum of between one and two Millions.

I shall, as opportunities offer, endeavour to acquire further information on this Subject, as it may possibly lead to the satisfactory conclusion of a most difficult business.

If it is probable that we shall ultimately be required to pay upon the Awards of the Commissioners a sum equal to or not far short of one for which the business could at once be settled, Would it not be the part of a wise Policy to Engage to pay such sum by installments or in some other convenient manner? All further Expense to Individuals, as well as to the Public would in this mode of Settlement be saved; we should moreover escape the embarrassment of any future disagreement among the Commissioners, and consequent misunderstanding between the two Countries; the trouble and vexation of numberless Law-suits would be prevented, and instead of the dissatisfaction and ill-will towards the Government that they would unavoidably excite, a General Release to the Debtors would be a boon that could not fail to produce opposite Sentiments. With perfect respect & Esteem, I have the honor to be, Dear sir, Your ob. & faithful servant.

RUFUS KING

From Rufus King

Letterbook Copy, King Papers, New-York Historical Society

Private & Personal
Dear Sir,[9]   London, April 22, 1800
In order that the President may have all the information in my power to communicate on the subject of my official Letter of this date, I have concluded to send you copies of the private Letters which passed between Lord Grenville and me on that Subject.[1] I desire for obvious reasons that this Letter may not be considered as belonging to your office, or in any respect as a public communication. The more I think of the overture for the Settlement of the Claims of the British Creditors by the payment of a gross sum to their Government to take them off our hands, the better I like it. I am aware of many

9. This letter appears to have arrived late in July and to be the letter mentioned in JM to John Adams, Aug. 1, 1800, but see Timothy Pickering to JM, Dec. 27, 1800.

1. The enclosures are letters exchanged between Grenville and King, indicating a complete breakdown in negotiations over art. 6 of the Jay Treaty. See the letterbook copies, in King Papers, New-York Historical Society.

objections to the Scheme, but admitting their force will not the measure still be a wise one? and may not the proposition be so made as to insure its success with Congress? The business of the Commission here could, as I conceive, be soon brought to a close; and there would, I think, be no difficulty in a satisfactory arrangement upon this Subject, provided the Claims of the British Creditors were disposed of.

This sort of Settlement might moreover afford an opportunity to obtain the possession of the Maryland Bank Stock which is the everlasting Subject of fair Words that are intended to mean nothing. With sincere regard and Esteem &c

R K

To William F. Ast

ALS, Henry E. Huntington Library

Sir   Philadelphia, April 23, 1800

I have receivd yours of the 23d. inst.[2] The stamp office law has been totally misrepresented.[3] It never was in contemplation to oblige persons having occasion for stamps to send for them to the seat of government. The present regulation is nothing more than one calculated to prevent fraud but the existing offices are all kept up & stamps may be obtaind at them as heretofore.

2. Ast, of the Mutual Assurance Society in Richmond, had obviously written JM after hearing of the passage of the new stamp act. Ast's letter has not been found, but see William Miller to Ast, May 21, 1800, Incoming Correspondence, Mutual Assurance Society Papers, Virginia State Library. JM mailed this letter to Ast in Richmond, and it is postmarked Apr. 22 in Philadelphia. The reference to Ast's letter of Apr. 23 must be an error.

3. In 1797 Congress had adopted an act "laying duties on stamped vellum, parchment, and paper," specifying that the stamped paper be available in offices of supervisors of revenue throughout the country. Unstamped paper might be used for legal documents provided a stamp was purchased and affixed by the proper official before the document could become valid. 1 Stat. 527–532.

Robert Goodloe Harper introduced a bill to establish a central stamp office on Mar. 3, 1800, presumably to eliminate the widespread distribution of stamps and the resulting possibility of fraud. After debate and amendment of the bill by the Senate, agreement was reached on Apr. 15. The act did in fact provide that paper deposited in an office of the supervisor of revenue would be sent to Washington for stamping, although the procedure for using unstamped paper by paying an additional fee and obtaining official endorsements was retained. *Annals of Congress*, X, 510, 582, 656, 657, 659, 668, 1475–1478; 2 Stat. 40–42.

Apparently general confusion over the act increased. At the following session, Congress repealed every section of the 1800 act except the one permitting the use of unstamped paper by paying the duty and obtaining endorsements on the document in the local office of the collector of the revenue. *Annals of Congress*, X, 1557; 2 Stat. 109–110.

If the directors send a petition I shall certainly present it tho I do not beleive it will succeed. I am Sir very respectfully, Your Obedt

J MARSHALL

It will be too late to take up the subject in the present Congress.

Committee Report

Printed, [U.S. Congress, House], *Report of the Committee to whom was referred the bill sent from the Senate, intituled "An Act Prescribing the Mode of Deciding Disputed Elections of President and Vice-President of the United States"* (Philadelphia, 1800)

Philadelphia, April 25, 1800

[The committee agrees to the said bill with the following amendments.[4]]

STRIKE out from the word "assembled," in the second line of the first section to the end of the bill, and insert in lieu thereof the following—

That on the   next following the day when a President and Vice-President shall have been voted for by electors it shall be the duty of the Senate and House of Representatives of the United States to choose by ballot in each house four members thereof: And the persons thus chosen shall form a joint committee and shall have power to examine into all disputes relative to the election of President and Vice-President of the United States, other than such as may relate to the number of votes by which the electors may have been appointed.[5] *Provided always*, that no person shall be capable of serving on this committee who shall be one of the five highest candidates from among whom a President of the United States may be chosen by the House of Representatives in case no person should be found

---

4. When the House failed to agree to alterations in the bill sent from the Senate, a select committee was appointed on Apr. 21, consisting of JM, as chairman, and Samuel Sewall, Chauncey Goodrich, Robert Goodloe Harper, John Nicholas, John Dennis (1771–1806), and James A. Bayard. On Apr. 25 JM reported this radically revised version, later referred to as "Marshall's amendment" by Thomas Jefferson. *Journal of the House of Representatives . . . first session of the Sixth Congress*, III (Washington, D.C., 1826), 675; *Annals of Congress*, X, 683; Jefferson to James Madison, May 12, 1800, Jefferson Papers, Library of Congress.

For JM's earlier involvement, see Amendment, *ca.* Apr. 16, 1800.

5. John Nicholas's motion to delete this section of the bill was defeated on Apr. 29. A second attempt to omit it failed on May 1. *Annals of Congress*, X, 691–692, 694.

to have a majority of the whole number of the votes of the electors appointed by the different States.[6]

SEC. 2. *And be it further enacted*, That the President of the Senate shall deliver to the members of this joint committee appointed from the Senate, all the petitions exceptions and memorials against the votes of the electors or the persons for whom they have voted together with the testimony accompanying the same and all documents relative thereto of which he may be possessed, other than those inclosed in the packets containing the certificates of the votes of the electors; And the Speaker of the House of Representatives shall deliver to the members of the joint committee appointed from that House, all the documents relative to the votes for President and Vice-President of which he may be possessed.

SEC. 3. *And be it further enacted*, That the joint committee shall meet on every day (Sunday excepted) from the time of their appointment until they make their report—Six members of whom, there must be three from each house, may proceed to act. If any member of the committee appointed by either House should die, or become unable to attend after his appointment, the committee before they proceed further shall notify both Houses of such death or inability; and the House by which such member was appointed, shall immediately proceed to choose another member, by ballot, to supply such vacancy.

SEC. 4. *And be it further enacted*, That the joint committee shall have power to send for persons and papers, to compel the attendance of witnesses, to administer oaths or affirmations to all persons examined before them, and to punish contempts of witnesses refusing to answer, as fully and absolutely as the Supreme Court of the United States may or can do in causes depending therein: and the testimony of all witnesses examined before the committee, shall be reduced to writing by the clerk of the committee, and shall be signed by the witness after his examination is closed: And if any person sworn and examined before this committee, shall swear or affirm falsely, such person, being thereof convicted, shall incur the pains, penalties and disabilities, inflicted by the laws of the United States, upon wilful and corrupt perjury.

SEC. 5. *And be it further enacted*, That it shall be the duty of the Marshals of the several districts of the United States, and of their deputies, to serve all process directed to them, and signed by the

6. This provision most likely was the one added on May 1, the only alteration in the select committee's draft that the House would accept. *Ibid.*, 696.

chairman of the joint committee; and for such services they shall receive the fees allowed for services of similar process, issued by the Supreme Court of the United States; all witnesses attending the committee in consequence of summons or other process, shall receive the same compensation as witnesses attending the Supreme Court of the United States.

SEC. 6. *And be it further enacted*, That the joint committee shall appoint a clerk who shall keep a journal of their proceedings under their direction to be reported to the Senate and House of Representatives.

SEC. 7. *And be it further enacted*, That before the houses shall assemble for the purpose of counting the votes, each house shall choose, by ballot, two members thereof as tellers, whose duty it shall be to receive the certificates of the electors, from the president of the Senate, after they shall have been opened and read, and to note in writing, the dates of the certificates, the names of the electors, the time of their election and the time and place of their meeting, the number of votes given, and the names of the persons voted for; and also the substance of the certificates from the executive authority of each state, accompanying the certificates of the electors; and the minutes thus made by the tellers, shall be read in the presence of both houses, and a copy thereof entered on the journals of each.

SEC. 8. *And be it further enacted*, That so soon as the joint committee shall have made the examinations and taken and digested the testimony, a report of their proceedings shall be made both to the Senate and House of Representatives, and shall be inserted on the journals of each House. The said report shall contain all the petitions, exceptions and memorials against the votes of the electors or the persons for whom they have voted together with the whole testimony, and arranging with each petition, exception, memorial and vote, the testimony relative thereto, but without giving any opinion thereon. The report shall also contain a copy of the law, resolution or act of the state legislatures respectively, under which the electors of the president and vice president of the United States, whose votes are to be counted, were chosen. So soon as this report shall have been made and entered on the journals the Senate and House of Representatives shall meet at such place as may be agreed on for the purpose of counting the votes for president and vice president of the United States. The names of the several states shall then be written under the inspection of the speaker of the House of Representatives, on separate and similar pieces of paper, and folded up as nearly alike as may be, and put into a ballot box, and shaken by a member of the House of Representatives, to be named by the speaker thereof, out of which box shall be drawn, the paper on which the names of the states are written one at a time, by a member of the Senate, to be named by the president thereof, and so soon as one is drawn the packet containing the certificates from the electors of that state shall be opened by the president of the Senate, and shall then be read, and then shall be read also the petitions, depositions and other papers and documents concerning the same, and if no exception is taken thereto, the votes contained in such certificate shall be counted; but if any exception be taken, the person taking the same shall state it directly, and not argumentatively, and sign his name thereto, and if it be founded on any circumstance appearing in the report of the joint committee, and the exception be seconded by one member from the Senate, and one from the House of Representatives, each of whom shall sign the said exception, as having seconded the same, then each house shall immediately retire, without question or debate to its own apartment, and shall take the question on the exception without debate, by ayes and no's.[7] So soon as the question shall be taken in either house, a message shall be sent to the other, informing them that the house sending the message is prepared to resume the count, and when such message shall have been received by both houses, they shall again assemble in the same apartment as before, and the count shall be resumed. And if the two houses have concurred in rejecting[8] the vote or votes objected to, such vote or votes shall not be counted, but unless both houses concur such vote or votes shall be counted. If the objection taken as aforementioned shall arise on the face of the papers opened by the president of the Senate in presence of both houses, and shall not have been noticed in the report of the joint committee, such objection may be referred to the joint committee to be examined and reported on by them in the same manner and on the same principles as their first report was made, but if both houses do not concur in referring the same to the committee, then such objection shall be decided on in like manner as if it had been

7. On Apr. 30, Albert Gallatin proposed altering this procedure to provide for an immediate vote on the exception, without debate, and without retiring into separate houses. His motion was defeated by two votes. A second attempt was defeated on May 1. *Ibid.*, 692, 695.

8. The Senate voted to change this word to "admitting." This alteration was opposed by Robert Goodloe Harper and James A. Bayard when it came back to the House, and they persuaded their colleagues to reject this change. When the Senate insisted on its alteration, the bill died. *Ibid.*, 176, 179, 709–710, 713.

founded on any circumstance appearing in the report of the committee. The votes of one state being thus counted, another ticket shall be drawn from the ballot box, and the certificate and the votes of the state thus drawn shall be proceeded on as is herein before directed, and so on, one after another until the whole of the votes shall be counted. The two houses may adjourn from day to day, passing over Sunday, until the count shall be completed. When a motion for adjournment shall be made by a member of either house and seconded by a member from each house, the question thereon shall be taken in the two houses separately and if they do not concur, they shall proceed in the count.

SEC. 9. *And be it further enacted,* That when the joint committee shall have been duly formed according to the directions of this act, it shall not be in the power of either house to dissolve the committee, or to withdraw any of its members.

SEC. 10. *And be it further enacted,* That it shall be the duty of the executive authority of each state, to cause three copies of the law, resolution, or act of the state legislatures respectively, under which electors are chosen or appointed, to be made, certified under the seal of the state, and delivered to the electors in such state before they give their votes, and the electors shall annex one of the said copies to each list of their votes, and it shall be the further duty of the executive authority of each state as soon as may be and within   days after the appointment therein of electors of president and vice-president of the United States to cause three other copies of the said law, resolution or act together with a complete list of the electors appointed and the time of their election to be made and certified as aforesaid and to transmit them inclosed, noting on each the contents of the packets, one to the president of the Senate, one to the speaker of the House of Representatives and one to the secretary of state of the United States: And it shall be the duty of the post-master-general and post-master at the seat of government to whom or to whose knowledge such packets may come to deliver them to the officers respectively to whom they may be directed, or in case of the absence from the seat of government of such officer, to deliver the packet to him directed to the secretary of the Senate, the clerk of the House of Representatives or to the chief clerk of the department of state, as the case may be. And it shall hereafter be the duty of the electors to express specially in their certificates, the time, the place, and the manner of giving their votes.

SEC. 11. *And be it further enacted,* That all petitions respecting the election of president and vice-president of the United States, shall be presented and read in the Senate of the United States, and then be transmitted to the House of Representatives, where they shall be read and afterwards delivered to the joint committee; but no petition shall be received after the   ; nor shall any petition against the qualifications of a candidate or elector, or for improper conduct in an elector, be received, unless ten days notice thereof in writing be previously given to the person whose qualifications are contested, or whose improper conduct is petitioned against.

SEC. 12. *And be it further enacted*, That persons petitioning against any of the votes given by any of the electors of president and vice-president of the United States and persons desirous of supporting such contested votes may respectively apply to any judge of the courts of the United States, or to any chancellor, justice, or judge of a superior or county court, or court of common pleas of any state, or to any mayor, recorder or intendant of a town or city, who shall, thereupon, issue his warrant of summons, directed to all such witnesses as shall be named to him by such applicant, or his agent duly authorised for that purpose, and requiring the attendance of such witnesses, before him, at some convenient time and place, to be expressed in the warrant, in order to be then and there examined, in the manner herein after provided, touching the subject matter of the aforesaid application.

SEC. 13. *And be it further enacted*, That every such witness, as is above-mentioned, shall be duly served with such warrant, by a copy thereof being delivered to him or her, or left at his or her usual place of abode; and that such service shall be made a convenient time before the day on which the attendance of such witness is required, which time the magistrate issuing the warrant is hereby authorised and required to fix, for each witness, at the time of issuing it, having respect to the circumstances of such witness, and the distance of his or her residence from the place of attendance.

SEC. 14. *And be it further enacted*, That any person, being summoned in the manner above directed, and refusing or neglecting to attend, pursuant to such summons, unless in case of sickness, or other unavoidable accident, shall forfeit and pay the sum of twenty dollars, to be recovered with costs of suit, by the party at whose instance the warrant of summons was issued, and for his use, by action of debt in any court, or before any other tribunal of the United States, or any state, having jurisdiction to the amount of such penalty.

SEC. 15. *And be it further enacted*, That persons desirous of taking testimony either to support a petition against any contested votes for president and vice-president of the United States or to support any such vote or votes shall previously advertize the time and place for taking such testimony together with the points intended to be established thereby for   weeks successively, in some one of the gazettes published at the seat of government of the state in which the votes to which the testimony is to relate were given; provided there be a gazette published at the seat of government, and in some one of the gazettes near the place at which the testimony is to be taken if there be any gazette published nearer such place than the seat of government.

Sec. 16. *And be it further enacted*, That all witnesses who shall attend in pursuance of the said summons and all other witnesses who shall be produced at the time and place aforesaid shall then and there be examined on oath or affirmation by the magistrate who issued the warrant of summons aforesaid, or in case of his absence by any other such magistrate as is authorized by this act to issue such warrant, touching all such matters and things respecting the votes about to be contested or supported as may have been suggested in the notice herein before directed to be published; the testimony given on which examination together with the questions proposed to the witnesses respectively, the said magistrate is hereby authorized and required to cause to be reduced to writing in his presence and to be duly attested by the witnesses respectively; after which he shall transmit the said testimony duly certified under his hand, covered and sealed up to the president of the Senate; together with a copy of the warrant of summons and notification issued in that behalf and the original affidavit proving the service of such notification.

Sec. 17. *And be it further enacted*, That in case any judge, justice, chancellor, mayor, recorder or intendant as is aforesaid, to whom the application herein mentioned shall be made, shall, by reason of sickness, necessary absence, or unavoidable accident, be rendered unable to attend at the time and place fixed for the examination aforesaid, it shall be lawful for him to certify the matter, and the proceedings had by him in that behalf, to any other magistrate of any of the descriptions aforesaid, which said magistrate thereupon, shall be, and hereby is authorized to attend at such time and place, and to proceed touching the said examinations, in all respects, as the magistrate issuing the warrant of summons might have done, by virtue of this act.

Sec. 18. *And be it further enacted*, That when no such magistrate as is herein authorized to receive applications as aforesaid, and proceed upon them, shall reside within any district for which an election about to be contested shall have been held, it shall be lawful to make such application to any two justices of the peace residing within the said district, who are hereby authorized in such case, to receive such application, and jointly to proceed upon it in the manner herein before directed.

SEC. 19. *And be it further enacted,* That every witness attending by virtue of such warrant of summons as is herein directed to be issued, shall be allowed the sum of seventy-five cents for each day's attendance, and the further sum of five cents, for every mile necessarily travelled in going and returning, which allowance shall be ascertained and certified by the magistrate taking the examination, and shall be paid by the party at whose instance such witness was summoned: and such witness shall have an action for the recovery of the said allowance, before any court or magistrate having competent jurisdiction, according to the laws of the United States, or of any state, in which action the certificate of the magistrate taking the said examination shall be evidence.

Sec. 20. *And be it further enacted,* That each judge, justice, chancellor, mayor, recorder, intendant and justice of the peace, who shall be necessarily employed, pursuant to the directions of this act, and all sheriffs, constables, or other officers who may be employed to serve any of the warrants of summons or notifications herein provided for, shall have and receive from the party at whose instance such service shall have been performed, such fee or fees, as are or may be allowed for similar services in the states wherein such service shall be rendered, respectively.

From Rufus King

LS, RG 59, National Archives

[*April 26, 1800, London.* In dispatch no. 69,[9] King notifies the government that he sent Lord Grenville an extract of his dispatch no. 67 in order to ensure his ability to correct mistakes in reporting on their conversations. He encloses a reply from Grenville that cautions King about relating Gren-

---

9. The copy marked "triplicate" arrived on June 25, and JM sent it to John Adams the following day. See JM to Adams, June 26, 1800, and Adams to JM, July 5, 1800. The original dispatch did not arrive until Aug. 9, on which day it was endorsed by JM.

ville's informally expressed opinions of people. King adds, "On the Supposition that a new Commission is appointed, I perceive fewer difficulties in the arrangement suggested by his Lordship in respect to the Proceedings of the Board of Commissioners, than with regard to the Courts." He closes with news from the Continent.]

Amendments

Printed, [U.S. Congress, House], *Mr. Nicholas's Motion, for Amending the Bill to Provide for the Execution of the Twenty Seventh Article of the Treaty of Amity, Commerce and Navigation with Great Britain (With the amendments of Mr. Marshall thereto.)* (Philadelphia, 1800)

[Philadelphia, April 29, 1800]

PROVIDED,[1] That where any person is charged, before a judge or justice, with having committed murder, within the meaning of the aforesaid twenty seventh article of the Treaty, and it shall appear, upon examination, that the act wherewith he is charged, was committed on board some ship or vessel of war belonging to his Britannic Majesty's navy, or in resisting the authority claimed over him, as belonging to such ship or vessel; and the person so charged shall, *on oath*, alledge in his defence, that he is a citizen of the United States, and that he was impressed on board the ship or vessel to which he is said to have belonged; it shall be the duty of the judge or justice to commit him only for safe keeping, during such time as, in the opinion of the said judge or justice, shall be necessary to *examine into such allegation*: and it shall be the duty of the judge or justice, to summon *such* witnesses, *not exceeding five in number, as shall be named by the prisoner; and also to summon such other witnesses as the prisoner shall satisfy him are material to prove him to be a citizen of the United States, to appear before him on a day and at a place to be named by himself, of which the person making the requisition shall have reasonable notice,* and to take their evidence, *as well as such counter testimony as may be adduced,* in writing, if such witnesses reside within the district where application is made, *and report the same*

1. On Apr. 2, John Nicholas introduced two amendments to a bill regarding the extradition clause of the Jay Treaty. The first was defeated on Apr. 28. *Annals of Congress*, X, 654, 691. When debate resumed on Apr. 29, JM proposed alterations to Nicholas's second amendment, which are rendered here in italics. When considerable opposition to JM's suggestions emerged, the House decided to postpone debate until Nicholas's second amendment could be printed with JM's proposed changes. Congress adjourned, however, without further debate on the bill. *Ibid.*, 691.

with his opinion thereon to the President of the United States; but if they reside elsewhere, within the United States, it shall be the duty of the said judge or justice to report the case to the President of the United States, together with the names and places of residence of the witnesses, on whose evidence the person charged shall rely: and the President of the United States is hereby authorized and empowered, to cause the examination of such witnesses to be taken in writing before some person authorized to administer oaths, and the examination so to be taken, to be transmitted to the said judge or justice, who shall *cause notice thereof to be given to the person making the requisition under the treaty as aforesaid, and shall allow a reasonable time for the production of any counter testimony, after which the whole of the testimony, with the opinion of the judge or justice thereon, shall be transmitted to the President of the United States; and if such opinion shall be that the person charged is a citizen of the United States, then he shall be considered as having been impressed,* unless *satisfactory* evidence be produced on the part of his Britannic Majesty, that the person charged as aforesaid, entered voluntarily on board such ship or vessel.

Committee Report

Printed, [U.S. Congress, House], *Report of the Committee to whom was referred, so much of the President's Speech, as relates to "A revision and amendment of the Judiciary System"* (Philadelphia, 1800)

[*ca. May 1, 1800, Philadelphia.* As part 2 of its report,[2] the committee submits a bill dealing with the administration of justice in the federal courts. Chief among its features is provision for bringing bills of exception and cases stated in the U.S. Circuit Courts before the U.S. Supreme Court. The bill also directs provisions for appointing commissioners and deputy marshals in U.S. District and Circuit Courts, for using examinations by commission and interrogatories, and for such other matters as pleadings, judgment on awards, taking of verdicts, and costs.]

2. The committee chairman, Robert Goodloe Harper, presented this report on May 1. The report and the accompanying bill were both read and ordered committed to the Committee of the Whole for consideration the following week. Apparently the bill was allowed to die during the final days of the session, for it was not discussed after May 1. *Annals of Congress,* X, 694; *Journal of the House of Representatives . . . first session of the Sixth Congress,* III (Washington, D.C., 1826), 688.

For the other work of the committee, see Committee Report, Mar. 11, 1800, and Legislative Bills, calendared at Mar. 11 and 31, 1800. See also Congressional Career: Editorial Note, Dec. 4, 1799.

Deed

Deed Book Copy, Office of the Clerk of Hardy County, Moorefield, W.Va.

[*May 4, 1800 (Hardy County, Va.*). By his attorney, Rawleigh Colston, JM conveys 1.5 acres in the South Branch Manor to John Rennick for £1 12s. 6d. The deed was recorded in the District Court at Hardy County on Sept. 9, 1800.]

Deed

Deed Book Copy, Office of the Clerk of Hardy County, Moorefield, W.Va.

[*May 7, 1800 (Hardy County, Va.*). By his attorney, Rawleigh Colston, JM conveys 17.5 acres in the South Branch Manor to Joseph Obannon for £5. The deed was recorded in the District Court at Hardy County on Sept. 9, 1800.]

To John Adams

ALS, Adams Papers, Massachusetts Historical Society

Sir   Philadelphia, May 8, 1800

I was informd yesterday afternoon that you had done me the honor to name me as the successor of Mr. McHenry.[3]

While I avow the impression made on me by this additional mark of your confidence—an impression which no time will efface—I must pray you sir to withdraw the nomination.

No man is more intimately persuaded than myself, of the wisdom of that political system which has been adopted by the government of my country, nor of the unvarying patriotism with which it has been pursued. It is therefore with peculiar regret I assure you that my private affairs claim an immediate attention incompatible with public office & oblige me to decline the honorable station you woud

3. Adams had sent JM's nomination for secretary of war to the Senate the previous day, and it was approved on May 9. JM recalled the circumstances of this unexpected action in John Stokes Adams, ed., *An Autobiographical Sketch by John Marshall* . . . (Ann Arbor, Mich., 1937), 27–28. See also Theodore Sedgwick to Rufus King, May 11, 1800, in King, ed., *Life and Corres. of Rufus King*, III, 239, and John Adams to the Senate, May 7, 1800, Records of the U.S. Senate, RG 46, National Archives.

have assignd me.[4] I am Sir with the most respectful esteem, Your Obedt. Servt.

J MARSHALL

From Charles Lee

Copy, Pickering Papers, Massachusetts Historical Society

Sir   Philadelphia, May 13, 1800
    The President of the United States being desirous of availing the public of your services, in the room of Timothy Pickering, Esqr. as Secretary of State, has been pleased, by and with the advice and consent of the Senate to appoint you to that office. I have now the honor to enclose the commission, to request you to be pleased to signify to me as early as possible your acceptance of the same, and to express to you the sentiments of respect, with which, I am, your most obed. servt.

CHARLES LEE
now executing the office of Secretary of State

Commission

Copy, RG 59, National Archives

Philadelphia, May 13, 1800
JOHN ADAMS, President of the United States of America.
    To all who shall see these presents—GREETING:
    KNOW YE, That reposing especial trust and Confidence, in the Patriotism, Integrity and abilities of JOHN MARSHALL of Virginia, I have nominated and by and with the advice and consent of the Senate DO appoint him Secretary of State, and do authorize and empower him to execute and fulfil the duties of that office according to Law; and to have and to hold the said office, with all the powers privileges and emoluments to the same of right appertaining, during the pleasure of the President of the United States for the time being.[5]

4. On the same day JM obtained permission to be absent for the remainder of the session. He left for Richmond to attend the meeting of the U.S. Circuit Court. See Congressional Career: Editorial Note, Dec. 4, 1799.

5. Adams nominated JM and Samuel Dexter (1761–1816) on May 12, 1800. The Senate confirmed his nominations on May 13. See Nomination, May 12, 1800, Virginia Historical Society, and Resolution of Consent, May 13, 1800, Entry 342, Senate Confirmations of Presidential Appointments, RG 59, National Archives.

IN TESTIMONY WHEREOF, I have caused
these Letters to be made Patent and the
seal of the United States to be hereunto
affixed. GIVEN under my Hand at the city
of Philadelphia the Thirteenth day of May
in the year of our Lord, one thousand eight
hundred, and of the Independence of the
United States of America, the twenty fourth.

[seal]

JOHN ADAMS

By the President

Charles Lee
now Executing the office of
Secretary of State

From American Envoys

ALS, RG 59, National Archives

[*May 17, 1800, Paris.*[6] The American envoys write to the secretary of
state, acknowledging his letters[7] and describing the contents of their last
dispatch of Apr. 18. They enclose copies of letters that give information
respecting the progress of the negotiation.[8] This progress has been hindered
by the illness of Talleyrand, who, as minister of exterior relations, has been
instructing the French ministers in the negotiations. Nonetheless, the American envoys have persevered in pressing "*the whole length of the proposd treaty
with a view of avoiding all useless discussion, of fixing the attention* of the Ministers
to *the real point of difference.*" The envoys also write: "*Our success is yet doubtful.
The french think it hard to indemnify for violating engagements unless they can thereby
be restored to the benefits of them.*" The envoys conclude with news of the European campaign and of French impressment of American vessels.]

6. The letter is endorsed "recd. aug. 22d 1800, Ex," although it is likely another copy
arrived much earlier. The words in italics were originally in code and were decoded by a
State Department clerk.
JM sent this dispatch to Adams with no covering letter on Aug. 24. He sent the
enclosed decrees to Adams in his letter of Aug. 25. See JM to Adams, Aug. 25 and Sept.
12, 1800, and Adams to JM, Sept. 4, 1800.
7. See Timothy Pickering to American Envoys, Feb. 14 and Mar. 7, 1800, Ellsworth
Letterbook, Connecticut Historical Society. The former letter is also printed in *Amer.
State Papers, Foreign Relations*, II, 324.
8. The enclosed letters are French Ministers to Envoys, May 6, 1800, and Envoys to
French Ministers, May 8, 1800, printed in *Amer. State Papers, Foreign Relations*, II, 319–
321. The first letter explained the French belief that the negotiators must determine the
principles governing relations between the two nations before indemnities could be discussed—an allusion to the French insistence that the Treaty of 1778 must be recognized
before claims could be made. The envoys' letter stated that American claims were based

From Timothy Pickering

AD, RG 59, National Archives

[Washington, May 17, 1800]
Memorandum.

Barbary Affairs.

There are three lists of *Regalia*, that is, of maritime & military stores, for Tunis.

No. 1. In Capt. O'Brien's journal concerning Tunis, p. 14.—*there* marked No. 3. & called *determined* terms.[1]

No. 2. The articles as demanded by the Bey of Capt. Eaton, in 1799, increased by larger dimensions of plank & scantling, and by the addition of 200 quintals of cordage, equal to 10 tons.[2]

No. 3. A list (herewith) which I think was made out for General Stevens,[3] noting the difference between Tunissian & American quintals, and proposing sizes of timber & plank larger than O'Brien's & less than Eatons. In fact, to load the Hero, it was necessary to take such plank as could be found at market. The invoice in the office will show what articles were sent in the Hero, Capt. Robinson,[4] last winter, for Tunis. General Stevens is providing the residue. But it may be expedient to enquire of him whether there be any articles

---

on the Treaty of 1778 for violations prior to July 7, 1798, when Congress voided the treaty because of French unwillingness to honor it, and on the law of nations subsequent to July 7, 1798; the envoys believed therefore that claims could be considered before principles of a treaty were discussed.

1. See "Captain O'Brien's Negotiations in Barbary 1796–1797," Consular Despatches, Algiers, II, RG 59, National Archives. Richard O'Brien (*ca.* 1758–1824) was U.S. consul at Algiers.

2. The Treaty of Peace and Friendship between Tunis and the United States was concluded at Tunis on Aug. 28, 1797, and was signed with alterations on Mar. 26, 1799. The final treaty was ratified by the Senate on Jan. 10, 1800. William Eaton (1764–1811), who with James L. Cathcart (1767–1843) and O'Brien represented the United States at the extended negotiations, reported that the bey accepted the 1797 treaty with three alterations: "The consent of the Bey for six months forbearance in expectation of the regalia of maritime and military stores—His *demand* for a present in jewels—and his *request* for a cruiser." See Miller, ed., *Treaties*, II, 420.

3. Ebenezer Stevens (1751–1823) was a New York City merchant and major general of the state militia.

4. The *Hero*, Capt. John Robinson, arrived in Tunis on Apr. 12, 1800, after setting sail in the first week of February.

which cannot conveniently be obtained at New-York. Perhaps the Navy Department can furnish the Cannon, of the kind (heavy ones) which it may be desirable to discard from the American Navy.

Algiers.

The lists (within) of merchandize, signed by O'Brien April 2. 1799, was furnished the late purveyor.[5] He shipped a part in the Sophia. The bill of lading & invoice are in the office. The remainder to be sent in the Washington frigate, daily expected round from Newport. This merchandize is for the purpose of forming in Algiers a fund for paying the debts & answering demands, on acct. of the U.States for all the three Barbary Regences of Algiers, Tunis & Tripoli.

The other lists, for the Regency & the Dey, require attention: the articles not already sent in the Sophia, should go in the Washington. Some of the articles of merchandize cannot be got in america, or at least in the quantities demanded. Consult Dr. Gillaspey,[6] who was employed by Mr. Francis to procure the articles referred to in the items distinguished by Note No. 1. to Note No. 5.

Mr. Humphreys[7] is sawing some pine logs into the large plank for Algiers. If he has orders for the purpose, he will see to the selection of the planks (oak as well as pine) and timber for Algiers.

It appears by Capt. O'Brien's dispatches, that in February last he made a lumping settlement with Algiers, of which the following is the result.

The Military and naval stores stipulated at the making of peace, were estimated by Mr. Donaldson[8] at $57,500. With an addition of $4150. for an after demand: but that the Deys Secretary after this declared that the latter sum must be increased to

$ 7 500.

57,500

making in the whole .... Dollars 65 000.

5. See Richard O'Brien to Pickering, Apr. 12, 1799, Pickering Papers, Massachusetts Historical Society. Israel Whelen (1752–1806) succeeded Tench Francis (1730–1800) on May 13, 1800. For more information on Whelen's appointment, see Harold C. Syrett et al., eds., *The Papers of Alexander Hamilton*, XXIV (New York, 1976), 552.

6. George Gillaspy was the naval doctor in Philadelphia.

7. Joshua Humphreys (1751–1838) was a shipbuilder and naval architect. On June 28, 1794, he was appointed naval constructor for the United States.

8. Joseph Donaldson, Jr., was the chief negotiator for the treaty between the United States and Algiers that was signed on Sept. 5, 1795, and ratified by the Senate on Mar. 7, 1796.

The amount of the stores actually delivered at Algiers, as *there* rated, was only .... 66,096.
(as by O'Brien's acct. No. 24.)

*But O'Brien assured the Dey & Ministry that the stipulated stores for the *peace*, amounted only to 60,000 dollars.[9]

The Purveyor in 1796, estimated the cost of these stores and their freight to Algiers, at .... $120,037.
But experience has proved that they would cost much more. And for

The annuity of 12 000 sequins, equal only to .... $ 21,600.

Congress have actually appropriated Per Ann....... $ 72,123.

which for two years, would be $144,246

But by taking the annuity in Cash, at 12,000 sequins—for 2 years 24,000. equal .... $43,200. only
And putting the two armed schooners at
30,000 sequins[1] = ... 54,000.

There remained paid towards the 3d. years annuity ... $ 10,800.
*And the surplus of stores actually delivered beyond the stipulation for the peace[2] .... 6,096.
$ 16,896.

Remain to be paid of the 3d year's annuity .... 4,704.
$ 21,600.

Arrears of 3d years annuity .... Dollars 4,704.
Annuity for the 4th year, ending Septr. 5. 1799 .... 21,600.

To Thomas Hungerford

ALS, Virginia Historical Society

Dear Sir[3]   Richmond, May 22, 1800
    Your letter of the 6th. of May reachd me by last nights mail.[4] It had traveld to Philadelphia & returnd to this place. If I had even been in Philadelphia it woud have been out of my power to have renderd you any service.

    9. This sentence was inserted later by Pickering.
    1. The word "sequins" was added in a different hand.
    2. This sentence was inserted later by Pickering.
    3. This is item no. Mss2M3567a7 in the society's collections. This letter is addressed to Hungerford (*ca.* 1739–1803) in Westmoreland, Va.
    4. Not found.

The land warrant is not evidence that you servd to the end of the war. In order to have obtain your final settlements if you have not drawn them the returns in the office woud have been examind which show the names of all those who were in service to the end of the war. If you had even been found on the returns it woud not have availd you because there is an act of limitations which woud now be an absolute bar to the claim.[5] I return you the warrant & am dear Sir, Your obedt

J Marshall

From Rufus King

ALS, RG 59, National Archives

[*May 22, 1800, London.* In his dispatch no. 71,[6] King sends news of an attempted assassination of King George III at a theater in London on May 15. The remainder of the letter contains news of events on the Continent.]

From Rufus King

ALS, RG 59, National Archives

No. 72.
Dear Sir[7]   London, May 25, 1800

I yesterday received a letter from Mr. Smith at Lisbon, inclosing a letter and several Papers dated in October last from Mr Eaton our Consul at Tunis.[8] According to Mr. Eaton's representation, the

---

5. "An Act regulating the grants of land appropriated for military service" had an act of limitation set for Jan. 1, 1800. In 1799, however, the limitation was extended until Jan. 1, 1802, when "all warrants or claims for lands on account of military services, which shall not, before the day aforesaid, be registered and located, shall be for ever barred." 1 Stat. 490 (1796), 724 (1799).

6. See JM to John Adams, July 24, 1800, by which he forwarded this letter to the president.

7. JM endorsed the duplicate of this letter "Recd. July 23, 1800" and forwarded it to John Adams in his letter of July 24.

8. See William Eaton to King, Mar. 31 and Apr. 1, 1800, Consular Despatches, Tunis, I, RG 59, National Archives, with Eaton's enclosure of the list of jewels for the bey of Tunis. This list is also included in King, ed., *Life and Corres. of Rufus King*, III, 247. William L. Smith's letter to King merely recommended that King assist in acquiring the jewels for the bey.

Smith sent JM two reports on this problem, the earlier of which arrived on July 19, and the latter on the same day as King's dispatch no. 72. On June 4, he wrote that he had sent the bey's dagger to King to be mounted with gold and diamonds. See Smith to [JM], May 6, 7, and June 4, 1800, Diplomatic Despatches, Portugal, V, RG 59, Natl. Arch.

Peace, which he states to have been concluded with the Bey of Tunis, is in danger of being broken, by the Delay that has arisen in the delivery of the stipulated Supply of military and naval stores, and for want of what is called the customary present of Jewels, which it is alledged the persons who negotiated the Treaty sanctioned the Bey's expectation of receiving. The object of Mr Eatons letter to me is to engage me to purchase and send to Tunis the Jewels and other articles, a list of which he has inclosed, estimated by the Bey to be worth forty thousand Dollars, but which Mr. Eaton supposes may be purchased in England for half that Sum. The military Stores, which Mr Eaton thought of entering into a Contract with certain English Traders at times to supply, giving them Bills on me, have according to Mr Smith's information been sent from the U.S. Mr Smith who I presume is acquainted with the state of our Barbary affairs, gives no explicit opinion concerning the purchase of these Jewels, tho I conclude from the tenor of his Letter that he is on the whole rather disposed to acquiesce in the demand: but as I am entirely without information or authority on this subject, & have no knowledge whatever respecting the intentions & measures of the Government, I shall not without a direct & explicit request from Mr Smith comply with Mr. Eaton's demand. I will however immediately apply to Mr Boulton of Bermingham, who is able to manufacture and prepare, on lower Terms than any other, the articles enumerated in the list of Jewels, for an estimate of the Price at which he will engage to supply them.[9] This Estimate I will send to Mr. Smith with an answer corresponding with the tenor of this Letter. I submit to your consideration whether it will not be expedient, by some means or other, that I should be made acquainted with the situation of our Barbary connections, if there is any probability that I am from time to time to be called upon to excercize a Discretion concerning them. Should Mr Smith, before I can receive your answer to this Letter, ask my assistance in the Execution of his orders, I shall give it in the best way in my power. But uninformed as I am, I shall do nothing of my own Discretion, nor shall I hereafter be inclined to interfere on any occasion, unless I hear from you, that such interference, may in the presidents Opinion be necessary: in this case, I must repete the Observation, it will be proper that I should be kept fully acquainted with the situation of our Barbary affairs. With perfect Respect & Esteem, I have the honor to be Dr. Sir, Yr. Ob. & faithful Sert.

RUFUS KING

9. See King to [JM], calendared at June 6, 1800.

From Jonathan Trumbull

ALS, Jonathan Trumbull, Jr., Papers, Connecticut Historical Society

Sir[1]   Hartford, May 30, 1800

In compliance with the terms & provisions of an Act of Congress passed at their lasst session, I have the Honor to transmit to the office of the Secretary of State for the U States, the enclosed Act of Renunciation & Deed of Cession, on the part of the State of Connecticut, of the Jurisdiction of that Territory commonly called the Western Reserve of Connecticut, for the observation & acceptance of the President of the U States.[2]

When received I beg the favor of your giving me early information of their being placed in your hands & lodged in your office for the purpose mentioned.[3] With high regard & consideration I am, Sir, Your Obedt Servant

JONA TRUMBULL

Law Papers, May 1800

U.S. Circuit Court, Va.

Backhouse's Administratrix v. Hunter (debt for $8,238.44), special verdict, AD, U.S. Circuit Court, Va., Ended Cases (Unrestored), Virginia State Library.

Backhouse's Administratrix v. Hunter (debt for $16,000.00), special verdict, AD, U.S. Circuit Court, Va., Ended Cases (Unrestored), Va. State Lib.

Secretary of State

EDITORIAL NOTE

Near the end of the first session of the Sixth Congress, John Marshall left Philadelphia for Richmond, hoping to rebuild his law practice during the summer recess. One month later, however, he was in Washington as the newly appointed secretary of state. His tenure in this position, though brief, was marked by the same quiet but

1. Trumbull (1740–1809) was governor of Connecticut at this time.
2. See 2 Stat. 56–57. This act is printed in Carter, ed., *Terr. Papers, NW*, III, 84–86. See also Committee Report, calendared at Mar. 21, 1800, Legislative Bill, calendared at *ca.* Mar. 21, 1800, and Speeches, calendared at Apr. 7 and 8, 1800.
3. See JM to Trumbull, June 9, 1800.

determined efficiency that had characterized his career in public office up to that point.

When John Adams finally decided, late in his term as president, to reorganize the cabinet he had inherited from George Washington, he appointed Marshall—without his consent—secretary of war. Marshall was on the verge of leaving for Richmond, and he politely refused the position.[4] His loyal support of Adams and of Adams's administration, however, made Marshall an obvious choice for a cabinet post. It is not surprising, therefore, that a few weeks later Adams tried once again to get Marshall to join the executive branch by nominating him as the successor to Timothy Pickering.[5] Marshall's strategic position in Congress as leader of the southern Federalists, his diplomatic experience in France, and his loyalty were substantive reasons for appointing him to the cabinet; the impending presidential election of 1800 made consolidation of the administration especially important. Consequently, Adams sent Marshall's nomination as secretary of state to the Senate on May 13, again neglecting to obtain the Virginia congressman's consent.[6]

Marshall was in Richmond attending court when he heard of this second nomination by Adams. His return home had given him a new perspective on accepting a position in the cabinet, which had been missing in Philadelphia. The law practice he had left the previous fall was difficult to rebuild. Clients were reluctant to turn to him for legal assistance because he had a second session of Congress to attend the following winter and would not be on hand to shepherd litigation through the courts. Furthermore, Marshall's political foes had regrouped for the upcoming presidential election, and their attacks on him were stronger than ever. Aware that a Republican victory in the fall was a real possibility, he was unwilling to be defeated for reelection. As secretary of state, Marshall would be able to serve through the remainder of Adams's term and return to his law practice without suffering the personal pain of electoral defeat. Marshall believed, moreover, that his involvement in elective politics had lessened his desirability as an attorney. By accepting appointment to the cabinet, he would escape the image of being a "political man" and hold an office for which he considered himself well qualified. Accordingly, he accepted the president's appointment by writing Charles Lee, the acting secretary of state, sometime in the last week of May.[7]

The president had already set out for Washington, where he intended to meet with the new secretaries to see that their departments were properly established in the new capital. Both Lee and Benjamin Stoddert, secretary of the navy, wrote to Adams with the good news of Marshall's acceptance, hoping to reach the president in the course of his journey southward.[8] By the time Adams had reached Frederick, Maryland, on June 1, he had received word that Marshall had accepted the appointment and would be arriving in Washington soon after the president.[9]

4. See John Stokes Adams, ed., *An Autobiographical Sketch by John Marshall* . . . (Ann Arbor, Mich., 1937), 27, and JM to John Adams, May 8, 1800.
5. See Congressional Career: Editorial Note, Dec. 4, 1799.
6. See Commission, May 13, 1800.
7. Adams, ed., *Autobiographical Sketch*, 28–29; Charles Lee to John Adams, May 29, 1800, Adams Papers, Massachusetts Historical Society.
8. Charles Lee to Adams, May 28 and 29, 1800, and Benjamin Stoddert to Adams, May 28, 1800, Adams Papers.
9. William Smith Shaw to Abigail Adams, June 1, 1800, Adams Papers (mistakenly filed under June 5).

The *Register* of the Department of State indicates that Marshall assumed his duties officially on June 6, but this date is incorrect. He left Richmond on June 5, the day after the U.S. Circuit Court adjourned, sharing a coach with Samuel Chase, the associate justice who had just presided over the famous trial of James T. Callender. On June 7, Marshall was in Alexandria, and he probably did not arrive in Washington until the following day. Adams, Marshall, and Samuel Dexter, the secretary of war, lodged together in the Washington City Hotel, across from the rising Capitol, where they worked for one week before Adams left to spend the summer in Quincy.[1]

The president no doubt discussed three areas of the nation's foreign affairs that were of paramount concern to him: (1) the mission to France; (2) relations with Great Britain; and (3) relations with the Barbary powers.[2] The so-called Ellsworth Mission to France had been launched the previous November, and Marshall, with the rest of the members of Congress, had followed the news of the arrival of the envoys in Paris. Significant information was slow in coming, however, and Marshall and Adams had little to discuss until August. At that time the news was not encouraging, and both men began to face the possibility of a failed mission. In the course of the negotiations, however, the envoys determined to disregard their specific instructions and to deal with the French on what appeared to be acceptable terms. Thereafter, an agreement was quickly arrived at, and by the end of September the envoys left Paris. News of this success did not reach Washington until December, whereupon Adams sent the Convention of 1800 to the Senate for approval. John Marshall played only a minor role in these negotiations. When Adams despaired over the lack of progress in reaching an agreement and intimated to Marshall that he might ask Congress to declare war against France, Marshall counseled patience, confident that the new government under Napoleon was more inclined to develop a peaceful relationship with the United States than was the government he had negotiated with during the XYZ affair. In the end his counsel reinforced the president's determination to obtain a new treaty.[3]

Marshall had to deal more immediately with the dispute with Great Britain over article 6 of the Jay Treaty. Both the Philadelphia and the London commissions, one meeting to settle the debt issue and the other to discuss seizure cases, had broken off negotiations the previous summer. Timothy Pickering had been slow in dealing with the resulting impasse, and Adams had been preoccupied with the French mission and the difficult session of Congress. Three months before he was removed from office, Pickering had sent new instructions to Rufus King, but the British were

1. U.S. Department of State, *Biographic Register* (Washington, D.C., 1937), 325; *Virginia Federalist* (Richmond), June 7, 1800, 3; William Smith Shaw to Abigail Adams, June 8, 1800, and John Adams to Abigail Adams, June 13, 1800, Adams Papers; and Federal Writers' Works Progress Administration, *Washington: City and Capital* (Washington, D.C., 1937), 627. On Callender's trial, see James Morton Smith, *Freedom's Fetters: The Alien and Sedition Laws and American Civil Liberties* (Ithaca, N.Y., 1956), 356.

2. The best general account of these and other issues and JM's experience with them as secretary of state is Andrew J. Montague, "John Marshall," in Samuel Flagg Bemis, ed., *American Secretaries of State and Their Diplomacy*, II (New York, 1927), 247–284.

3. See the correspondence between the envoys and JM and between JM and Adams. See also Alexander DeConde, *The Quasi-War: The Politics and Diplomacy of the Undeclared War with France, 1797–1801* (New York, 1966), 223–258, and Albert Hall Bowman, *The Struggle for Neutrality: Franco-American Diplomacy during the Federalist Era* (Knoxville, Tenn., 1974), 386–414.

not mollified. In April, Lord Grenville hinted that a lump-sum payment, by avoiding the inevitable disagreements arising from a joint commission, might end the dispute most easily. King's report of this conversation with Grenville reached Washington after Marshall had become secretary of state, and Marshall advised Adams to accept the idea. Encouraged by the president, Marshall sent King formal instructions to negotiate a lump-sum settlement with the British and end the diplomatic stalemate. This action did not result in the final settlement of the issue because the Pitt government resigned before details could be agreed upon. The tense relationship with England was greatly eased, however, and the foundation for a settlement was laid.[4]

In September, Marshall sustained the spirit of conciliation by formulating lengthy instructions for King designed to settle other differences existing between the two countries. Andrew J. Montague extravagantly termed this dispatch "a document ranking among the very greatest of American papers, and perhaps unequalled in the diplomatic contributions of the English-speaking world."[5] Marshall wrote that the British should not be allowed to blame the difficult relationship between the two countries on the president's decision to send a new mission to France. He argued that America was trying to maintain neutrality in the current war between France and England and that in pursuance of that policy, "we have avoided, & we shall continue to avoid, any political connections which might engage us further than is compatible with the neutrality we profess, and we have sought, by a conduct just & friendly to all, to be permitted to maintain a position which, without offence to any, we had a right to take." The United States had prepared for war out of necessity, and it was a situation in which "we are placd—not by our own acts—but by the acts of others; & which we change, so soon as the conduct of others will permit us to change it."[6] These instructions reveal Marshall at his best, having mastered the issues confronting the nation from abroad and having matured in his own long-standing support of Federalist foreign policy.

Affairs on the high seas made the official policy of neutrality difficult to maintain in 1800, particularly as diplomatic relations became more complicated following Napoleon's accession to power. Complaints of impressments, confiscations, or violations of foreign nations' rights arrived at the State Department with increasing frequency. These events affected United States negotiations with France and England, as well as with Spain. Throughout his tenure, Marshall remained temperate in his actions and defended American neutrality in statements that clearly explained the role the United States was pursuing in relation to these European nations.

The irritation caused by the Barbary powers demanded an inordinate amount of Marshall's time. Treaties between the United States and Algiers, Tunis, and Tripoli had been ratified by 1799, and Adams had appointed consuls in anticipation of the establishment of normal diplomatic relations. In return for a tribute of money, naval and military supplies, and jewels (in the case of Tunis), the Barbary powers agreed to allow American shipping to pass unmolested.[7] The effect of carrying out the terms

4. See Bradford Perkins, *The First Rapprochement: England and the United States, 1795–1805* (Berkeley, Calif., 1967), 116–120, 126. See also the exchange of correspondence between Rufus King and JM and between JM and Adams.

5. Montague, "John Marshall," in Bemis, ed., *Secretaries of State*, 265.

6. JM to King, Sept. 20, 1800.

7. See Glenn Tucker, *Dawn like Thunder: The Barbary Wars and the Birth of the U.S. Navy* (Indianapolis, Ind., 1963), 107–127.

of these treaties occupied Marshall and the purveyor of goods for the United States, Israel Whelen, to a degree disproportionate to the importance of American relations with these countries. Marshall tried for weeks to obtain a reliable statement of the country's account with the Barbary powers. The attempt in the aftermath of the Jay Treaty at settling accounts with Great Britain through a lump-sum payment suggested to Marshall that a similar settlement with the bey of Tunis might be successful in ridding the United States of much troublesome business.[8] No settlement was effected, however, and throughout the summer Marshall and Whelen purchased supplies and shipped goods to the Mediterranean pirates according to the terms of the treaties.

In addition to keeping abreast of the foreign affairs of the United States, Marshall spent some of his first month in the department supervising the many domestic duties that were required of it.[9] Among these were the granting of patents, copyrights, and passports, the taking of the census, the recording of land patents, the supervision of the Mint (which had remained in Philadelphia), the printing and distribution of the laws of the United States, the preparation and delivery of commissions of appointment, and the large and complicated responsibility of supervising the territories of the United States. The administration of justice fell to the State Department during this period, as well, the role of the attorney general being merely advisory. An immediate and highly important responsibility was supervising the work of the commissioners appointed to oversee the construction of the public buildings in the new capital. This work became more pressing in the fall as Congress prepared to convene and the Adamses planned to move into the new president's house.

While Marshall was secretary of state, Adams retained his direction over the nation's foreign policy, just as he had while Pickering served as head of the department. Marshall's impact during his brief tenure may have been greater than is generally believed, however, because he helped to implement policies his predecessor had tried to stymie. Adams's prolonged absence during the summer of 1800 added stature to Marshall's role as advisor, and his advice was clearly accepted on several significant occasions. Adams seldom if ever rescinded Marshall's actions, and he never returned a letter of instruction prepared by his secretary of state. Indeed he often sent on these instructions immediately, highly pleased with their contents. At the same time, Marshall did not attempt to control or direct American foreign policy, and he clearly viewed his role as that of secretary. Adams had complete confidence in Marshall's loyalty and in the Virginian's support of his attempt to maintain peace. Furthermore, Adams respected the experience Marshall had acquired in Paris, and he hoped to use Marshall's position as leader of the southern Federalists to strengthen his chances for reelection to the presidency in the fall. These two men worked well together; certainly theirs was the most harmonious and compatible relationship that had existed between any president and secretary of state

8. See Timothy Pickering to JM, May 17, 1800, JM to Israel Whelen, calendared at June 28, 1800, and JM to Richard O'Brien, July 29, 1800. O'Brien suggested that $30,000 might satisfy the Algerines.

9. Much of this kind of work is described in Gaillard Hunt, *The Department of State of the United States: Its History and Functions* (Washington, D.C., 1893), 80–86, and U.S. Department of State, *History of the Department of State of the United States . . .* (Washington, D.C., 1901), 22–25. See also Leonard D. White, *The Federalists: A Study in Administrative History* (New York, 1948), 128–144.

up to that point in the young republic. Abigail Adams said the nation needed "cool dispassionate Heads, as well as honest Hearts" during those difficult months of 1800.[1] Marshall fit the description as well as anyone in the party, and better than most.

From Rufus King

ALS, RG 59, National Archives

[*June 6, 1800, London.* King relates in dispatch no. 74[2] that he was "mistaken in supposing the Jewels enumerated in Mr. Eaton's Note[3] could be obtained at Birmingham: Mr. Boulton informs me that these articles are not made there; and I have taken measures to ascertain their cost, should we be obliged to purchase them, in London."

He further writes, partially in code, "In conversation with the *Lord chancelor*[4] a few days ago, he remarked, speaking of *the sixth article of the treaty* that the *best manner of* settling the *late difference & avoiding future disagreements woud be the payment of a gross sum* and that he never knew *an arbitration* which did not come to something of this sort."

King concludes with news of European military and diplomatic affairs.]

To James Monroe

ALS, Executive Papers, Virginia State Library

Sir[5]   Alexandria, June 7, 1800

Having been appointed by the President of the United States to the office of secretary of State I am no longer a representative in congress of the district for which I was elected. I shoud have sooner notified this vacancy to you had I been certain that it woud have existed. With very much respect, I am Sir your obedt

J MARSHALL

1. Abigail Adams to John Quincy Adams, May 15, 1800, Adams Papers.
2. JM wrote on the verso, "No. 74, recd Septr. 4th. 1800," but on another copy JM wrote, "No. 74, recd Aug. 9th. 1800." This dispatch is printed in King, ed., *Life and Corres. of Rufus King*, III, 252–253.
3. See William Eaton to King, Apr. 1, 1800, Consular Despatches, Tunis, I, RG 59, National Archives. See also King to [JM], May 25, 1800, on jewels for the bey of Tunis.
4. Words in italics represent words that were originally in code. The lord chancellor was Alexander Wedderburn, Lord Loughborough (1733–1805).
5. James Monroe had been elected governor of Virginia on Dec. 19, 1799. The Council of State called for an election to fill JM's seat on June 14. See *Journals of the Council of the State of Virginia*, June 14, 1800, Virginia State Library.

From John Steele

DS, RG 59, National Archives

[*June 7, 1800 (Washington)*. Enclosing a commission appointing Thomas Taylor of Richmond a customs official, Steele[6] advises JM that Oliver Wolcott wants the president to reconsider his appointment. Wolcott believes William Davies is better qualified because of "his standing in society . . . and that if the President had been apprized of his pretensions the commission would have been offered to him in the first instance." He quotes from a letter received from William Heth strongly recommending Davies. Steele wants JM to obtain the president's final decision as soon as possible.]

From William Tazewell

ALS, RG 59, National Archives

Dr. Sir   [Williamsburg], June 8, 1800

Your exertions in Congress in favor of the payment of my demand upon Government call forth my most grateful acknowledgments.[7]

The deduction that has been made on my acct. is a heavy stroke upon me, it leaves me out of pocket just about what I should have gained by my secretaryship had I declined going to London (an expedition I always thought very unnecessary) & returned to America with Mr. Gerry. But this my evil Stars forbad. I endeavour however to bear the blow with patient resignation, as when I view the respectable names of some of the members that voted against me, I am almost persuaded that it comes from the hand of justice. Tho' I shall ever be of opinion that the part of the Acct allow'd viz expences of capture was undoubtedly the most disputable. How after terminating my commission on my arrival in London any posterior expences

6. Steele (1764–1815), comptroller of the Treasury, was responsible for the settling of public accounts. See Noble E. Cunningham, Jr., *The Process of Government under Jefferson* (Princeton, N.J., 1978), 99–101.

William Davies (1749–1821), formerly a customs official in Petersburg, was granted the position of collector of the port of Richmond. On Sept. 13, 1800, he was recommended for collector of customs at Norfolk, a position left vacant by the death of Otway Byrd. See Oliver Wolcott to John Adams, Sept. 13, 1800, Adams Papers, Massachusetts Historical Society. See also William Davies file, Letters of Application & Recommendation during the Administration of John Adams, 1797–1801, RG 59, National Archives, and *Amer. State Papers, Miscellaneous*, I, 275.

7. See Legislative Petition, Mar. 13, 1800.

should be allow'd me I can not comprehend; but this is perhaps to be attributed to my own imbecility.

I here enclose you my Acct. stated as I suppose tis intended it should stand. In your last you mention that I am not to be allow'd for my passage home.[8] I conclude you meant my passage from London in case I had not been captured; Have therefore charged my passage from Lisbon, being one of the expences incur'd by capture.

The charge for the first item you find I have left blank as I can not suppose government will take advantage of my having charged 112 1/2 dollars per month when I expected to be paid up to my arrival in Philadelphia & settle at the same rate for the few weeks they admit me to have been occupied in the execution of my commission. This mode of charging never came into my head till I rec'd Mr. Gerry's letter in Philadelphia in which you have seen stated that he expected me to be paid for my "services & expences till my arrival in Philadelphia."

Considering that I am to pay my own expencess of living & traveling in England & thence home, I hope 400 dols. will not be regarded an unreasonable charge; It is much less, I am fully convinced, than any young man in Paris could have been engaged to do the business for, leaving out of the question, the sacrifices my particular situation render'd it necessary I should make on undertaking it.

Should you not think yourself authorised to allow this, I will write to Mr. Gerry & know what compensation he contemplated my receiving when he employed me, & be finally regulated by what he shall say. I am anxious the business should be closed for a plurality of reasons, but more especially that I am anxious to settle my debt to you. Mr. Pickering, after my arrival in America, paid a Bill for me drawn in favor of Bulkely & Son Lisbon, and advanced me some money to bear my expences from Philadelphia to Virga. The amount you will find in an acknowledgment given him in his official capacity. With the most sincere esteem & respect I remain Yr Obt. Sert.

WILLIAM TAZEWELL

My Relation L. Waller Tazewell is spoken of here as your successor in Congress, also Col. S. Griffin.[9]

W. T.

8. Neither Tazewell's account nor JM's letter to Tazewell has been found. See Timothy Pickering to JM, Apr. 1, 1800, for the source of this disallowance. See also Tazewell to JM, Aug. 22, 1800.

9. Littleton Waller Tazewell (1774–1860) was elected to replace JM in Congress. Samuel Griffin (1739–1810) did not run for office.

To Jonathan Trumbull

ALS, Jonathan Trumbull, Jr., Papers, Connecticut Historical Society

Sir   Washington, June 9, 1800
Your letter of the 30th. of May accompanying an act of renunciation & deed of cession on the part of the State of connecticut, of the jurisdiction of that territory commonly calld the western reserve of connecticut, has been receivd, & the accompanying papers have been laid before the President.

He thinks them sufficient & has directed them to be deposited in the office of State for the purposes for which the deed was executed. With very much respect & consideration, I have the honor to be, Your obedt Servt

                                                    J MARSHALL

From Rufus King

ALS, RG 59, National Archives

[*June 11, 1800, London*. King notifies the State Department, in dispatch no. 75,[1] that Benjamin West, president of the Royal Academy and a native-born American, has submitted a design for a monument in memory of George Washington.]

To David Jones

ALS, American Baptist Historical Society, Rochester, N.Y.

Dear Sir[2]   Washington, June 12, 1800
I receivd your letter inclosing a bill stating your case in which you wishd me to institute a suit in chancery. Having left the bar for a short time I placd your papers in the hands of Mr. Randolph. I did this in consequence of the desire you expressd in your letter to employ him in the cause.[3] I am Sir very respectfully, your obedt. Servt

                                                    J MARSHALL

1. This letter is printed in King, ed., *Life and Corres. of Rufus King*, III, 255. West's design has not been found, but see King to West, June 9, 1800, *ibid.*, 254–255. West (1728–1820) was president of the Royal Academy from 1792 to 1820. His design was not used when the monument was begun in 1833.

2. JM addressed this letter to "The reverend David Jones, Grave creek, To be sent to the post office, Wheeling."

3. The letter enclosing a bill and mentioning Edmund Randolph has not been found. See JM to Jones, Aug. 2, 1800. See also Vol. III, 69.

From Rufus King

ALS, RG 59, National Archives

[*June 12, 1800, London.* King writes, in dispatch no. 76,[4] that as he has not heard from William L. Smith about the jewels for the bey, he has hopes that Smith has been able to avoid the demand since the jewels cannot be obtained in Birmingham. The jewels in London could not be procured for less than £7,000 sterling. "The principal articles could not immediately be furnished at any price, as they are never made except by order, and it would require a year to complete them."]

To Arthur St. Clair

LS, The Rosenbach Foundation, Philadelphia

Sir[5]   Washington, June 12, 1800

I have the honor to enclose, for your information, a copy of An Act of Congress, entitled, "An Act to divide the Territory of the United States, North West of the Ohio, into two seperate governments;"[6] and to be, With great respect, your Excellency's, Most obed. servt.

J. MARSHALL

From James Williams

ALS, RG 59, National Archives

[*June 12, 1800, Annapolis.* Williams writes that a ship he loaded with goods bound for Havana in December was captured by an armed schooner flying French colors but manned by Spanish sailors. The ship was taken to Havana and condemned there. Williams encloses an invoice of the cargo and a protest filed with the Spanish government by the U.S. consul at Havana.[7]]

4. This dispatch was received by the State Department on Aug. 23, 1800, and is printed in King, ed., *Life and Corres. of Rufus King*, III, 256.

5. St. Clair (1734–1818) was appointed governor of the Northwest Territory upon its formation in 1789 and served until Nov. 22, 1802.

6. See 2 Stat. 58–59. This act is printed in Carter, ed., *Terr. Papers, NW*, III, 86–88.

7. See JM to Williams, June 16, 1800. Williams (d. *ca.* 1818) was a merchant from Annapolis, Md.

From Winthrop Sargent

LS, RG 59, National Archives

[*June 15, 1800 (Natchez)*. Sargent[8] complains of the misrepresentation of his territorial government to Congress by Narsworthy Hunter on behalf of some of the inhabitants of Mississippi.[9] Sargent says that "the change in Government which it appears he [Hunter] has nearly effectuated—So far from giving satisfaction to a discontented party, will but multiply and increase complaint within the Territory." He is surprised that Hunter's representation to Congress has been given more credence than his own.

Sargent replies to several charges of misconduct made against him, averring that he has been working under many hardships. His actions have been misinterpreted; for example, "the appointment of Officers Civil and Military and the visit made to Mr. Ellicot[1] seem to be the great Crimes of the Governour, as charged by Cato West and Mass." Sargent protests the charges made by some of the inhabitants of Mississippi and desires to efface the unfavorable impression made on the federal government by their claims of injustice.]

To William Vans Murray

Letterbook Copy, RG 59, National Archives

[*June 16, 1800, Washington.* JM writes on behalf of Jeremiah Yellott, of Baltimore, whose vessel and cargo had been seized by French privateers

8. Sargent (1753–1820) was confirmed governor of the Mississippi Territory on June 28, 1798. This letter was written to Timothy Pickering but received by JM.

9. See Carter, ed., *Terr. Papers, Mississippi*, III, 45–105, for the state papers relating to this letter. See also *Amer. State Papers, Miscellaneous*, I, 203–206, 207, 214, 233–241; *Annals of Congress*, X, 1376–1397; Sargent to JM, calendared at Aug. 25, 1800, and Sargent to JM, Sept. 5, 1800. The case against Sargent was dismissed on Mar. 3, 1801. *Annals of Congress*, X, 1074.

Narsworthy Hunter was sent by a committee to Washington to present to Congress the grievances of the inhabitants of Mississippi. Sponsored by William C. C. Claiborne (1775–1817) and Thomas T. Davis, his petition urged that Mississippi's territorial government be expanded to allow for the popular election of one house and that land grants made before the Pinckney Treaty should be legally confirmed. The main topic of debate both in Congress and in Sargent's letter, however, was Sargent's alleged despotism. For more information on the controversy, see Robert V. Haynes, "The Revolution of 1800 in Mississippi," *Journal of Mississippi History*, XIX (1957), 234–251.

1. Andrew Ellicot (1754–1807), surveyor of the boundary between the United States and Spanish territory, had exacerbated already existing animosity between a group of inhabitants, which was headed by Cato West (*ca.* 1750–1819), of Natchez, and represented in Congress by Hunter, and the federal government.

during a voyage from the Dutch East Indies to Baltimore.[2] When it was taken into Curaçao, the captain, Isaac Philips, demanded protection under terms of the Batavian Republic's proclamation of 1798. The governor's council in Curaçao had denied the petition and ordered the vessel and cargo sold. JM asks Murray to offer Yellott assistance with the government in Holland.]

To James Williams

ALS, RG 76, National Archives

Sir[3]   Washington, June 16, 1800
    I have receivd your letter of the 12th. inst. together with an invoice of the goods shipd on board the schooner Brothers & the protest of her captain. The claim will be transmitted to our minister at Madrid. I am Sir very respectfully, Your obedt. Servt.

J MARSHALL

From Charles Lee

ALS, RG 59, National Archives

Sir   Alexandria, June 17, 1800
    The papers herewith sent refer to the case of Capt. Jones which was considered in Philadelphia when it was thought best not to direct a noli prosequi;[4] because Capt. Jones was absconding from justice,

2. This letter is printed in *Quasi-War with France Docs.*, V, 189. Yellott's ship, the *Mary*, was captured in Feb. 1800 by the *Renommé*. The proclamation of 1798 stated that the "captors of any Dutch neutral vessel bound from one dutch port to another, or to a neutral port, who shall bring their prize within the Dutch Jurisdiction are rendered liable not only to restitution of the prize, but also to a pecuniary penalty." See Murray to Jacob Spoor, Dutch minister of marine, Sept. 15, 1800, Murray Letterbooks, I, Pierpont Morgan Library; and Murray to Spoors, Mar. 14, 1799, and Murray to Timothy Pickering, June 13, 1799, Pickering Papers, Massachusetts Historical Society. See also Murray to JM, Nov. 10, 1800, and JM to Murray, Jan. 11, 1801.
    3. The letter is addressed to "James Williams esquire, Annapolis," and is filed under "Claims Disallowed."
    4. Capt. Levin Jones, of the brigantine *David Stewart*, was indicted for the homicide of William Davis, one of his crew. A number of citizens of Baltimore had requested that the president issue a nolle prosequi because the crew was on the verge of a mutiny at the time of the homicide. Pickering had urged that the application not be granted. See Timothy Pickering to John Adams, Mar. 29, 1800, Pickering Papers, Massachusetts Historical Society. The enclosures have not been found.

and the homicide did not appear sufficiently excused according to the affidavits laid before the President. Perhaps further proofs may be offered or the President may review what have been already considered. Yet Capt. Jones remains out of the hands of justice. I submit to you to take such steps as may be thought proper; and to this purport I have written to Genl. Smith.[5] I am with the greatest respect & esteem Sir your most obedient Servant

CHARLES LEE

From John Adams

ALS, RG 59, National Archives

Sir[6]   Philadelphia, June 20, 1800
The inclosed Letter from John Lasher[7] resigning his office of Surveyor and Inspector of the Customs for the Port of New York I received last night.

I believe you have Blank Commissions in your office one of which I pray you to fill up with the Name of William S. Smith[8] of New York: or if you have not a blank you will please to make out a Commission for him and send it to me for signature: for it is my Judgment that he ought to be appointed to succeed Mr Lasher in preference to any other Candidate. With great regard, I am Sir, your most obedient & humble Servant

JOHN ADAMS

From Israel Whelen

LS, RG 59, National Archives

[*June 23, 1800, Philadelphia.* Whelen reports the arrival of the armed ship *George Washington* and requests instructions for loading it for Algiers. He also sends the claim of Wharton & Lewis[9] for payment of an insurance premium taken for the *Sophia.*]

5. Lee's letter to Smith, probably Samuel Smith, the prominent Baltimore merchant and politician, has not been found.
6. A note on the verso indicates that this letter arrived on June 24.
7. Not found.
8. Smith (1755–1816), Adams's son-in-law, expressed appreciation for this post in Smith to John Adams, July 18, 1800, Adams Papers, Massachusetts Historical Society. For an account of the difficulties with Smith's appointment, see Alexander Hamilton to James Ross, Dec. 18, 1800, in Harold C. Syrett et al., eds., *The Papers of Alexander Hamilton*, XXV (New York, 1977), 265.
9. For a copy of the claim, see Wharton & Lewis to Israel Whelen, June 5, 1800, Miscellaneous Letters Received, RG 59, National Archives.

To John Adams

ALS, Adams Papers, Massachusetts Historical Society

Sir   Washington, June 24, 1800

I receivd to day your letter of the 20th. inst. & immediately transmitted to the secretary of the treasury a commission for Mr. Smith.

After considering Mr. Kings letter of the 7th. of April[1] it appears to me most adviseable still to press an amicable explanation of the 6th. article of our treaty with Britain. Whatever the present temper of the cabinet may be a moment may present itself in the course of the summer or autumn when a disposition more favorable to an accomodation conforming to the real principles of the contract may be found. To give our minister the chance of availing himself of such a disposition it woud seem necessary at least to suspend our assent to the proposd change in the mode of constituting the board of commissioners. I have conversd with the secretaries of war & of the navy[2] on this subject & they both concur with me in sentiment concerning it. Will you sir be pleasd to give your directions after you shall have decided on the course to be pursued? I cannot help fearing that an intention on the part of the British ministry exists to put such a construction on the law of nations or so to practice under their construction as to throw into their hands sums equivalent to the probable claims of British creditors on the United States.[3]

Repeated complaints are made to this department of the depredations committed by the Spaniards on the American commerce. Is it proper that our minister at Madrid shoud receive any instructions on this interesting subject?

Some Portuguese sailors are at Norfolk in Virginia in great distress. There is neither a minister, consul or any other authorizd agent of Portugal in the United States who can make the necessary provision for them. I have deemd it proper, shoud an application I am about making to Mr. Da Costa fail, to make the necessary advances for them & to transmit to Mr. Smith the claim on the Portuguese government which these advances may authorize. If you disapprove

1. See Rufus King to [JM], Apr. 7, 1800.
2. Samuel Dexter and Benjamin Stoddert (1751–1813) were secretary of war and secretary of the navy, respectively.
3. JM had not yet received word from King that Lord Grenville was considering a lump-sum settlement, although JM might have known that the idea was considered by the British at the time the Jay Treaty was being negotiated. See John Bassett Moore, ed., *International Adjudications Ancient and Modern . . .* , III (New York, 1931), 353.

of this be pleasd to state your disapprobation that I may if in my power adopt such measures as you may deem eligible.[4] With the most perfect respect I remain Sir, Your Obedt. Servt.

J MARSHALL

From Henry A. and John G. Coster

ALS, RG 76, National Archives

[*June 24, 1800, New York.* The Costers, natives of Prussia but now American citizens, complain of the capture of their ship, *Charlotte*, by a British frigate as it was bound for Amsterdam.[5] The ship was then condemned in Halifax at a very heavy loss to the Costers, who "have Carried on a Considerable Trade to most every part of the world, & Can assure you that we have payd lately every year from 35 to 40/m Ds. in our Customhouse for inward Duty." They ask JM to intercede on their behalf.]

From Israel Whelen

LS, RG 59, National Archives

[*June 25, 1800, Philadelphia.* Whelen informs JM that he has just received a letter from Ebenezer Stevens, who writes that he has chartered the *Anna Maria*, purchased a cargo, and therefore has drawn on Whelen for $3,450, payable in 20 days. Whelen reports that he was unable to accept the bill because he had received no instructions from the State Department on the subject, nor had he any funds on hand for the purpose.[6]]

4. For Adams's reaction to Spanish depredations and the plight of the Portuguese sailors, see Adams to JM, July 5, 1800.

5. See Timothy Pickering to Rufus King, July 2 and Aug. 6, 1799, Pickering Papers, Massachusetts Historical Society. For JM's response to this letter, see JM to King, Sept. 9, 1800.

6. Whelen enclosed the note from Stevens and his reply to Stevens in this letter. See Stevens to Whelen, June 24, 1800, and Whelen to Stevens, June 25, 1800, Miscellaneous Letters Received, RG 59, National Archives. Whelen's reply to Stevens is printed in *Barbary War Docs.*, I, 361.

The letter is endorsed "recd. 28 June." See JM to Whelen, calendared at June 28, 1800.

To John Adams

ALS, Adams Papers, Massachusetts Historical Society

Sir   Washington, June 26, 1800
I receivd yesterday a letter from Mr. King of which the inclosd is a copy.[7] His number 67 to which he refers & which seems necessary in order to explain the present actual state of the negotiation with England has not yet been receivd. The letter which I now forward shows that some progress towards an agreement has been made which it may perhaps be necessary to understand before further instructions shall be given.[8] I am Sir with the most perfect respect, Your Obedt. Servt.

J MARSHALL

To David Lenox

Letterbook Copy, RG 59, National Archives

[*June 26, 1800, Washington.* JM writes to Lenox, who was U.S. agent in Great Britain, enclosing proof of the American citizenship of John Grayson. Grayson had been impressed by the British navy. JM requests that Lenox renew Grayson's claim with the documents that he is supplying.]

From Timothy Pickering

Draft, Pickering Papers, Massachusetts Historical Society

Dear Sir;   Philadelphia, June 27, 1800
Mr. Dennie[9] will have the honor to present to you this letter. Desirous of being at the seat of government and to be relieved from the

7. See Rufus King to [JM], calendared at Apr. 26, 1800, which was enclosed with this letter.

8. JM sent King's dispatch no. 67 of Apr. 22, 1800, to Adams on July 21. See also Adams to JM, July 5, 1800.

9. Joseph Dennie (1768–1812), an essayist and staunch Federalist, was a personal secretary to Pickering when he was secretary of state. Dennie's name is included on the List of State Department Officers, 1800, Madison Papers, Library of Congress. Dennie afterward took an editorial position with the *Gazette of the United States* (Philadelphia) and in 1801 became the editor of *The Port Folio*, a literary periodical. His friend was Gen. Lewis L. Morris (1760–1825). For more information, see Harold Milton Ellis, *Joseph Dennie and His Circle: A Study in American Literature from 1792 to 1812* (Austin, Tex., 1915).

drudgery of editing a newspaper for a very inadequate compensation, his friend Genl. Morris recommends him for a place in the department of State. But I cannot, because I ought not, to conceal from you, that Mr. Dennie's habits and literary turn—I should rather say, his insatiable appetite for knowledge, useful as well as ornamental, render his service as a clerk less productive than the labours of many dull men. He still wishes however, to renew his attendance in the department of State, to make a fresh essay to serve his country, provide for his own support, and promote his ultimate views of rendering, in another line, more important benefits to his fellow citizens and to mankind. He, therefore, being a perfect stranger to you, has asked of me a letter of introduction. You will be gratified by the proofs he will give you of an enlightened mind, and with his amiable manners: and I am sure you will be inclined to the most liberal indulgence of his laudable propensities. I am with very great respect and with esteem, dear Sir, yr. obt. servt

T. PICKERING

To James A. Bayard

ALS, Boston Public Library

Dear Sir   Washington, June 28, 1800
    I had to day the pleasure of receiving your favor of the 25th. inst.[1]
    The application of Bishops Asbury & Watcoat[2] will unquestionably be attended to, & government will, doubtless, give its countenance to the mission they propose. So far as a letter from me will be useful in ensuring their missionaries all proper respect they may command it. The mode of obtaining the necessary passports is prescribd in the 4th. vol. of the laws of the United States page 530. The President has not authorizd this department to grant them. In obtaining them however no difficulty I presume will exist.
    There is at present no vacancy among the clerkships in the department of State. Shoud one be made your recommendation will certainly be respected.
    Every fountain of inteligence, I mean of such as is connected with

1. Not found.
2. Francis Asbury (1745–1816) and his associate Richard Whatcoat (1736–1806) were Methodist bishops who oversaw the carrying of Methodism into the remote parts of the United States.

fact, is I beleive entirely dry, or if not so, the current which flows from them has been diverted into some other channel, so that not a drop refreshes this office. By way of compensation however for this, the spring which is in the keeping of the Aurora & other fountains supplied by fancy in the keeping of those who hold the Aurora in deservd execration, seem uncommonly full. Concerning them nothing is worth saying but that almost every thing which is said is untrue, & that of the thousand ancedotes relative to our domestic affairs which are reported & receivd as unquestionable, scarcely one has any other than an imaginary existence. With great & real esteem, I am dear Sir your affectionate Servt.

J MARSHALL

To Israel Whelen

Printed extract, Charles Retz, Inc., Catalog No. 16 (New York, 1944), 30

[*June 28, 1800, Washington.* "It is at present impracticable for me to obtain correct information respecting our affairs with the Barbary Powers. . . ."[3]]

From Israel Whelen

LS, RG 59, National Archives

[*June 28, 1800, Philadelphia.* Whelen reports that he has had some difficulty in finding an order for goods to be sent by the *Sophia* because of the confusion left by his predecessor, Tench Francis. He and Francis's clerk, William Govett, have found only one list. "There must however have been other orders either verbal or written because in the Invoice of goods sent by the Sophia, there are a number of articles constituting three fourths of the Cargo, that are not mentioned in either of the lists of articles in the above mentioned paper. . . . Mr. Govett says he understood that some articles were substituted for others that were scarce, or could not be obtained. Whether this was done in consequence of subsequent communications from Mr. OBrien, or previous arrangements, which Government did not chuse to vary from, may be known in your office." Whelen asks questions on the substance of the list he has found in his office. Also he requests additional revenue to purchase the articles on the list for the *Sophia.* Whelen concludes

3. This letter is a response to Whelen to JM, calendared at June 25, 1800.

his letter by asking for permission to provide Ebenezer Stevens with the means to complete the orders Stevens has received.[4]]

To John Adams

ALS, Adams Papers, Massachusetts Historical Society

Sir Washington, June 30, 1800

The inclosd communication was transmitted to this department in a letter dated the 14th. of Jany. last.[5] In a letter receivd from Mr. Adams dated the 7th. of April[6] at Berlin he says that the negotiations between France & Austria were not supposd to be entirely broken off. The points of difference were that France claimd the Rhine as a boundary & that Austria insisted positively on the total evacuation of Swisserland & also probably on the restoration of the Netherlands. Mr. Walcott arrivd on saturday. I am Sir with the most perfect respect, your obedt.

J MARSHALL

Note

Berlin ce 28. Decembre. 1799

Les vexations inouies que les Barbaresques ont depuis quelque tems plus que jamais exercés contre le commerce de la Mediterrannée, le prix auquel on achète d'eux de paix dont on ne peut pas calculer la decrée, & les pretentions toujours plus exagerées qu'ils ont fait valoir même au milieu de la paix, ont fait naitre a sa Majesté le Roi de Suéde l'idée de protiger le commerce dans ces parages d'une manière plus sûre moins conteuse, & plus convenable à la dignité, & à l'independence des nations commercantes. Il n'y en a pas certainement ou plus efficase que l'union des puissances interessées, pour etablir des convois reglées. Il seroit question d'entretenir un certain nombre des frigattes dans la Medeterrannée, de fixer les epoques, les stations, & les courses necessaires pour protiger leurs navires.

Le Roi a ordonné au Soussigné de proposer aux Serenissimes Etats Unis

---

4. JM requested Benjamin Stoddert, secretary of the navy, to supply the information requested in Whelen's letter. See Stoddert to Whelen, July 3, 1800, *Barbary War Docs.*, I, 362–363. See also Whelen Letterbook, June 27, 1800, Letters Sent by Purveyor of Public Supplies, RG 45, National Archives.

5. See John Quincy Adams to [JM], Jan. 14, 1800. The note that Adams sent has not been found, but a copy in JM's hand is here enclosed. See Adams's reply to the enclosure in Adams to JM, July 11, 1800.

6. This is probably Adams's dispatch no. 162, discussed in JM to John Quincy Adams, July 24, 1800. Letter not found.

de l'Amerique par son ministre plenipotentiaire a la cour de Prusse de s'unir avec lui pour cet objet. Aucune puissance n'a si cherement acheté la paix avec les Barbaresques, ni tant souffert de leurs pretentions multipliées, que les Etats Unis de l'Amerique. Ils ont presque payé le triple des sommes donnée par le Dannemarc & la Suéde. Il parait par consequence de leur interêt d'accepter une proposition, qui, sans presenter aucune sorte d'inconvenient, offre la perspective agréable de voir cesser une espèce de tribut aussi peu honorable qu'extremement onéreux, & auquel on ne peut pas prèvoir des bornes.

L'assistance donnée l'année passée dans la Mediterrannée mutuellement par les Frigattes Suedoises & Denoises aux navires marchands des deux nations ont eu un succes qui repond parfaitement de la necessité de l'union proposée.

Laurent d'Engestrom

From Commissioners of the District of Columbia

Letterbook Copy, RG 42, National Archives

Gentn:[7]   Washington, July 3, 1800

The Pavement having commenced and the Contractors for Stone having made some progress in the delivery of that article, we wish a sufficient sum to be placed at Bank to our credit, to meet the expenses incurred & daily arising; to prevent frequent applications, it may perhaps be best to place four or five thousand Dollars at once, to our Credit.

It is also necessary to determine whether the Pavement is to be continued to Rock Creek on Pennsylvania Avenue, or is to diverge to the present Bridge from about Sq 74, as our Road must be governed by the direction of the Pavement. We are, Gentn, &c.

G. Scott
W. Thornton

7. This letter is addressed to the secretaries of state, war, navy, and the Treasury. Gustavus Scott (d. 1800) and William Thornton were appointed to the board of commissioners of the District of Columbia in 1794. For more information on the commissioners, see Wilhelmus Bogart Bryan, *A History of the National Capital* . . . , I (New York, 1914), 237–238, 413.

To Richard Law

Transcript, Beveridge Papers, Library of Congress

Sir:[8]   Washington, July 3, 1800

I had the honor of receiving to-day your letter of the 27 June.[9] The acts of the last session of Congress shall certainly be transmitted to you so soon as they shall be printed. On inquiry I am informed that the acts which compose the 4th volume of the laws of the United States were immediately forwarded to you at the close of each session. If these have miscarried, & you will please to notify me thereof, I will make a point of immediately furnishing other copies. With very much respect, I am, Sir, your obdt.

J MARSHALL

From Israel Whelen

LS, RG 59, National Archives

[*July 3, 1800, Philadelphia*. Whelen reports that he will be able to purchase the cargo for the *Sophia* with the credit that JM mentioned in his letter of June 28. Today he intends to "get the Guns on Board that were borrowed from the Dey, as the Captain wishes them for Ballast."[1] Joshua Humphreys, naval constructor for the U.S. Navy, has reported that the last cargo delivered to Algiers was in bad condition and that the supplies on hand have been too long exposed to the water and weather.]

Deeds

Deed Book Copies, Office of the Clerk of Hardy County, Moorefield, W.Va.

[*July 4, 1800 (Hardy County, Va.*). By his attorney, Rawleigh Colston, JM conveys parcels of land in the South Branch Manor to George Harness, Sr., 300 acres for £63 18s., and to John Harness, 5.75 acres for £1 9s. 6d. Both deeds were recorded in the District Court at Hardy County on Sept. 9, 1800.]

8. Richard Law (1733–1806), of New Haven, Conn., was a U.S. District Court judge. He was also mayor of New Haven from 1784 to 1806.

9. Not found.

1. Whelen recorded that he sent eight 20-pound cannons to Algiers by the *George Washington* in July 1800. These cannon were "said to replace so many heretofore sent by the Dey of Algiers to the Navy Department." See Statement of Account of Israel Whelen with the United States, July 1800–Dec. 1801, *Barbary War Docs.*, I, 648.

From John Adams

ALS, RG 59, National Archives

Dear Sir   Quincy, July 5, 1800

I have received your favour of the 24th of June and thank you for transmitting to the Secretary of the Treasury a Commission for Mr Smith. If Mr Smith, for any reason, should decline this appointment, my opinion is that Mr William Morris, of New York, at present Deputy Collector is next in the Line of Merit and you may send a Commission to him.

I concurred with you and the gentlemen you consulted in opinion, that it would be prudent to direct Mr King to use his best Endeavours to bring the British Government to some explanations, untill I recd yours of the 26. of June with a Copy of Mr Kings Letter of 26 of April, when I fully agreed with you that it will be proper to wait for Mr Kings Number 67.[2]

All the Complaints made to your department, of depredations committed by the Spaniards on the American Commerce, I pray you to transmit to our Minister at Madrid, with Instructions to make friendly representations and endeavor to obtain Justice.

I approve of your sentiments concerning the Portuguese Sailors. The Duties of Humanity will never be neglected I hope by the American Government.[3]

I arrived here on the third.[4] With great Esteem, I am, Sir your most obedient & humble Servant.

JOHN ADAMS

From Rufus King

LS, RG 59, National Archives

[*July 5, 1800, London.* In dispatch no. 77, King relates news of Europe. He states that relations between Austria and England are poor, the war

2. Rufus King's dispatch no. 67 probably arrived late in July. See King to [JM], Apr. 22, 1800.

3. See JM to Adams, June 24, 1800.

4. Adams left Washington on June 15 or 16. See Adams to Abigail Adams, June 13, 1800, and James Calhoun to Adams, June 16, 1800, Adams Papers, Massachusetts Historical Society.

in Italy is going badly, and war has recurred in Egypt. King concludes, "The Reputation and influence of this Country upon the Continent, if I am not mistaken, are at this time, at a lower ebb than they have been at any period of the war. This certainly is not the present situation of France."[5]]

From William L. Smith

LS, RG 59, National Archives

[*July 5, 1800, Lisbon.* Smith acknowledges receipt of Timothy Pickering's letters of Mar. 22 and May 7, 1800. He reports that nothing has occurred respecting a commercial treaty with Portugal and that he suspects that Portugal does not desire to establish commercial relations with the United States. Smith also has spoken to a representative of the Ottoman Empire on the subject of a commercial treaty.

He writes, "By the last Accts. all was well in the three Regencies; but our peace with those powers must always be precarious, untill we establish a character in the Mediterranean as a naval power. One Portuguese 64 compelled Tripoli to pay Portugal for a peace, & induced Tunis to request a Truce for three years. These facts, while they indicate the true policy of our government, warn us to prepare in season for a complete state of peace between Portugal & the three Regencies; a negociation with Algiers is already on foot. I am happy to find by your last that a ship of some force will soon appear in the Mediterranean."

Smith also encloses an article[6] from a French newspaper about Algiers. It is copied from an English paper and has no other foundation than a letter of Richard O'Brien's that was written some months ago.]

From Carlos Martínez de Yrujo

Translation Copy, RG 59, National Archives

Sir[7]   Philadelphia, July 7, 1800
    When I noticed in the Gazettes the circumstances of the capture,

---

5. This dispatch was received on Aug. 23, 1800. See JM to John Adams, Aug. 23, 1800, by which he transmitted this dispatch. The letter is printed in King, ed., *Life and Corres. of Rufus King*, III, 266–267. See also Adams to JM, Aug. 30, 1800 (first letter).

6. The article in the French newspaper was discussed in David Humphreys to [JM], June 27, 1800, Diplomatic Despatches, Spain, V, RG 59, National Archives. Humphreys quotes the following: "Le Dey d'Alger n'ayant pas reçu les présens qu'il attendoit des Etats Unis d'Amerique, vient d'ordonner à tous ses bâtimens de s'emparer des vaisseaux Americains."

7. Carlos Fernando Martínez, marqués de Yrujo (1763–1824), was appointed Spanish minister to the United States in 1795.

at Puerto Plata, Island of St. Domingo, of the French vessel Sandwich by a large part of the crew of the American Frigate Constitution, commanded by Capt. Talbot,[8] I determined to represent to you this aggression upon the Spanish Territory, and to claim from the justice of the Government of the U.S. the restitution of that captured vessel. But as from the tenor of the last treaty of peace between Spain and the French Republic, doubts might be raised concerning the lawful ownership of Puerto Plata, in which the crew of the Constitution took possession of the said french vessel, I thought it convenient, before I should apply to you, to obtain the necessary information for the regulation of my conduct in consequence of it. This information is in part founded on the tenor of the three documents, of which I enclose copies,[9] whence you will observe, that Puerto Plata was always considered as Spanish Territory; and the informal information I have acquired on this subject does not leave me the least doubt in the assertion, that it ought yet to be considered as Spanish Territory. It is certain that by the last treaty of peace between Spain and the Republic the part which formerly belonged to Spain was ceded to the latter; but it is equally so, that this clause of the said treaty has not yet been executed; that the military posts of the said Spanish port continue garrisoned by the King's troops; that the Spanish flag is planted in them; and that *not only the military authority, but also the civil, is placed in Spanish Subjects, who exercise it in the name of the King my master and not of the French Republic.* In the said Port Plata there was a Spanish officer with some men, at the time when the boats of the Constitution committed the insult, not only by cutting out the said vessel, but by taking possession by surprize of the only battery, of three guns, and spiking and rendering them useless. These cannon belonged to the King, my Lord; and the flag of truce, which was employed to communicate with the commandant of the American Seamen was also Spanish. In one word, there is no circumstance which constitutes the right of sovereignty, which was not exer-

8. For an account of the capture that was written by an officer on board the *Constitution*, see *Claypoole's American Daily Advertiser* (Philadelphia), June 10, 1800. On May 12, 1800, Silas Talbot (1751–1813), captain of the U.S.S. *Constitution*, had captured the *Sandwich*, a French armed privateer, in a Spanish port. For documents relating to the capture, see *Quasi-War with France Docs.*, V, 500–506, 509, 513–514, VI, 18, 150, 211, 320. See also correspondence with Adams and additional correspondence with Yrujo on the capture.

9. Enclosed with this letter is an extract from the records of the tribunal of commerce, which describes American recognition of Spanish authority over Puerto Plata, and a translation copy of Minuty to du Ponceau and Joseph Philippe Létombe, both in Notes from Foreign Legations, Spain, II, RG 59, National Archives.

cised by the servants of the King of Spain, as well in the said Porto Plata as in the rest of the Island belonging to him.

Altho' the cession to the French Republic by the last treaty, is solemn and explicit, you are not ignorant of the opinion of the publicists, that the property and sovereignty commence only at the moment of possession; and the French Republic not having yet taken it of the Spanish port, and the King, my master, continuing to exercise all his rights, *as he did before the treaty*, it is evident, that the port ceded by him, and of course Puerto Plata, ought to be yet considered as Spanish; that the attack made on the French vessel, the Sandwich, is a violation of the territory of His Majesty, and an infraction of the friendship, which happily reigns between the King, my master, and the U.S. of America: and I am not able to conceive, that the said insult can be approved by the American Government, but am obliged to attribute it merely, either to the hardihood of Capt. Talbot or his ignorance of the circumstances I have mentioned. Wherefore I consider it my duty to represent to you the insult committed by the said Capt. Talbot, and to claim (as I do) from the equity of the Government of the United States, the restitution of the said French vessel, with her cargo, to whom they may belong, as a satisfaction for the said offence, which I do not consider as voluntary.

I offer myself anew, for this reason, to your disposal, and pray our Lord to preserve your life many years. I kiss your hand, Your most obed. & faithful servt.

CARLOS MRTNZ DE YRUJO

From Carlos Martínez de Yrujo

ALS, RG 59, National Archives

[*July 8, 1800, Philadelphia.* Yrujo writes in Spanish to JM on a subject he has already introduced in a communication to Timothy Pickering. He has warned Pickering of William A. Bowles's[1] arrival in the Bahamas and of Bowles's preparations to provoke hostilities against the Floridas by inciting

---

1. William A. Bowles (1763–1805) was an adventurer whose efforts to establish an independent Indian state in Florida caused Spanish-American diplomatic havoc. Early in 1800 he led an expedition of Creeks against the Spanish and captured the Spanish fort of St. Marks. See J. Leitch Wright, Jr., *William Augustus Bowles: Director General of the Creek Nation* (Athens, Ga., 1967).

Indians in violation of art. 5 of the Pinckney Treaty.[2] Yrujo notes that the newspapers have published accounts of Bowles's capture of the fort of St. Marks of Apalache in Florida. Because of this victory various Indian tribes have united with Bowles, creating a dangerous situation for both Spain and the United States. Yrujo suggests that U.S. troops join with Spanish troops in curbing Bowles's activities. He requests information on the measures that the American government might take.[3]]

From John Adams

ALS, RG 59, National Archives

Dear Sir   Quincy, July 10, 1800
    Inclosed are a Number of Petitions for Pardons of Fines and Imprisonments, which cannot be granted.[4] They ought however to be filed in the office of State. I am with great regard yours

J. ADAMS

From Commissioners of the District of Columbia

Letterbook Copy, RG 42, National Archives

Gentn,[5]   Washington, July 10, 1800
    We have the honor of your favor of the 8th,[6] and shall press forward the Pavement as fast as possible. We have no doubt it will be complete by the middle of Octo, if no delay arises from the Contractors for the delivery of stone. We presume you mean the Pavement to be continued on Pennsylvania Avenue to Rock Creek and shall act accordingly. To render both the Pavement and Road dry, several deep and long Ditches must be cut from Pennsylvania Avenue, to the

---

2. In art. 5 of the Pinckney Treaty, the United States and Spain agreed to "maintain the peace and harmony among the several Indian Nations who inhabit the country adjacent to the lines and Rivers which by the proceeding Articles form the boundaries of the two Floridas." See Miller, ed., *Treaties*, II, 322–323.
3. See also Yrujo to John Adams, July 22, 1800, Notes from Foreign Legations, Spain, II, RG 59, National Archives.
4. This letter was received on July 19, 1800. The enclosures have not been found.
5. This letter, although addressed to the secretaries of the Treasury, of war, and of the navy, was doubtless intended for JM also.
6. Not found, but see Commissioners of the District of Columbia to JM, July 3, 1800.

waters of Tyber Creek; and a Bridge must be erected over Tyber Creek. We are not able at present to calculate the precise cost of all these operations, and therefore beg leave to recommend to you to appropriate no part of the ten thousand Dollars to any other object, until the way between the Capitol and Rock Creek is complete.

We request that the Secretary of the Treasury will be so good as to order the four thousand Dollars mentioned in your letter, to be placed to our Credit in the Bank of Columbia. We are, &c.

G. SCOTT
W. THORNTON

From James McHenry

Drafts, William L. Clements Library, University of Michigan

[*July 10, 1800, Baltimore.* Having learned of the death of U.S. marshal Jacob Graybell, McHenry recommends as his successor Archibald Campbell,[7] of Baltimore, in one letter and Richard Keene,[8] a native of the Eastern Shore, in another.]

From John Adams

ALS, RG 59, National Archives

Dear Sir   Quincy, July 11, 1800

I received, only last night, your favour of the 30th of June.

There is no part of the Administration of our Government which has given me so much discontent as the negotiations in the mediterranean, our ill success in which, I attribute to the diffidence of the agents and Ministers employed in them, in soliciting Aid from the French and the English and the Russians. Mr D'Engestrom has too much reason to reproach us, or to commisserate us, for paying the Tripple of the Sums given by Sweeden and Denmark.[9]

---

7. Archibald Campbell was navy agent at Baltimore.

8. Richard Reynal Keene (b. *ca.* 1777) was employed as a law clerk by Luther Martin from 1799 to 1802. See Paul S. Clarkson and R. Samuel Jett, *Luther Martin of Maryland* (Baltimore, 1970), 197.

See also John Adams to JM, July 25 and 27, 1800. JM enclosed other recommendations from McHenry in his letter to Adams of July 29, 1800.

9. See John Quincy Adams to [JM], Jan. 14, 1800.

As, however, the Promisses of the United States although made to their hurt, ought to be fulfilled with good Faith, I know not how far We can acceed to the Proposition, of Uniting with Sweeden and Denmark in appointing in concert with them and others Convoys for their and our Trade. Convoys for our own Trade I suppose We may appoint at any time and in any seas to protect our Commerce, according to our Treaties and the Law of Nations. If, indeed the Barbary Powers or any of them should break their Treaties with us and recommence hostilities on our trade We may then be at Liberty to make any reasonable arrangements with Sweeden and Denmark.

You will be at no loss to instruct Mr Adams to give a polite and respectfull answer to Mr D'Engestrom, according to those principles if you approve them.[1] I am Sir with great Esteem, your humble sert

J. ADAMS

From John Adams

ALS, RG 59, National Archives

[*July 14, 1800, Quincy*. Adams sends JM a letter from Johann Wilhelm von Stein that is written in German. He requests that a State Department clerk translate it for his and JM's edification.[2]]

From John Adams

ALS, RG 59, National Archives

Dear Sir   Quincy, July 19, 1800

Inclosed are Letters proper to be deposited in your office and submitted to your consideration,

1.   from Mr Jonathan R. Wilmer,[3] soliciting the office of Marshall of Maryland

1. See JM to John Quincy Adams, July 24, 1800.

2. JM enclosed the translation in his letter to Adams of July 26, 1800. For the German letter and translation, see von Stein to Adams, Mar. 1, 1800, Adams Papers, Massachusetts Historical Society.

3. The enclosures have not been found. Since JM was absent from the State Department, Adams was probably sending these letters to be routinely filed.

The first four letters are applications for the office of marshal of Maryland, the incumbent having died in office. See James McHenry to JM, calendared at July 10, 1800.

Wilmer was a Maryland merchant and lawyer who served on the Governor's Council from 1797 to 1801. See Wilmer to Adams, July 12, 1800, Adams Papers, Massachusetts Historical Society.

2   A Letter from Judge Chase[4]
3. A Letter from Mr Luther Martin recommending Thomas Chase Esq.
4. A Letter from Richard Raynall Keene, with a Number of Papers inclosed which I pray you to inclose to him after you have read them.
5   from Elias Backman Consul in Sweeden with an account inclosed.[5]
6   A Letter from Mr Mayer[6] late Consul in St Domingo
7. a Letter from David Brown soliciting a Pardon of a Fine & Costs.

I am Sir with great regard yours

J. ADAMS

To John Adams

ALS, Adams Papers, Massachusetts Historical Society

Sir   Washington, July 21, 1800

With this you will receive a copy of Mr. Kings letter No. 67 to which the letter formerly transmitted to you refers.[7]

If the proposition of paying a sum in gross to the British government in lieu of & in satisfaction for the claims of British creditors shoud be deemd to merit attention, can it afford just cause of discontent to France?

You will receive also dispatches from the American envoys at Paris which reachd me by the last mail & have just been decypherd.[8] I hasten to transmit the originals to you & have not taken copies as doing so woud have producd some delay & it is not probable that any accident can prevent their safe return to the office of state.

On the information given by these dispatches it woud be rash to

---

4. Judge Samuel Chase (1741–1811) recommended his son, Thomas, for the position of marshal; however, neither his, Martin's, nor Keene's letter has been found.

5. Backman's letter was written on May 14, 1800. See JM to Backman, Dec. 22, 1800. For Backman's account, see Account of Disbursements for Accounts of United States, Sept. 1797 to Oct. 1799, Consular Despatches, Göteborg, I, RG 59, National Archives.

6. Jacob Mayer.

7. Rufus King to [JM], Apr. 22, 1800 (first letter), and King to [JM], calendared at Apr. 26, 1800.

8. The dispatches are possibly those of the American Envoys to [JM], calendared at Apr. 18, 1800. For Adams's reply, see Adams to JM, July 31, 1800 (first letter).

form any decisive judgement respecting the issue of the embassy, but I am much inclind to think the negotiation will not speedily be terminated. The French government may be inclind to protract it in the expectation that the events of this campaign in europe & certain possible political events in America may place them on higher ground than that which they now occupy.

The instructions given in your letter of the 11th. of July relative to the convoys in the mediterranean shall be immediately obeyd.[9] With very much respect & attachment, I am Sir your obedt. Servt.

J MARSHALL

From John Adams

ALS, RG 59, National Archives

Dear Sir   Quincy, July 21, 1800

Inclosed is a Letter from General Forrest, recommending his Nephew Mr Joseph Forrest to be Marshal in the place of Mr Greybell deceased, and another Letter from Mr. Wilmer soliciting the place for himself.[1] The Letter of Mr Wilmer is so confidential in its nature, and so liable to the imputation of indelicacy, if it should be seen by uncandid Persons that I pray you to return it to me, after you have read it. I hope you will weigh the qualifications and Merits of all the Candidates and favour me with your opinion. Hitherto without having formed any decided opinion, I feel most inclined to Mr Chase: partly from a personal knowledge of the young Gentleman partly from the Merits of his Father, and partly from the Recommendation of Mr Martin, and the promisses of both to advise him.[2] I am Sir &c

J. ADAMS

9. See John Adams to JM, July 11, 1800, and JM to John Quincy Adams, July 24, 1800.

1. See Jonathan R. Wilmer to Adams, July 12, 1800, Adams Papers, Massachusetts Historical Society. The letter from Forrest has not been found.

2. Thomas Chase did not receive the appointment despite Luther Martin's recommendation and the friendship of his father, Samuel Chase, with the president. See JM to Adams, July 29, Aug. 1 and 2 (first letter), and Adams to JM, Aug. 13, 1800.

From John Adams

ALS, RG 59, National Archives

Dear Sir   Quincy, July 23, 1800
I received this morning Mr Wagners Letter of the 12th[3] and return
the blank Commission signed, to be filled up in your office. I have
read all the Letters and recommendations, and continue inclined to
fill the blank with the Name of Thomas Chase Esq, according to the
recommendation of his Father and Mr Martin but if you are aware
of any serious Objection or give a decided preference to any other, I
shall pay a defference to your opinion. I return all the Letters. My
next Inclination is to Mr Wilmer. I See no propriety in giving the
place to any who have been distinguished by their Zeal in opposition
to the Government, though that is not always a decisive objection. I
am Sir with great Regard &c

                                                        J. ADAMS

The President requests the Secretary of State to transmit him a copy
the laws enacted the last session of Congress.[4]

To John Jay

ALS, Jay Papers, Columbia University Library

Sir   Washington, July 23, 1800
    A short absence from this place has prevented an earlier acknowl-
edgement of the receipt of your letter of the 28th. of June.[5]
    An application on the part of Mr. Gray has been made to this de-
partment & his case has been enquird into.[6] I am sorry to find that
the affair of the Dover Cutter was settled by Mr. Carmichael with
the Spanish Government in March 1784, & that he receivd on that
account three hundred[7] pounds sterling.[8] His estate is said to be
insolvent.

3. Jacob Wagner had written to Adams, in JM's absence, about the appointment of
a marshal for the Maryland census. Wagner enclosed a blank commission for marshal to
be filled out before Aug. 1, 1800. He also enclosed various letters of recommendation for
candidates from Luther Martin and others. See Wagner to Adams, July 12, 1800, Adams
Papers, Massachusetts Historical Society. The enclosures have not been found. See also
Adams to JM, July 19 and 21, 1800.
    4. This postscript was added in a hand other than that of John Adams.
    5. Not found. JM had left Washington after July 3 and had returned July 19.
    6. Not found.
    7. JM here inserted "1800$."
    8. The case of the *Dover Cutter* was an action of claims for money by an American

I have informd Mr. Gray that no further claim can be supported against the spanish government & that his only remedy if any is by petition to Congress for the sum receivd by Mr. Carmichael.[9] With very much respect & esteem, I am Sir your obedt.

J MARSHALL

To Timothy Pickering

ALS, Pickering Papers, Massachusetts Historical Society

Dear Sir   Washington, July 23, 1800

The inclosd[1] was receivd to day with a number of public letters from Europe & was carelessly opend without adverting to the direction—but on opening it the address showd the letter to be from your son & consequently private. Without reading one other word I inclose it to you & am truely sorry that it has been opend.

The inteligence from our envoys at Paris furnishes no data from which to infer either their success or failure. With much respect & esteem, I am dear Sir your obedt.

J MARSHALL

To John Adams

ALS, Adams Papers, Massachusetts Historical Society

Sir   Washington, July 24, 1800

I transmit you two letters No. 71 & 72. receivd from Mr. King.[2]

---

captor of an English prize brought into a Spanish port, Teneriffe in the Canary Islands. The proceedings were instigated under the Jay-Gardoqui Treaty in 1786, with William Carmichael (d. 1792) representing American interests as chargé d'affaires in Spain. Carmichael had initially served as Jay's secretary on his mission to Spain.

For more information on Carmichael, see Samuel Gwynn Coe, *The Mission of William Carmichael*, Johns Hopkins University Studies in Historical and Political Science, XLVI (Baltimore, 1928), and Samuel Flagg Bemis, *Pinckney's Treaty: America's Advantage from Europe's Distress, 1783–1800* (New Haven, Conn., 1960), 166–168.

9. Neither Gray's petition nor a letter from JM to Gray has been found.

1. The enclosure is not filed with this letter. The letter from Pickering's son might have been from either John Pickering, Jr. (1777–1846), or Timothy Pickering, Jr. (1779–1807), both of whom were in Europe and both of whom wrote to their father in the spring of 1800. See Timothy Pickering, Jr., to Timothy Pickering, Apr. 7, 1800, and John Pickering, Jr., to Timothy Pickering, May 7, 1800, Pickering Papers, Massachusetts Historical Society.

2. See Rufus King to [JM], calendared at May 22, 1800, and King to [JM], May 25, 1800.

Respecting the jewels for Tunis I think it proper to observe that on looking into the correspondence between this department & Consul Eaton I perceive a letter which states the demand of them as an encroachment which ought to be resisted as long as possible but which in the last necessity must be submitted to, & in that event it is recommended to him to have them purchasd in England. Yet I think it necessary to receive your further instructions before I write to Mr. King on the subject.

I transmit you also a letter addressd to Mr. Adams our minister at Berlin.[3] If it receives your approbation it is probable that Mr. Shaw will have an opportunity of giving it a conveyance & I shall wish to know you approve it that a duplicate & triplicate may be forwarded. I transmit it to you because there are in it some sentiments further than those containd in your letter. Shoud you wish any change, be pleasd to note it & return the letter.

No other copies of the letters from Mr. King have reachd this department nor are copies taken of those which I transmit. With very much respect & attachment, I remain Sir your Obedt. Servt.

J MARSHALL

To John Quincy Adams

LS, Adams Papers, Massachusetts Historical Society

No. 1. Triplicate[4]

Sir,   Washington, July 24, 1800

The duplicate of your No. 160 & the first of 161 and 162 were received on the 29th. of June.[5]

The proposition made by the Minister of Sweden for employing in the Mediterranean a number of frigates, in concert between the United States, Sweden and Denmark, for the purpose of protecting their commerce, has been laid before the President.[6]

---

3. See JM to John Quincy Adams, July 24, 1800. William Shaw (1778–1826) was the president's personal secretary.

4. The letter is addressed to Adams, "Recommended to the care of the American Consul at Hamburg." It is endorsed "Recd & ford. By YhS, J. Pitcairn" and "21. Octr. 1800 recd:, 7. Novr. do. Ansd." Adams received another copy on Oct. 25. For Adams's reply, see Adams to JM, Nov. 7, 1800.

5. See Adams to [JM], Jan. 14 and Mar. 8, 1800. Dispatch no. 162 is Adams to Secretary of State, Apr. 7, 1800.

6. See the note from Engëstrom, enclosed in JM to John Adams, June 30, 1800.

He is far from being pleased with the State of our affairs with the Barbary powers: but he conceives that the engagements of the United States, tho' unreasonably burthensome, ought to be performed. He is not satisfied that in the existing state of those engagements, good faith will permit us to unite with other powers, in appointing, in concert with them, convoys for their and our trade. There is indeed cause to apprehend that the Barbary powers or some of them, will break their treaties with us, and recommence hostilities on our Commerce. In such an event the United States will be at perfect liberty, and will be well disposed, to make any reasonable arrangements with Sweden and Denmark, for the purposes mentioned in the note of the Swedish Minister.

You will be pleased Sir to make a respectful communication to Baron D'Engerstrom conforming to these principles.

Until the differences between the United States and France shall be so far accommodated, as that actual hostilities shall cease between them, to station American frigates in the Mediterranean would be a hazard, to which our infant Navy ought not perhaps to be exposed. I am, Sir, with very much respect and esteem, Your Obedt. Servant,

J MARSHALL

From John Adams

ALS, RG 59, National Archives

Dear Sir   Quincy, July 25, 1800

I have received Mr Wagners Letter of the 15th inclosing a Certificate of the Mayor of Baltimore Mr Calhoun in favour of Mr Cornelius Howard Gist to be Marshall, and a Letter from Mr Hollingsworth to Mr Wolcott to the same effect, these Papers I return inclosed.[7]

I have since recd a Letter of Mr Wagner of the 16th inclosing a Letter of Mr Wm Wilson, requesting to be appointed Marshall; another from Mr McHenry recommending Mr Archibald Campbell: another from Mr Campbell requesting the appointment.[8] All these papers I return inclosed.

7. See Jacob Wagner to Adams, July 15, 1800, Adams Papers, Massachusetts Historical Society. James Calhoun (d. 1816), mayor and a leading merchant of Baltimore, recommended Gist, who was a sheriff at this time. Zebulon Hollingsworth (1735–1812) was U.S. district attorney at Baltimore. The enclosures to Wagner's letter have not been found.

8. See Wagner to Adams, July 16, 1800, Adams Papers. The letters of William Wilson and Archibald Campbell have not been found. For McHenry's recommendation, see McHenry to JM, calendared at July 10, 1800.

What am I to think of Mr Guest who is represented as a Man of sound political Principles and yet as opposed to the Administration of our Government. The Inference is that the Administration is opposed to sound political Principles.

After weighing all Things I remain in favour of Thomas Chase Esq and next to him Mr Wilmer. However, your Situation and means of Information are so much better than mine, and my Confidence in your Judgment and Integrity so entire, that I pray you to fill the blanks in the Parchment with the name that you prefer. With great Esteem,

J. ADAMS

To John Adams

ALS, Adams Papers, Massachusetts Historical Society

Sir[9]   Washington, July 26, 1800

I receivd by the last mail your letter of the 19th. inst. inclosing several papers which are disposd of according to your directions.

You will receive herewith a translation of the german letter which was addressd to you. The calculations & the poem referd to, it was deemd unnecessary to translate.[1]

The spanish minister has on the part of his sovereign claimd the restoration of the Sandwich capturd by Capt. Talbot in porto del plato as having been taken in a spanish port.[2] Porto del plato is in that part of St. Domingo which was by treaty stipulated to be surrenderd to France but which has still in fact remaind in the possession & under the government of the spanish crown. I supposd it to be perfectly clear that the capture was not authorizd & that it was an unintentional violation of the rights of Spain. I consulted the heads of departments on the case & they all concurd with me in opinion respecting it. Under these circumstances it was beleivd that it woud be more agreeable to you that I shoud immediately act than that an answer shoud be withheld until your opinion coud be obtaind. I have therefore directed the Sandwich to be given up to the minister of his Catholic Majesty. I hope Sir you will not be dissatisfied with this measure.

9. This letter is endorsed "ansd. Aug. 11, 1800."
1. See Adams to JM, July 14, 1800.
2. See Carlos Martínez de Yrujo to JM, July 7, 1800.

I transmit you by this mail a letter receivd some time past from the spanish minister respecting Genl. Bowles.[3] I have informd him that the letter is laid before you & have requested him to furnish this department with such further information as he may receive & may chuse to communicate.

I have mentiond to the heads of departments the suggestion containd in Mr. Kings letter concerning the payment of a gross sum in satisfaction of the claims of the British creditors under the 6th. article of our treaty of amity &c with that nation. It is their opinion that the proposition merits consideration & they think that if a sum not exceeding five milion of dollars or perhaps a milion sterling woud be receivd that sound policy woud direct the compromise. I am greatly inclind to beleive that we shall never be able to extricate ourselves from this affair on better terms. I am Sir with respectful attachment, Your Obedt. Servt.

J MARSHALL

From John Adams

ALS, RG 59, National Archives

Dear Sir   Quincy, July 27, 1800

I have received Mr Wagners Letter of the 17th.[4] and have read Mr W. Mathews's application for the office of Marshall, and Mr McHenrys Letter to you in favour of Mr William Wilson. These Papers I return inclosed, together with the Passport for the Ann Maria, signed. With great Esteem &c

J. ADAMS

To John Adams

ALS, Adams Papers, Massachusetts Historical Society

Sir[5]   Washington, July 29, 1800

I receivd last night your letter of the 21st. inclosing one from Genl. Forrest & one from Mr. Wilmer which I return to you.[6]

3. See Yrujo to JM, calendared at July 8, 1800. JM's reply has not been found.
4. See Jacob Wagner to Adams, July 17, 1800, Adams Papers, Massachusetts Historical Society. The enclosures to Wagner's letter have not been found.
5. The letter is endorsed "Gen. Marshall, rec & ans. 7 Aug, Marshall of Maryland."
6. The letter from Jonathan R. Wilmer is enclosed with this letter.

As the applicants for the office of Marshal for this district are almost entirely unknown to me I thought it most proper to consult Mr. Stoddart on the subject. He says that Mr. Chase is, he beleives, qualified for the office, but that in his opinion it woud be unadviseable to appoint him. Mr. Chase is a young man who has not yet acquird the public confidence, & to appoint him in preference to others who are generally known & esteemd, might be deemd a meer act of favor to his Father. Mr. Stoddart supposes it ineligible to accumulate, without superior pretensions, offices in the same family.

Mr. Forrest he says deserves the character Genl. Forrest has given him, but he has lately obtaind the benefit of a legislative act of bankruptcy, & this will probably be deemd by others as well as yourself an objection to his filling such an office as that of Marshal.

Mr. Stoddart balances between Mr. Beale whose recommendations I transmitted to you some few days past[7] & Major Hopkins who has been prevented from obtaining so many letters as he coud have commanded in support of his application by an apprehension that he is too late. His feelings & friendship are apparently in favor of Mr. Beale who was a meritorious officer in our revolution war, & was also an officer much respected in one of the disbanded regiments. But to Mr. Beale the same objection lies as to Mr. Forrest. The opinion of his honesty & worth is universal but he broke as sheriff & has been releivd by an act of Assembly.

To Major David Hopkins Mr. Stoddart thinks there is no objection & he beleives the appointment will give general satisfaction. Common opinion he says concurs with the character given of this gentleman by Mr. Davidson in the inclosd letter.[8] I am Sir with the highest respect, Your Obedt. Servt.

J MARSHALL

To Richard O'Brien

LS, Historical Society of Pennsylvania

Sir   Washington, July 29, 1800
The George Washington sails immediately for Algiers With a

7. The recommendation for Lloyd Beale (1756–1817) has not been found.
8. See the recommendation of John Davidson for Hopkins (1753–1824), July 14, 1800, enclosed with this letter.

JULY 29, 1800 [193]

cargo according to the invoice and bill of lading inclosed.[9] The cargo I hope will reach you in good order, and in time for the purposes of our government.

The Sophia, Captain Smith has arrived, and has brought letters from yourself and from Consul Eaton. Another vessel for the mediterranean will, I hope, sail in a short time with such further articles as may be necessary.

I find it difficult from the papers in this Department to ascertain the precise state of our accounts with the Barbary powers.[1] I shall be much obliged to you and to Consuls Eaton and Cathcart to make out a perfect and complete statement, if you have it in your power, to do so, shewing the claims of the different regencies, and the produce and application of every cargo which has arrived, and exhibiting also with precision the present state of their demands.

It is very much to be wished that a sum in specie could be fixed on for the annuities instead of the specific articles now called for. It would simplify the accounts and greatly ease the United States. The sum of thirty thousand dollars, which you mention, would certainly be more desirable, than the present annuity to Algiers.

It is very much the wish of our government to preserve its peace with the mediterranean powers, and to perform all its engage[*ments*] but the burthensome caprices of the Barbary sovereigns cannot always be submitted to. It will very much tend to secure the preservation of peace and the punctuality of the payment, to commute the annuity to a sum in specie.

I will mention to the President, who is now in Massachusetts the proposition for sending to Algiers a man to make powder. I am, Sir, very respectfully, Your obt. Servt.

J MARSHALL

9. The invoice and bill of lading have not been found, but see Statement of the Account of Israel Whelen with the United States, July 1800–Dec. 1801, *Barbary War Docs.*, I, 648. See also List of Timber and Naval Stores for Algiers, enclosed in John Leamy to Jacob Wagner, July 29, 1800, Consular Despatches, Algiers, V, RG 59, National Archives.

1. See Whelen to JM, calendared at June 28, 1800. For further discussion of the difficulties encountered in lading the *George Washington*, see Whelen to Benjamin Stoddert, July 24, 1800, Miscellaneous Letters Received, RG 59, National Archives. See also Whelen to Richard O'Brien, July 29, 1800, *ibid.*

From John Adams

ALS, RG 59, National Archives

Dear Sir   Quincy, July 30, 1800
I have recd your favour of the 21st and have read the respectable Recommendations inclosed in favour of Mr Lloyd Beal and Mr Bent Rawlings to be Marshall of Maryland. I return all these Letters to you in this.[2]
With the Advantages of Mr Thomas Chase in the opportunity to consult his Father and Mr Martin, I still think that his appointment is as likely to benefit the public, as that of any of the respectable Candidates would be. Your knowledge of Persons Characters and Circumstances are so much better than mine, and my Confidence in your Judgment and Impartiality so entire, that I pray you, if Mr Chase should not appear the most eligible Candidate to you, that you would give the Commission to him whom you prefer. With great regard &c

                                                    J. ADAMS

To Israel Whelen

[*July 30, 1800.* JM discusses the sale of the brigantine *Sophia.* Listed in Samuel T. Freeman Co., Auction Catalog (Philadelphia, Nov. 30, 1961), item 683. Not found.]

From John Adams

ALS, RG 59, National Archives

Dear Sir   Quincy, July 31, 1800
In the night of the 29th your favour of the 21 was left at my house. Mr Kings Letter shall be soon considered;[3] at present I shall confine myself to the Dispaches from our Envoys in France.
The Impression made upon me, by these Communications is the same with that which they appear by your Letter to have made upon

2. The letter and enclosures have not been found.
3. See Adams to JM, Aug. 1, 1800.

you. There is not sufficient Grounds on which to form any decisive opinion of the Result of the Mission. But there are reasons to conjecture that the French Government may be inclined to explore all the resources of their diplomatic Skill to protract the negotiation. The Campaign in Europe may have some weight: but the Progress of the Election in America may have much more. There is reason to believe that the Communications between the Friends of France in Europe and America are more frequent and constant as well as more Secret than ours: and there is no room to doubt that the French Government is flattered with full Assurances of a change at the next Election which will be more favourable to their Views.

McNeil, it appears was arrived at Havre, the latter part of May.[4] Our Envoys will probably insist on definitive and categorical Answers and come home, according to their Instructions, either with or without a Treaty. On this Supposition We need say no more upon the Subject. Another Supposition is however possible and in order to guard against that I shall propose to your consideration and that of the heads of departments the propriety of writing to our Envoys by the Way of holland and England or Hambourg, or any other more expeditious and certain conveyance. The Question is what We shall write?

There are but two points which appear to me to deserve a further Attention, and indeed their present Instructions are Sufficient upon these heads.

I always expected, that our Envoys would be hard pressed to revive the old Treaty to save its Anteriority, as they say they shall be. I cannot see however that We can relax the Instruction on that head. Perhaps it may be necessary to repeat and confirm it.

The other Point relates to a discontinuance of our Naval protection of our Commerce and to opening our Commerce with France. But We have no official or other authentic Information that the French have done any Thing to justify or excuse Us in the Smallest Relaxation. And indeed nothing they can do, short of a Treaty, would justify me in taking one Step. I therefore think that our Envoys may be instructed to be as explicit, as decency and delicacy will admit in rejecting all propositions of the kind. I return you all the Papers relative to this subject. With great regard &c

JOHN ADAMS

4. Daniel McNeill (1748–1833), captain of the *Portsmouth*, left the United States in Apr. 1800 carrying dispatches to the envoys. William R. Davie returned with him on the trip back in late October. See Blackwell P. Robinson, *William R. Davie* (Chapel Hill, N.C., 1957), 355.

From John Adams

ALS, RG 59, National Archives

Dear Sir   Quincy, July 31, 1800

Last night, the Consul of Spain Mr Stoughton, came out to Quincy upon the important Errand of delivering to me, in my own hand, according his own account of his orders, the inclosed Letter demanding of the Government a fullfillment of the fifth Article of our Treaty with Spain.[5] Although I see no sufficient reason in this case, for deviating from the ordinary course of Business, I shall take no exception to this Proceeding on that account: but I desire you to communicate this Letter to the Secretary at War, and concert with him the proper measures to be taken. Orders I think should be sent to Mr Hawkins and to General Wilkinson,[6] to employ every means in their Power to preserve the good Faith According to the Stipulation in this fifth Article of the Treaty with Spain. And I also desire you would write a civil and respectfull Answer to this Letter of the Chevalier,[7] still the Minister of the King of Spain, assuring him of the sincere Friendship of the Government for the Spanish Government and Nation and of our determination to fullfill with perfect good faith the Stipulations in the Treaty and informing him [*that*] orders have been given or shall be immediately given to the officers of the United States civil and military to take all the measures in their Power for that Purpose. With great regard &c

JOHN ADAMS

From Israel Whelen

Letterbook Copy, RG 45, National Archives

[*July 31, 1800, Philadelphia.* Whelen reports that he will put the *Sophia* up for public auction on Aug. 11, 1800, at 69 days credit. He has written to Capt. John Smith, requesting him to furnish an inventory and description of the vessel for advertisement.]

5. Carlos Martínez de Yrujo to Adams, July 22, 1800, Notes from Foreign Legations, Spain, II, RG 59, National Archives. See Yrujo to JM, calendared at July 8, 1800, and Miller, ed., *Treaties*, II, 322–323.

6. Benjamin Hawkins (1754–1818) held the post of agent to the Creeks and general superintendent to all Indian tribes south of the Ohio River. See "Letters of Benjamin Hawkins, 1796–1806," *Collections of the Georgia Historical Society*, IX (1916), 7–12. James Wilkinson (1757–1825) was a brigadier general and at this time senior officer in the U.S. Army.

7. See JM to Yrujo, Aug. 12, 1800.

From Carlos Martínez de Yrujo

LS, RG 59, National Archives

[*July 31, 1800, Philadelphia.* Yrujo acknowledges receipt of JM's letter of July 25, 1800,[8] in which JM assured him that the French vessel, *Sandwich,* with its cargo, would be restored to its owners. He thanks JM for his punctuality in responding and for the justice of the United States's decision. Yrujo also informs JM that he has written to President Adams[9] on the subject of William A. Bowles further to expedite a decision on the case, and he again urges the United States to take immediate action to fulfill art. 5 of the Pinckney Treaty with Spain. This letter is written in Spanish.]

To John Adams

ALS, Adams Papers, Massachusetts Historical Society

Sir   Washington, August 1, 1800

I receivd to day your letter of the 23d. ultimo. As I am uncertain what will be your wish respecting the marshal of Maryland after considering the opinion of Mr. Stoddart which I communicated to you some few days past, I shall not fill up the commission until I receive an answer to that letter.[1] Altho this may be in a slight degree inconvenient yet I suppose the public service cannot suffer materially by the delay.

By this mail you will receive a letter from the Prince regent of Portugal announcing another birth with an answer prepard for your signature.[2]

Since writing to you last I have receivd a letter from Mr. King recommending an agreement with the British government for a sum in gross in lieu of claims under the 6th. article of our treaty with that nation.[3] With very much respect & attachment, I remain Sir your obedt

J Marshall

8. Not found.

9. See Yrujo to Adams, July 22, 1800, Notes from Foreign Legations, Spain, II, RG 59, National Archives.

1. Adams responded to this letter in Adams to JM, Aug. 11, 1800.

2. These letters have not been found, but see Adams to JM, Aug. 11, 1800.

3. This letter is probably Rufus King to [JM], Apr. 22, 1800 (second letter).

From John Adams

ALS, RG 59, National Archives

Dear Sir[4]   Quincy, August 1, 1800

I have twice read the dispatch of Mr King No. 67[5] inclosed in your favour of the 21. of July.

I am glad to see, that Lord Grenville expressed his opinion that the new board ought to proceed in a different manner from their Predecessers, by deciding cases singly one after another instead of attempting to decide them by general Resolves and in classes.

The Idea of paying a gross sum to the British Government in lieu of and in satisfaction for the Claims of British Creditors seems to me to merit Attention and mature Consideration.[6] There will be great difficulties attending it, no doubt. How can We form an estimate, that will satisfy the American Government and the British Government? How shall the Claims of British Creditors be extinguished, or barred from Recovery in our Courts of Law? Shall the Claim of the Creditor be transferred to our Government, and how? or shall it be a total Extinguishment of Debt and Credit between the Parties? How will the British Government apportion the sum among the British Creditors? This, however is their Affair.

You ask an important Question, Whether such an Arrangement can afford just cause of discontent to France. But I think it must be answered in the Negative. We acknowledge our Citicens in debt to British subjects. We surely have a right to pay our honest debts in the manner least inconvenient to ourselves: And no foreign Country has any thing to do with it. I think I should not hesitate on this Account.

The difficulty of agreeing upon a sum is the greatest; but I am inclined to think this may be overcome.

If nothing of this kind can be agreed on, And the British Government refuse all explanations, I think that good faith will oblige Us to try another board and I have so little objection to the modes of appointing a new board, suggested to Mr King by our Government or by the British Government that I am content to leave it to Mr King to do the best he can. I shall keep the Copy of Mr Kings dis-

---

4. JM endorsed the letter "recd. Aug. 9th, 1800."
5. Rufus King to [JM], Apr. 22, 1800 (first letter).
6. On the subject of a lump-sum payment, see JM's response to this letter, in JM to Adams, Aug. 12, 1800. See also Adams to JM, Aug. 11, 1800.

patch No. 67 presuming that you have the original. With great regard &c

J. ADAMS

To David Matthew Clarkson

Letterbook Copy, RG 59, National Archives

Sir:[7]   [Washington], August 1, 1800

I am just informed that two American seamen Daniel Tripe and Benjamin Yeaton are in prison at Point Peter Guadaloupe and that the government of that place refuses to exchange them and threatens to punish them as criminals.[8] The offence committed is said to have been the rescue of their vessel, in doing which the prize master was killed.

As the fact is completely justifiable by the laws and usages of war, it will not authorize the revenge which the government of Guadaloupe proposes to exercise on these prisoners. Nor will the Government of the United States permit such practices to remain unpunished: however, retaliation may wound the feelings of humanity, a just regard for the lives of our citizens and a sound policy will compel us to resort to it.

I must therefore request that you will endeavour to have these men exchanged, and that, if it is pretended that they ought to be detained as criminals and to be punished as murderers, you remonstrate against an act alike lawless and inhuman, and make such declarations as you may believe will be productive of good, of the certainty, that the American Government will retaliate. I am Sir, &c. &c.

J. MARSHALL

To John Adams

ALS, Adams Papers, Massachusetts Historical Society

Sir[9]   Washington, August 2, 1800

I have just receivd your letter of the 25th. of July inclosing the

---

7. David Matthew Clarkson was U.S. agent at St. Kitts.

8. See JM to John Adams, Aug. 2, 1800. For further information on the incident, see Job Wall to [JM], June 6, 1800, in *Quasi-War with France Docs.*, VI, 20–21.

9. This letter is endorsed "Washington City, Sec. of State, rec 10th Aug, Ans 13th."

recommendations of several gentlemen for the vacant office of marshal for this district.

I am sensible of the confidence you place in me, when you authorize me to fill the commission with the name of such person, as on the best information I can collect, shall appear most proper; & I shoud not have hesitated to insert the name of Mr. Chase had I not supposd that the reasons assignd against his appointment by Mr. Stoddart, had some weight, & might probably produce a change in your wishes on that subject. I shall therefore postpone filling up the commission until I receive your answer to my letter stating Mr. Stoddarts observations on the different candidates.[1]

I have just receivd a letter from a Mr. Richard Tripe of Dover in New Hampshire[2] stating that his son Daniel Tripe & another sailor are now detaind in prison in Guadaloupe, that the government of that island refuses to exchange them & threatens to prosecute & punish them criminally. Their offense is having retaken the Rebecca Henry the vessel in which they had saild from Portsmouth & which had been capturd by a french privatier, & having killd the prize Master in the act of rescuing the vessel. The next day the Rebecca Henry was taken by another privatier from the same island & carried into Guadaloupe. In such a case it seems to me proper to remonstrate against such a prosecution & to threaten retaliation if the prisoners shoud be executed. I shall however suspend my letter til I receive your instructions on the subject.

The commissioners under the Spanish treaty have awarded in favor of Messrs. Gregorie & Pickard of Boston the sum of $8487 \frac{2\frac{1}{2}}{100}$ dollars which award has been presented to the Spanish government & payment thereof has been refusd because Mr. Viar[3] the Spanish commissioner has not signd it. His reason for withholding his signature is that Messrs. Gregorie & Pickard have become American citizens since the acknowledgement of our independence by the British government in 1783.

This act appears to me to be a direct violation of our treaty with Spain & I presume ought to be complaind of thro' our Minister at

1. See JM to Adams, July 29, 1800.

2. The letter from Richard Tripe (1720–1811) has not been found, but see JM to David Matthew Clarkson, Aug. 1, 1800.

3. Josef Ignacio de Viar was a Spanish commissioner under the Pinckney Treaty. For more discussion on the subject, see JM to David Humphreys, Sept. 23, 1800. See also Adams to JM, Aug. 13, 1800.

Madrid. With the most respectful attachment, I remain Sir your obedt. Servt.

J MARSHALL

To John Adams

ALS, Adams Papers, Massachusetts Historical Society

Sir   Washington, August 2, 1800
I transmit you a letter receivd some time past from Mr. Sitgreaves[4] as being connected with the letters of Mr. King on the same subject. I am Sir with very much respect, Your obedt Servt.

J MARSHALL

From John Adams

ALS, RG 59, National Archives

Dear Sir[5]   Quincy, August 2, 1800
Last night I recd your favour of the 24. of July. The Letter to Mr Adams dated the 24th. of July I have read, and as I see no reason to desire any alteration in it, I shall give it to Gen. Lincoln the Collector at Boston[6] to be by him sent to Hamburg or Amsterdam by the first good opportunity. The Duplicate and Triplicate you may send by such opportunities as may be presented to you.

Mr Kings dispatches No. 71. and 72 I have read and if you think it proper you may authorize Mr King, if he thinks it proper to communicate to the Court, in any manner he thinks most decent the Congratulations of His Government and if he pleases of the President on the Kings fortunate Escape from the attempt of an assassin.[7]

The mighty Bubble, it seems is burst, of a projected Combination of all the North of Europe against France. This mighty design which was held up in terror before my Eyes, to intimidate me from Sending

4. Enclosure not found, but see Samuel Sitgreaves to Timothy Pickering, Mar. 18 and 23, 1800, Pickering Papers, Massachusetts Historical Society. Sitgreaves (1764–1824) was an American commissioner under art. 6 of the Jay Treaty.

5. This letter was received on Aug. 10, 1800.

6. Adams sent JM's letter to John Quincy Adams by Benjamin Lincoln (1733–1810).

7. See JM to Rufus King, Aug. 16, 1800.

Envoys to France, is evaporated in smoke. Indeed I never could hear it urged against the Mission to France without Laughter.

The Jewells for Tunis are a more serious Object. When I read over all the Dispatches from the Barbary States I remember your Predecessor consulted me concerning these Jewells. His opinion was that it was best to make the Present rather than hazard a Rupture. After the Expenditure of such great sums, I thought with him that it would be imprudent to hazard an interruption of the Peace on Account of these Jewells, and I presume he wrote to Mr Eaton or Mr Smith Accordingly.[8] I am still of the same opinion.

I see no objection against requesting Mr Smith and all the Consuls in the Barbary States to keep Mr King informed of the general state of affairs. It will be of Service to the Public, that our Minister at London should know as much Information as possible concerning our affairs in those Countries. I return Mr Kings Dispatches 71. & 72. With high regard &c

JOHN ADAMS

To an Unknown Person

ALS, Library of the Supreme Court of the United States

Sir   Washington, August 2, 1800

Your letter of the 16th. ultimo was receivd during my absence from this place.[9] As an appeal has been prayd by Brothers Casters & Co. from the decree of the court of Vice Admiralty in Halifax, the decision of the superior court will show what principle will regulate the conduct of Britain in similar cases. When that shall have been ascertaind I have no doubt that the course of the American government will be such as the interests, the honor & the justice of the United States require.[1] In the meantime shoud I give you an opinion it woud

8. See Timothy Pickering to John Adams and Pickering to William Eaton, Jan. 17, 1800, Pickering Papers, Massachusetts Historical Society. For JM's reply to King, see JM to King, Aug. 16, 1800.

9. Not found.

1. JM might have been referring to the British policy of capturing neutral ships with enemy merchandise on board. This development was reported to him in William Armstrong to JM, July 17, 1800, British Spoliations, RG 76, National Archives. For the same or a similar case, see Henry A. and John G. Coster to JM, calendared at June 24, and JM to Rufus King, Sept. 9, 1800.

Experience with British colonial vice admiralty courts caused the State Department to place reliance upon the High Court of Admiralty to correct unjust decrees. When the High Court affirmed a decree deemed prejudicial to American interests, the State Department then framed its protest, usually transmitted through the U.S. minister in London.

be only that of a private individual & of consequence it woud be un-important & perhaps improper. I am Sir very respectfully, Your Obedt.

J MARSHALL

To David Humphreys

Letterbook Copy, RG 59, National Archives

Sir: Washington, August 2, 1800

I have the honor to enclose a copy of a letter written to you by Mr. Lee, while exercising a temporary agency in this Department. I also transmit a letter from the President to the King of Spain,[2] in answer to his communication of the birth of a grandson, a copy of which is enclosed for your inspection. I am Sir, &c. &c.

J. MARSHALL.

To David Jones

ALS, American Baptist Historical Society, Rochester, N.Y.

Dear Sir[3] Washington, August 2, 1800

I have just seen your letter of the 9th. of July which was receivd while I was absent from this place.[4] I have transmitted the record to Mr. Randolph[5] to whom I gave your papers as you had mentiond your wish to employ him. I am uncertain whether he has instituted the suit or not but I incline to beleive he has not. It will be well for you to write to him on this subject. I am Sir very respectfully, Your obedt. Servt

J MARSHALL

2. Neither enclosure has been found.
3. JM addressed this letter to "The reverend David Jones, Wheeling."
4. Letter not found.
5. Edmund Randolph. See JM to Jones, June 12, 1800.

To John Adams

ALS, Adams Papers, Massachusetts Historical Society

Sir   Washington, August 4, 1800
    I transmit you two letters relative to the consul at Madeira & an oration which I presume the inclosd letter informs you was forwarded to this office by the author for you.[6] I am most respectfully, Your obedt

J MARSHALL

To Job Wall

Letterbook Copy, RG 59, National Archives

Sir: Washington, August 4, 1800
    Your bill on the Secretary of State in favor of Capt. Joseph Dacosta, for three thousand dollars dated the 12th. of May in this year has been presented to this Department.[7] With much regret I have permitted it to be protested.
    You have not furnished any accounts of the expenditure of the monies already placed in your hands, nor do I know in what manner so considerable a sum as you have drawn for can have been employed in your department for the public use. The expenses of relieving our seamen are so considerable, that unless the fund be husbanded with correct economy, it will be exhausted, before the new appropriations can be made. It will be adviseable for you to transmit immediately your accounts, or it will be impossible that your drafts can be honored.
    Your bond is rejected, because the security you have given is not a resident of the United States. I am Sir, &c. &c.

J. MARSHALL

To Harrison Gray Otis

ALS, Otis Papers, Massachusetts Historical Society

Dear Sir   Washington, August 5, 1800
    I wrote to you a few days past[8] that I had paid Mr. Dexter forty

6. For details on these letters, see Adams to JM, Aug. 15, 1800.
7. See Wall to [JM], May 14, 1800, printed in *Quasi-War with France Docs.*, V, 514–515. Wall, U.S. consul at St. Bartholomew, replied to JM's letter on Oct. 6, 1800, in Consular Despatches, St. Bartholomew, I, RG 59, National Archives.
8. Not found.

dollars for you which he had promisd shoud be paid you by his nephew. He has since given me the inclosd draft. If you have receivd the money you will please to give the draft to Mr. A. Dexter & if you have not receivd it the exhibition of the bill will I presume secure it.

Ill news from Virginia. To succeed me has been elected by an immense majority one of the most decided democrats in the union.[9]

In Jersey too I am afraid things are going badly. In Maryland the full force of parties will be tried but the issue I shoud feel confident woud be right if there did not appear to be a current setting against us of which the force is incalculable.

There is a tide in the affairs of nations, of parties, & of individuals. I fear that of real Americanism is on the ebb. Your

J MARSHALL

From Arthur St. Clair

Draft, Ohio State Library

Sir,[1]   Cincinnati, August 5, 1800

I have been honored with your Letter of the 9th. of June relating to the Connecticut reserve, and also that of the 12th. of the same Month covering the Act for dividing this territory.[2] In pursuance of the first a County called Trumbull has been erected, comprehending all the Land contained within the Boundaries by which the reservation was made, when the cession of the Claim of Connecticut to western Lands generally was accepted by Congress. In that County an unfortunate accident has happenned already, the killing of two Indian Men and the wounding two Children of which I recd. the account this morning in a Letter from Colo. Hamtramck the enclosed a copy of it.[3] I shall send another to the Secry. of War. There has been for a considerable time past a great restlessness amongst the Indian Tribes, and some of them have been committing depredations upon other tribes, and much appearances that War between them would be kindled, while others have been stealing many horses

9. Littleton Waller Tazewell took JM's seat in Congress on Nov. 26, 1800. He defeated John Mayo.

1. This letter is printed in Carter, ed., *Terr. Papers, NW*, III, 101–102.

2. The letter of June 9, 1800, has not been found; the act referred to is in 2 Stat. 56–57 and was passed on Apr. 28, 1800. See also JM to St. Clair, June 12, 1800.

3. John Francis Hamtramck (1754–1803) was an officer in the infantry stationed in Pittsburgh. The copy of the letter from Hamtramck to St. Clair has not been found.

from the white people, which is a common prelude to hostilities. I am persuaded that, if they do not quarrel amongst themselves, it will not be long that they will be at peace with Us, to obviate however as much as possible the ill effects of this present affair I shall go to the County of Trumbull immediatly and, if the Circumstances will justify it, appoint a special Court of Oyer and terminer for the trial of the person who is taken. I have the honor to be with great Respect, Sir, yr. obedt Servt.

AR. ST. CLAIR

From Israel Whelen

LS, RG 59, National Archives

[*August 6, 1800, Philadelphia.* Whelen reports that Capt. John Smith of the *Sophia* has presented a bill for payment. Smith has also shown him Richard O'Brien's draft for $1,244, a copy of which has been sent to the State Department. Smith has left samples of two kinds of nails for which he understands requisitions have been made. "Much of the Timber now on hand has been injured by the weather. I am getting it Sorted and piled, what is unfit for shipping had I presume better be disposed of before it is entirely lost. I cannot but believe that contracting for the delivery of the particular kinds of timber or plank that may be wanted, would be a more oeconomical plan than to purchase rafts & have them sawed." Whelen also requests $48,000 to pay for the articles he purchased for the *George Washington* and to defray the expenses of the *Sophia*.]

From John Adams

ALS, RG 59, National Archives

Dear Sir   Quincy, August 7, 1800
    Inclosed is a Letter from a worthy Clergyman of Braintree who has invented a very ingenious machine to facilitate that necessary domestic operation called Washing;[4] which, by the concurrent testi-

---

4. See Rev. Ezra Weld to Adams, Aug. 6, 1800, Miscellaneous Letters Received, RG 59, National Archives. Weld's patent was finally granted on Sept. 17, 1800. His previous patent, granted on June 26, 1799, was deemed inadequate by the State Department. See *Amer. State Papers, Miscellaneous*, I, 426, 427, and Timothy Pickering to Weld, Aug. 21, 1799, and Feb. 21, 1800, Pickering Papers, Massachusetts Historical Society.

mony of those who have Used it, saves, two days labour out of three.

A Patent was granted him long ago: but by the inclosed Letter it was sent back for some Amendment. I pray you to send on his Patent as soon as may be. You will find it and the Letters concerning it in the office no doubt. With Sincere regard &c

J. ADAMS

From John Adams

ALS, RG 59, National Archives

Dear Sir   Quincy, August 7, 1800

I inclose to you a Letter from Governor Trumbull of Connecticutt, a Petition for a Pardon from Isaac Williams in Prison at Hartford for Privateering under French Colours.[5] His Petition is seconded by a number of very respectable People. I inclose many other Papers relative to the subject, put into my hands yesterday by a young Gentleman from Norwich his Nephew. The Mans Generosity to American Prisoners, his refusal to Act and resigning his Command when he was ordered to capture American Vessells, his present Poverty and great distress are Arguments in favour of a Pardon and I vow I feel somewhat inclined to grant it. But I will not venture on that Measure without your Advice and that of your Colleagues. I pray you to take the opinion of the heads of departments upon these Papers and if they Advise to a pardon you may send one. With high Esteem &c

J. ADAMS

See also JM to Adams, Aug. 16, 1800.

Until 1802, when a separate patent office was established, the State Department granted patents and copyrights. See Noble E. Cunningham, Jr., *The Process of Government under Jefferson* (Princeton, N.J., 1978), 92.

5. Williams (1758–1844) became a naturalized Frenchman in 1792 and accepted a commission in the French navy. He served in the French navy until war broke out between France and the United States, when he returned to his home in Norwich, Conn. He was charged in federal court with accepting a foreign commission and warring on British shipping while he was an American citizen. On Sept. 17, 1799, he was found guilty on both counts, ordered to pay a fine of $2,000, and sentenced to eight months in jail. In May 1800, unable to pay the fine, he was retained in prison. For Trumbull's letter and Williams's petition, see Jonathan Trumbull to Adams, July 30, 1800, and "Petition of Isaac Williams," July 18, 1800, filed under pardon no. 29, Petitions for Pardon, RG 59, National Archives. Also filed under pardon no. 29 are the transcript of record for the trial and testimonials to Williams's character and health.

A pardon was granted to Williams on Aug. 16, 1800. See JM to Simeon Baldwin, Aug. 16, 1800. For JM's opinion on the case, see JM to St. George Tucker, Nov. 27, 1800.

From John Adams

ALS, RG 59, National Archives

Dear Sir   Quincy, August 7, 1800

I have just recd your favour of July 29th. The Merit of Judge Chase, of which I have been a Witness at times for Six and twenty years are very great in my estimation: and if his sons are as well qualified as others, it is quite consistent with my Principles to consider the sacrifices and services of a Father, in weighing the Pretensions of a Son. The Old Gentleman will not probably last very long, and it can hardly be called accumulating offices in a Family, to appoint the son of a Judge of the United States, Marshall of a particular state. However I have so much defference for the opinion of Mr. Stoddert, especially in an Appointment in his own state, that I will waive my own Inclination in favour of his Judgment and consent to the appointment of Major David Hopkins.[6] With great regard

J. ADAMS

From Israel Whelen

Letterbook Copy, RG 45, National Archives

[*August 7, 1800, Philadelphia.* In reply to JM's letter of Aug. 4,[7] Whelen requests information on the *George Washington* for insurance purposes and asks "whether she is *ordered* to stop at any port or place previous to her arrival at Algiers, otherwise the underwriters will endeavour to evade payment in Case of loss." He assumes that he can obtain insurance at 5% or 6% premium, although he has written to Ebenezer Stevens[8] for insurance rates in New York for both the *George Washington* and the *Anna Maria.*]

6. For information on this appointment, see Adams to JM, July 21, 1800. See also Adams to JM, Aug. 13, 1800.
7. Not found.
8. Ebenezer Stevens's reply to Whelen is in *Barbary War Docs.*, I, 336.

To John Adams

ALS, Adams Papers, Massachusetts Historical Society

Sir Washington, August 8, 1800

I herewith transmit to you a letter from Mr. King,[9] which I only receivd yesterday, accompanying a complaint made by the Swedish chargé des affaires against two American Captains for an injury done a swedish vessel & an insult offerd to their flag. I have written to day to the collector of Charleston South Carolina[1] at which port the two persons complaind of were commissiond requesting him to have their conduct enquird into. In the mean time I presume it will be adviseable to write to Mr. King requesting him to assure the representative of his Swedish majesty that such conduct if intentional will be strongly discountenancd by the American government which has set on foot enquiries concerning it.

In fact I suppose that the American Captains proceeded under the mistake that the swedish cutter was a french privatier & I presume that some general declarations of good will & respect on our part will be all that can be requird from us. I postpone writing to Mr. King til I receive your instructions.[2] I remain Sir with very much respect, Your obedt. Servt

J Marshall

To Mary W. Marshall

ALS, Marshall Papers, Swem Library, College of William and Mary

My dearest Polly [Washington], August 8, 1800

I have this moment receivd yours of the 5th.[3] & cannot help regreting that it affords me no hope of seeing you soon or that you are perfectly well.

I am delighted with the account you give me of Mary's dinner

9. See Rufus King to Timothy Pickering, Sept. 11, 1799, printed in King, ed., *Life and Corres. of Rufus King*, III, 103–104. For the complaint of the chargé d'affaires and the protest of the captain of the Swedish ship, see George de Silverhjehm to King, July 26, 1799, and Protest of Capt. A. G. von Gerdlen, July 26, 1799, *ibid.*, 80–83.

1. JM's letter to James Simmons (1761–1815), collector of the port of Charleston, has not been found.

2. See Adams to JM, Aug. 18, 1800, and JM to King, Aug. 26, 1800.

3. Not found.

with you & of John's good breeding. Tell him I say he is a fine boy for his attention to his sister & his love for his Mama.

I approve of your sending the boys up the country.

I receivd a letter from Tom[4] inclosing the sermon I wrote for but he did not say a single word about you. This was a cruel disappointment to me because I cannot flatter myself with respect to you that silence is an evidence of good health. I am my dearest Polly, your

J MARSHALL

From John Adams

ALS, RG 59, National Archives

Dear Sir[5]   Quincy, August 11, 1800

On Saturday night I recd your favour of the 26. Ult. The German Letter proposing to introduce into this Country; a Company of schoolmasters, Painters Poets &c all of them Disciples of Mr Thomas Paine, will require no answer. I had rather countenance the Introduction of Ariel and Caliban with a Troop of Spirits the most mischievous from Fairyland.

The Direction to deliver the Sandwich to the Spanish Minister, on the requisition of the King of Spain, as the Case is stated, no doubt accurately, in your Letter I believe was right, and it was better to do it promptly than wait for my particular orders in a Case so plain.[6]

Respecting Bowles, I wrote you on the 31st. of July that I thought General Wilkinson and Mr Hawkins should be written to. I now add that I think the Governors of Georgia, Tennessee, & the Mississippi Territory should be written to, to employ all the means in their Power to preserve the good faith of the United States According to the fifth article of the Treaty with Spain. How far it will be proper to order Gen. Wilkinsen to cooperate with the Spanish Government or military forces, it will be proper for the heads of Departments to consider. I can see no Objection against ordering them to join in an Expedition against Bowles, wherever he may be, in concert with the Spanish forces at their request. The only danger would arise from Misunder-

---

4. The letter from JM's son has not been found.
5. JM endorsed the letter "recd. Aug. 22d. 1800."
6. See Carlos Martínez de Yrujo to JM, July 7, 1800, and JM to Adams, July 26, 1800.

standings and disagreements between the officers or Men.

In my Letter of 31. Ult I also requested you to give, a civil Answer to the Chevalier, assuring him of our Sincere Friendship for the Spanish Government and Nation and of our Resolution to full fill the Treaty with good faith &c. This Letter I hope you recd.

On the 1st. of August I wrote you on the subject of a sum in gross to be paid instead of going through all the Chicanery, which may be practicable under the Treaty. I most perfectly agree with You and the Heads of Departments, that the Proposition merits serious attention. My only objection to it is one that cannot be seriously mentioned. I am afraid that as soon as this Point of dispute is removed, such is their habitual delight in Wrangling with Us, that they will invent some other. Some Pretext or other for venting their spleen and ill humour against Us they will always find. This however cannot be gravely urged as a reason against settling this quarell. I am willing you should write to Mr King Instructions on this head.[7] Take the opinion however of the heads of departments on the Letter before you send it. If they are unanimous with you for going as far as a million, in the Latitude to be given to Mr King in the negotiation, I will agree to it. With the Utmost Esteem

JOHN ADAMS

From John Adams

Letterbook Copy, Adams Papers, Massachusetts Historical Society

[*August 11, 1800, Quincy.* Adams requests that Frederick Butler,[8] of Wethersfield, Conn., be granted a patent for a tin cook stove.]

From John Adams

ALS, RG 59, National Archives

Dear Sir   Quincy, August 11, 1800

I have recd your favour of Aug. 1st.

I wrote you, on the 7th of this month my Consent to the appoint-

7. See JM to Adams, Aug. 23, 1800, and JM to Rufus King, Aug. 23, 1800 (first letter).

8. Butler's patent for a machine for cooking was granted on Aug. 22, 1800. See *Amer. State Papers, Miscellaneous,* I, 427.

ment of Major David Hopkins to be Marshall conformably to the advice of Mr Stoddert.

The Letter from the Prince Regent of Portugal, announcing another Birth, with the Answer prepared for my signature I find not among the Papers. It has not arrived to me.[9]

I embrace with pleasure the Recommendation of Mr King, of an Agreement with the British Government for a sum in gross in lieu of Claims under the 6th article. Can any plan be devised, to induce the Debtors to contribute some proportion of the Money? With the highest regard &c

J. ADAMS

To Jonathan Dayton

ALS, Charles G. Slack Collection, Marietta College Library

[*August 11, 1800, Washington.* JM writes in reply to Dayton's letter of Aug. 5, 1800,[10] that the patent applied for by a Mr. Brooklyn[1] may have already been granted to Silas Betts of New York.]

To Timothy Pickering

ALS, Pickering Papers, Massachusetts Historical Society

Dear Sir   Washington, August 11, 1800

I receivd your letter[2] inclosing one to Genl. Pinckney which I have forwarded to him. What you say of Major Mountflorence & Mr. Mitchell will certainly be attended to.

9. See JM to Adams, Aug. 1, 1800. The letter arrived soon after. See Adams to JM, Miscellaneous Letters Received, RG 59, National Archives.

10. Not found. Dayton (1760–1824), of New Jersey, had been Speaker of the House in 1799 and then served in the Senate from 1799 to 1805.

1. Silas Betts's patent on an improvement in a tide waterwheel was granted on Mar. 18, 1797. There is no patent listed as being granted to Brooklyn, although a patent was granted to Aaron Brookfield on Oct. 24, 1800, for an invention that raised water for mills. See *Amer. State Papers, Miscellaneous*, I, 425, 427.

2. Pickering's letter has not been found, but see Memorandum, Aug. 2, 1800, Pickering Papers, Massachusetts Historical Society, in which Pickering notes that he sent JM a letter on that date. The letter enclosed a letter to Charles Cotesworth Pinckney in which Pickering "mentions the reasons why M[ountflorence] had not been further employed and the different opinions concerning him." James C. Mountflorence and John Mitchell were applying for positions as consuls at Paris and Le Havre, respectively. See Mitchell to Pickering, Apr. 15, 1800, *ibid*.

I transmit you two letters which have come under cover to the secretary of state. I am sir very respectfully, Your obedt. Servt

J MARSHALL

From Israel Whelen

LS, RG 59, National Archives

[*August 11, 1800, Washington*. JM writes in reply to Dayton's letter of Aug. 5, 1800,[10] that the patent applied for by a Mr. Brooklyn[1] may have already been granted to Silas Betts of New York.]

To John Adams

ALS, Adams Papers, Massachusetts Historical Society

Sir   Washington, August 12, 1800

I send you the copy of a letter transmited to this department by the Chevallier de Yrujo.[3]

Your letter of the 31st. of July, inclosing one addressd to yourself personally, by the minister of his Catholic Majesty,[4] was receivd on the 9th inst., & I have, in conformity with your wish, consulted with the Secretary of war on the means proper to be usd on the occasion. He will write to Colo. Hawkins requesting him to continue his endeavors to detach the indians from Bowles, & to suppress his party. Those endeavors have already been usd, & I beleive successfully. A friendly deputation from the creek nation, with pacific objects, has visited the Seminoles, & it is hop'd will be too powerful for the *mischief makers*.

Their endeavors will be aided by the recapture of St. Marks, an event mentiond by Colo.Hawkins in a letter of the 10th. of July. A Mr. Gilabert, who exercises the powers of government at Pensacola in the absence of the governor who commands the expedition against Bowles, expresses his satisfaction at the friendly conduct of the United States, & I shoud conceive from his letters to Mr. Hawkins, that he neither expected nor wishd further efforts on our part than such as

3. See Carlos Martínez de Yrujo to JM, calendared at July 31, 1800.
4. See Yrujo to Adams, July 22, 1800, Notes from Foreign Legations, Spain, II, RG 59, National Archives.

have been already made. It does not appear to me that the Spaniards require any military aid: nor do I suppose they woud be willing to receive it. A body of American troops in either of the Floridas woud excite very much their jealosy, especially when no specific requisition for them has been made & when their own force is entirely competent to the object.[5]

The Spanish minister woud appear to suspect that Bowles is supported by the British government. Altho that suspicion may have some appearances in its support, yet I am strongly inclind to belive the fact to be otherwise. Mr. Liston calld on me the other day in his passage through this city & read me part of a letter receivd by the last packet from Lord Grenville,[6] requesting him to give the most positive assurances to the American government that the British government gave no aid support or direction to Bowles, nor did he act in any manner whatever by their authority. Unless some strong counter testimony existed I shoud suppose these assurances deservd credit.

I shall write a letter to the Chevallier conforming to your instructions.[7]

I have also receivd your two letters one of the 31st. of July returning the dispatches from our ministers at Paris & the other of the 1st. of August concerning the dispatch from Mr. King No. 67.

If the payment of a sum in gross, in lieu of what might be awarded under the 6th. article of our treaty with Britain, shoud be decided on, there will certainly be much difficulty in estimating its amount; nor will it be possible to say precisely what its amount shoud be. We may conjecture & can only conjecture what sum, on our construction of the article, ought to be awarded against us; but when we recollect the extravagant pretensions of a majority of the board of Commissioners, & that however the persons may be changd, yet the majority must continue to be constituted in a manner unfavorable to the

5. Benjamin Hawkins's letter has not been found.

The Spanish had formally surrendered the fort of St. Marks on May 19, 1800. Gov. Vincente Folch, Spanish governor of West Florida, had led an expedition to recapture the fort from William Bowles and his band of Creek Indians. Bowles had asked the British for help in wresting this area from Spanish control, and the episode had become a source of difficulty for the United States. The Spanish recaptured the fort on June 23, 1800. See J. Leitch Wright, Jr., *William Augustus Bowles: Director General of the Creek Nation* (Athens, Ga., 1967), 127–131, 136.

6. See Grenville to Robert Liston, May 9, 1800, F.O. 115/8, Public Record Office. See also Liston to JM, Aug. 25, 1800, for Liston's formal statement of British policy with regard to Bowles.

7. Not found, but see JM to Liston, Sept. 6, 1800.

United States, we shall have cause to apprehend that, tho those pretensions may in part be receded from, yet sums will be awarded against us, exceeding what justice & a sound impartial construction of the article, woud warrant. Under these circumstances it woud I think be the real interest of the United States to pay, perhaps something more than we beleive to be really due, rather than risk the arbitration.

The claims of the British creditors woud not by such a compact be extinguishd as against American debtors. Our courts woud still be open to them & their rights woud be the same as heretofore : but their claim against the American nation for those debts which had been lost or diminishd by impediments created by the diffirent states woud be extinguishd by the new compact & the receipt on the part of their government of the stipulated satisfaction for such claims.

I doubt whether under such an arrangement it woud be necessary to obtain an assignment of the claims of the creditors—but if this be requird, it may be done.

France I beleive woud have no just cause to complain of such a transaction. With the most respectful attachment, I remain Sir your obedt. Servt.

J MARSHALL

From John Adams

ALS, RG 59, National Archives

Dear Sir   Quincy, August 13, 1800

In Answer to yours of the 2d, I have agreed to the Appointment of Major David Hopkins to be Marshall of Maryland,[8] according to the Advice of Mr Stoddert, although it was a great disappointment and Mortification to me to loose the only opportunity I shall ever have, of testifying to the World the high opinion I have of the Merits of a Great Magistrate by the appointment of his son to an office for which he is fully qualified and accomplished.

I agree with you that a Letter should be written to the Government of Guadaloupa remonstrating against the Treatment of Daniel Tripe and another Sailor, and holding up the Idea of Retaliation.

8. Hopkins's commission was issued on Aug. 15, 1800, and was countersigned by JM. See Temporary Presidential Commissions, 1789–1909, RG 59, National Archives.

I agree too that Complaint should be made, through Mr Humphreys, to the Spanish Court of the Violation of their Treaty in the Case of Gregorie and Pickard of Boston.[9] With cordial Esteem &c

                                                                    J. ADAMS

P.S. I return Mr Sitgreavess Letter recd in yours of Aug. 2d.

From William L. Smith

LS, RG 59, National Archives

[*August 13, 1800, Lisbon.*[1] Smith writes that he has received the letter of May 22 from the State Department[2] that informed him of the two vessels chartered to carry cargo to Tunis and Algiers. This, he says, will "induce a continuation of that Tranquillity which subsisted at the date of the last Advices, but which will be ever precarious, untill consolidated by the exhibition of our Naval Ressources & Spirit in the Mediterranean."

He also reports on correspondence with the consuls in Algiers, Tunis, and Tripoli.[3] He received a letter from Richard O'Brien dated July 15, 1800, which relates that the United States is in debt to the Bacris[4] for $110,000, besides being in arrears to the Regency. O'Brien writes, "We must act with more Energy or war will be the result; the consequences you have an example of in the Danish affairs at Tunis & Algiers;[5] we should have a few of our large Frigates in the Mediterranean."

Smith has received no recent letters from William Eaton but is expecting information on the gift of jewels for the bey from the president. Smith's opinion is that the bey's "extravagant demand ought to be resisted as long as possible."

Smith refers to a letter from Eaton[6] regarding the nature of a demand made by the bey of Tripoli. Should the bey persist in his demand and "our

9. For JM's letter on Tripe and the Boston firm, see JM to Adams, Aug. 2, 1800.

1. This dispatch was received by the State Department on Oct. 14, 1800.

2. Not found. Charles Lee was acting secretary of state from May 13 to June 5, 1800. The *George Washington*, an armed merchantman, was sent to Algiers and the *Anna Maria* to Tunis in Aug. 1800.

3. Not found.

4. The Bacris were bankers in Algiers from whom the United States borrowed money.

5. On June 28, 1800, the bey of Tunis declared war on Denmark after capturing eight Danish merchant ships, despite the Danes having paid regular tribute. See Glenn Tucker, *Dawn like Thunder: The Barbary Wars and the Birth of the U.S. Navy* (Indianapolis, Ind., 1963), 116. See also James L. Cathcart to [JM], Aug. 14, 1800, Consular Despatches, Tripoli, I, RG 59, National Archives, and William Eaton to Richard O'Brien, June 28, 1800, *Barbary War Docs.*, I, 362.

6. See William L. Smith to [JM], May 7, 1800, Diplomatic Despatches, Portugal, V, RG 59. See also JM to Rufus King, Aug. 16, 1800; and King to Smith, Oct. 8, 1800, in King, ed., *Life and Corres. of Rufus King*, III, 319.

governmt. find it convenient to send some Frigates up the straights, a quarrel with Tripoli would be rather favorable to our affairs. Consul Cathcart's narrative of Commodr. Campbell's[7] expedition against that nest of Pirates (in the Office of State) will shew the facility with which it may be awed into good behavior, & the happy influence of such acts on the other Regencies."

Smith concludes his letter with news of an aborted attempt made by Campbell to blockade Algiers and by assuring the State Department that he will deliver the president's answer to the letter from the prince regent of Portugal.]

From John Monroe

ALS, RG 59, National Archives

[*August 14, 1800, Lexington, Ky.* Monroe[8] applies for the office of federal attorney in Kentucky. He reminds JM of their acquaintance in Virginia and adds that Bushrod Washington can testify to his ability to discharge the duties of the office he solicits.]

From Israel Whelen

LS, RG 59, National Archives

[*August 14, 1800, Philadelphia.* Whelen writes for an additional sum of $10,000 to pay for the *George Washington*'s cargo and to cover Ebenezer Stevens's draft. He asks whether he should separate the accounts of the *George Washington*'s and *Anna Maria*'s cargoes.[9] Joshua Humphreys estimates that more than three times the amount of timber that was taken by the *George Washington* is still sound for shipment to Algiers and Tunis. Whelen has insured the cargo of the *George Washington* for $40,000 at 5% interest and will insure the *Anna Maria* in New York at a cheaper premium, or 7% interest, than can be obtained in Philadelphia. He encloses a duplicate receipt for $40,000 received on Aug. 14 from the Treasury of the United States for the Barbary negotiations.]

7. Not found, but see Charles Lee to Cathcart, May [13], 1800, Consular Despatches, Algiers, V, RG 59. Comdr. Hugh George Campbell (1760–1820).

8. A John Monroe was federal attorney for western Virginia in 1802. See *Amer. State Papers, Miscellaneous*, I, 303.

9. See Stevens to Whelen, Aug. 8, 1800, in *Barbary War Docs.*, I, 366–367.

From John Adams

ALS, RG 59, National Archives

Dear Sir   Quincy, August 15, 1800

I received, but last night your favour of the 4th. I have read the Papers enclosed.   1. the Letter from Mr Robert Waln.   2 The Letter from Gid Hill Wells   3. The representation of three Masters of Vessells Thos Choate Robert Forrest and Knowles Adams, relative to the Consulate at Madeira.[1]

If there is a necessity of removing Mr John Marsden Pintard a native American and an old Consull, why should We appoint a Foreigner in his stead? Among the Number of Applications for Consulates, cannot We find an American capable and worthy of the Trust? Mr Lamar is a Partner in a respectable House: but it is said to be an English or rather a Scotch House.[2] Why should We take the Bread out of the mouths of our own children and give it to Strangers? We do so much of this, in the Army, Navy, and especially in the Consulships abroad that it frequently gives me great anxiety.

If however, you know of no American fit for it, who would be glad of it, I shall consent to your giving the Commission to Mr Lamar; for it seems to me from these last representations there is a necessity of removing Mr Pintard. With high Esteem

J. ADAMS

N.B. I return you all the Papers.

1. None of the letters transmitted by JM has been found, although Robert Waln (1765–1836) in a letter to Albert Gallatin in 1801 wrote that a representation had been made to the secretary of state by a number of Philadelphia merchants, stating that "the long absence of Mr. Pintard and other circumstance rendered it highly necessary to appoint some other person to that Office and recommending Mr. Marien Lamar a native of Maryland and a partner in one of the most respectable houses in the Island as his successor. From the information then received it was expected that an appointment wou'd have been immediately made, but nothing has been done in the business." See Waln to Gallatin, June 6, 1801, Letters of Application & Recommendation during the Administration of Thomas Jefferson, 1801–1809, RG 59, National Archives.

Choate was the captain of the *Betsey*, and Knowles Adams (d. 1799) was the captain of the *Mary Ann*. See *Quasi-War with France Docs.*, IV, 58, III, 170–173, 436.

2. John Marsden Pintard (1760–1811), U.S. consul at Madeira, was accused of abusing the privileges of his office. The controversy over his dismissal and the consequent appointment of his successor continued from 1797 until 1803, when Marien Lamar (d. *ca.* 1807), of Maryland, a merchant in Madeira, was appointed consul. For biographical information on Pintard and Lamar, see *Letters of John Pintard to His Daughter* (New-York Historical Society, *Collections*, LXX–LXXIII [New York, 1937–1940]), and Harold Dihel LeMar, *History of the Lamar or Lemar Family in America* (Omaha, Nebr., 1941). For letters of recommendation for Lamar and for Pintard's cousin, Lewis Searle

From American Envoys

LS, RG 59, National Archives

Sir   Paris, August 15, 1800

Having ascertained by an interview with the French Ministers soon after our note to them of the 8th of May (a copy of which you have doubtless received)[3] that as we refused to assume the former treaties they could proceed no further without new instructions, and that a report on the state of the negotiation was preparing for the Minister of Exterior Relations, and ultimately for the Premier Consul, we judged it expedient, in order to obviate an apprehension that our Government contemplated further grants to the prejudice of France, and to diminish the hazard of sending off the business to the Premier Consul, then with the army in Switzerland who in a *moment*[4] *of agitation* might pronounce definitively upon it, to propose the following clause as an addition to the 32d Article of our project viz.

Nor will either of the said Parties while they continue in amity make a treaty with any foreign Sovereign or State stipulating *for the privatiers & prizes of* such Sovereign or State *an asylum in the ports of either* unless they shall have *assured to each other such right of asylum* for the *privatiers & prizes of each in the ports of the other*. And it was accordingly sent with the note marked A.[5]

Embarrassing as the delay for new instructions was foreseen to be, it was neverthess deemed inexpedient in the then critical state of European affairs to *treat as a studied delay*.

On the 1st of June we addressed the Note marked B and on the 5th. received an answer marked C.

Soon after the Premier's return from Italy [*the*] Note Marked D was sent.

Pintard (1773–1818), see Letters of Application & Recommendation, 1801–1809, RG 59. See also John Marsden Pintard, [*Letters to Timothy Pickering, Secretary of State, and the President of the United States* (New York, 1800)]; Pickering's comments on Pintard's actions and his recommendation of Lamar, in Pickering to Adams, Dec. 17, 1799, and Jan. 30, 1800, Adams Papers, Massachusetts Historical Society; Pintard's defense of his actions, in Pintard to JM, Nov. 7, 1800; and additional correspondence between JM and Adams on Pintard.

3. This note is enclosed in American Envoys to [JM], calendared at May 17, 1800, and is printed in *Amer. State Papers, Foreign Relations*, II, 320–324.

4. The italicized words, originally in code, were decoded by JM.

5. The documents marked A through G are enclosed with this letter and also have been printed. *Ibid.*, 326–330.

The requested interview took place on the 11th. of July, and altho' the French Ministers declared that they had not received further instru[ctions] yet as they expressed a willingness to converse upon the subject, a conversation was entered upon, which had for it's object to ascertain with more precision the grounds of difference between us. Their observations led to, and finally terminated in this position, that to be deprived of her former priviledges in the ports of the United States, and that too in favor of an enemy, and at the same time to be called upon for compensation was derogatory to the honor of France.

At a further interview on the 15th of July we brought forward in order to remove what seemed to be the difficulty at the interview on the 11th of July, a written proposal *to suspend the actual payment* of indemnities *on the condition of replacing* France in the *privileges she contended for*. A condition which our Government *might or might not perform after it* should have *further seen the political state of europe* and also been better able *to estimate a promise of indemnity*.

The proposition was as follows viz.

Indemnities to be ascertained, and secured in the manner proposed in our project of a treaty, *but not to be paid until* the United States shall *have offerd to France an article* stipulating *free admission in the ports of each* for the *privatiers & prizes of the other to the exclusion* of their *enemies* nor *unless the article* shall be offered *within seven years* Such *article to have* the same *effect in point of priority as* a similar *provision had in the treaty of 1778.*

An immediate reply to the proposition was not pressed or wished; there was no difficulty however in perceiving that the impression was not perfectly satisfactory.

On the 23d of July the note was sent marked [E] which throws some further light on the two preceding conferences.

On the 27th of July the Note marked F was recd. To this no answer was returned as it had become useless to pursue the subject of it.

The note marked G purporting to be predicated on the new instructions was received the 11th of August. This note is now under consideration and will not be formally answered, untill there has been an interview to ascertain *some points.*

It has however become manifest that *the negotiation must be abandoned or our instructions deviated from.* Should the latter *be ventur'd* upon, which from present appearances is not improbable, the *deviation will be no greater* than a *change of circumstances* may be *presumd to justify.*

The success of the French in Italy produced an Armistice, and has since opened with the Emperor a negotiation for peace, which is yet pending. The result is daily and anxiously expected.

Captn. McNiell with the Portsmouth arrived safe at Havre the 23d of May, where he yet remains. The dispatches sent by him were duly received. We have the honor to be, Sir, with very high respect, your most obedient

OLIV. ELLSWORTH
W: R: DAVIE
W. V. MURRAY

From David Humphreys

LS, RG 59, National Archives

[*August 15, 1800, Madrid*.[6] In dispatch no. 245, Humphreys reports on his activities and accounts as minister to Spain. Enclosed is his expense account for 1799 to 1800, including $820 for "Gratifications paid to persons about the Palace by indispensable Custom." He claims that living expenses are "dearer here than in any other Capital of Europe" and that most other governments make special allowances for their diplomats.

Word has been received that France may be preparing to invade Portugal or extort more money as a condition of peace. Rumor also says that the American envoys have left Paris without agreement on a treaty. In a coded portion of his letter, which JM decoded, Humphreys reports on a confidential letter received from Paris informing him that the negotiations are continuing, but he fears the demands for compensation by France will prevent a treaty. "*You will recollect that our treaty with France had been declard void by congress. France thinks compensation can be made only on the idea that the treaty is in force or on its being revivd which cannot be done without infracting the british treaty.* This was the 24th. of July."]

From Israel Whelen

LS, RG 59, National Archives

[*August 15, 1800, Philadelphia*. Whelen writes that Ebenezer Stevens[7] requests $16,000, owed to John Murray & Son, for the cargo delivered at Tunis by the *Hero*. Whelen requests instructions on how to proceed.]

6. JM wrote on the duplicate of this dispatch that it was received on Nov. 4, 1800. Italics indicate words originally in code.

7. Whelen enclosed the letter from Stevens in this letter. See Stevens to Whelen, Aug. 14, 1800, Miscellaneous Letters Received, RG 59, National Archives.

To Carlos Martínez de Yrujo

ALS, Adams Papers, Massachusetts Historical Society

Sir[8]   Washington, August 15, 1800

The President of the United States has transmited to this department your letter of the 22d. of July addressd personally to him,[9] with
directions to assure you in the most explicit manner, of the continuing sincere friendship of this government for the spanish government
& nation, & of its fix'd determination to fulfill with perfect good faith
the stipulations of the treaty enterd into with his Catholic Majesty.
Orders corresponding with this determination have been long since
given to the proper officers both civil & military.

Early in the last session of Congress an act was passd subjecting to
fine & imprisonment, any person residing within the United States
or its territory, who shoud send any talk, speech, message, or letter,
to any indian nation tribe or chief, with an intent to produce a con-
travention or infraction of any treaty or other law of the United
States.[1]

In the spirit of this law directions were immediately given to watch
the conduct of William A. Bowles, & to prevent, so far as we coud
prevent, even with a military force, if under existing circumstances
the use of such means shoud be deemd adviseable, any expedition
against the dominions of spain; to be carried on by indians residing
within the boundaries of the United States.

Colo. Hawkins agent for the United States with the indians of the
southern department has, in pursuance of instructions which have
been given him, usd, we beleive successfully, the influence of his
government with those tribes, to preserve among them a pacific
temper & conduct towards the dominions & subjects of his Catholic
Majesty. These measures have producd a deputation from the Creek
nation to the Seminoles for the purpose of inducing them to restrain
the *Mischief makers* who have followd the standard of Bowles & we
have no reason to doubt its success. A Mr. Gilabert, the gentleman
who at present exercises the powers of government at Pensacola, has

8. JM prepared this copy for Adams and enclosed it in JM to Adams, Aug. 16, 1800.
9. See Carlos Martínez de Yrujo to Adams, July 22, 1800, Adams Papers, Massachusetts Historical Society.
1. 2 Stat. 6–7. The act for the preservation of peace with the Indian tribes was passed
on Jan. 17, 1800. See *Annals of Congress*, X, 23, 26, 1436.

unequivocally expressd his sense of the kind offices renderd by Mr. Hawkins.[2]

The recapture of St. Marks of which we are informd in a letter dated the 10th. of July, connected with the means of pacification which have been usd under the authority of the United States, will, we are persuaded, effectually disarm Bowles & disperse his party. I am Sir with very high respect, Your obedt. Servt.

J MARSHALL

To John Adams

ALS, Adams Papers, Massachusetts Historical Society

Sir[3]   Washington, August 16, 1800

I have transmited to Major Hopkins a commission as marshal for the district of Maryland. This step was taken with reluctance because your preference seemd to be in favor of Mr. Chase.

The petition of Isaac Williams with the accompanying documents was, in conformity with your direction laid before the heads of departments & by their unanimous opinion the fines are remited. I have inclosd his pardon to the marshal for the district of connecticut.[4]

Mr. Wagner has transmited to Mr. Weld his papers with instructions which when complied with, will authorize the issuing of an amended patient.[5]

I have written to Mr. King as you directed,[6] requesting him to present, if he shoud deem it adviseable, to his Britannic majesty the congratulations of the President & Government of the United States on his fortunate escape from the meditated blow of an assassin, & I have also requested him to purchase the jewels for the Bey of Tunis. I wait only for your decision respecting the stipulation proposd of a sum in gross in lieu of the claims of the British creditors on the government of the United States to prepare a letter to him on that subject also. In such a letter the ultimate sum shoud your opinion be that such an

---

2. See also JM to Adams, Aug. 12, 1800.

3. The letter is endorsed "Secretary of State, rec. 25 Aug. An 26."

4. See JM to Simeon Baldwin, Aug. 16, 1800. See also Adams to JM, Aug. 7, 1800 (second letter).

5. See Adams to JM, Aug. 7, 1800 (first letter).

6. See Adams to JM, Aug. 11, 1800, and JM to Rufus King, Aug. 16, 1800.

agreement may be enterd into, must be mentiond. I stated to you that the secretaries with whom I had consulted on this subject were all of opinion that it woud be adviseable to give five milion of dollars in satisfaction of all claims under the 6th. article of our treaty. Mr. Lee to whom I also spoke on the subject seemd to think that sum too considerable. Without doubt Mr. King will make the best possible bargain & therefore it is only for us to state the ultimatum. If you will favor me with your directions on this subject I will immediately pre- pare & transmit for your consideration a letter respecting it.[7]

I inclose you the copy of a letter which I sent yesterday to the Chevallier de Yrujo.[8] Since its date the secretary of war has shown me dispatches from Colo. Hawkins stating that an expedition is about to be carried on by the creeks aided by some American troops for the purpose of punishing & reducing to a quiet & orderly behavior some indians who have carried on an expedition against & done some mischief to the Spanish settlements. I am Sir with the most respectful attachment, Your Obedt. Servt

J MARSHALL

From John Adams

ALS, RG 59, National Archives

Dear Sir   Quincy, August 16, 1800
The inclosed Letter from Cotton Tufts[9] Esq one of the most re- spectable Men in our State I pray you to file with all the other appli- cations for Consulships, that it may be considered in due time. I am with the greatest regard &c

J. ADAMS

7. See JM to King, Aug. 23, 1800 (first letter).
8. See JM to Yrujo, Aug. 15, 1800.
9. The letter from Cotton Tufts (1732–1815), a physician, a caretaker, and a relative of Adams, has not been found. Turell Tufts mentioned that Dr. Tufts had written a recommendation for him for a post as consul to Bordeaux, in Turell Tufts to JM, Dec. 4, 1800. See also Turell Tufts to Adams, Aug. 8, 1800, Adams Papers, Massachusetts Historical Society.

To Simeon Baldwin

ALS, Collection of Susan H. Elias, Haverford, Pa.

Sir[1]   Washington, August 16, 1800

In conformity with the directions of the President a pardon has been granted to Isaac Williams.[2] To ensure its safe & speedy conveyance I take the liberty of commiting it to your care. Let it be transmited to the Marshal or any of his deputies. I am Sir very respectfully, your obedt. Servt.

J MARSHALL

To Rufus King

LS, RG 59, National Archives

No: 1

Dear Sir,   Washington, August 16, 1800

Your letters to No: 74 inclusive have been received. The President directs me to request that you will, if under existing circumstances you shall yourself deem it adviseable, offer to the King of Great Britain, in terms corresponding with the friendly dispositions he continues to manifest, his congratulations, and if you think proper that of the American government, on the fortunate escape of his Majesty from the blow of an assassin which so seriously endangered his life.[3]

With the claim of jewels on the part of the Bey of Tunis the President is by no means satisfied. To purchase them however, he deems the less evil, and therefore wishes the commission of Mr. Eaton to be executed. The President is of opinion that you should be kept regularly informed of the actual state of our affairs with the Barbary powers, and has desired me to give instructions to that effect to our Minister at Lisbon and to our Consuls with those regencies.[4]

1. JM addressed this letter to Baldwin, "Clerk of the court of the United States, New Haven, Connecticut." Baldwin (1761–1851) was clerk of the U.S. District and Circuit Courts of Connecticut from 1789 to 1806. He served as clerk at Williams's trial.

2. See John Adams to JM, Aug. 7, 1800 (second letter), and Pardon of Isaac Williams, Aug. 16, 1800, Pardons & Remissions, I, RG 59, National Archives.

3. King responded to this letter on Oct. 26, 1800. See also King's instruction to William L. Smith, Oct. 8, 1800, in King, ed., *Life and Corres. of Rufus King*, III, 319.

4. See John Adams to JM, Aug. 2, 1800.

I hope in a few days to receive directions on the interesting subject of the 6th: Article of our Treaty of Amity &c. with Great Britain.[5] With the most entire respect and esteem, I Remain Dear Sir, Your obedient Servant

J MARSHALL

To Timothy Pickering

ALS, Pickering Papers, Massachusetts Historical Society

Dear Sir   Washington, August 16, 1800

I inclose you a letter receivd in a packet from Consul Eaton at Tunis.[6]

I have receivd your letter covering one from Mr. OBrien[7] respecting the money he wishes shoud be paid to his mother & will take measures to make the necessary remitance.

Mr. Cist unfortunately applied to me with your letter of the 2d. of August[8] for the current business of this office after I had engagd it to another. But for this circumstance your recommendation woud certainly have been decisive. I am dear Sir with much respect & esteem, Your obedt. Servt.

J MARSHALL

5. See Adams to JM, Aug. 22 and 26, 1800.

6. William Eaton forwarded this letter in Eaton to JM, July 21, 1800, RG 59, National Archives. See Eaton to Pickering, May 13, 1800, Pickering Papers, Massachusetts Historical Society. Pickering wrote on the last page of this letter, "forwarded from City of Washington by Genl. Marshall in his letter of Augt. 16."

7. This letter has not been found, although Pickering noted in a memorandum that he wrote to JM, "enclosing Capt. Richard O'Brien's letter of May 6, 1800, desiring money for the public service, and that his mother Rebecca Arrundell may be paid 200 dollars a year out of his Salary." Memorandum, Aug. 7, 1800, *ibid*.

8. This letter has not been found, but see *ibid*., Aug. 2, 1800, where Pickering notes that he wrote JM "recommending Mr. Cist."

John Adams had written to Pickering on Apr. 23, inquiring about hiring a printer in the service of the government. Perhaps Pickering was recommending Charles Cist (1738–1805), who printed many government documents, to be the official government printer. See Adams to Pickering, Apr. 23, 1800, *ibid*.

From John Adams

ALS, RG 59, National Archives

Dear Sir   Quincy, August 18, 1800

I believe you will find in the office that either the original or a Duplicate of Mr Kings Triplicate Dispatch of Sept. 11 1799[9] has been before received and perhaps your Predecessor wrote to Mr King upon the subject. Be this as it may.

With you I presume it was a Mistake of the American Captains in thick and hazy Weather. But still it is proper that you should write to Mr King in the manner you propose and the letter you have written to the Collector of Charleston S. C. is a very proper one, that he may make an investigation of the Facts.[1]

Our Courts of Judicature are the proper Trybunals for the injured to resort to for Justice: or the owners or Captains of the American Letter of Marque ought voluntarily to make satisfaction if they were intentionally guilty of any outrage, which I think however is not probable. With great Esteem

JOHN ADAMS

I return Mr Kings Dispatch.

From Israel Whelen

LS, RG 59, National Archives

[*August 18, 1800, Philadelphia*. Whelen writes that in his letter of Aug. 15, 1800, he stated he had not yet seen George Harrison[2] or William Govett. In this letter he takes the opportunity of conveying information received from Govett.

The *Hero* was chartered by Tench Francis from John Murray & Son to take a load of timber and timber products to Algiers. The ship was loaded at Philadelphia and sailed at the end of 1798. Due to a violent storm, the bulk of its cargo was ruined or used to repair damage to the ship at Jamaica. It

---

9. See Rufus King to Timothy Pickering, Sept. 11, 1799, in King, ed., *Life and Corres. of Rufus King*, III, 103–104.

1. See JM to Adams, Aug. 8, 1800.

2. George Harrison was navy agent at Philadelphia and was also agent for the estate of Tench Francis. For a more complete history of the *Hero*, see *Barbary War Docs.*, I, 347–348.

then put in at New York, new cargo was assembled, and its destination was changed to Tunis, where it has since arrived. The bill of lading for $15,135.59, was shown to Whelen. Whelen reports that the accounts were never settled between Francis and Ebenezer Stevens and that no copies of letters from Francis are extant. Thus, the only information available on the subject is from Stevens's letters or from Govett's and Stevens's memories of the transactions.]

From David Humphreys

ALS, RG 59, National Archives

[*August 19, 1800, Madrid.* Humphreys, in dispatch no. 246, sends news of the negotiations at Paris[3] and a report of the capture of an American ship, *Swansbury*, by a French privateer and a Spanish gunboat.[4]]

To Mary W. Marshall

ALS, Marshall Papers, Swem Library, College of William and Mary

My dearest Polly[5]   [Washington], August 20, [1800]

I have just returnd from a visit to Mount Vernon where I passd an evening. Mrs. Washington askd me to bring you to see her when you shoud visit this city. She appears tolerably cheerful but not to possess the same sort of cheerfulness as formerly. You as a widow woud I hope show more firmness.

Tell Jaqueline I was much pleasd with his letter.[6] If he will keep his word & get a lesson every day while Mr. Burns is absent & will afterwards continue to get a few extra lines he will soon overtake the class he ought now to be in. Farewell my dearest Polly, I am your ever affectionate

J MARSHALL

3. Enclosures not found.
4. JM endorsed the letter on the verso "No. 246, recd. Novr. 4th. 1800. First mention made of a capture for a breach of the blockade of Gibraltar."
5. The letter, postmarked in Washington on Aug. 19, is addressed to JM's wife in Richmond.
6. The letter from JM's son has not been found.

From John Adams

ALS, RG 59, National Archives

Dear Sir   Quincy, August 22, 1800

I received last night, your favour of the 12th and am very happy to find that a Correspondence upon terms of friendship and good humour has at length taken Place between the office of state and the spanish Minister. I am entirely of your opinion and approve of all you have done. The Declaration of Mr Liston and Lord Grenville are to me satisfactory.

If the Relation between American Debtors and British Creditors should not be altered, and our Courts should be left open to the latter to recover their just dues, in all Cases, where any thing can be recovered I should hope that a Less sum than a Million sterling would suffice. I agree however With you and the heads of departments that it [*is*] better to pay more than We conjecture is due than go through all the trouble and run all the risk of the arbitration. I think with you that an assignment of the Claims would give more trouble than profit: Yet some mouths might be stopped by such a stipulation. I must be of little Consequence. With great esteem &c

JOHN ADAMS

From William Tazewell

ALS, RG 59, National Archives

Dr. Sir   Williamsburg, August 22, 1800

Your very acceptable favor of the 15th Inst. came to hand yesterday. In regard to the act of Congress respecting my Acct. as I ever have been I still remain fully persuaded that every exertion in your power was call'd forth in my favor, & am grateful accordingly.[7]

I have never seen the law relative to my demand & in course can not calculate with any degree of precission what tis meant should be paid me. If you will have the goodness to inform me what the sum is small or great (I am anxious to bring the business to a conclusion on any terms) a receipt shall be immediately forwarded you for the

7. JM's letter has not been found. For information on Tazewell's claim, see Legislative Petition, Mar. 13, 1800, and Tazewell to JM, June 8, 1800.

Amt. on receiving which perhaps t'will be in your power to render the money payable in Richmond.

In all, I received from Mr. Gerry precisely six hundred dollars as my receipt to him will shew. When he drew in my favor t'was for so many *dollars* for which I recd. french coin at the rate, if I recollect right of 5 livres 8 sous per. dollar.

I have no friend or acquaintance in the federal City I can take the liberty of appointing to settle the business for me, indeed my full conviction that your adjustment will be as favorable to me, as your duty to yourself & Country will admit, precludes the necessity of any such appointment. With the most sincere esteem & regard, Yr. Obt. Sert.

W. TAZEWELL

If tis not too much out of your way, will you give me your opinion in regard to the expediency of my coming to settle in the fedl. City? My practice here tho' as extensive as I could possibly have anticipated; from local circumstances is much more limitted than I could wish.

W.T.

To John Adams

ALS, Adams Papers, Massachusetts Historical Society

Sir[8]   Washington, August 23, 1800

I receivd by yesterdays mail your two letters of the 11th. inst. & that which coverd the duplicates of the letter to the Prince Regent of Portugal which will be sent by the first opportunity.

Instructions to Mr. King respecting an agreement for a sum in gross in compensation for the claims of British creditors under the 6th. article of our treaty of amity with Britain are prepard & will if approvd, be transmited to him. I understand your opinion to be that the explanatory articles if attainable, are preferd to any other mode of accomodating the differences which producd the dissolution of the board lately siting at Philadelphia, & that the next most eligible mode is the substitution of a sum in gross as compensation for the claims of the creditors on the United States. On this idea the letter to Mr. King is drawn. For many reasons I am myself decidedly of the

8. The letter is endorsed "Washington Aug 23d, Sec of State, rec 29th, ans 30, Mr Kings letter, No 77."

same opinion & I beleive there is with respect to it, no difference among the heads of departments.[9]

I showd Mr. Dexter your letter expressing your wish that the Governors of Georgia Tenessee & the Mississipi territory shoud be written to, requesting them to use all the means they possess to comply with the engagements of the United States to Spain. The last inteligence from Colo. Hawkins which has been communicated to you in letters you had not receivd on the 11th. of August, induces us to beleive that the measures taken already by the United States, in aid of the force employd by Spain, will have completely effected the object for which that force was employd. Under this impression it is supposd most adviseable to defer writing the letters to the Governors until further information reaches us, or until your further opinion shall be receivd.[1]

I am happy that the orders given respecting the Sandwich meet your approbation.

I inclose you the copy of a letter just receivd from Mr. King.[2] The new York papers will give you a still more full account of the affairs of Italy. The letter was receivd last night. I am Sir with very much respect, your obedt. Servt.

J Marshall

From John Adams

ALS, RG 59, National Archives

Dear Sir   Quincy, August 23, 1800

Inclosed is a Letter from Col. Norton of Martha's Vineyard and Copy of a Certificate from Sir Guy Carlton.[3] If Norton should make

9. See JM to Rufus King, Aug. 23, 1800 (first letter). Adams approved the letter to King in Adams to JM, Aug. 30, 1800 (first letter).

1. The letters of Benjamin Hawkins have not been found. See Adams to JM, Aug. 30, 1800 (first letter).

2. See King to [JM], calendared at July 5, 1800.

3. Beriah Norton (1734–1820), a prominent militia officer in the American Revolution, wrote to claim reimbursement for supplies furnished to British troops on Martha's Vineyard during the war. See Norton to Adams, Aug. 6, 1800, Miscellaneous Letters Received, RG 59, National Archives. The certificate from Carleton (1724–1808), commander of British troops in Canada during the Revolution, is enclosed with Norton's letter. See also Charles Edward Banks, *The History of Martha's Vineyard . . .* , III (Baltimore, 1966 [orig. publ. Edgartown, Mass., 1911]), 379.

Norton had already written to Timothy Pickering about his claim, but Pickering refused to respond to it. Jacob Wagner wrote to Pickering for additional information on you a Visit, it is my desire that you would attend to his story and give him a Letter to Mr King, requesting Mr King to give him any Aid in his Power, without committing his Government. I wish you to write at the same time a private Letter to Mr King expressing it to be at my request cautioning him against lending Money to Norton: for a burned Child dreads the fire. This Man took me in for fifty Guineas when I was in London no part of which shall I ever see. Norton's Cause I believe is just. But he is an insinuating, slippery Body. With great Esteem &c

JOHN ADAMS

To Alexander Hamilton

ALS, Hamilton Papers, Library of Congress

Dear Sir   Washington, August 23, 1800

I receivd to day your letter of the 19th. inst. accompanying a memorial from the governor General of the Danish West india islands respecting the conduct of some of our ships of War.[4]

This paper shall be immediately communicated [to th]e secretary of the Navy.

Our dispatches from Paris come no later than the 17th. of May. There is in them nothing on which a positive opinion respecting the result of that negotiation can be formd.

Connecting tho these state of things with european events which have since happend & with inteligence from America which has since reachd them, I shall not be surprizd if the paragraph from St. Sebastians shoud be true. With very much respect & esteem, I am dear Sir your obedt.

J MARSHALL

---

the case on Aug. 18, 1800. See Norton to Pickering, Apr. 26, 1800, and Wagner to Pickering, Aug. 18, 1800, Pickering Papers, Massachusetts Historical Society. See also Norton's petition reported to Congress, in *Amer. State Papers, Claims*, I, 226.

For JM's letter to Rufus King, see JM to King, Nov. 4, 1800.

4. Letter not found. For further information, see Harold C. Syrett *et al.*, eds., *The Papers of Alexander Hamilton*, XXV (New York, 1977), 80–81, where this letter is printed.

To Rufus King

LS, Henry E. Huntington Library

No. 4

Dear Sir,[5]   Washington, August 23, 1800

Your letter stating your negotiations with Lord Grenville respecting the differences which have arisen in executing the 6 Article of our treaty of Amity, Commerce and Navigation with Great Britain,[6] have been laid before and considered by the President.

He still retains the opinion that an amicable explanation of that Article is greatly to be desired, and therefore receives with much regret the information, that the British cabinet is indisposed to enter on the discussion of this interesting subject.

He perceives with a concern not entirely unmixed with other sensations, that the secession of two commissioners from the Board lately sitting in Philadelphia has been attributed, not to its real cause, but to motives which in no instance have ever influenced the American Government.

That Government is, as it has ever been, sincerely desirous of executing, with perfect and scrupulous good faith, all its engagements with foreign Nations. This desire has contributed, not inconsiderably, to the solicitude it now manifests, for the explanatory articles you have been instructed to propose.

The efforts of the American commissioners to proceed and decide on particular cases, instead of laying down abstract principles believed to be untrue in themselves, ought to have rescued their government from suspicions so very unworthy, and so little merited by the general tenor of its conduct.

The resolutions maintained by a majority of the late Board of commissioners, are such as the government of the United States can never submit to. They are considered, not as constructive of an existing treaty, but as imposing new and injurious burthens, unwarranted by compact, and to which, if in the first instance plainly and intelligibly stated, this government never could and never would have assented.

This opinion is not lightly taken up. It is a deep and solemn conviction produced by the most mature and temperate consideration

5. The letter is endorsed "Sec State No. 2.23 Aug. 1800, Recd. 14 Novr., 6 Art: of Eng. treaty."

6. King to [JM], Apr. 22, 1800 (first letter).

we are capable of bestowing on the subject.

This being the fixed judgment of the United States, it is impossible not seriously to apprehend, unless we could forget the past, that no attempt by arbitration to adjust the claims of individuals under the 6 Article of the treaty, previous to an explanation of it by the two governments, can be successful. A second effort at this adjustment by the proposed modification of the Board, while the principles heretofore contended for, receive the countenance of the British Government, would most probably, unless indeed the Board should again be dissolved, subject us to the painful alternative, of paying money which, in our best judgment, the commissioners had no power to award, or of submitting the public faith to imputations from which it could only be freed by a correct and laborious investigation of the subject. In a situation presenting to us only such an alternative, we are extremely unwilling to be placed.

It is then very seriously desired, that the explanations required by this Government, should be made. They are believed to be so reasonable in themselves, and to be so unquestionably in the spirit, and to the full extent to the existing treaty, that it is hoped the difficulties on the part of the British cabinet may yet be removed.

The President therefore requests that you will take any proper occasion, should one in your judgment present itself, to renew your application to Lord Grenville on this subject. Perhaps a change of temper may be produced by a change of circumstances, and there may be a state of things in which you may perceive a disposition favourable to the accomplishment of an object which ought to be desired by both nations, because it is just in itself, and because it will remove a subject of controversy which may, in the course of events, have a very unhappy influence on that good understanding and friendly intercourse, which it is the interest of both to preserve.

The note of the 18 of April addressed to you by Lord Grenville,[7] stating the determination of the British cabinet, not to modify, but to reject without discussion, the explanatory Articles proposed by you, on the part of the United States, assumes as the base of its decision, a principle not only so different from those admitted by this government, but so different from those recognized by both Nations in the Treaty of Amity negotiated between them, and which ought therefore to be adhered to in all explanations of that treaty, as to warrant

7. The note was enclosed in King's dispatch no. 67, Apr. 22, 1800, and is printed in full in *Amer. State Papers, Foreign Relations*, II, 395–398.

a hope, that the determination announced in that note, may not be unalterable.

His Lordship assumes as a fact that "the 4th Article of the treaty of Peace not having been duly executed on the part of the United States, the British Government withheld the delivery of the forts on the frontier of Canada, in order that these might serve as a pledge for the interests and rights secured to the British creditors under that Article."

But this is a fact which the American Government has ever controverted, and which has never yet been established.

Without entering into the always unavailing and now improper discussion of the question—which Nation committed the first fault? —it ought never to be forgotten that the treaty in which the claim of the British creditors on the United States originated, was avowedly entered into for the purpose of terminating the differences between the two Nations, "in such manner as, without reference to the merits of their respective complaints and pretensions, may be the best calculated to produce mutual satisfaction and good understanding."

In questions growing out of such a treaty neither nation can be permitted to refer to and decide the merits of those respective complaints and pretensions, by asserting that the other, and not itself has committed the first fault.

Lord Grenville then proceeds on the idea that the commissioners appointed by the American Government have withdrawn from the Board, merely because awards were rendered against their opinion, and on claims which they believed to be unjust.

But this idea is neither warranted by the conduct or declarations of the American Commissioners or of the government which appointed them. It has been and still is expressly disavowed. The commissioners and their government acquiesced under opinions which they conscientiously believed to be formed on erroneous principles, but on principles submitted by the treaty to their decision. Awards conforming to such opinions, unless by mutual consent the subject shall assume some other form, will be paid by the United States. It was not until a majority of the Board had proceeded to establish a system of rules for the government of their future decisions, which, in the opinion of this government, clearly comprehended a vast mass of cases never submitted to their consideration; that it was deemed necessary to terminate proceedings believed to be totally unauthorized, and which were conducted in terms and in a spirit, only calculated to destroy all harmony between the two Nations.

We understand the treaty differently from what Lord Grenville would seem to understand it, when he says that the decision of the Board constituted according to the provisions of that instrument "was expressly declared to be, in all cases, final and conclusive."

These terms have never been understood by us as authorizing the Arbiters to go out of the special cases described in the instrument creating and limiting their powers. The words "all cases" can only mean those cases which the two nations have submitted to reference. These are described in the preceding part of the Article, and this description is relied on by the United States, as constituting a boundary, within which alone the powers of the commissioners can be exercised. This boundary has, in our judgment, been so totally prostrated, that scarcely a trace of it remains. The reasoning on which we have formed this judgment, it would be unnecessary to detail to you, because you are in perfect possession of it.

Believing the British cabinet disposed to act justly and Honorably in a case, in which we conceive their reputation as well as ours to be concerned, we have been confident in the opinion, that to obtain their serious attention to the subjects of differences between the two Nations, was to secure the establishment of that reasonable and *liberal* construction of the Article, for which America has contended. We shall abondon this opinion with reluctance and regret.

Altho' the President decidedly prefers the amicable explanations which have been suggested, to any other mode of adjusting the differences which have arisen in executing the 6th. Article of our treaty with Great Britain, yet it is by no means the only mode to which he is willing to resort. He does not even require that you shall press this proposition in a manner which in your judgment may lessen the probability of settling existing differences, or further than may comport with the interests of the United States. Your situation—your full and near view of all the circumstances which can influence the negotiation, enable you to decide, more certainly than can be done on this side the Atlantic, on the precise course which it may be most advantageous to pursue. To your discretion therefore the President entirely submits this part of the subject.

If the explanatory Article so much desired by the United States be attainable, the substitution of a gross sum, in full compensation of all claims made or to be made on this goverment, under the 6th Article of our treaty of Amity, Commerce and Navigation with his Britannic Majesty, is deemed the most eligible remaining mode of accommodating those differences which have impeded the execution of that Article.

It is apparent that much difficulty will arise in agreeing on the sum which shall be received as compensation. The ideas of the two governments on this subject appear so different, that, without reciprocal sacrifices of opinion, it is probable they will be as far from agreeing on the sum which ought to be received, as on the merits of the claims for which it will be paid. This difficulty is perhaps increased by the extravagant claims which the British Creditors have been induced to file. Among them are cases believed to be so notoriously unfounded, that no commissioners retaining the slightest degree of self respect, can establish them. There are many others where the debtors are as competent to pay as any inhabitants of the United States. And there are others where the debt has been fairly and voluntarily compromised by agreement between creditor and debtor. There are even cases where the money has been paid in specie and receipts in full given. I do not mention there distinct classes, as comprehending all the cases of claims filed, which can never be allowed, but as examples of the materials which compose that enormous mass of imagined debt, which may by its unexamined bulk obstruct a just and equitable settlement of the well founded claims which really exist.

The creditors are now proceeding, and, had they not been seduced into the opinion that the trouble and expense inseparable from the pursuit of old debts might be avoided by one general resort to the United States, it is believed they would have been still more rapidly proceeding in the collection of the very claims, so far as they are just, which have been filed with the commissioners. They meet with no obstructions either of law or fact which are not common to every description of creditors, in every country, unless the difficulty with respect to interest during the War, may be so denominated. Our Judges are even liberal in their construction of the 4th Article of the treaty of Peace, and are believed in questions growing out of that treaty, to have manifested no sort of partiality for the debtors. Indeed it is believed that, with the exception of the contested Article of war interest, and possibly of claims barred by the Act of limitations during the War, the United States are justly chargeable with the debts of only such of their citizens, as have become insolvent subsequent to the peace, and previous to the establishment of the Federal Courts. This opinion is founded on a conviction that our Judges give to the 4th Article of the Treaty of Peace, a construction as extensive as ought to be given to it by commissioners appointed under the 6 Article of the Treaty of Amity, commerce & Navigation.

Those who have attended most to this subject are of opinion, that the sum which might properly be awarded against the United States, would fall far short of any estimate which has probably been made of it in England, or by the British creditors or agents in this Country. We are however sensible that commissioners acting within their powers may extend the sum further than justice or a fair construction of the Article would extend it, and we have been taught to apprehend a construction of which, at the ratification of the Treaty, no fear was entertained. From this persuasion and from a solicitude to perform what even rigid and unfavourable Judges may suppose to be injoined by good faith, the interests of the United States may require, and the President is therefore willing that the agreement should not be strictly limited by the sum for which in our own opinion we ought to be liable. He will be satisfied with *four*[8] *million of Dollars*. He will not consent to exceed *One Million* sterling.

If a gross sum in satisfaction of all other claims be accepted, you will of course stipulate for the lowest possible sum, and for the most favourable instalments which may be attainable.

Should it be found impossible to negotiate reasonable explanatory articles, or to agree on a sum to be received as compensation for the claims of the creditors, much doubt is entertained concerning the proposition for new modeling the Board as proposed by the British Minister. While the government itself professes to approve the conduct of its late commissioners, much fear is entertained that their successors may bring with them, those extravagant and totally inadmissible opinions which have dissolved the past, and will most probably dissolve any future Board. Before the United States proceed to take a new step in a case where experience has done so much to teach them caution, some assurances of the temper in which the commissioners to be appointed will meet, ought to be received. And yet we are not satisfied that good faith does not require that, notwithstanding the past, we should consent to make a second effort for the execution of the 6th. Article of the treaty in the forms it has prescribed.

On this part of the subject however the President has come to no determination. So soon as his decision shall have been made, it shall be communicated to you. With very much respect & Esteem, I am Dear Sir, your Obt. Servt.

J MARSHALL

8. The italicized words, originally in code, have been taken from the letterbook copy in Instructions to U.S. Ministers, V, RG 59, National Archives.

To Rufus King

ALS, Morristown National Historical Park

Private

Dear Sir   Washington, August 23, 1800

I have just addressd to you a letter on the subject of the differences existing between the United States & Great Britain respecting the execution of the 6th. article of our treaty with that nation. There are some statements omited in that letter which I deem it proper to make.

The gentlemen concernd in the administration of our government who are best informd respecting the claims of British creditors under the article in question, are of opinion that, on a fair & honorable construction of that article, they woud not exceed two milion, or at most two & a half milion of dollars. My own estimate accords with theirs. On that however I do not much rely, because I have not examind the particular cases of demand for compensation which have been on the United States. You will readily perceive what *a*[9] *sacrafice we make for the preservation of peace* & of *the* public *faith* shoud we *appease* the existing differences *by the payment of* such a *sum as is contemplated.*

There are other considerations (but these are my own suggestions & have not even been communicated to those with whom I act, which lead to a decisive *preference* of the *explanatory articles* shoud they *be attainable.*

A variety of causes among wh I am sorry to place the *contin*[*ued impress*]-*ments of our seamen & the unpunished depredations on our commerce have combined* to increase considerably the [*irritation*] *of the public mind in* [*Amer*] *at the Bri*[*tish*] *Govt an agreement to pay even a reasonable sum in gross* will be considerd & represented as a *disgraceful sacrafice with wh the Govt have purchased the* continuance of a *humiliating* [   ] *peace.*

Any attainable *Sum will exceed* the calculations made in America & being a *new Step voluntarily taken* shoud be enterd into with caution.

These considerations will not & ought not to induce the government of the United States to decline a measure of public utility. But they increase & justly increase our preference for the explanatory articles shoud it be found practicable to obtain them.

---

9. The words in italics indicate words originally in code. These words have been decoded by King and by the editors.

We are just informd tho not officially or certainly, that our negotiations with France have terminated, not in a treaty. The difficulties which are stated to have prevented the success of this mission were considerable, yet I am strongly inclind to the opinion that the successes of Buonaparte in Italy, & *the Election of N Y* have contributed to its failure. This event in the existing state of things renders the situation of the United States delicate & critical. Their conduct I trust will not vacillate—but will continue to be firm & moderate.

Your number 77 is just receivd.[1] I am dear Sir with very much respect & esteem, Your obedt. Servt

J MARSHALL

To John Adams

ALS, Adams Papers, Massachusetts Historical Society

Sir   Washington, August 25, 1800

When I forwarded the last dispatches from our envoys in Paris I omited unintentionally to transmit with them the decrees which accompanied them & which I now inclose.[2]

The state of the negotiation on the 17th. of May, considerd in connection with the subsequent military operations of the Armies, & with the impression which will probably be made by the New York election, gives the appearance of truth to the inteligence in the papers from St. Sebastians. We ought not to be surprizd if we see our envoys in the course of the next month without a treaty. This produces a critical state of things which ought to be contemplated in time.[3]

The question whether hostilities against France, with the exception of their west india privatiers, ought to be continued, if on their part a change of conduct shall be manifest, is of serious & interesting magnitude & is to be viewd in a variety of aspects.

I inclose you also dispatches just receivd from the isle of France which exhibit a state of things at that place essentially different from what had been supposd.[4]

1. King to [JM], calendared at July 5, 1800.
2. These decrees are filed following this letter in Adams Papers, Massachusetts Historical Society.
3. See JM to Alexander Hamilton, Aug. 23, 1800, and Harold C. Syrett *et al.*, eds., *The Papers of Alexander Hamilton*, XXV (New York, 1977), 80–81.
4. The dispatches from George Stacey, U.S. vice-consul at Mauritius, an island off the east coast of Madagascar, were enclosed with this letter and are dated Feb. 23 and

I have receivd your letter of the 15th. of Aug. respecting the consulate at Madeira. As you do not approve entirely of Mr. Lamar I certainly shall not commission him for the present. I will make the necessary inquiries for an American by birth & have no doubt that one can be found who is fit for the office. It is only on failing to find such a person that I think myself authorizd by you to appoint Mr. Lamar. I find among the names which have been formerly presented for that office to this department a Mr. Terry I beleive a spaniard who is very strongly recommended by Mr. Smith our minister at Lisbon, a Mr. Baretto a native of Madeira who is also strongly recommended, a Mr. John Leonard a native, I beleive, of New Jersey & a Mr. Henry Preble recommended for Marseilles & Cadiz particularly, but who has made a general application & will probably be pleasd with an appointment to Madeira. The application of Mr. Leonard was strongly supported but as it was made in 1799 he may possibly have turnd his attention to other objects. I am Sir with the highest respect, your obedt. Servt

J MARSHALL

From Robert Liston

AL, RG 59, National Archives

Philadelphia, August 25, 1800
R. Liston presents his respects to Genl. Marshall, Secretary of State.[5]

At a short distance of time from the appearance of the person of the name of Bowles among the Indian Tribes on the frontiers of the

---

Mar. 15, 1800. Stacey stated that on Aug. 29, 1799, the Directory reversed their proclamation of Jan. 18, 1798, which decreed that neutral ships having English merchandise on board would be considered as English ships and seized as prizes of war. Stacey wrote that "in consequence of these proceedings, I presume there can be no risque in American Vessels carrying on commerce again with this place." Also enclosed are the communications from the French government that reinstated Stacey as vice-consul with the attendant duties of that office and that apologized for previous actions. For a history of American trade with the Isle de France and for related documents, see A. Toussaint, ed., *Early American Trade with Mauritius* (Port Louis, Mauritius, 1954).

5. For JM's reply, see JM to Liston, Sept. 6, 1800. See also correspondence with Adams on William A. Bowles. Liston received his instructions from his government in Lord Grenville to Liston, May 9, 1800, F.O. 115/8193, Public Record Office.

Spanish Territories and those of the United States (towards the beginning of this year) I communicated to the Secretary of State (Colonel Pickering) such explanations respecting the countenance which that man had received from the Governors of some of the British Islands in the West Indies, as seemed to me to be perfectly satisfactory to the Federal Government. And when I had last the honour of seeing you, Sir, in the City of Washington, I confirmed those explanations by express order from His Majesty's Government. But finding that groundless charges and offensive surmises on this subject are not only still propagated in newspapers, but are published by persons high in office in certain states of the Union, I think it my duty, Sir, to repeat in writing what I had the honour of stating to you in conversation: that you may have it in your power, if you should at any time judge it necessary, to meet these insidious calumnies by a flat and formal contradiction.

The King's commands were that I should declare in the most unequivocal manner that His Majesty's Ministers are entirely unacquainted with any hostile designs which Mr Bowles may meditate in the Indian Territory; and that he has no authority, commission, instruction or promise of support from His Majesty's Government. The King's Ministers have had no other knowledge of his proceedings than that he solicited and received permission to proceed to the West Indies, for the purpose of endeavouring to procure a safe passage from thence to his native Country: that during his residence in Barbadoes, Jamaica, and at the Bahamas, he obtained from the Governors of those respective Islands, some small pecuniary assistance in order to supply his immediate wants; and that no other convenient opportunity occurring, he was allowed to take his passage on board one of His Majesty's Ships of war to the Continent of America.

I cannot end this note without repeating the expression of my regret at the ready credit which seems to be given in this country to every groundless report of hostile measures or designs on the part of Great Britain. I had fondly hoped that the conduct of the King's Government during the time I have had the honour of being employed in my mission here, would have established a degree of confidence in His Majesty's friendly intentions towards the United States, which would have precluded the necessity of such explanations as the present.

From Winthrop Sargent

Printed, *Annals of Congress*, X, 1381–1389

[*August 25, 1800 (Natchez)*. Sargent writes to protest the proceedings in the House of Representatives that direct censure toward himself and the judges of the Mississippi Territory, and he specifically protests the motion of Representative Thomas T. Davis[6] to curb Sargent's executive powers. Sargent defies Davis and his supporters to establish that he acted, in conjunction with the judges of the territory, as a despot, that he ignored the wishes of a majority of the citizens of the territory, or that he practiced avarice, extortion, and favoritism in appointing men to civil and military office.

Sargent claims that in governing the Mississippi Territory he has followed practices that had precedent in the practices of the Northwest Territory. There, the governor and judges legislated law, and the judges were allowed to exact fees for legal functions. He denies that he has tried to usurp the powers of the court, and he asserts that the characters of the judges of the territory are satisfactory.

Sargent concludes by reiterating his original complaint that "the honorable Mr. T. T. Davis, of Kentucky, seems to the Governor and Judges of the Mississippi Territory to have been unnecessarily severe. Towards the former he has practised most wanton and unwarrantable cruelty. He has given publicity to one of his letters seemingly intended only for his constituents, but which has circulated in the Northwestern Territory, where my very interesting concerns, where almost all my pecuniary affairs are afloat, calculated evidently to impress the people with such sentiments as may do me irreparable injury."[7]]

To John Adams

ALS, Adams Papers, Massachusetts Historical Society

Sir   Washington, August 26, 1800
    I receivd this morning your letter of the 18th. returning the com-

---

6. Sargent responded specifically to Davis's motion of May 14, 1800. *Annals of Congress*, X, 717–718. Davis accused Sargent of abusing the power to adopt laws for the territory by "usurping an authority of making new laws, not to be found amongst the laws of the individual States, by prescribing penalties inconsistant with the Constitution of the United States, and by combining with the said Judges in enacting laws for the purpose of exacting sums of money from the inhabitants of said Territory." *Ibid.*, 718.

7. Sargent's case was dismissed Mar. 3, 1801, with the recommendation that no further action be taken against him. See *ibid.*, 1074. See also Sargent to [JM], calendared at June 15, 1800.

plaint of the Swedish chargé d'affaires & immediately wrote to Mr. King such a letter as you say you approve of.[8]

I inclose you a letter from the governor of the Indiana territory respecting the appointment of Judges.[9] The opinion that the laws of the old territory do not operate in the new, whether well or ill founded furnishes a strong argument in favor of making these appointments at an earlier date than had been contemplated.

I recollect a conversation with you on this subject at this place & that you then expressd a determination to appoint Mr. William Clarke the present attorney for the United States in Kentucky, first Judge. I beleive there is no cause for altering this determination.

Governor Harrison takes a strong interest in the appointment of Major Henry Vanderburgh[1] as one of the Judges. In addition to his letters he has in several private conversations given me personal assurances of his high opinion of this gentleman. It is probable that a more eligible appointment cannot be made.

I send you also some recommendations of young Mr. Griffin.[2] With the late Judge Blair you are acquainted. Mr. Andrews whose name is subjoind to that of Mr. Blair is one of the professors in the University of William & Mary & is a gentleman of acknowledgd worth.

I send you also some recommendations of Mr. Claiborne[3] the brother of the member for Tenessee. I am Sir with the utmost respect & attachment, Your obedt.

J MARSHALL

8. See Adams to JM, Aug. 18, 1800, and JM to Rufus King, Aug. 26, 1800.

9. Not found. William Henry Harrison (1773–1841) was appointed governor of the Indiana Territory on May 12, 1800, and served in that capacity until 1813.

1. William Clarke (d. 1802) and Henry Vanderburgh (1760–1812) each received a recess appointment on Oct. 4, 1800. See Clarence E. Carter, "William Clarke, First Chief Justice of Indiana Territory," *Indiana Magazine of History*, XXXIV (1938), 1–13, and Mary Kay Bonsteel Tachau, *Federal Courts in the Early Republic: Kentucky, 1789–1816* (Princeton, N.J., 1978), 116–117.

2. John Griffin (*ca.* 1769–*ca.* 1842) received an appointment as judge at the same time as Clarke and Vanderburgh. He was the son of Cyrus Griffin, judge of the U.S. District Court of Virginia. His recommendations were from John Blair and Robert Andrews. See Francis S. Philbrick, ed., *The Laws of Indiana Territory, 1801–1809* (Illinois State Historical Library, *Collections*, XXI [Springfield, Ill., 1930]), ccxxxvi. See also Adams to JM, Sept. 5, 1800 (second letter), and additional correspondence on the appointment of judges for the Indiana Territory.

3. Nathaniel Herbert Claiborne (1777–1859) later became a representative from Virginia. His brother, William C. C. Claiborne, a representative from Tennessee from 1797 to 1801, became governor of the Mississippi Territory in 1801 and of the Orleans Territory in 1803.

From John Adams

ALS, RG 59, National Archives

Dear Sir   Quincy, August 26, 1800

I recd last night your Letter of the 16th. I am well satisfied with all its Contents. The only Thing which requires any observation from me is the proposed Instruction to Mr King. As far as I am able to form a Conjecture, five millions of Dollars are more than sufficient, provided The British Creditors are left at Liberty to prosecute in our Courts and recover all the Debts which are now recoverable. I agree however with the heads of departments that it is better to engage to pay, by Installments or otherwise as may be agreed the whole sum, than be puzled and teased with a New Board and two or three Years of incessant Wrangles. I should be for instructing Mr King to obtain the lowest sum possible, but to go as far as five millions, rather than fail. I wish Mr King to be furnished with as many reasons as can be thought of, for reducing the sum. I pray you to prepare a Letter to Mr King as soon as possible: and as We are all so well agreed in all the Principles I do not think it necessary to transmit it to me.[4] Lay it before the heads of departments and if they approve of it, I certainly shall not disapprove it. And you may send it if opportunity occurs, without further Advice from me.

Whether it will be adviseable to stipulate for a transfer to the United States, of such Claims as the British Government shall think fit to discharge in Consequence of this arrangement, I wish you to consider. I believe it will occasion more trouble and expence too than profit. With great regard

J. ADAMS

To Thomas Claxton

Letterbook Copy, RG 45, National Archives

Sir   Washington, August 26, 1800

By an act of Congress passed on the 24th of Ap. 1800[5] the sum of

---

4. The letter of instruction had already been prepared. See JM to Rufus King, Aug. 23, 1800 (first letter).

5. 2 Stat. 55. See *Annals of Congress*, X, 1493–1495.

Fifteen thousand dollars was appropriated for the purpose of providing furniture for the house erected in the City of Washington for the accomodation of the President of the United States to be applied under the direction of the Secretaries of the four Executive Departments.

We hereby Constitute you the Agent for executing the above mentioned direction of Congress, and we engage to allow you for your services the sum of $250. in addition to the reasonable expences of any Journies to Baltimore or Philadelphia for the purpose of procuring furniture.

It will be necessary to ascertain the quantity and description of furniture on hand, which being done you will take orders for supplying what is deficient. If the fund is sufficient, two Rooms, that is the oval room on the second floor intended for the Drawing Room of Mrs. Adams, & the Northwest Room on the first floor, intended as the Drawing Room of the President, may be richly furnished. We wish the other Rooms to be furnished in a plain and elegant manner, avoiding expence as much as possible.

If you wish for particular instructions on any point, you will state your inquiries in writing. We are &c[6]

To Rufus King

LS, RG 59, National Archives

Duplicate
No 4
Dear Sir,   Washington, August 26, 1800
By a variety of accidents your No 50 accompanying a complaint made by the chargé d'affaires of his Swedish Majesty, against two American letters of Marque, was prevented from reaching me until about a fortnight past. I immediately directed the case to be enquired into, and transmitted your letter with the documents annexed to the President.[7]

I cannot believe that the insult or injury has been intentional, and therefore persuade myself that the Swedish government will not be disposed to treat this as a serious affair.

6. This letter was signed by the secretaries of state, war, the navy, and the Treasury.
7. See John Adams to JM, Aug. 18, 1800.

However this may be the President desires you to assure the representative of Sweden in London, of the friendly dispositions of the American government and of its sollicitude to avoid giving any just cause of dissatisfaction to that of Sweden: and further that directions have been given to enquire into the case, and that, if any intentional insult has been offered to the flag of his Swedish Majesty the United States will take the proper means to repair the injury and to show their marked disapprobation of such conduct.

For the private loss which may have been sustained our Courts will afford an adequate remedy. With very much respect and esteem, I am, Dear Sir, Your obedient

J MARSHALL

To William L. Smith

Letterbook Copy, RG 59, National Archives

[*August 26, 1800, Washington.* JM encloses John Adams's "answer to the letter of the Prince Regent of Portugal, announcing the birth of a daughter, and a copy of the same for your own inspection."[8]]

To John Adams

ALS, Adams Papers, Massachusetts Historical Society

Sir   Washington, August 27, 1800

I transmit you some dispatches lately receivd from the Judge of the Kentucky district.[9] I hope the resistance he mentions to the execution of the judgements of the court of the United States exists no longer.

I inclose you also two letters from Mr. Yznardi[10] & a copy of one to him from Don Urquijo.[1]

I can scarcely beleive that our envoys have embarkd for the Hague.

8. See JM to Adams, Aug. 23, 1800, which mentions this letter.
9. The dispatches from Harry Innes have not been found. Adams replied to this letter in Adams to JM, Sept. 5, 1800 (first letter). For a study of Innes and the Kentucky court system, see Mary Kay Bonsteel Tachau, *Federal Courts in the Early Republic: Kentucky, 1789–1816* (Princeton, N.J., 1978).
10. Not found, but see Josef Yznardy to Timothy Pickering, Apr. 3, 1800, Consular Despatches, Cadiz, I, RG 59, National Archives.
1. See Mariano Luis de Urquijo to Josef Yznardy, Jan. 13, 1800, *ibid.* Urquijo (1768–1817) was Spain's secretary of state for foreign affairs.

Mountflorence I shoud think must have been mistaken.

The letter of Don Urquijo merits some attention. The conduct of the spanish government towards that of the United States has furnishd cause for complaints much more serious & extensive than have ever been made. To me it seems that compensation for every American vessel condemnd by the french consular courts in the dominions of spain is justly demandable from the spanish government & that it is not yet too late to make the demand. I am Sir with respectful attachment, Your obedt. Servt.

J MARSHALL

From Commissioners of the District of Columbia

Letterbook Copy, RG 42, National Archives

Sir,   Washington, August 27, 1800

The present deranged state of our finances, and the failure of the Sales to give them any effectual aid, render it necessary that the Executive should be informed of the state of our affairs.

We believe that twenty five thousand Dollars in addition to our own resources would carry us through the Season and finish all the public Buildings now on hand. We had every reason to hope that the present Sales would have raised that sum, and left a sufficient Balance to satisfy the last loan from the State of Maryland. The Property advertised at the low Rate of eighty Dollars per standard lot, ought to have raised one hundred and eight thousand Dollars. It is reduced to a certainty that six thousand Dollars will not be raised out of this fund, so as to be brought into active operation this Season—and we cannot calculate that all our other outstanding Debts, amounting to near forty thousand Dollars (exclusive of the sums due from Morris and Nicholson)[2] will yield us much more than that sum.

Under such prospects, we think it our Duty to lay this state of our affairs before you, and if you judge it proper, before the other Executive Officers, or the President of the United-States.

2. Robert Morris and John Nicholson, of Philadelphia, speculated together in property in Washington, D.C., during the 1790s. They had a contract to pay the commissioners $62,214 for lots they had purchased for development. Nicholson died on Dec. 5, 1800, in debtors' prison. See Robert D. Arbuckle, *Pennsylvania Speculator and Patriot: The Entrepreneurial John Nicholson, 1757–1800* (University Park, Pa., 1975), esp. 114–138.

Should a more detailed state of our funds and resources be judged necessary, a member of our Board, will at any time attend to give the necessary Information. We are, &c.

G. SCOTT
W. THORNTON

To Henry M. Rutledge

Printed extract, Carnegie Book Shop, Catalog No. 155 (New York, 1950), 14

[*August 27, 1800, Washington.* JM writes about election activity and the effect of Indian negotiations on South Carolina and observes, "The late intelligence from Europe wears the appearance of magic. That the Alps & Italy should be conquered in a month is more like fable than history. . . ."]

From Israel Whelen

LS, RG 59, National Archives

[*August 27, 1800, Philadelphia.* Whelen reports accounts of the *George Washington* and the *Sophia.* He has not yet paid Richard O'Brien's draft in favor of Capt. John Smith for port charges at Algiers, nor has he received the $10,000 needed to discharge these expenses. Also included with this letter is the bill of lading for the *Anna Maria,* which JM forwarded to William Eaton on Aug. 30, 1800.]

From Israel Whelen

LS, RG 59, National Archives

[*August 27, 1800, Philadelphia.* Whelen asks if the *Anna Maria* is to have orders to touch at any port previous to her arrival at Tunis. He needs this information for insurance purposes.]

To Timothy Pickering

ALS, Pickering Papers, Massachusetts Historical Society

Dear Sir   Washington, August 28, 1800
I receivd last night a packet from Mr. King with the inclosd letter to you.[3]

3. See Rufus King to Pickering, July 25, 1800, Pickering Papers, Massachusetts Historical Society, which is printed in King, ed., *Life and Corres. of Rufus King,* III, 281–282.

Our last dispatches from Paris do not come later than the 17th. of May. From their contents no conclusion can be drawn with any sort of certainty respecting the fate of the embassy. I am dear Sir with much respect & esteem, your obedt.

J MARSHALL

To John Adams

ALS, Adams Papers, Massachusetts Historical Society

Sir   Washington, August 30, 1800
   I have just receivd your letter of the 22d. & am happy that the pro-ceedings with the spanish minister have your approbation.
   I inclose you a letter from Mr. Stevens which represents the part of St. Domingo which had adherd to Rigaud as being completely reducd under the dominion of Toussaint.[4]
   I transmit you also a letter from a Mr. Mitchell of Charleston in South Carolina & a letter I have receivd from Mr. Humphries.[5] I am Sir with very much respect & attachment, your obedt. servt.

J MARSHALL

From John Adams

ALS, RG 59, National Archives

Dear Sir   Quincy, August 30, 1800
   I recd last night your favour of the 23d. My Ideas are perfectly con-formable to yours in your Instructions to Mr King as you state them to me. The explanatory Articles if attainable are preferred to any other mode. The next most eligible is the substitution of a sum in gross. That sum to be as small as can be agreed to or will be agreed to by the British Government: But to agree to five millions of Dollars rather than fail of explanations and substitutions both: and be com-

   4. See Edward Stevens to JM, Aug. 2, 1800, RG 59, National Archives, although the ALS was not received by the State Department until Sept. 18; see also Adams to JM, Sept. 9, 1800. André Rigaud (1761–1811), a leader of the mulatto rebellion on Santo Domingo, fled to France on July 29, 1800. For a history of the Haitian rebellion and of Rigaud, see Thomas O. Ott, *The Haitian Revolution, 1789–1804* (Knoxville, Tenn., 1973), 114–118.
   5. The letter from John H. Mitchell has not been found. See David Humphreys to JM, June 27, 1800, RG 59, which was received by the State Department on Aug. 26.

pelled to agree to a new Board and all their delays and Altercations.

The proposed Letters to the Governors of Georgia Tennessee and Missisippi, will I presume be unnecessary.

Mr Kings Letter of the 5th of July is a melancholly picture of Britain.[6] Alass how different from that held up to view in this Country twelve Months ago, to frighten me from sending to France! However Mr King is somewhat of a Croaker, at times. He is apt to be depressed by what he thinks a train of unfortunate Events. There is enough however of likeness in his Drawing, to give great Spirits and a high tone to the French. It will be our Destiny for what I know, Republicans as We are, to fight the French Republic alone. I cannot account for the long delay of our Envoys. We cannot depart from our honor nor violate our faith to please the Heroic Consul. With very great Esteem &c

J. ADAMS

From John Adams

ALS, RG 59, National Archives

Dear Sir   Quincy, August 30, 1800

The enclosed Letter from Mr Boudinot[7] recommending Mr Isaac Barnet I pray you to file among the Applications for the Consulate at Bourdeaux.

The enclosed Letter from Governor St Clair[8] though a private one, is, I think proper for you to peruse, as We shall e'er long have to consider of a Nomination of a Governor. After you have perused it you may let the other Gentlemen read it, and then return it to me. With sincere Esteem

J. ADAMS

6. See Rufus King to [JM], calendared at July 5, 1800.

7. This letter from Adams is printed in Carter, ed., *Terr. Papers, NW*, III, 103. The letter from Elias Boudinot (1740–1821) has not been found, but see Vol. III, 326–327.

8. See Arthur St. Clair to Adams, Adams Papers, Massachusetts Historical Society. JM returned this letter on Sept. 8. See JM to Adams, Sept. 8, 1800.

To William Eaton

ALS, Stark Library, University of Texas

Sir[9]   Washington, August 30, 1800
    The Anna Maria sails immediately for Tunis with a cargo which
I hope will reach you in good order. I send you a copy of the invoice
bill of lading & charter party.[1]
    Your letters by Mr. Shaw & by the Hero have been receivd.[2] The
President has, but with very much reluctance consented to direct the
purchase of the jewels. The exorbitant & unwarrantable demands of
the barbary powers sit very uneasy on us & are submited to with
difficulty. For the jewels meerly we are unwilling to go to war & thus
lose the benefit of the heavy expenses already incurd. But this system
of heavy exaction must not be continued. You must persevere in your
endeavors so long as you may safely do so, to avoid entirely or
diminish this demand. It may be that Mr. King may find some difficulty or delay in obtaining the jewels & on that account as well as
others it is probably most adviseable to suspend any actual promise
on this subject as long as possible.
    The residue of the stores will be prepard & expedited as soon as
can be done.
    It is the wish of the President that you shoud keep Mr. King in-
formd of the state of our affairs with the barbary powers.
    I have directed your bill for the six thousand dollars receivd from
Mr. Robinson to be paid. I am Sir respectfully your obedt. Servt.
                                                        J MARSHALL

From Samuel and Miers Fisher

ALS, RG 76, National Archives

[*August 30, 1800, Philadelphia.* The Fishers seek to revive their request for
assistance from the State Department, first made in 1799. Their ship, the
Sussex,[3] was captured by Spanish privateers and condemned in Pontevedra.

    9. A note on the verso indicates that this letter was "Recd Dec. 1, Ann Maria's invoice
$11355:31, Do. charter party 16000:, [for a total of] Drs. 27355:31."
    1. See Bill of Lading for the *Anna Maria*, Aug. 25, 1800, Miscellaneous Letters Re-
ceived, RG 59, National Archives.
    2. See Eaton to Timothy Pickering, Mar. 31, 1800, Consular Despatches, Tunis, I,
RG 59. See also John Adams to JM, Aug. 2, 1800.
    3. For an account of the *Sussex*, which was condemned in 1797, see Memorial of

Having related their story, the writers conclude: "We therefore earnestly request that thou willt instruct our Minister at Madrid to take Such Measures in our Behalf as thine & his *diplomatic Skill* will better point out than any Small Knowledge of ours on Such a Subject enables us to ask for."]

To Ebenezer Stevens

ALS, Ebenezer Stevens Papers, University of Virginia Library

Sir[4]   Washington, August 30, 1800
    In the letter to Consul Eaton are the invoice bill of lading & charter party of the Ann Maria.[5]
    I send you also the letter to her Captain[6] containing his instructions & a special passport signd by the President. For the mediterrenean pass application must be made as in other cases to the collector of the port.
    She has liberty to touch at Gibralter for information but is not bound to do so. Insurance is to be made by the Purveyor.
    If by any strange revolution we shoud be at war with Tunis it will I presume be improper to bring back the cargo. I am Sir your obedt.
                                                    J MARSHALL

To Israel Whelen

ALS, Historical Society of Pennsylvania

[*August 30, 1800, Washington.* JM transmits $10,000 to Whelen.[7] He also directs a remittance of $16,000 on account of the *Hero* with an injunction to close entirely the transactions. "The anne Maria has liberty but is not absolutely orderd to touch at Gibralter."]

Samuel Fisher, July 9, 1821, filed following Samuel and Miers Fisher to JM, calendared at Sept. 8, 1800. See also JM to David Humphreys, Sept. 23, 1800, and the Fishers to JM, Dec. 23, 1800.
    4. This letter is in response to Stevens's letter of Aug. 26, RG 59, National Archives, which was received by the State Department on Aug. 29, 1800.
    5. See JM to William Eaton, Aug. 30, 1800.
    6. The letter to Capt. George G. Coffin has not been found.
    7. For Whelen's reply, see Whelen to JM, calendared at Oct. 16, 1800. See also Ebenezer Stevens to Whelen, Sept. 30, 1800, enclosed in Whelen's letter of Oct. 18, Miscellaneous Letters Received, RG 59, National Archives.

From Carlos Martínez de Yrujo

LS, RG 59, National Archives

[*September 1, 1800, New York.* Yrujo writes that in compliance with JM's letter[8] he had authorized Citizen Arcambal to receive the *Sandwich* and her cargo from Richard Harison, U.S. attorney for the district of New York. He has since learned that Harison referred Arcambal to the marshal of the district, Aquila Giles. Giles declared that he had no authority in the action and could not make restitution. Yrujo therefore protests the U.S. government's procrastination and demands once again the return of the *Sandwich*.[9] This letter is written in Spanish.]

From John Adams

ALS, RG 59, National Archives

Dear Sir   Quincy, September 2, 1800

On the last of August at night I recd a Packett containing a Letter from our Envoys of May 17th. A Memorial of our Envoys to the French Ministers of May 8. in answer to one of those Ministers to ours of the 16 floreal 8 year. These I return inclosed. There was no Letter from you, nor any other Paper in the Packett.[1] You will know whether I recd all the Papers you sent. If not the Packet has been opened and pilfered.

The Dispatches need no comment. I agree with our Gentlemen that their success is doubtfull. With sincere Esteem

JOHN ADAMS

From David Humphreys

ALS, RG 59, National Archives

[*September 2, 1800, Madrid.* Humphreys, in dispatch no. 248, sends several

8. Not found.

9. See JM to John Adams, Sept. 6, 1800 (first letter), and Adams to JM, Sept. 17, 1800 (third letter). See also additional correspondence on the *Sandwich* case.

On Sept. 5, 1800, the case of Talbot v. *Sandwich* was brought before the U.S. District Court for New York. The libel was dismissed and the ship ordered to be restored to her captain. See the Decree of the District Court, enclosed in Yrujo to JM, Oct. 15, 1800, Notes from Foreign Legations, Spain, II, RG 59, National Archives.

1. The enclosed documents are printed in *Amer. State Papers, Foreign Relations*, II, 295–301. See also JM to Adams, Sept. 12, 1800.

enclosures: a letter from the acting first minister of state in Spain, Mariano Luis de Urquijo, complaining of "excesses committed by some armed vessels of the United States on the Spanish commerce in America"; a petition of Mary Murphy, widow of Michael Murphy, late U.S. consul at Malaga, asking Congress to approve financial assistance for the support of her family; and a published account of military news in Europe. In a postscript added on Sept. 5, Humphreys notes that Gen. Louis-Alexandre Berthier has arrived in Madrid from France and that he has spoken to the general.[2]]

To John Adams

ALS, Adams Papers, Massachusetts Historical Society

Sir   Washington, September 3, 1800
   I have receivd your letter respecting Mr. Nortons claim & shall observe your instructions.[3]
   There appears to be considerable delicacy in engaging in the support of a claim founded on provisions furnishd the British army during our revolution war.
   I inclose you a letter from Mr. Wilkins to Mr. Harrison & from Mr. Harrison to me recommending a Mr. Hollingsworth as a Judge in the Indiana territory.[4] I am Sir with the most respectful attachment, Your obedt. Servt

J Marshall

From Israel Whelen

ALS, RG 59, National Archives

[*September 3, 1800, Philadelphia.* In reply to JM's letters of Aug. 27 and

2. A notation in JM's hand indicates that this letter arrived on Nov. 20, 1800. The enclosures are filed following this letter in Diplomatic Despatches, Spain, V, RG 59, National Archives.
   Napoleon sent Berthier (1753–1815) to Madrid to negotiate with Spain for Louisiana, the Floridas, and 10 warships in exchange for territory in Italy. Napoleon's wish to conciliate the United States by terminating the Quasi-War developed from his plan to acquire an American empire. The day after the convention of Mortefontaine was signed, Berthier signed the secret treaty of Ildefonso with Spain, which exchanged a kingdom in Italy for Louisiana and 6 warships. See Alexander DeConde, *This Affair of Louisiana* (New York, 1976), 91–97.
   3. See Adams to JM, Aug. 23, 1800.
   4. The letters from John Wilkins to William Henry Harrison and from Harrison recommending John Hollingsworth (1752–1808) have not been found. See Adams to JM, Sept. 13, 1800.

30, Whelen reports that he has written to Ebenezer Stevens requesting that all accounts on the *Hero* be closed. Whelen, apparently in response to a suggestion made by JM, argues that a ship of war is not suitable to transport bulky articles such as lumber. The small quantity of lumber loaded on the *George Washington* proves his point. He suggests that providing him with a list of articles to be purchased for shipment as early as possible will permit him to obtain better prices, and "if you are pleased to trust the management of the business hereafter to me," it would save money to ship lumber directly from Portsmouth or another eastern port. In any case, he cannot estimate loading time without a complete cargo list. JM's letter of Aug. 27, 1800, has not been found.]

From Oliver Wolcott

LS, RG 59, National Archives

[*September 3, 1800 (Washington)*. Wolcott sends JM several documents[5] relating to a claim of Arnold Henry Dohrman[6] to a township under authority of the Oct. 5, 1787, act of Congress. Wolcott believes Dohrman's claim is valid, and he thinks JM should issue the grant.]

From John Adams

ALS, RG 59, National Archives

Dear Sir   Quincy, September 4, 1800

I have recd your favour of August 25th. I am of your opinion that We ought not to be surprized if We see our Envoys in the Course of a few Weeks or days, without a Treaty. Nor should I be surprized if they should be loaded with Professions and Protestations of Love, to serve as a substitute for a Treaty. The state of Things will be so critical that the Government ought to be prepared to take a decided Part. Questions of Consequence will arise, and among others, whether the President ought not at the opening of the session to recommend to

5. A note on the verso indicates that the documents were returned to Wolcott. The documents are enclosed in JM to Samuel Dexter, Dec. 10, 1800, filed in Committee on Claims, RG 233, National Archives.

6. Dohrman (1749–1813) was given a grant of money and a township by Congress. The bill for his relief passed on Feb. 26, 1801, and Dohrman moved to Steubenville, Ohio, in 1809. For more information on Dohrman, see William T. Hutchinson and William M. E. Rachal, eds., *The Papers of James Madison*, II (Chicago, 1962), 34. See also *Annals of Congress*, X, 752, and JM to Nathaniel Macon, Jan. 16, 1801.

Congress an immediate and general Declaration of War, against the French Republic. Congress has already in my Judgment as well as in the opinion of the Judges at Phyladelphia, declared War, within the meaning of the Constitution, against that Republic, under certain restrictions and Limitations.[7] If War in any degree is to be continued, it is a serious question whether it will not be better to take off all the Restrictions and Limitations. We have had wonderful Proofs that the Public mind cannot be held in a state of suspense. The Public opinion it seems must always be [a][8] decided one whether in the right or not. We shall be tortured with a perpetual Conflict of Parties, and new and strange ones will continually rise up, untill We have either Peace or War. The Question proposed by you, is also of great magnitude. I pretend not to have determined either in my own mind: but I wish the heads of departments to turn their Thoughts to the subject and view it in all its lights.

The Dispatches from the Isle of France are unexpected. Four or five Parties have in succession had the Predominance in that Island, and the old Governor had gone along with each in its turn. We ought to be cautious in that Business.

I should prefer Mr Lamar so strongly recommended, to any Spaniard or Madeira Man. If you can find a sound native American well qualified, appoint him if not, I will agree to Mr Lamar.

I will return the Papers by a future opportunity. With sincere Esteem &c

JOHN ADAMS

From John Adams

ALS, RG 59, National Archives

Sir   Quincy, September 5, 1800

I hope, as you do, that the Resistance to the Execution of the Judgments of the Courts of the United States in Kentucky as represented by Judge Harry Innes exists no longer.[9] I return you all the Papers.

7. The Supreme Court had ruled in Aug. 1800 that limited hostilities, authorized by the legitimate authority of two governments against each other, constitute a public war and render the two nations enemies to each other. See *Bass* v. *Tingy*, 1 U.S. (4 Dall.) 731–735. See also Thomas B. Adams to John Adams, Aug. 10, 1800, Adams Papers, Massachusetts Historical Society, in which Adams's son informs him of the Court's decision.

8. This word is included in the letterbook copy of the letter.

9. See JM to Adams, Aug. 27, 1800.

Mounflorence's Information was that our Envoys "were ready to depart for Havre De Grace, where they intended to embark for the Hague." This was probably *given out* by the French, to conceal something from the Public, what that something was you may conjecture as well as I. They would not be anxious to conceal a settlement to mutual satisfaction.

I agree with you that very serious tho friendly remonstrances ought to be made to Spain. I can even go as far as you and demand Compensation for every American Vessell condemned by the French Consular Courts in the Dominions of Spain.

I return all the Papers relative to this subject. With sincere Esteem &c

JOHN ADAMS

From John Adams

ALS, RG 59, National Archives

Sir   Quincy, September 5, 1800

I should rather have waited, till nominations could be made to the senate, when We might have had opportunity to make more Inquiries but as Mr Harrison seems so anxious, and you seem to be satisfied, I am willing to appoint Mr William Clark, Major Henry Vanderburgh and Mr John Griffin.[1] I am Apprehensive that this will be suspected to be a Compliment to his Father and that other Candidates may be named of riper Age: but he cannot be deficient in Law or the French Tongue, His Fathers Profession would insure him the first and the last is spoken by his Mother like a Paris Lady. The Recommendation of Judge Blair has great weight with your sert

JOHN ADAMS

I return you all the papers.

1. See JM to Adams, Aug. 26, 1800. See also temporary commissions for William Clarke, Henry Vanderburgh, and John Griffin, Temporary Presidential Commissions, 1789–1909, RG 59, National Archives.

From Winthrop Sargent

Draft, Sargent Papers, Ohio Historical Society

Mississippi Territory, September 5, 1800

Anxious Sir in the Extreme to preserve a good name *which* in a Service of much Toil and no inconsiderable share of Peril I had essayed to attain, I have presumed to address two long Letters, bearing Date June the 15th: and August the 25th: to the Department of State—to illustrate public Transactions as well as the proceedings of *some* of this people, and avert the Curse of Infamy which *seemed* indelibly accosting to my Official Character: Copies of *those* Letters have been transmitted to my most respected President, and I can nothing doubt a Conclusion honourable to myself and the Judges from the *due* Impression upon his and your mind.

Justice will mercifully ordain that *they* be submitted to the Senate —to continue our *political* Existence and, *what* is of infinitely dearer Consideration in my mind, the good Opinion of Individuals in that honourable Body, to whose wisdom and Virtues I render the Tribute of Reverence and Admiration. But when I *feelingly* consider Sir the Publicity of evil Report; *that* an *Indictment* has been preferred against me before the first Tribunals upon Earth—for Matter enough—to anathematize me in the minds of the great & the good; AND that the *same* may not be *traversed*—a tacit Acquittal is not Sufficient.

To Friends of Sensibility—Americans of acknowledged worth— to an august Executive, whose Confidence we have enjoyed, we owe a public Explanation.

For an Offspring in whom we are to be perpetuated, and to *whom* we had proudly calculated upon handing down a reputation, undefiled we must *take Care* that the Sons shall not blush because their Fathers have been defamed. 'Tis therefore I most respectfully solicit, *that* to the volume of Accusation, and preceedings of the honourable house of representatives (criminating the Governeur and Judges of this Territory) and printed by ORDER, my Letters of Illustration may ingenuously be added.

We have been humiliated before our Friends and the World in the publication uttered under an Authority we are bound to respect and diffused to the remotest parts of the Union.

To the Equity of the same Source therefore we appeal for the requested mode of Exoneration.

If however in this *seemingly* rational Solicitation we are not to be indulged, the Gentleman who obligingly takes charge of my Letter of the 25th: ult: and its Accompaniments will ask from you a Copy thereof, and that of the 15th: of June also for the Press—PROVIDED my printing the same for Information of Gentlemen of Congress and my Friends shall not to *you* seem improper. With every sentiment of the most unfeigned Respect, I have the honour to be, sir, your Obdt Humble Servt

W S

To John Adams

ALS, RG 59, National Archives

Sir   Washington, September 6, 1800

I receivd a few days past a letter from the chevallier de Yrujo complaining that the marshall for the district of New York says he has no authority to deliver up the vessel capturd by Capt. Talbot in the puerto plata.[2] I have taken measures which will I presume occasion the delivery of this vessel, unless under the idea that the government has no right to interpose, so far as the captors are interested, Capt. Talbot shall refuse (as I conjecture his agent must already have done) to submit to the decision of the executive. I cannot beleive that Capt. Talbot will act so indiscreetly; but as in this I may be disappointed, it becomes necessary to consider the situation in which his refusal will place the subject, & to decide provisionally, on the course which in that event, it will be proper to pursue.

If the executive of the United States cannot restore a vessel capturd by a national ship, in violation of the law of nations, it is easy to perceive how much inconvenience may result from such defect of power. Cause of war may be given by those who of all others are, perhaps, most apt to give it, & that department of the government, under whose orders they are placd, will be unable to correct the mischief. On the other hand as there is an inchoate interest in the captors, there is some doubt concerning the right of the executive to affect this interest, & much delicacy in exercising it. It is only in plain cases such as I take this to be that the exercise of such a right, was it even unquestionable woud be recommended. Sir William Scott I observe lays it down as law, that, in England, there is a right in the captors to proceed with the prosecution of the vessel, against the will

2. See Carlos Martínez de Yrujo to JM, calendared at Sept. 1, 1800.

of the crown. He does not however state any case in which such proceedings have been had.[3]

Shoud this point be contested, I must request your instructions in the case. To me it seems unadviseable that the executive shoud decide absolutely on the question, & that it woud be proper to submit it to the court. To obtain their judgement respecting it I know of no mode more proper than to request the attorney for the district to enter immediately on the record the directions given him from this department to dismiss the prosecution, & the claim of the captors to proceed—leaving it to the court to decide whether in such a state of things further proceedings can or cannot be maintaind. Shoud the court determine to proceed & the capture shoud afterwards be decided to have been unlawful, & without probable cause, I presume Capt. Talbot will have no pretext for applying to the United States to be reimbursd any damages which may be awarded against him.

I cannot doubt sir the acquiescence of Capt. Talbot under the decision made by the executive, but it is necessary to prepare for a state of things which, tho not probable, is entirely possible. I am Sir with the most perfect respect & attachment, Your obedt. Servt

J Marshall

To John Adams

ALS, Adams Papers, Massachusetts Historical Society

Sir   Washington, September 6, 1800

I receivd last night your letter of the 26th. of august.

The more I think on the proposition of giving a gross sum in lieu of the claims of the British creditors on the government of the United States, the more difficulty appears to me to attend the subject. On the one side I am convincd that the sum we shall be under the necessity of giving, if we come to any agreement, must be more considerable than is really due, & on the other I am equally well persuaded, that any commissioners, with the majority against us, unrestraind by previous explanatory articles, will award against us a still larger sum than any we will submit to give. Under these circumstances it appears

3. The first edition of Scott's (1745–1836) decisions was published in 1798 by Christopher Robinson and must be the volume referred to here, although the case in question cannot readily be determined. See Christopher Robinson, *Reports of Cases argued and determined in the High Court of Admiralty, commencing with the judgments of the Right Hon. Sir William Scott* (London, 1798).

to me that the most eligible mode of proceeding is to press for the explanatory articles, but if they be totally unattainable to agree on the gross sum, if such an agreement can be made without exceeding the limits you have prescribd.

I have prepard a letter to Mr. King which has been approvd by the heads of departments & in conformity with your direction will be immediately dispatchd to him.[4]

I will also order a copy to be made for your consideration.

I send you a copy of a note receivd from Mr. Liston. Tho no particular expressions in it may be deemd exceptionable, yet the whole together, has an appearance of discontent & irritation, which I think he ought not to have permited himself to have manifested. I regret very much that I cannot submit to your consideration, before it is transmited, my answer to this letter; but it seems to me that an answer ought not to be delayd until your sentiments respecting it can be obtaind. Under this conviction & in the hope that the answer will not be dissatisfactory to you, I have written a letter to Mr. Liston of which I inclose you a copy.[5]

The enormous abuses & injuries our commerce has sustaind from the lawless depredations of privatiers fited out or mand in the ports of Spain, & the manifest violations of the law of nations & of our treaty which the consular tribunals of France have been allowd to commit in that country, seem to me to require from the United States a very serious remonstrance. As my view of this subject may be as well considerd in the form of a letter to Mr. Humphries as any other I am preparing one which when finishd I will transmit to you.[6]

I have just receivd a letter from Mr. Stevens stating the entire pacification of the south of St. Domingo & enclosing a letter to him from Genl. Toussaint expressing the Generals wish that our commerce may now be extended to that part of the island. The heads of departments are all of opinion that this shoud be done. If you entertain the same opinion it will I presume be necessary to issue a proclamation notifying this regulation. I have inclosd you a proclamation for your consideration.[7]

4. See JM to Rufus King, Sept. 9, 1800.
5. See Robert Liston to JM, Aug. 25, 1800, and JM to Liston, Sept. 6, 1800.
6. See JM to David Humphreys, Sept. 8, 1800.
7. See Edward Stevens to JM, Aug. 14, 1800, RG 59, National Archives, which enclosed the letter of Toussaint Louverture to Stevens, Aug. 2, 1800. See also Proclamation extending trade to the entire island of Hispaniola, Proclamations, RG 11, Natl. Arch.

If this commerce shoud be extended Mr. B. Dandridge a young gentleman of very considerable merit, who was first secretary to Mr. Murray & afterwards to Mr. King & is now a merchant in Alexandria applies for a consulate.[8] I am Sir with the most respectful attachment, Your obedt. Servt

J MARSHALL

From John Adams

Letterbook Copy, Adams Papers, Massachusetts Historical Society

Dear Sir   Quincy, September 6, 1800
I transmit you a letter from William Wetmore[9] Esqr. of Castine in the District of Maine, to be filed & considered in time & in case. Mr. Whetmore is one of the remaining characters, whom I knew as a student in a Barristers office, when I was at the bar. What other applications may be presented I know not. With sincere regard

To Robert Liston

Presscopy, Adams Papers, Massachusetts Historical Society

Washington, September 6, 1800
J Marshall presents his respects to Mr. Liston Minister plenipotentiary &c of his Britannic Majesty to the United States.[1]
The verbal communications respecting William A. Bowles which you made to me while in Washington, were immediately transmited to the President. I have since receivd a letter from him stating his entire satisfaction with the assurances you then gave, & have now repeated in writing that this adventurer has receivd no authority, commission, instruction, or promise of support from the ministers of his Britannic Majesty, & that they are entirely unacquainted with any hostile designs he may meditate in the indian territory.[2]

8. See Adams to JM, Sept. 17, 1800 (second letter). Bartholomew Dandridge (d.1802) was appointed U.S. consul at Aux Cayes, Haiti. See Commission to Bartholomew Dandridge, Dec. 12, 1800, Commissions to Consuls, RG 59.
9. Not found. Wetmore (1749–1830) opened a law office in Castine, Maine, in 1795 and was appointed justice of the peace for that district in 1801. See Clifford K. Shipton, *Biographical Sketches of Those Who Attended Harvard College in the Classes 1768–1771* (Boston, 1975), 447–451.
1. See Liston to JM, Aug. 25, 1800.
2. Letters not found.

The President sir gives the most implicit faith to these declarations of your government made through you, & on this subject is at perfect ease.

I have no knowledge of the information you may have given my predecessor relative to this affair, nor of the means you may have enabled him to use for the purpose of removing suspicions which, tho unfounded, as I am happy to beleive, in fact, your candor will admit, were not entirely unsupported by appearances. I must however be permited to say, that I have no reason to doubt the willingness with which he woud have freed the British government, or any other at peace with the United States, from imputations known to be unwarranted by facts. For myself I can assure you sir, that I shall, at all times, with much pleasure, & in this I shall faithfully represent the feelings of the President, do ample justice to your government & yourself.

If groundless charges & offensive surmises on this subject, are still propagated in newspapers, & publishd by persons high in office in certain States of the union, I beg you to beleive that these charges & surmises receive no countenance from the government of the United States. To that government they are always causes of infinite regret, & woud be prevented if the means of prevention existed. Your knowledge of the state of the press in our country must satisfy you, that newspaper calumnies are not imputable to our government, &, without going far back you may find examples in your own of the impunity with which a foreign friendly nation may be grossly libeld.

If too ready a credit is given in this country to every groundless report of hostile measures or designs on the part of Great Britain, be assurd, sir, the government regrets, with you, that such a temper shoud exist. While we cherish the beleif that the government you represent does not authorize a conduct in its officers calculated to excite such a temper, & admit that the belligerent state of your nation renders it difficult to prevent all acts of aggression, yet, perhaps, in examining the practice of your officers employd in the business of impressment, of [*your   , & of*] your courts of Vice admiralty, you will perceive, at least some of the causes, by which this temper may have been producd.

Allow me sir, on this occasion to express the conviction I feel that your conduct during your mission here, has been entirely calculated to ensure the confidence & friendship of the nation to which you are deputed, & to add the most explicit assurances of my very high & sincere respect & esteem for your person & character.

To John Adams

ALS, Adams Papers, Massachusetts Historical Society

Sir   Washington, September 8, 1800

The papers from Govr. St Clair have been read by the heads of departments & are now returnd.[3]

On receiving your letter respecting the consulate in the island of Madeira I wrote to Mr. Bayard who I found had on a former occasion recommended in very strong terms for a different consulate, a Mr. Leonard, & have receivd an answer from which I now transmit to you. I transmit with it a certificate from Don Lewis Roderigues Villares who has something to do with the government of Madeira, conceiving that you woud wish to see these papers before you decide absolutely respecting Mr. Pintard.[4]

Shoud you decide on removing that gentleman I am persuaded that a more proper successor than Mr. Lamar coud not be selected. He is a native American, born in Maryland. His long establishd commerce with Madeira & the high respectability of his house enable him to be of more service to the Americans trading to that island than perhaps any other person who coud be appointed.

I have directed a copy of a letter prepard to Mr. Humphries to be inclosd to you. The list of condemnations in Spain transmited by Mr. Young who has acted under Mr. Humphries shows that the depredations complaind of even in Europe have been immense.[5]

If you will please to suggest such alterations as you may wish in the letter (provided you are of opinion that such a representation ought to be made to the court of Madrid) I will immediately make them—if you approve the letter as it is I will on being informd of your determination forward a duplicate & triplicate to Mr. Humphries. That now transmitted to you Mr. Shaw may have an opportunity of sending by the way of Boston.

In the Genl. Green came passengers the adjutant Genl. & the comissary of the army of the north from St. Domingo. They spoke of having dispatches for our government but passd through this place

3. See Adams to JM, Aug. 30, 1800 (second letter).

4. Samuel Bayard had married a sister of John Marsden Pintard. Neither JM's correspondence with Bayard or the certificate to Villares has been found. See additional correspondence on Pintard.

5. See JM to David Humphreys, Sept. 8, 1800. The list sent by Moses Young, U.S. consul at Madrid, has not been found.

without seeing me & I have not since heard of them. I am Sir with the highest respect, Your obedt. Servt.

J MARSHALL

To Samuel and Miers Fisher

ALS, RG 76, National Archives

[*September 8, 1800, Washington.* JM acknowledges receipt of the Fishers' letter of Aug. 30, agreeing that their case deserves the attention of the U.S. government. He intends to demand compensation from Spain as soon as President Adams consents.[6]]

To David Humphreys

LS, The Rosenbach Foundation, Philadelphia

No. 2.

Sir   Washington, September 8, 1800

From the commencement of the present war, which has raged so long and with so much violence in Europe, the efforts of the United States to maintain a fair and an honest neutrality have been unremitted. The unvarying object of our government has been, by avoiding strict political connections with any nation, by performing with scrupulous good faith its engagements to all, and by affording equally to all, where uncontrouled by express stipulations, those benefits and advantages, which the laws and usages of nations permit, and which friendship and social intercourse enjoin, to entitle ourselves to those privileges, which of right belong to a nation at peace.

Towards Spain this has been the uniform course of the American Government. The neighbourhood of her possessions to our country, the reciprocal benefits, which may result from that neighbourhood, while a good understanding subsists between the two governments, and the mischiefs they can, with so much facility, inflict on each other, in case of war, form, in addition to our general love of peace, the strongest motives for wishing to preserve it with Spain. It is not recollected or believed, that the Government of the United States

6. See JM to David Humphreys, Sept. 23, 1800, and Samuel and Miers Fisher to JM, calendared at Aug. 30 and Dec. 23, 1800.

has, from the day of its foundation, afforded any cause of complaint to His Catholic Majesty or to his subjects.

With this fair and upright conduct on our part, we had a right to expect, and we have now a right to require, some attention on the part of Spain, to those duties towards the United States, which her own particular engagements, as well as the laws and usages of nations, bind her to perform.

This reasonable expectation has been entirely disappointed. The aggressions committed by the subjects of His Catholic Majesty on the property of the citizens of the United States, are totally incompatible with real peace. It is impossible that this state of things can continue. Injuries repeated and unredressed must at length compel the injured to use their own means to obtain that justice to which all are entitled.

To avoid an event so truly deprecated by us, the President expressly directs, that you lay before the Spanish government, in terms of respect, manifesting, at the same time, the peaceful dispositions of the United States and their earnest sollicitude for the preservation of a good understanding with His Catholic Majesty, and a friendly intercourse with his dominions, the very weighty causes of serious dissatisfaction to which the conduct of Spain has given birth.

These complaints are founded on,

1st. The capture of our merchant vessels by privateers, manned in whole or in part by Spaniards, and fitted out in Spanish ports.

2nd. The condemnation of our vessels, however captured, in the courts of Spain.

1st. Privateers manned, in whole or in part, by Spaniards, and fitted out in the ports of Spain, having commissions from the French Republic, cruize on the American commerce both in Europe and the West Indies, and capture our merchantmen to a great and ruinous extent.

This practice is in such direct and open opposition both to the laws of nations and our subsisting treaty, that we are unwilling, not with standing the continued repetition of the offence, to believe that it can have been sanctioned by the Government of Spain. The President therefore relies confidently on the success, which must attend your representations on this subject.

The United States have been reduced to the painful necessity of arming for defence against France. In this contest Spain has been considered and treated by the American Government, as a neutral and friendly power. Tho' belligerent, as it respects France and her European enemies, she has been supposed to be neutral as between France and the United States.

If this be her real position (and she has enjoyed all its advantages) then with its privileges are connected correspondent duties, which she cannot permit herself to neglect. One of these duties, of high and unquestionable obligation, is to withhold from the enemy of the United States, all aid in the prosecution of hostilities, not stipulated by preexisting treaties. To permit her to fit out privateers in the ports of Spain and to man them with Spanish subjects, is to give her the most efficient aid, and that aid, which of all others is most injurious to the United States. Nor is it recollected, that she is bound by any pre-existing treaty to furnish this aid. The extent of this practice in Europe, is a fact which has certainly not escaped your observation. You will be able to enforce your representations on this subject, by the statement of particular cases within your own knowledge. In the West Indies it has prevailed to a degree, which scarcely our love of peace can tolerate. The superiority of our naval force in those seas, has enabled us so to environ Guadeloupe, that privateers from that Island, experience considerable difficulty in prosecuting from thence their piratical depredations. This however affords no safety to American commerce. From the ports of His Catholic Majesty, privateers are fitted out, under French commissions, manned in whole or in part with Spanish subjects, and issue in swarms, which spread over the ocean, and capture indiscriminately every American vessel they fall in with, of inferior force. Thus to disable Guadeloupe from doing essential injury avails us nothing. It only changes the quarter from which the attack proceeds.

We are well aware, that Spain, being engaged in a common war with France against England, may find some difficulty in preventing entirely all abuse of the privilege of fitting out privateers in her ports for the purpose of cruizing against a nation, with which his Catholic Majesty is at war. If cases had seldom occurred, in which this privilege had been abused, to the great injury of the United States, and if proper means had been used to discourage the practice, this government would not have deemed it a subject of sufficient magnitude to induce the very serious remonstrance you are now instructed to make. But the cases have been so multiplied, the practice has been so open and so systematic, it has been so fostered by the security, prizes made by such privateers find in the Spanish ports, that the United States can no longer consider such captures otherwise than if made by privateers acting under the authority of His Catholic Majesty, and the President feels himself bound by the high duties his station imposes on him, to use all the means he possesses to prevent a repetition of such real injuries, and to obtain for our citizens compensation for the past.

In addition to the general principles, which regulate the conduct of nations at peace with each other, our treaty[7] has been considered as containing stipulations, which ought further to have restrained the practices complained of. The first article, which promises a firm and inviolable peace and sincere friendship between the two governments, and the subjects of the one and the citizens of the other, means nothing, if it leaves the subjects of His Catholic Majesty at liberty to plunder with impunity the citizens of the United States. That the commission under which they cruize is granted by the French Republic, constitutes, when the purpose of the commission becomes thus open and notorious, no solid defence for the measure. Indeed in the present state of the parties, Spain as well as France being at war with Britain, the very act of commissioning privateers, equipped and manned in the Spanish ports, by any other than the Spanish government, becomes evidence of an intent to cruize on nations with whom Spain is at peace.

The provisions of the 14th. article of our treaty have also been considered as prohibiting any Spanish subject from taking a commission from France, while that nation is in hostility with the United States.[8]

2d. The merchant vessels of the United States, prosecuting a peaceful and lawful commerce, have been, when captured and carried into the ports of Spain, condemned, with their cargoes, as good prize to the captors.

The frequency and notoriety of these condemnations render unnecessary the recital of particular cases. Should however instances in support of the complaint be required, you, sir, are already but too amply furnished with the means of complying with this request. The long list, which has been lately transmitted to this department by Mr. Young,[9] is a document, which, independent of the transactions in the West Indies, evidences but too conclusively the truth of this complaint.

---

7. See the Treaty of Friendship, Limits, and Navigation of 1795, known as the Pinckney Treaty, in Miller, ed., *Treaties*, II, 318–338.

8. *Ibid.*, 328.

9. See JM to John Adams, Sept. 8, 1800.

The losses thus sustained by American citizens are immense. They demand the intervention of the Government. This intervention can no longer be withheld. No considerations which exist could justify a silent acquiescence on our part, under national injuries so extensive and so apparent.

The merchant vessels of a nation at peace with another can only, if captured on the high seas, be justly adjudged to be prize by that other, when such vessels shall have violated either the law of nations or some existing treaty. When either of these causes can be with truth alledged, the adjudication is not complained of. It is only in cases where no law, whether established by the common consent of the civilized world, or by particular compact, between the two governments, has been infracted, no rule, which governs the conduct of belligerent and neutral powers towards each other, has been broken, by the vessel condemned, that the United States complain of, and expect compensation for the injury.

It is perfectly understood, that many of these decisions, alike unjust and injurious, have been made by the French consular tribunals established in Spain. This circumstance in no degree weakens the claim of the United States on the Spanish government. That complete and exclusive jurisdiction within its own territory is of the very essence of sovereignty, is a principle which all nations assert. Courts, therefore, of whatever description, can only be established in any nation, by the consent of the sovereign power of that nation. All the powers they possess must be granted by, proceed from, and be a portion of, the Supreme authority of that country in which such powers are exercised. Of consequence foreign nations consider the decisions of such tribunals in like manner as if made by the ordinary tribunals of the country. A government may certainly, at its discretion, permit any portion of its sovereignty to be exercised by foreigners within its territory: but for the acts of those to whom such portions of sovereignty may be delegated, the government remains, to those with whom it has relations, as completely responsible, as if such powers had been exercised by its own subjects named by itself. The interior arrangements, which a government makes, according to its will, cannot be noticed by foreign nations, or affect its obligations to them. Of consequence the United States can consider the condemnation of their vessels by the French tribunals in Spain, no otherwise, than if such condemnations had been made in the ordinary tribunals of the nation.

Where vessels so condemned have been captured by privateers

equipped in the ports of his Catholic Majesty, or manned in whole or in part by his subjects, the hostility of the act is rendered still more complete.[1]

In the one case or in the other, the aggressions complained of are totally incompatible with those rules, which the law of nations prescribes for the conduct of a neutral power.

They are also considered as violating the 6th. article of our treaty with Spain.[2] By that article each nation binds itself to protect, by all means in their power, the vessels and other effects belonging to the citizens or subjects of the other, which shall be within the extent of their jurisdiction by sea or land, and to use all their efforts to recover and cause to be restored to the right owners, their vessels and effects, which may have been taken from them within the extent of their said jurisdiction.

When an American vessel has been brought within the extent of the jurisdiction of His Catholic Majesty by a privateer, which, having been equipped in whole or in part in the ports of Spain, could not lawfully capture her, the casus foederis occurs, and Spain is bound by solemn treaty, to protect such vessel by all means in her power, and to use all her efforts to recover and cause such vessel to be restored to her right owners. In similar situations, such is the uniform conduct of the United States. Instead of pursuing this course, prescribed alike by the law of nations and by particular compact, American vessels, thus circumstanced, have been declared lawful prize.

Neither the frequency nor the long continuance of these aggressions have as yet induced the United States to make reprisals. A strong solicitude to preserve a good understanding with Spain, a hope, that amicable representations, by calling the attention of the Government to injuries it cannot have designed to commit, may, by arresting their progress for the future and obtaining compensation for the past, reestablish that cordial friendship between the two nations, which can only be preserved by reciprocal justice, induce the grave and serious remonstrance, which the President now directs.

1. A notation on the manuscript, "Vat. B.3.S.15.95.97.102.104.," indicates that JM was referring to Emmerick de Vattel, *The Law of Nations*, book III, on war. The sections cited maintain that soldiers may not be enlisted in a foreign country without permission and that those who associate with one's enemies are to be considered enemies also. Neutrals are obliged to avoid any act of assistance in the absence of treaty obligation. See Emmerick de Vattel, *The Law of Nations* . . . (New York, 1796), 365–366, 396–397, 400–401.

2. Miller, ed., *Treaties*, II, 323.

While you state the complaints of the United States respectfully, but with plainness and with truth, you will also do justice to the dispositions of this government. Your assurances of its amicable temper, of its real solicitude to dissipate, by its own moderation, and the establishment of such principles as are dictated and required by justice, all causes of discontent between the two nations, cannot be stronger than those dispositions will warrant.

If the same just and friendly temper be manifested on the part of Spain, no difficulty can exist to obstruct the accommodation we wish. The United States ask only what, under similar circumstances they would not hesitate to grant.

You will claim from the Spanish government,

1st.   That efficient measures be taken to prevent the equipping or manning of vessels in the ports of Spain, designed to cruize on the commerce of the United States, and that decisive orders be given to the proper officers to effect the restoration to the owners of all vessels with their cargoes so taken, and which may be brought within the extent of the jurisdiction of His Catholic Majesty:

2ndly.   That means be taken to prevent the condemnation of any American vessels or cargoes in Spain, by any tribunal whatever, on principles incompatible with the law of nations, or our treaty with His Catholic Majesty: And

3rdly.   That in all cases, where American vessels or cargoes have been captured by privateers, equipped or manned in whole or in part in the ports of His Catholic Majesty, and all means in his power have not been used to restore them; and in all cases where such vessels and cargoes have been condemned either by the French Consular Tribunals in Spain, or the ordinary Tribunals of the country, contrary to the law of nations, and the subsisting treaties between the two powers, full compensation be made by the Government of Spain to the owners of such vessels and cargoes.

These demands on our part are rendered indispensable by the high duties of every government to itself, and to that people, whose interests it superintends. His Catholic Majesty is urged to accede to them by his sacred regard for that honor, justice and good faith, which have so long influenced the conduct of the Spanish Government.

The principles by which they are to be governed having been accurately detailed, commissioners may be appointed to ascertain the amount of damages. For this object the 21st. article of our present treaty presents a model to which we have no exception.[3]

3. *Ibid.*, 335–337.

Should our present negotiations with France terminate happily, we are perswaded, that no difficulties will exist in making such arrangements for the future, as will effectually secure the continuance of harmony and good understanding between the two nations. Indeed it will only be necessary to enforce the observance of engagements which already exist. But however that negotiation may terminate, compensation for past depredations on our commerce must be insisted on. Neither that respect, which is due to its own character, nor that justice, which is due to its citizens, will permit the Government of the United States to dispense with the performance of a duty of such high obligation.

An expectation, that His Catholic Majesty would depute to the United States a Minister, with adequate powers, disposed to keep up the relations of amity, required by the interests of both nations, and to whom this government might honorably make such communications as the state of things should render necessary, has, with other causes, prevented an earlier representation on the important subjects of this letter. It is still wished, that the minister, who is to replace the Chevalier de Yrujo may have full powers for the accommodation of all existing differences. If however their adjustment at Madrid should be preferred by the Spanish Government, the President charges you with the necessary arrangements, which must there be made. Your knowledge of the importance of this charge to the honor and interests of your country will of course induce you to give it all your attention, and to press its speedy completion with as much zeal as a proper respect for the government of Spain will permit you to use. I am, sir, with very much respect, Your obed. servt.

J Marshall

To John Adams

ALS, Adams Papers, Massachusetts Historical Society

Sir   Washington, September 9, 1800

I now send you a copy of the letter transmited to Mr. King. I wrote him also privately stating the best opinion here to be that not more than two milion of Dollars coud justly be chargeable to the United States under the treaty.[4] I am Sir with the highest respect, Your obedt. Servt.

J Marshall

4. See JM to Rufus King, Aug. 23, 1800 (both letters).

From John Adams

ALS, RG 59, National Archives

Dear Sir   Quincy, September 9, 1800

Mr Stevens's Letter inclosed in yours of the 30th. seems to require a Proclamation to open the Trade between the United States and the Ports of St. Domingo which were lately in the Possession of Rigaud and I am ready to agree to it, whenever you and the heads of Departments shall be satisfied.

Mr Mitchell of Charleston promises great Things, and he may be able to perform them for any thing that I know. But I have no intimation that Mr Boudinot[5] will resign and I can promise no Office beforehand. It has been the constant Usage, now near twelve years for the President to answer no letters of solicitation or Recommendations for Office. I know of no coins of Gold better executed than our Eagles nor of silver than our dollars. The Motto of the Hotel de Valentinois in which I lived at Passy was si sta bene, non si move, if you stand well stand still. The Epitaph stava ben ma por stare meglio sto qui, I was well, but by taking too much Physic to be better lo here I lie is a good Admonition. I will not be answerable for the correctness of my Italian: but you see I have an idle morning or I should not write you this common place.

I return you Mr Humphries's Letter and inclose that of Mr John H. Mitchell, and that of Mr Stevens. With sincere regard &c

JOHN ADAMS

To Rufus King

LS, RG 59, National Archives

Sir   Washington, September 9, 1800

The ship Charlotte, belonging to Messrs. Costers[6] of New York, and bound thence for Amsterdam, was captured some months ago by the British frigate Cleopatra, and condemned in the Court of Vice Admiralty at Halifax. Those Gentlemen have appealed from the sentence of that Court, thro' the intervention of their friends Messrs.

5. Elias Boudinot was director of the Mint from 1795 to 1805.
6. See Henry and John Coster to JM, calendared at June 24, 1800. See also JM to an unknown person, Aug. 2, 1800.

Phyn, Inglis and Co. of London, and have requested me to bespeak your good offices in their favor, in case they may need them: which I request you to grant them, so far as may be proper and customary. I have the honor, sir, to be, with great respect, Your most obed. servt.

J MARSHALL

Deed

Deed Book Copy, Office of the Clerk of Hardy County, Moorefield, W.Va.

[*September 9, 1800 (Hardy County, Va.*). By his attorney, Rawleigh Colston, JM conveys 53.25 acres in the South Branch Manor to Job Welton for £13 6s. 3d. The deed was recorded in the District Court at Hardy County on Sept. 9, 1800.]

From Israel Whelen

LS, RG 59, National Archives

[*September 10, 1800, Philadelphia.* Whelen reports that Messrs. Yard and Cramond gave him a good recommendation respecting Mr. D'Arey. Because D'Arey has no real estate in the United States, Mr. Yard will sign a bond as security for him.]

To John Adams

ALS, Adams Papers, Massachusetts Historical Society

Sir   Washington, September 12, 1800

Your letter of the 2d. inst. returning the dispatches from our envoys of the 17th. of May, is just receivd. I now perceive that my having omited to accompany those dispatches with a letter requires an apology. After decyphering it, I had been engagd with the heads of departments until it became necessary to forward the package immediately to you, or to lose a mail which I was not inclind to do, & on that account, only inclosd the papers themselves, intending to write the next day.

Mr. Yznardi is here but as yet has made me no communications. I am Sir with every sentiment of respect, your obedt. Servt.

J MARSHALL

From John Adams

ALS, RG 59, National Archives

Dear Sir   Quincy, September 13, 1800

I have recd your favour of the third. There is indeed so much deli-cacy in engaging in the support of a Claim founded on provision furnished the British Army during the revolutionary War that I would not consent that Mr King should interpose officially in the Business, of Col Norton.[7]

I return the Letter of Willm. H. Harrison to you and Mr John Wilkins's Letter to him recommending Mr John Hollingsworth of Kentucky to be a Judge in the Indiana Territory. In my late tour to the City of Washington, I became acquainted at Baltimore on my return, with two Gentlemen of this Name and at head of Elk with a third all Brothers I presume of the Gentlemen in Question and all very respectable Men.[8]

I am apprehensive We may be hurried by Governor Harrisons impatience into some appointments which may not give general satisfaction. I know not Mr Hollingsworth Age or Accomplishments well enough to make a Comparison of them with those of Mr Griffin. I must rely much on your Inquiries and Judgment.

Where is the Portsmouth and her illustrious Charge?[9] Are they gone to Petersbourg to join in the armed Neutrality? With great regard &c

J. ADAMS

7. JM presented Beriah Norton's claim to Rufus King in JM to King, Nov. 4, 1800.
8. For information on the Hollingsworths, see [Joseph Adger Stewart], *Descendants of Valentine Hollingsworth, Sr.* (Louisville, Ky., 1925).
9. The *Portsmith*, Capt. Daniel McNeill, arrived at Norfolk the first week in December carrying William R. Davie and with him the convention of Mortefontaine. See Blackwell P. Robinson, *William R. Davie* (Chapel Hill, N.C., 1957), 356.
    Russia joined with Prussia, Sweden, and Denmark in an anti-British league of armed neutrality in 1780 and again in 1801 to protect their commerce from search and seizure by British sea power. See Alexander DeConde, *The Quasi-War: The Politics and Diplomacy of the Undeclared War with France, 1797–1801* (New York, 1966), 251–253.

To Thomas Bulkely

Letterbook Copy, RG 59, National Archives

[*September 13, 1800, Washington*. Acting at the request of Lewis A. Terascon, a merchant in Philadelphia, JM asks Bulkely to assist Terascon in his difficulties with the Spanish over the capture of his brigantine, *Sea Nymph*, which was taken into Lisbon by a British armed ship. JM refers to a letter from Bulkely of June 27, which has not been found, in which he mentioned the capture.]

To John Gavino

Letterbook Copy, RG 59, National Archives

[*September 13, 1800, Washington*. JM writes a letter similar to the one of the same date to Thomas Bulkely asking Gavino, U.S. consul at Gibraltar, to assist Terascon. He adds, however, that "the captors have threatened to send the papers to Gibralter, in order that the vessel and cargo may be there adjudicated, and where it is said they expect to find less difficulty of obtaining a condemnation than in England." JM wants Gavino to help prevent that if possible.]

To Timothy Tinsley

ALS, Washburn Papers, Massachusetts Historical Society

[*September 13, 1800, Washington*. In response to a request from Tinsley, JM informs him that he has sent his application for appointment as collector of Norfolk to the secretary of the Treasury, although he believes that Oliver Wolcott has already decided on someone else.[1] JM closes with a remark about the lack of news regarding the negotiation with France, adding, "It is probable that their late victories & the hope which many of our papers are well calculated to inspire, that America is prepard once more to crouch at her feet, may render ineffectual our endeavors to obtain peace."]

1. See John Steele to JM, calendared at June 7, 1800.

To Elbridge Gerry

ALS, Collection of Sol Feinstone, Washington Crossing, Pa.

Sir   Washington, September 15, 1800
   The President has directed me in settling your account, to continue your salary to the time claimd by yourself.[2] There remains therefore nothing to be adjusted in order to conclude this business but the item respecting the proportion of cabin stores with which you are chargeable.
   Colo. Pickering supposd you to be accountable for one half & on that principle settled with the captain.[3] I inclose you a copy of the account of stores & am informd that the captain states a large proportion of them to have been purchasd at your request.
   If this principle adopted by my predecessor is agreeable to you be pleasd to write with ink the pencil'd figures & return the account signd & an order for the balance in favor of any person whatever which I will immediately pay. If you disapprove of the amount of the item respecting cabin stores, be pleasd to lay the subject before the President whose directions will be promptly obeyd. I am Sir very respectfully, Your obedt. Servt.

J MARSHALL

From Joseph Nourse

Letterbook Copy, RG 53, National Archives

[*September 15, 1800 (Washington)*. In a circular letter intended for several officers of government, Nourse, register in the Treasury Department, requests an estimate of expenses for the remainder of 1800 and for 1801 in order to assist the secretary of the Treasury in proposing a budget for 1802.[4]]

   2. See Account of Elbridge Gerry, 1797–1799, Entry 221, Despatches & Accounts of Elbridge Gerry, RG 59, National Archives. See also Gerry to JM, Sept. 17, 1800.
   3. See Timothy Pickering to Gerry, June 20, 1799, Pickering Papers, Massachusetts Historical Society. See also Gerry to JM, Oct. 11, 1800.
   4. See Statement of Accounts, Sept. 30, 1800.

To John Adams

Printed, The Meridian Bookshop, Inc., Catalog No. 48 (n.p., 1936), 50

Washington, September 16, 1800

Your letter is here before me as I think over the contents and the information it contains.[5] In response to your inquiry as to the status of Col. Miller, as far as I am able to determine he is in the service of the United States. Nothing could successfully come of so mean a plot to defeat the honourable intents and purposes of so worthy an officer and gentleman as Col. Palmer of Massachusetts. The family are neighbours; and if any word of recommendation might be needed, I know of none better qualified than the continental general was when he nominated the Col. as his aide. I shall place the matter in the hands of Mr. Dexter, and I assure you, Sir, that careful consideration will be given the charges which I am sure are political. Thanking you for advising me of the case, I am, Sir, your obdt. humble Servt.

J. MARSHALL.

To John Adams

ALS, Adams Papers, Massachusetts Historical Society

Sir   Washington, September 17, 1800

I have receivd your several letters of the 4th. & 5th. inst.

It is certainly wise to contemplate the event of our envoys returning without a treaty, but it will very much depend on the inteligence & assurances they may bring, what course sound policy will direct the United States to pursue. I am greatly disposd to think that the present government is much inclind to correct, at least in part, the follies of the past. Of these none were perhaps more conspicuous or more injurious to the french nation than their haughty & hostile conduct to neutrals. Considerable retrograde steps in this respect have already been taken & I expect the same course will be continued. Shoud this expectation not be disappointed there will be security—at least a reasonable prospect of it—for the future & there will exist no cause of war, but to obtain compensation for past injuries.

5. The letter from Adams has not been found. In the absence of a manuscript copy of this letter, it is impossible to determine JM's authorship, which seems questionable from the contents of the letter.

This I am persuaded will not be deemd a sufficient motive for such a measure.

I inclose you commissions for the three Judges of the Indiana territory.[6] If you shoud be disinclind to the appointment of Mr. Griffin you will be pleasd to retain the commission made out for him & signify to me the name of the person you prefer. Another commission shall immediately be forwarded. If Mr. Griffin is a young man of competent talents I shoud not think his age an objection—I am not however acquainted personally with him, tho I know & respect his family.

When I left Richmond to fill the office to which you were pleasd to call me there was some private business which very much requird my personal attention & which remains undone. It will be a considerable inconvenience & perhaps injury to me if it is not completed this fall. I therefore propose, if it is not disagreeable to you to be in Richmond for a fortnight about the first of october.[7] That time will I trust enable me to transact some private affairs which I cannot commit to others & which are interesting to me. I am Sir with the most respectful attachment, Your obedt

J MARSHALL

From John Adams

ALS, RG 59, National Archives

Dear Sir   Quincy, September 17, 1800

In Consequence of the Information transmitted in your Letter of the 6. I think it most equitable to suspend the Removal of Mr Pintard for the present. I am glad to find that Mr Lamar is a native American and now agree with you that, whenever Mr Pintard must be removed, a more proper Person cannot probably be selected than Mr Lamar.[8]

I have read with Care your Letter to Mr Humphries[9] and find it

---

6. The temporary commissions were signed on Oct. 6, 1800, and the permanent commissions, on Dec. 12, 1800. See Temporary Presidential Commissions, 1789–1909, and Permanent Presidential Commissions, 1789–1802, RG 59, National Archives.

7. JM returned to Richmond to argue the case of Mayo v. Bentley before the Court of Appeals. 8 Va. (4 Call) 528 (1800). See Albert J. Beveridge, *The Life of John Marshall*, II (Boston, 1916), 494.

8. See JM to Adams, Sept. 8, 1800.

9. See JM to David Humphreys, Sept. 8, 1800.

so well conceived considerd and expressed, that I have directed Mr Shaw to send it from Boston. The Duplicate and Triplicate you may convey whenever you find opportunities. With great respect &c

J. ADAMS

I return the Papers respecting Pintard.

From John Adams

ALS, RG 59, National Archives

Dear Sir   Quincy, September 17, 1800

I agree entirely with your sentiments relative to Explanations with the British Government and a gross sum, and am happy to learn that you have prepared a Letter to Mr King, according to the Principles understood between us, which has been approved by the heads of departments.[1] This Letter may be sent without further Advice from me.

Mr Liston, apparently had, Un peu de l heumeur, when he wrote his note of the 25 of August. Your Letter in Answer to it, is very proper.[2] This Gentlemans Conduct on the whole has been wise and agreeable.

I return the Proclamation for opening the trade with St. Domingo signed. I know Mr Dandridge so well that I am very willing you should give him a Consulate.[3] With sincere Attachment &c

J. ADAMS

From John Adams

ALS, RG 59, National Archives

Dear Sir   Quincy, September 17, 1800

In Answer to your favour of the 6th. I agree upon the whole with you.

The Law considers the whole of the Island of St. Domingo as a Dependance of France, which raises some doubt of the Power of the

1. This letter is in response to JM to Adams, Sept. 6, 1800 (second letter).
2. See JM to Robert Liston, Sept. 6, 1800.
3. See Proclamation extending trade to the entire island of Hispaniola, Proclamations, RG 11, National Archives; and JM to Adams, Sept. 6, 1800 (second letter).

Executive to discharge and restore the Vessell captured by Captain Talbot. If therefore the interested should insist on the Judgment of the Judiciary, the plan you propose will be the safest. Capt. Talbot, I am convinced will make no difficulty: but his officers and Men may.

Sir William Scotts Law, that there is a Right in the Captors to proceed with the Prosecution against the Will of the Crown, seems to be in point. With sincere Attachment &c

J. ADAMS

From Elbridge Gerry

Letterbook Copy, Gerry Papers, Library of Congress

Sir   Cambridge, September 17, 1800
Having had the honor, yesterday, of an interview with the President, I was informed, on enquiry, that you had not made a report to him, for liquidating my account. The President likewise desired me to write to you for information, whether you had considered the subject & come to a decision.[4] I remain Sir, respectfully & your very huml sert.

From Israel Whelen

LS, RG 59, National Archives

[*September 17, 1800, Philadelphia.* Whelen reports on a visit with Andrew Ellicott made to learn the location of instruments used to determine the boundary between the United States and the Floridas. Ellicott told him he would write the State Department.[5] Whelen requests direction on paying accounts relating to the *Anna Maria* and the *Sophia.*]

From John Adams

ALS, RG 59, National Archives

Dear Sir   Quincy, September 18, 1800
I recd last night and have read this morning the Copy of your

4. Gerry had not received JM's letter of Sept. 15. See also Gerry to JM, Oct. 11, 1800.
5. See Ellicott to JM, Sept. 23, 1800, Entry 391, Letters Received by the State Department, 1799–1804, III, RG 76, National Archives.

Letter to Mr King inclosed in your favour of the 9th. I know not how the subject could have been better digested.

An Idea has occurred to me, which I wish you would consider. Ought not something to be said to Mr King about the other Board, that I mean in London. We understand it no doubt, all along, that those Commissioners are to proceed and their Awards to be paid. But should not something be expressed concerning it in the new Arrangement, whether by Explanations or a composition for a gross sum. Can it be stipulated, that the gross sum, if that should be accepted should be paid in whole or in Part to American Claimaints before the Board in London, in satisfaction of Awards in their favour? These perhaps would loan the Money to Government and receive Certificates on Interest as the Merchants have for ships. I only hint the thing for consideration: am not much satisfied with it. With great regard &c

J. ADAMS

To Rufus King

ALS, The Carl H. Pforzheimer Library, New York City

No. 5

Dear Sir[6]   Washington, September 20, 1800

It is the hope & expectation of the President that your negotiation with Lord Grenville, concerning contraband of war & the impressment of our seamen, which had progressd considerably, & been broken off in consequence, as is here understood, of the differences between the two nations respecting the construction of the 6th. article of their treaty of amity, commerce & navigation, has been, or will now be, renewd.

Shoud it have been intended to proceed pari passu with these subjects, yet your instructions respecting the claims of British creditors on the United States, having, as we hope, enabled you to place that business in a train for adjustment, we are sanguine in our expectations concerning the other objects of the negotiation.

Shoud you be unable to obtain—what is most desird because most

6. For the background of this important letter of instruction, see Secretary of State: Editorial Note, June 6, 1800, and JM's correspondence with King and John Adams on Anglo-American negotiations over the terms of the Jay Treaty. See also Adams to JM, Oct. 3, 1800.

just—explanatory articles placing the original treaty on its true ground, or even to settle this difference on the terms stated in my No. 2,[7] terms of the liberality of which I am more & more convinc'd, yet we perceive no reason growing out of this misunderstanding, which shoud obstruct the progress of an agreement on subjects, the present practice on which so seriously threatens the peace of the two nations.

The 7th. article of the treaty of amity, commerce, & navigation, corresponds with the 6th., & proceedings under both have been suspended. It is not my purpose to show that these two measures, viewd together, are injurious to the United States, because we do not complain, for the present, of the suspension, which has taken place, of the proceedings of the board lately siting in London. But certainly, as the one measure completely balances the other, this misunderstanding can furnish to the British government no plausible pretext, for taking other steps unfriendly in themselves, or for refusing to take such as justice & friendship indispensably require.

We trust then that, whatever may be the fate of the propositions respectively made, concerning the differences under the 6th. & 7th. articles of our late treaty, the negotiations relative to contraband & impressments will now progress, without further interuption, to a happy conclusion.

Shoud this hope be disappointed the practices of depredating on our commerce & impressing our seamen, demand & must receive the most serious attention of the United States.

The unfeignd solicitude of this government to preserve peace with all, & to obtain justice by friendly representations to the party commiting injuries, rather than by a resort to other means, induces it now to wish, that any misjudgement respecting its views & intentions, which may have been formd in the british cabinet, & which may have promoted dispositions unfavorable to that perfect harmony which it is the interest of both nations to cherish, may be completely corrected. For this the President has great & just reliance on you. If impressions of any sort have been made, impairing that conciliatory temper which enables one nation to view with candor the proceedings of another, the President hopes that your perfect knowledge of the principles which influence the government you represent, will enable you to meet & to remove them.

That such impressions have been made by connecting two mea-

7. JM to King, Aug. 23, 1800 (first letter).

sures entirely independent of each other is greatly suspected.

The secession of the American commissioners from the board lately siting at Philadelphia, & the recommencement of negotiations with France, may have been united together as parts of one system, & been considerd as evidencing a temper less friendly to Great-Britain than had heretofore guided our councils.

You have been assurd that the suspension of further proceedings on the claims of british creditors against the United States, is attributable, exclusively, to the wild, extensive, & unreasonable construction put, by the commissioners of that nation, on the article they were appointed to execute; a construction which, as we think, at once prostrated the words & spirit of the article, & overleapd all those bounds, within which, by common consent, their powers were limited. You know too well the integrity of this government to doubt the sincerity with which this opinion is avowd, & you possess too perfectly the reasoning on which it has been formd, to feel any difficulty in supporting it. In fact we beleive that the points of difference need only be considerd, to produce in every inteligent mind the conviction, that the American government is, at least, sincere in the opinion it has maintaind.

Being entirely persuaded of the vast injury & injustice which woud result from executing the 6th. article according to the strange system devisd by a majority of the commissioners, a sense of duty & of national honor, as well as a wish to preserve a solid & lasting peace between the two countries, renderd indispensable the step which has been taken. Had the United States been at open & declard war with France, without a prospect of speedy pacification, the same causes must have inducd the same measure.

The suspension then of the commission at Philadelphia was not influencd by the probability of negotiating with France, nor have these two measures any tendency to explain each other.

It is equally true that neither of them proceeds from a temper in the United States hostile to, or even indifferent about a good understanding with, the british government.

The one has been shown to be a necessary measure of defence against, what was beleivd to be, an unauthorizd attack on the interests of the United States, which, it was conceivd, the british government woud not have sanctiond. The other is a necessary consequence of the well digested political system which this government adopted early in the present war, & has uniformly sought to maintain.

The United States do not hold themselves, in any degree, responsible to France or to Britain, for their negotiations with the one or the other of those powers. But they are ready to make amicable & reasonable explanations with either.

In this spirit their political system may be reviewd.

It has been the object of the American government from the commencement of the present war, to preserve between the belligerent powers, an exact neutrality. Separated far from Europe, we mean not to mingle in their quarrels. This determination was early declard, & has never been changd. In pursuance of it we have avoided, & we shall continue to avoid, any political connections which might engage us further than is compatible with the neutrality we profess; and we have sought, by a conduct just & friendly to all, to be permited to maintain a position which, without offence to any, we had a right to take.

The aggressions, sometimes of one, & sometimes of another belligerent power, have forcd us to contemplate, & to prepare for, war, as a probable event. We have repeld, & we will continue to repel, injuries not doubtful in their nature, & hostility not to be misunderstood. But this is a situation of necessity, not of choice. It is one in which we are placd—not by our own acts—but by the acts of others; & which we change, so soon as the conduct of others will permit us to change it.

The regularly accumulating injuries sustaind from France had, in 1798, progressd to such a point, as to leave to the United States no reasonable ground of doubt, that war was to be expected, & that force & force only coud be relied on, for the maintenance of our rights as a sovereign & independent nation. Force therefore was resorted to: but in the very act of resorting to it our preference for peace was manifest, & it was apparent that we shoud return to our natural situation, so soon as the wrongs which forcd us from it shoud cease & security against their repetition be offerd. A reasonable hope that this state of things may be attaind, has been furnishd by the recent conduct & overtures of the french government. America meets these overtures, & in doing so, only adheres to her pacific system.

To impress more forcibly on the british cabinet the principles on which this government acts, it may not perhaps be improper, to point their attention to our conduct, during the most critical periods of the present war.

In 1793, when the combination against France was most formidable, when, if ever, it was dangerous to acknowledge her new government, & to preserve with it the relations of amity, which, in a different state of things, had been formd with the nation, the American government openly declard its determination to adhere to that state of impartial neutrality, which it has ever since sought to maintain; nor did the clouds which, for a time, lourd over the fortunes of the republic in any degree, shake this resolution.

When victory had changd sides, & France in turn threatend those who did not arrange themselves under her banners, America, pursuing, with undeviating step, the same steady course, negotiated with his Britannic majesty, a treaty of amity, commerce & navigation, nor coud either threats or artifices prevent its ratification.

At no period of the war has France occupied such elevated ground, as at the very point of time when America armd to resist her. Triumphant & victorious every where, she had dictated a peace to her enemies on the continent & had refusd one to Britain.

In the reverse of her fortunes, when defeated both in Italy & on the Rhine, in danger of losing Holland, before the victory of Massena had changd the face of the last campaign, & before Russia had receded from the coalition against her, the present negotiation was resolvd on. During its pendency the state of the war has changd, but the conduct of the United States sustains no alteration. Our terms remain the same. We still pursue peace. We will embrace it if it can be obtaind without violating our national honor or our national faith, but we will reject, without hesitation, all propositions which may compromit the one or the other.

I have thought it not entirely useless to notice thus briefly, the relative situation of the belligerent powers, at the several eras when important measures have been adopted by the American government, because the review will mark, unequivocally, the character of that government, & show how steadily it pursues its system, without regarding the dangers from the one side or the other, to which the pursuit may be exposd.

The present negotiation with France is a part of this system, & ought therefore to excite in Britain, no feeling unfriendly to the United States.

Perhaps the apprehension that an erroneous estimate may have been made in the british cabinet, of the views & intentions of this government, may be unfounded. If so, it will of course be unnecessary to attack prejudices which do not exist. If, however, such prejudices do exist, you will, by a plain & candid representation of the truth, endeavor to remove them.

The way being thus smoothd for the reception of our complaints, the peace & interests of the nation require, that they shoud be, temperately but very seriously, enforcd.

These complaints are occasiond by the conduct of the british government through its agents, towards our commerce & our seamen.

The depredations on our commerce have of late been so considerable, as even to give some countenance to the opinion, that orders have been receivd to capture every american vessel bound to an enemy port. It cannot be difficult for you to conjecture the effect of such a system.

In your correspondence with my predecessor I perceive that these subjects have been repeatedly taken up, & that, in your several representations to the ministers of his britannic majesty, you have done ample justice to your country.

I am directed by the President to express to you his wish that, unless this business be in a train for satisfactory adjustment, you once more call the very serious attention of the british government to the irritating & injurious vexations we sustain, & make one more solemn appeal to the justice, the honor, & the real interests of the nation.

Our complaints respecting the depredations on our commerce may be classd under the following heads.

1st. The construction given to the article of our treaty relative to contraband of war.

2dly. The extent given to the rule concerning blockaded ports.

3dly. The unjust decisions of their courts of Vice Admiralty, & the impunity which attends captures totally vexatious & without probable cause of siezure.

We will consider

1st. The interpretation given to the 18th. article of our treaty. Under the expression "and generally whatever may serve directly for the equipment of vessels" which closes the enumeration of prohibited articles, our merchant vessels have been siezd & condemnd, because a part of their cargoes consisted of such articles as may, by possibility, serve for the equipment of vessels, altho they are not generally so applied, but are most commonly usd for purposes of husbandry. Such are ticklenberg, oznaburgs, & small nails, which, in the courts of vice admiralty, have been adjudgd contraband of war.

This vexatious construction is beleivd to be as unjustifiable as it is unfriendly.

As the law of nations on this subject can only establish general principles, particular treaties supply this defect by defining, precisely, between the parties, the relative rights of each as a belligerent or neutral power.

Thus the law of nations is clearly understood to declare that articles exclusively usd in war, are contraband; & that all articles not usd in war are the objects of lawful commerce. But articles of promiscuous use, proper either for peace or war, may be, it has been contended, contraband or not, according to the circumstances.

Admiting this opinion to be correct, it woud seem to be a reasonable construction of the law, that the character of articles thus doubtful in themselves, shoud be determind by those circumstances which may ascertain the use to which they are to be applied. If the circumstances of the cargo & its destination show, unequivocally, that its application must be to military purposes, materials fit for both peace & war, may assume the character of contraband; but if those circumstances afford solid ground for the opinion that the suspected materials are designd only for the ordinary purposes of the nation, then there can be no just motive for interrupting a commerce which ought to be pronouncd lawful.

This principle woud seem to mark the boundaries of the conflicting rights of neutral & belligerent powers. For neutrals have a right to carry on their usual commerce & belligerents have a right to prevent them from supplying the enemy with instruments of war.

But in the application of the principle considerable difficulty exists. The two nations judge differently on the circumstances attending each case, & to prevent the quarrels which may grow out of this difference of judgement, a precise list of contraband is usually agreed on between them.

If however in the enumeration there can be an ambiguous expression, it ought to be expounded with a reference to those general principles, intended to have been renderd definite by the particular agreement, & the enquiry ought always to be made, whether the article was really designd for a prohibited object, or was transported for the ordinary purposes of commerce.

In the catalogue of contraband agreed on between the United States & Great Britain, there is one description which leaves to construction what specific articles it may comprehend. It is in the following words—"and generally whatever may serve *directly* to the equipment of vessels."

In construing this expression, the british courts of Vice Admiralty appear to consider it as including whatever might, by any possibility be applied to the equipment of vessels. Altho the article be in itself unfit & improper for that case, & therefore be not in common so applied, yet if it might by possibility, from a want of other proper materials, admit of such an application, the courts adjudge, altho such other materials be not wanting at the port of destination, that it is contraband of war.

This construction we deem alike unfriendly & unjust. We conceive that the expression which has been cited, comprehends only such articles, as in themselves are proper for, & in their ordinary use are applied to, "the equipment of vessels."

Under the british construction all operation is referrd to the word "directly." Expunge it from the sentence, and according to them, the sense will remain the same. But plain reason, & the soundest, & most universally admited rules of construction, forbid us to interpret by garbeling a compact. The word "directly" is an important word, which forms a necessary & essential part of the description, & must have been inserted for the purpose of having its due weight in ascertaining the sense of the article. We can discover no effect which is allowd to it, unless it be admited to limit the description to materials which in their ordinary use & common application are, in considerable quantities, proper for, or "serve directly to, the equipment of vessels." To exclude it, or to construe the article as if it was excluded, is to substitute another agreement for that of the parties.

We do not admit the expression we are considering to be in itself doubtful. But if it was so, rules of construction prescribd by reason, & adopted by common consent, seem to us, to reject the interpretation of the british courts.

As this contract is formd between a belligerent and neutral nation, it must have been designd to secure the rights of each, &, consequently, to protect that commerce which neutrals may lawfully carry on, as well as to authorize the seizure of articles which they may not lawfully carry to the enemy. But under the interpretation complaind of, not only articles of doubtful use with respect to the equipment of vessels, but such as are not proper for that purpose, or if proper only in very small quantities, & which therefore are not in common so applied, are, because they may by meer possibility admit of that application, classd with articles prohibited on the principle that they are for the purposes of war.

This construction ought to be rejected, because it woud swell the list of contraband to an extent which the laws & usages of nations do not authorize: it woud prohibit, as being for the equipment of vessels, articles plainly not destind for that purpose, but fited &

necessary for, the ordinary occupations of men in peace: and it woud consequently presuppose a surrender on the part of the United States, of rights in themselves unquestionable, & the exercise of which is essential to themselves, & not injurious to Britain in the prosecution of the war in which she is engagd.

A construction so absurd & so odious ought to be rejected. The cases on which this reasoning is founded, have, many of them, been, already, stated to you, & they are, in some instances I beleive, now depending in the court of Admiralty in Great Britain.

In addition to the injury of condemning as contraband, goods which cannot properly, be so denominated, seizures & confiscations have been made in cases, where the condemnation even of contraband, coud not have been justified.

Articles of that description are, only, by the treaty declard to be "just objects of confiscation, whenever they are attempted to be carried to an enemy."

We conceive it certain that vessels bound to New Orleans & laden with cargoes proper for the ordinary use of the citizens of the United States who inhabit the Mississipi & its waters, cannot, meerly on account of the port to which they are bound, be justly said to carry those cargoes to an enemy.

By the treaty with Spain, New Orleans is made, for the present, a place of deposit for the merchandizes & effects of our citizens. Merchandizes designd for the consumption of those citizens who reside on the Mississipi or its waters, & which is to be transported up that river, will, in the present state of its commerce, be, almost universally, shipd for New Orleans. This port being by stipulation, & of necessity, common to the subjects of Spain, & to the citizens of the United States, the destination of the cargo can be no evidence of its being designd for an enemy, &, therefore, liable to confiscation when composd of articles that might be usd in war. In justice other testimony to this point out always to be receivd.

But the destination to New Orleans ought rather to exempt from confiscation articles of ordinary use but which may also serve to the equipment of vessels. It is well known not to be a port usually resorted to for that object. The Spaniards do not there build or equip vessels, nor has it ever been a depot for naval stores. When then a vessel bound for New Orleans, containing a cargo proper for the ordinary use of those citizens of the United States who are supplied through that port, & evidence that it is designd for them, shall be capturd, such cargo is not "a just object of confiscation" altho a part of it shoud also be deemd proper for "the equipment of vessels," because it is not "attempted to be carried to an enemy."

2dly.   The right to confiscate vessels bound to a blockaded port has been unreasonably extended to cases not coming within the rule as heretofore adopted.

On principle it might well be questiond, whether this rule can be applied to a place, not completely invested by land as well as by sea. If we examine the reasoning on which is founded the right to intercept & confiscate supplies designd for a blockaded town, it will be difficult to resist the conviction that its extension to towns invested by sea only, is an unjustifiable encroachment on the rights of neutrals. But it is not of this departure from principle—a departure which has receivd some sanction from practice—that we mean to complain. It is that ports not effectually blockaded by a force capable of completely investing them, have yet been declard in a state of blockade, & vessels attempting to enter them have been seizd, &, on that account, confiscated.

This is a vexation proceeding directly from the government, & which may be carried, if not resisted, to a very injurious extent. Our merchants have greatly complaind of it with respect to Cadiz & the ports of Holland.

If the effectiveness of the blockade be dispensd with, then every port of all the belligerent powers, may, at all times, be declard in that state, & the commerce of neutrals be, thereby, subjected to universal capture. But if this principle be strictly adherd to, the capacity to blockade will be limited by the naval force of the belligerent, &, of consequence, the mischief to neutral commerce cannot be very extensive. It is therefore of the last importance to neutrals that this principle be maintaind unimpaird.

I observe that you have pressd this reasoning on the british minister, who replies that an occasional absence of a fleet from a blockaded port, ought not to change the state of the place.

Whatever force this observation may be intitled to where that occasional absence has been producd by accident, as a storm which for a moment blows off the fleet & forces it from its station, which station it, immediately, resumes, I am persuaded that where a part of the fleet is applied, tho only for a time, to other objects, or comes into port, the very principle requiring an effective blockade, which is that the mischief can then only be coextensive with the naval force of the belligerent, requires that during such temporary absence, the commerce of neutrals to the place shoud be free.

The next subject of complaint is

3dly. The unjust decisions of their courts of admiralty, & the impunity which attends captures totally vexatious & without any probable cause.

No source has been more productive than this of injury to American commerce. From none are we to apprehend more serious mischief or more uncontrolable irritation.

It is not to be expected that all the commanders of national ships, much less that the commanders of privatiers, shoud be men of correct conduct & habits. The temptation which a rich neutral commerce offers to unprincipled avarice—at all times powerful—becomes irresistable, unless strong & efficient restraints be imposed by the government which employs it. It is the duty of the government to impose such restraints. Foreign friendly nations who do not exercise against such cruizers their means of self protection, have a right to expect & to demand it. The failure to impose them exposes the belligerent government to the just reproach, of causing the injuries it tolerates.

The most effectual restraint is an upright judiciary which will decide impartially between the parties, & uniformly condemn the captor in costs & damages, where the seizure has been made without probable cause. If this practice be not honestly & rigidly observd, there will exist no restraint on the captors. Their greediness for gain will be checkd by no fear of loss, & indiscriminate captures will, consequently, be made. If the vessel shoud be adjudgd good prize, of which before an unjust tribunal there is, in all cases, considerable probability, the profit is theirs; if the vessel even be acquited, the loss falls entirely on the capturd. The numerous depredations consequent on such a state of things are inevitable. The loss to the neutral merchant is immence. His voyage becomes not only unprofitable but injurious to him.

This is the state of things in the british possessions in America. Their courts of vice Admiralty, whatever may be the case, seldom acquit, & when they do, costs & damages for detention are never awarded.

We know well that Judges are appointed whose duty it is to award costs & damages for detention, instead of confiscation, in cases of vexatious seizure; but we know too the tenure by which they hold their offices, the source from which they derive their profits, & we know their practice. We can only attribute this practice to their government, for it has been notorious, has been of long continuance,

& has never been checkd. It is not to be suppos'd that Judges circumstanc'd as are those of the courts of vice Admiralty, woud dare to pursue openly & invariably this vicious system, if it was known to be offensive to their government.

The existence of an appellate court does not remove the evil. The distance of that court, the expences & delays attendant on an appeal, the loss inseparable from a first condemnation tho it be afterwards reversd, render it a very inadequate remedy even in cases of unjust condemnation, & absolutely forbid any resort to it on a meer question of costs.

It is only by infusing a spirit of justice & respect for law into the courts of vice admiralty, that these excessive & irritating vexations can be restraind, & the imputations to which they subject the british government wipd away. This spirit can only be infusd by, uniformly discountenancing & punishing those who tarnish, alike, the seat of justice & the honor of their country, by converting themselves from Judges, into the meer instruments of plunder.

Until some such reform be made, the practices complaind of will continue, & must be considerd by foreign nations, as authorizd by, & proceeding from, the government which permits them.

The impressment of our seamen is an injury of very serious magnitude, which deeply affects the feelings & the honor of the nation.

This valuable class of men is composd of natives & foreigners who engage voluntarily in our service.

No right has been asserted to impress the natives of America. Yet they are impressd, they are dragd on board british ships of war with the evidence of citizenship in their hands, & forcd by violence there to serve, until conclusive testimonials of their birth can be obtain'd. These must, most generally, be sought for on this side the Atlantic. In the mean time acknowledgd violence is practisd on a free citizen of the United States, by compeling him to engage, & to continue in, foreign service. Altho the Lords of the admiralty uniformly direct their discharge on the production of this testimony, yet many must perish unreleivd, & all are detain'd a considerable time in lawless & injurious confinement.

It is the duty as well as the right of a friendly nation to require that measures be taken by the british government to prevent the continued repetition of such violence by its agents. This can only be done by punishing & frowning on those who perpetrate it. The meer release of the injurd, after a long course of service & of suffering, is no compensation for the past, & no security for the future. It is impossible not to beleive, that the decisive interference of the government in this respect, woud prevent a practice, the continuance of which must inevitably produce discord between two nations which ought to be the friends of each other.

Those seamen who, born in a foreign country have been adopted by this, were either the subjects of Britain or some other power.

The right to impress those who were british subjects has been asserted, & the right to impress those of every other nation has not been disclaimd.

Neither the one practice nor the other can be justified.

With the naturalization of foreigners, no other nation can interfere further, than the rights of that other are affected. The rights of Britain are certainly not affected by the naturalization of other than british subjects. Consequently those persons who, according to our laws, are citizens, must be so considerd by Britain, & by every other power not having a conflicting claim to the person.

The United States therefore require positively, that their seamen who are not british subjects, whether born in America or elsewhere, shall be exempt from impressments.

The case of british subjects, whether naturalizd or not, is more questionable; but the right even to impress them is denied. The practice of the british government itself, may, certainly in a controversy with that government, be relied on. The privileges it claims & exercises ought to be ceded to others. To deny this woud be to deny the equality of nations, & to make it a question of power & not of right.

If the practice of the british government may be quoted, that practice is to maintain & defend in their sea service, all those of any nation who have voluntarily engagd in it, or who, according to their laws, have become british subjects.

Alien seamen not british subjects, engagd in our merchant service, ought to be equally exempt with citizens, from impressment. We have a right to engage them, & have a right to, & an interest in their persons, to the extent of the service contracted to be performd. Britain has no pretext of right to their persons or to their service. To tear them, then, from our possession is at the same time an insult & an injury. It is an act of violence for which there exists no palliative.

We know well that the difficulty of distinguishing between native Americans & British subjects, has been usd, with respect to natives, as an apology for the injuries complaind of. It is not pretended that this apology can be extended to the case of foreigners, & even with respect to natives we doubt the existence of the difficulty alledgd. We know well that among that class of people who are seamen, we can readily distinguish between a native American & a person raisd to manhood in Great Britain or Ireland; and we do not perceive any reason, why the capacity of making this distinction, shoud not be possessd in the same degree, by one nation as by the other.

If therefore no regulation can be formd which shall effectually secure all seamen on board american merchantmen, we have a right to expect from the justice of the british government, from its regard for the friendship of the United States & its own honor, that it will manifest the sincerity of its wishes to repress this offence, by punishing those who commit it.

We hope, however, that an agreement may be enterd into, satisfactory & beneficial to both parties. The article which appears to have been transmited by my predecessor, while it satisfies this country, will probably restore to the naval service of Britain, a greater number of seamen than will be lost by it. Shoud we ever be mistaken in this calculation, yet the difference cannot be put in competition with the mischief which may result from the irritation justly excited, by this practice, throughout the United States. The extent & the justice of the resentments it produces, may be estimated, in Britain, by enquiring what impressions woud be made on them by similar conduct on the part of this government.

Shoud we impress from the merchant service of Britain, not only Americans but foreigners, & even british subjects, how long woud such a course of injury unredressd, be permited to pass unrevengd? How long woud the government be content with unsuccessful remonstrance & unavailing memorials? I beleive, sir, that only the most prompt correction of, & compensation for, the abuse, woud be admited as satisfaction in such a case.

If the principles of this government forbid it to retaliate by impressments, there is yet another mode which might be resorted to. We might authorize our ships of war, tho not to impress, yet to recruit, sailors on board british merchantmen. Such are the inducements to enter into our naval service, that we beleive even this practice woud, very seriously affect the navigation of Britain.

How, sir, woud it be receivd by the british nation?

Is it not more adviseable to desist from, & to take effectual measures to prevent, an acknowledgd wrong, than, by perseverance in that wrong, to excite against themselves the well founded resentments of America, & force our government into measures which may very possibly terminate in an open rupture?

As we are unacquainted with the present actual state of things in Europe, & the President has the most entire confidence in you, it is not his wish to injoin on you a representation to the ministers of his britannic Majesty, in the terms of this letter. It is only intended to convey to you the feelings & sentiments of the government & people of America, & to instruct you from the President himself, to call the very serious attention of the british government, in such terms of respect & earnestness as to yourself shall seem advisable, to the weighty subjects of complaint which have here been stated. With great & sincere respect & esteem, I am dear Sir your obedt. Servt.

J MARSHALL

From William L. Smith

LS, RG 59, National Archives

[*September 20, 1800, Lisbon.* Smith relates, in dispatch no. 39,[8] a portion of a letter to him of Aug. 16 from Richard O'Brien, consul at Algiers, who wrote that the United States is far behind in its payments to Algiers and that "Tripoli demands something extra, & that if war should take place with Barbary, we should suffer a commercial loss of two million of dollars annually, besides an annual expence in Cruizers of one & a half million." O'Brien related that Denmark and France have settled their difficulties with Algiers by paying large sums of money. Finally, Smith gives the latest news about military preparations in Portugal and the issue of quarantine and observes that tensions with Spain appear relaxed.]

From John Adams

Letterbook Copy, Adams Papers, Massachusetts Historical Society

[*September 23, 1800, Quincy.* Adams encloses a letter from Samuel Parkman, a citizen of Boston and a member of the Massachusetts legislature, who recommends George A. Cushings to be a consul at Havana. He also encloses a letter from François Truin. Adams asks JM to file both letters at the State Department. Neither of the enclosures has been found.]

8. This dispatch was received by the State Department on Nov. 22, 1800.

To David Humphreys

ALS, André deCoppet Collection, Princeton University Library

No. 3.

Sir　　　　　　　　　　　　　Washington, September 23, 1800

The President has directed me to request your particular attention to the claim of Messrs. Gregorie & Scobie on the government of Spain. This claim is precisely stated in their memorial which is inclosd markd No. 1.[9]

The award made in their favor on the 28th. day of May 1799 by Mr. Clarkson & Mr. Breck two of the commissioners appointed under the 21st. article of our treaty with his catholic majesty, for the sum of eight thousand four hundred & eighty seven dollars & two & one half cents will be transmited by those gentlemen to their correspondent in Spain.[1]

As this award is made in conformity with the treaty between the two nations, the faith of the spanish government is pledgd for its payment, & the President instructs you to claim a performance of the stipulation which has been enterd into.

We understand that the objection made by the court of madrid when this award was presented, was, that the Spanish commissioner had not signd it. The validity of this objection cannot be admited. His Catholic Majesty has bound himself in the most solemn form to pay any award made by two of the commissioners. The words of that part of the article are "The award of the said commissioners or *any two of them*, shall be final & conclusive, both as to the justice of the claim & the amount of the sum to be paid to the claimants; and his Catholic Majesty undertakes to cause the same to be paid *in specie*, without deduction, at such times & places, & under such conditions as shall be awarded by the said commissioners."

To refuse to pay in specie the sum thus awarded by two of the commissioners is to violate the plain words of the article, & consequently to break the faith of the nation.

---

9. The enclosures have not been found.

1. The Treaty of Friendship, Limits, and Navigation of 1795 was known as the Pinckney Treaty. Matthew Clarkson (1733–1800) and Samuel Breck were two of the three commissioners who formed a claims commission under the terms of art. 22 of the treaty. They met in Philadelphia from 1797 to 1799. See Samuel Flagg Bemis, *Pinckney's Treaty: America's Advantage from Europe's Distress, 1783–1800* (New Haven, Conn., 1960), 341–342, and John Bassett Moore, *History and Digest of the International Arbitrations to Which the United States Has Been a Party . . .* , II (Washington, D.C., 1898), 991–1005.

We cannot admit that in such a case, the award is to be revisd, & its merits reconsiderd. But if even this might be done, still the decision ought to be in favor of the claim.

The abstract herewith transmitted (No. 2) from the proceedings of the commissioners exhibit the motives which inducd Don Joseph Ignatius Viar the commissioner on the part of his Catholic Majesty, to with hold his signature. This is, that the claimants were not citizens of the United States at the time of the ⟨declaration⟩ acknowledgement of our independence by Great Britain.

The injury is admited & its amount correctly ascertaind. The persons who claim were, not only when the treaty was made, but also when the injury was sustaind according to our laws, citizens of the United States. In this state of things the treaty stipulates, "in order to terminate all differences on account of the losses sustaind by the *citizens of the United States* in consequence of their vessels & cargoes having been taken by the subjects of his Catholic Majesty" "that all such cases shall be referd to the final decision of commissioners."

The right of naturalizing aliens is claimd & exercisd by the different nations of Europe as well as by the United States. When the laws adopt an individual no nation has a right to question the validity of the act, unless it be one which may have a conflicting title to the person adopted. Spain therefore cannot contest the fact that these gentlemen are american citizens.

If this inadmissible power was to be set up by his Catholic Majesty, it ought to have been asserted when the treaty was formd. He ought then to have discriminated between our citizens. He ought then to have promisd compensation only for the capturd vessels & cargoes of those, who were citizens of the United States when our independence was acknowledgd by Great Britain. Not having done so then it is too late now to attempt this odious discrimination. He has promisd in terms which expressly include Messrs. Gregorie & Scobie, & every principle of good faith & national honor require, that he shoud perform the promise thus made.

We must suppose that this claim has been inadvertently rejected, & that, on calling the attention of the Spanish government to its real merits, it will, according to the stipulations of our treaty, be paid in specie. Payment in no other medium can be receivd.

Many citizens of the United States complain that contracts enterd into with the spanish government for metallic money have been dischargd, to their very great loss, in depreciated paper.

The injustice of this is manifest. Between discharging a debt by paying one half its nominal amount, & the whole of its nominal amount possessing only one half its real value, there is no difference.

To your remonstrances heretofore made on this subject, we observe that the minister of his Catholic Majesty has only replied—the absolute right of a sovereign nation on its own territory.

This right we mean not to question or impair. But coextensive & coeval with it, is the privilege of a foreign friendly nation, to complain of, & remonstrate against, such acts of sovereignty as are injurious to its citizens or subjects. This privilege we mean respectfully to exercise.

In contracts enterd into by individuals with a sovereign power, there exists no tribunal to enforce their performance. For this the good faith of the sovereign is alone relied on. This is held sacred, & is always pledgd to exempt from the operation of that paramount power over all transactions within its dominions, the engagements of the sovereignty itself.

The citizens of the United States therefore who have formd specie contracts with the spanish government hold as a pledge, the faith of that government solemnly plighted, that its power shall never be so exercisd, as to work injury or injustice to them. One of these cases is stated in the letter from Mr. Beverley markd No. 4.

Our merchants also complain that their property recapturd from the English instead of being restord ⟨on paying salvage,⟩ as is the universal rule, is confiscated.[2] Had we even been at war with England, American property capturd by their cruizers, & recapturd by those of a friendly power, ought to be restord to the original proprietor, on paying salvage. But being at peace with England & Spain, there can be no pretext for holding any portion of vessels & cargoes truely american, taken by the cruizers of one of these powers from the possession of those of the other. As there must be some general arrangement, for the purpose of ascertaining the compensation to which our merchants are individually entitled, for depredations commited on them by spanish cruizers, or by cruizers equipd in spanish ports, this class of confiscations, so far as respects the past, may be included in the general settlement. But it is hopd & expected that the court of Madrid will immediately take effectual measures, to prevent the continuance of an injury so totally indefensible.

In the course of the hostilities which have been carried on by France against the United States, american sailors capturd by french

2. See Humphreys's reply to this letter, Humphreys to JM, Jan. 13, 1801.

cruizers have been carried into Spain, & there treated by the government of the place as prisoners of war. See the document No. 5. This is so totally incompatible with that state of peace which is supposd to exist between the two countries, that we must beleive the practice need only be mentiond to the ministers of his Catholic Majesty to induce an immediate order for its suppression, & a prompt release of any Americans who may be now in that situation.

In my letter complaining of the depredations commited on our commerce by privatiers really spanish, but nominally french, I transmited you no documents authenticating the facts. These were so notorious, that evidence of them was deemd unnecessary, until a tribunal shoud be establishd for the examination of particular claims. But there are cases which involve such serious accusations against certain officers of the spanish government, that I think it proper to transmit you some of them. You will receive (No. 6) the papers relative to the Nancy & the Franklin two american vessels capturd by the Buonaparte, a spanish privatier ownd by several spaniards at Campeachy among whom are several high officers of the government, & cruizing under a commission which had expird & which was almost certainly forgd. We are confident that the ministers of his Catholic Majesty will hasten to punish a transaction so openly shameless as this.

I send you also a copy of the case of the schooner Nymph.[3] The documents which support the statement will if necessary be forwarded to you.

The case of the schooner Lydia Capt. Fearson, exhibits such a wanton & savage hostility against an unarmd & unresisting merchantmen, as ought to incapacitate the person who coud be capable of it from holding longer a commission which he disgraces, if indeed a commission such as his can be disgracd.

The case of the Orion Capt. Farmer is of the same complection.[4] In transactions of this sort, and there are very many of them, a government tenacious of its reputation, & of the friendship & good opinion of its neighbors, will not be content with compensating the injury sustaind. In addition to ample pecuniary retribution, its own honor requires that any imputation to which such offences might subject the nation, shoud be wip'd away by punishing the offenders.

The case of the Sussex Capt. Atkins belonging to Thomas Samuel

3. See JM to Thomas Bulkely, calendared at Sept. 13, 1800.
4. See Humphreys to JM, Feb. 24, 1801.

& Miers Fisher of Philadelphia, is well known to you.[5] I shoud request your particular attention to it, & that you woud present on their account a special claim for compensation to the Spanish government, if I did not deem it certain that some general settlement for depredations must be made in which this particular case woud be included.

The President of the United States requests that you will, with that firmness which is due to the wrongs of your country, & that respect which belongs to a government whose friendship we wish to cultivate, lay before the ministers of his Catholic Majesty these very serious & weighty complaints, which have been so long permited to remain unattended to. I am Sir with very much respect & consideration, your Obedt. Servt.

J MARSHALL

From David Humphreys

ALS, RG 59, National Archives

[*September 23, 1800, Madrid*. Having learned of JM's acceptance of the office of secretary of state by seeing his signature on a passport, Humphreys, in dispatch no. 250, sends his congratulations. He is not yet able to relay accurate information on the detention of the Baltimore ship *Catherine* by the Spanish. Apparently the ship signaled an English vessel, offering to help capture two armed ships from the Batavian Republic. He transmits a letter from Richard O'Brien of Aug. 16 that reveals the urgent need to satisfy the Barbary powers. Humphreys also outlines an agreement between Denmark and England concerning the capture of a Danish convoy in the Mediterranean, and he sends a prospectus "for the publication of my works."[6]]

5. See the Fishers to JM, calendared at Aug. 30, 1800, and JM to the Fishers, calendared at Sept. 8, 1800. See also Humphreys to JM, Feb. 24, 1801.

6. Notations on the original and on a duplicate copy indicate JM received these papers on Dec. 23, 1800.

The *Catherine* of Baltimore, Capt. James Mills, was detained in the harbor of Barcelona because the Spanish thought signals on board the ship were to help the English capture two Dutch ships. The Americans claimed that the lights instead were a message to the captain who was on shore. For an account of the controversy, see the enclosures in Humphreys to JM, Sept. 30, 1800, Consular Despatches, Spain, V, RG 59, National Archives. See also Frank Landon Humphreys, *Life and Times of David Humphreys: Soldier, Statesman, Poet*, II (New York, 1917), 277, 280–282, and Humphreys to JM, Nov. 27, 1800.

From Israel Whelen

LS, RG 59, National Archives

[*September 23, 1800, Philadelphia*. Whelen reports that Messrs. Yard and Cramond do not know whether Mr. D'Arey has any "Bank or Insurance Stock, Stock in the funds, or Commercial Partnership" in the United States. Whelen has just received a letter from Thomas Thompson of Portsmouth, N.H.,[7] informing him that a shipment of oars is to be expected soon. Thompson recommended chartering vessels at once to send to the Mediterranean because they can be procured on low terms and can be used to carry salt on the journey back. Whelen has also written to James Sheaffe of Portsmouth, N.H., to inquire about prices of masts, spars, planks, etc., and on what terms vessels can be obtained there.]

To John Adams

ALS, Adams Papers, Massachusetts Historical Society

Sir   Washington, September 24, 1800

I inclose you the last letter from Mr. Adams our minister at Berlin.[8] The subject on which it treats is a very interesting one.

At the same time I receivd from him another letter of an earlier date in which was transmited a certificate of the exchange of the ratifications of our treaty with Prussia.[9]

I send you by this days mail a letter prepard to Mr. King.[1] If you conceive that no such letter shoud be sent it may at once be suppressd. If you wish any changes in that now transmited I will on receiving your wish immediately obey it. If the letter as sent is satisfactory to you I must ask the favor of you to let Mr. Shaw forward it to Mr. King.

---

7. See Thompson to Whelen, Sept. 15, 1800, Miscellaneous Letters Received, RG 59, National Archives, enclosed with this letter.

8. See John Quincy Adams to [JM], June 28, 1800, RG 59, National Archives, in which Adams discusses art. 12 of the Prussian treaty, or the principle that free ships make free goods. For the text of the treaty, see Miller, ed., *Treaties*, II, 433–455. See John Adams's reply to this letter, Adams to JM, Oct. 3, 1800.

9. See John Quincy Adams to [JM], June 24, 1800, RG 59, which was received by the State Department on Sept. 23, 1800. The treaty was proclaimed in the United States on Nov. 4, 1800. See Proclamations, RG 11, Nat. Arch.

1. See JM to Rufus King, Sept. 20, 1800.

The vessel taken in Puerto Plata has been deliverd to the order of the Spanish Minister.[2] I am Sir with the most respectful attachment, your obedt.

To Rufus King

Letterbook Copy, RG 59, National Archives

[*September 24, 1800, Washington.* At the request of James Hillhouse, JM transmits a letter and a document respecting the impressment of Benjamin Eastman and urges King to help secure his release.]

From John Adams

Letterbook Copy, Adams Papers, Massachusetts Historical Society

[*September 25, 1800, Quincy.* Adams encloses two letters for JM to consider. One letter, from Elias Backman,[3] U.S. consul in Sweden, contains his accounts. The other letter is from C. Blackberd,[4] in London, who requests legal advice.]

From Francis Peyton

ALS, RG 45, National Archives

[*September 25, 1800, Richmond.* Peyton requests a post as surgeon that he has heard is available on board the *Warren*. He asks JM to apprise him of any appointments as surgeon that may be open at the Department of the Navy.]

To Israel Whelen

Extract, RG 59, National Archives

[*September 25, 1800, Washington.* JM informs Whelen that he has requested Col. Thomas Thompson of Portsmouth, N.H., to consult Whelen on what

2. See correspondence on the *Sandwich* case.
3. Backman's letter has not been found, but see his Account of Disbursements, Feb. 14, 1800, Consular Despatches, Göteborg, I, RG 59, National Archives.
4. See C. Blackberd to Adams, June 14, 1800, Adams Papers, Massachusetts Historical Society.

kind of timber would be proper to ship with the oars to make up a load for Algiers. He desires Whelen to add such timber as may be necessary, taking care that it has not already been procured and that it corresponds with the list with which Whelen has been furnished. See Whelen to Jacob Wagner, Oct. 4, 1800, RG 59, National Archives.]

To John Adams

ALS, Adams Papers, Massachusetts Historical Society

Sir   Washington, September 26, 1800

I inclose you a permit which has been solicited for the brig Amazon to carry several passengers to France.[5] I am Sir with the highest respect &c, Your Obedt. Servt.

J MARSHALL

From John Adams

ALS, RG 59, National Archives

Dear Sir   Quincy, September 27, 1800

Yesterday I recd the enclosed Letter of I. Cox Barnet at Bourdeaux of 27th. July.[6] This Letter being Addressed to the Secretary of state, I ventured to open and found in it only a private Letter to you. This I did not think myself warranted to open, though it may contain Intelligence of a public nature, and now transmit it to you in the same Enclosure which first covered it.

I have recd also your favour of the 12th. No Apology was necessary for inclosing the dispatches to me without a Letter any further than to inform me, that there was no Letter in order to remove an Anxiety arising from suspicion that the Mail might have been robbed of your Letter. With great regard &c

J. ADAMS

5. Enclosure not found. See Adams to JM, Oct. 5, 1800 (first letter).
6. Not found.

From John Adams

ALS, RG 59, National Archives

Dear Sir   Quincy, September 27, 1800

I recd yesterday the inclosed Letter[7] sent up from Boston with several others and large Packetts which appear to be only Newspapers. This is Duplicate of No. 244 from Mr Humphries at Madrid. Dated 29 July and Aug. 1.—Talleyrands reply to the french Minister "In the present state of the negociation bet. the U. S. and France you may inform Mr Humphreys that he shall not long have occasion to complain of any more Robberies (Brigandages) committed under the name of Privateering." This sentiment favours your Idea in your Letter of the 17th, "that the present french Government is much inclined to correct, at least in part the follies of the past." Enclosed is a private Letter to me from Mr King of 28 July,[8] which may reflect some light upon the disposition of the french Government about that time. They might be courting or flattering the northern Powers into an armed Neutrality.

The Envoys, when they come, will I hope be able to clear away all doubts, and shew Us plainly both our Duty and our Interest.

I return you the three Parchments Signed as Commissions for Clark, Vanderburgh and Griffin to be Judges in the Indiana Territory.[9]

I wish you a pleasant Tour to Richmond but I pray you to give such orders that if Dispatches should arrive from our Envoys, they may be kept as secret as the grave, till the senate meets.

On Monday the 13. of October I shall sett off from this place. Letters should not be sent to me to reach this place or Boston after that day.

I pray you to turn your reflections to the subject of Communications to be made to Congress by the President at the opening of the session and give me your sentiments as soon as possible in Writing.[1]

7. Not found.

8. See Rufus King to Adams, July 28, 1800, Adams Papers, Massachusetts Historical Society.

9. See commissions for William Clarke, Henry Vanderburgh, and John Griffin, Oct. 6, 1800, Temporary Presidential Commissions, 1789–1909, RG 59, National Archives.

1. JM's suggestions were contained in JM to Adams, *ca.* Nov. 15, 1800. For the finished text of the speech, see *Annals of Congress*, X, 723–725. See also Adams to JM, Sept. 30, 1800 (second letter).

The Constitution requires that he should give both information and Counsell. I am with a sincere Attachment

J. ADAMS

From John Adams

Copy, RG 59, National Archives

[*September 27, 1800, Quincy*. Adams transmits the petition of Philip Desch and Abraham Schantz, two ill federal prisoners held in Norristown, Pa. He also transmits certificates from two doctors asking for a pardon in order to save the prisoners' lives and a petition from 94 inhabitants of Norristown asking mercy. Adams asks JM and Charles Lee to examine the documents and send their opinion.[2]]

From John Adams

Letterbook Copy, Adams Papers, Massachusetts Historical Society

Dear Sir   Quincy, September 30, 1800
The enclosed letter[3] from Mr. William Rogers of N. York, requesting to be Consul at Bourdeaux I pray you to file with others, aiming at the same object. I am Sir with much respect,

From John Adams

AL, RG 59, National Archives

Dear Sir   Quincy, September 30, 1800
It is high time for me to request that you would seriously revolve in your thoughts the subject of Communications both of Intelligence And Advice to be made to Congress at the opening of the approaching session, and favour me with your sentiments upon the whole sub-

---

2. See Lee to JM, Oct. 13, 1800. Desch and Schantz, two participants in the Fries uprising, were released from prison because of their poor health. See Pardon for Philip Desch and Abraham Schantz, no. 31, Nov. 4, 1800, Pardons & Remissions, I, RG 59, National Archives, which was countersigned by JM.
3. Not found.

ject as soon as possible.[4] I shall leave this place on Monday the 13th of October. No Letters should be directed to me here, which are to arrive after that day.

From David Humphreys

ALS, RG 59, National Archives

[*September 30, 1800, Madrid.* In his dispatch no. 251, Humphreys reports on the capture of two armed vessels from the Batavian Republic by English ships in the harbor of Barcelona on Sept. 4. The American ship, *Catherine*, of Baltimore, had been detained because of her apparent signal of assistance in the capture. Humphreys sends copies of six letters between various officials, each pertaining to the affair, and he asks advice on how to proceed.[5]]

From Rufus King

Copy, RG 59, National Archives

[*September 30, 1800, London.* In his dispatch no. 84, King sends the latest news about the war in Europe, especially as it concerns Great Britain's role. He adds that he has tried to determine if the increasing interruption of American trade by English cruisers is the result of new orders, "or whether these increased irregularities proceed from the unchecked and base spirit of Plunder that influences so many of the English naval Commanders. The result of my Enquiries satisfies me that they are solely to be ascribed to the latter cause, which will gain strength, and continue to operate, until the Prize-Courts compel the Captors to give compleat indemnity to Neutrals for their losses, and the government shall be willing to discourage the pillaging spirit of it's Officers by a few instances of severe and exemplary Punishment." King closes with information regarding the successor to Robert Liston as minister to the United States.[6]]

4. See Adams to JM, Sept. 27, 1800.
5. See Humphreys to JM, calendared at Sept. 23, 1800.
6. The triplicate copy arrived at the State Department on Nov. 24, 1800. The original did not arrive until Dec. 27. This letter is printed in King, ed., *Life and Corres. of Rufus King*, III, 313–315. Anthony Merry (1756–1835) succeeded Liston, although he did not arrive in the United States until 1803.

Statement of Accounts

DS, RG 217, National Archives

Washington, September 30, 1800

THE UNITED STATES—DRS.

> To the Secretary of State, Clerks and Messenger in his Office, for one quarter's salary—ending on the 30th of Septr. 1800—viz.

To John Marshall, Secretary of State, at 5000 dollars per. ann.				1,250. –
" Jacob Wagner ..... Chief Clerk	" 1500	"	"	375. –
" Hazen Kimball .... Clerk	" 900	"	"	225. –
" Christopher S. Thom Do.	" 650	"	"	162.50
" John C. Miller ..... Do.	" 600	"	"	150. –
" Stephen Pleasonton . Do.	" 600	"	"	150. –
" William Crawford .. Do.	" 600	"	"	150. –
" Daniel Brent ...... Do.	" 800	"	"	200. –
" John Maul .... Messenger	" 350	"	"	87.50
				$2,750. –

Department of State, Washington, September 30, 1800

J MARSHALL Secretary of State.

Please to issue the warrant for the above Account in favour of Hazen Kimball.

J MARSHALL Secretary of State

Auditor's Office, October 1st: 1800 B MIFFLIN

To John Adams

ALS, Adams Papers, Massachusetts Historical Society

Sir   Richmond, October 1, 1800

I have receivd your three letters of the 17th. & your letter of the 18th. of Septr., & am very happy that the dispatches to Mr. King & Mr. Humphries have your approbation.

If without increasing the sum, the payments can be made as you suggest, I think it woud be a desirable stipulation. There can, as it appears to me at present, be no objection to stating the proposition to Mr. King, & requesting him to make the best of it which circumstances will admit.

Some private letters state the Portsmouth to have saild & others

that she was stopd as she was about to sail. The inteligence thus receivd is meer conjecture & not in any manner to be relied on. I am
Sir with the most respectful attachment, Your obedt. Servt.

J MARSHALL

From William Vans Murray

ALS, RG 59, National Archives

Sir,   Paris, October 1, 1800
    About a fortnight since I had the honour of receiving your letter
respecting Mr. Yellot's Ship & immediately addressed a note to Mr.
Spoors, minister of marine of the Batavian Republic for the purpose
of attaining the objects of your instructions.[7]
    This will go by my colleagues Mr. Ellsworth & Mr. Davie who
probably will leave Paris in two days. They will inform you of the
whole history of the negociation which terminated last night in the
signature of a Provisional Treaty of Amity & Commerce.[8] We were
all profoundly convinced that, considering the relations of the two
countries politically considered, the nature of our demands, the
present state of France & the state [of] things in Europe, it was our
duty & for the honour & interest of the government & people of the
United States, that we should agree to that Treaty, rather than make
none.
    As the copy of our journal was not completely ready I have re-
quested Mr. Davie to do me the favour of signing it with my name for
me.
    In ten days I hope to leave Paris for my post at the Hague—where
I shall have it more in my power, than here, to attempt to fulfill the
orders of government, on the Curaçao case.
    Wishing you a career in the department of State as agreeable as is
consistent with public cares, I have the honour to be, with perfect
respect, Sir, yr. mo. ob. svt. &c

W V MURRAY

7. See JM to Murray, June 16, and Murray to JM, Nov. 10, 1800. Murray's letter
was received by the State Department on Dec. 15, 1800.
8. See American Envoys to JM, Oct. 4, 1800.

From William Vans Murray

ALS, RG 59, National Archives

Private.

Sir,   Paris, October 1, 1800

An english agent settled here enables me to write by the way of England & to inform you, I hope the first, that last night we signed a provisional Treaty with France. Indemnities, wh. were impossible, together with the discussion about the abolished treaties, & consular convention,[9] to sleep till a more convenient time; & the restoration of unjudged cases, on very easy proof of neutrality, form the principal objects.

I thought it might be useful that you should know that we have arranged amicably with France & that possibly this note might reach you even before my colleagues who will depart in three days. I am with sincere esteem respectfully, Sir, Yr. mo. ob. svt. &c &c &

W. V. MURRAY.

From Commissioners of the District of Columbia

Letterbook Copy, RG 42, National Archives

Gentn,   Washington, October 2, 1800

We will thank you to order four thousand Dollars of the paving Money to be placed to our Credit at Bank, as we have advanced six hundred Dollars more than we have received. We are, &c

G. SCOTT
W. THORNTON

---

9. In Murray's letterbook copy, the English agent is identified as "Mr. E," and a note indicates that the provisional treaty was "changed to *convention* next day." See Murray Letterbooks, I, Pierpont Morgan Library.

On the American desire to call the agreement a convention rather than a treaty, see Alexander DeConde, *The Quasi-War: The Politics and Diplomacy of the Undeclared War with France, 1797–1801* (New York, 1966), 256.

From Alexander Hamilton

ALS, Collection of Alexander H. Sands, Richmond, Va.

Dr. Sir[1]   New York, October 2, 1800

Before this reaches you, you will no doubt have seen under the Paris heads an account of the suspension of the negotiation which has strong marks of being genuine. Inclosed is a comment[2] which I have thought it expedient *rather hastily* to make upon it, with an eye particularly to some elections in our neighbourhood.

If you agree with me in the concluding sentiments you will seriously consider the question I have statted as to the Power of the President to proclaim temporary suspensions of hostilities—Generals of Armies have a right exofficio to make truces. Why not the constitutional Commander in Chief!

If the President have the power another question will be whether the idea of periodical suspensions by his authority will not be better than an indefinite Legislative suspension. This might leave the matter in a situation to be managed according to circumstances relative to the future conduct of France.

These are immature thoughts only thrown out for your more deliberate consideration.

Of one thing I am sure that if France will slide into a state of Peace *de facto*, we must meet her on that ground. The actual posture of European Affairs & the opinions of our people demand an accommodating course.

I will make no ap[*ology*] for intimations dictated [*by*] my solicitude for the public well[*being*] & offered to one whom I always place among the number of my friends. Truly Yrs

                                              A HAMILTON

From John Adams

ALS, RG 59, National Archives

Dear Sir   Quincy, October 3, 1800

I have recd, last night, your Letter of 24. of Septr. I return you

1. For information on the contents of this letter, see Harold C. Syrett *et al.*, eds., *The Papers of Alexander Hamilton*, XXV (New York, 1977), 128–131.
2. The enclosure, which has not been found, was an article from *The Spectator* (New York), Oct. 8, 1800. See *ibid.*, 131–139.

Mr Adams's Letter of 28. of June. The Question whether Neutral Ships shall protect Ennemies Property is indeed important. It is of so much Importance that if the Principle of free ships free goods, were once really established and honestly observed it would put an End forever to all maritime War and render all military Navies useless. However desireable this may be to Humanity, how much soever Phylosophy may approve it, and Christianity desire it, I am clearly convinced it never will take place. The Dominant Power on the Ocean will forever trample on it. The French would despise it more than any nation in the World if they had the maritime Superiority of Power, and the Russians next to them. We must treat the subject with great attention and if all other Nations will agree to it We will. But while one holds out We shall be the Dupes if We agree to it. Sweeden and Denmark, Russia and Prussia might form a rope of Land: But no dependence can be placed on such a martime Coalition. We must however treat the subject with great respect.

If you have received a Certificate that the Ratifications of the Treaty with Prussia are exchanged, should not a Proclamation issue as usual to publish it?

I have read with some Care and great pleasure your Letter to Mr King of 20 of Septr. I think it very proper that such a Letter should be sent and I am so fully satisfied with the Representations and Reasonings in it, that I shall give it to Gen. Lincoln the Collector of Boston to be sent by the first good opportunity to London. I am, sir with very great regard, &c

JOHN ADAMS

From David Humphreys

ALS, RG 59, National Archives

[*October 3, 1800, Madrid*.[3] Four couriers have arrived from Paris bringing news of the negotiations between France and Germany. "The delivery to the French of those Keys of Germany, Ulm, Ingolstadt & Philipsbourg, is considered as being the immediate opening to a Continental Peace." Humphreys encloses a letter of Napoleon to his deputies, Sept. 23, 1800, which has not been found. On Oct. 7, Humphreys sends a postscript informing

3. The quadruplicate copy of this letter was received by the State Department on Dec. 10, 1800.

JM of the 45-day extension of a truce between France and Germany. He also reports "that Malta was surrendered to the English & Neapolitans on the 4th of Sepr."]

From Caleb P. Wayne

Draft, Dreer Collection, Historical Society of Pennsylvania

Sir,[4]   Philadelphia, October 3, 1800

Some time has elapsed since I addressed myself to the Hon Bushrod Washington, soliciting the printing of the Life of the late President of the U. S. & requesting to be informed whether he contemplated disposing of the Copy right &c.[5] In answer to my Letter, he replys under date of Sep 18 that my request relative to printing should be duly considered, when the work was ready for Press; & requested me in the interval to make any propositions, for the copy right as he should prefer disposing of it in that way & observed that as it was probable he should soon proceed on the Southern Circuit, he wished me to address any letters on this subject to you, whom he had duly authorized. In consequence of which I have used the freedom of addressing you, & as I am unacquainted with the extent of the work it is not in my power to state any specific propositions. If Judge Washington's expectations were stated I could immediately determine as to the probability of a purchase. If any Information can be furnished on this head it will confer an obligation. Parden the freedom I have used & permit me to assure you that, With sentiments of Profound Respect, I am sir, your most obedt. & Hble. Servt

C. P. WAYNE

4. This letter marks the beginning of a lengthy correspondence between JM and Caleb Parry Wayne (1776–1849), who became the publisher of JM's *Life of Washington*. Wayne had recently moved to Philadelphia from Boston and was at this time publisher of the *Gazette of the United States*. See Benjamin Franklin V, ed., *Boston Printers, Publishers, and Booksellers: 1640–1800* (Boston, 1980), 480; H. Glenn Brown and Maude O. Brown, "A Directory of Book-Arts and Book Trade in Philadelphia to 1820 . . . ," *Bulletin of the New York Public Library*, LIV (1950), 139; and Clarence S. Brigham, comp., *History and Bibliography of American Newspapers, 1690–1820*, II (Worcester, Mass., 1947), 913.

5. See Bushrod Washington to Wayne, Apr. 11 and Sept. 18, 1800, Dreer Collection, Historical Society of Pennsylvania. In the former letter Washington informed Wayne that JM was "to write the history." Two years of negotiation followed before agreement was reached on the purchase of the copyright. See Albert J. Beveridge, *The Life of John Marshall*, III (Boston, 1916), 223–228.

From American Envoys

LS, RG 59, National Archives

Sir,   Paris, October 4, 1800

The undersigned have the honor to present to you a journal of their proceedings, and a Convention in which those proceedings have terminated.[6]

The claim of indemnities brought forward by them, was early in the negociation connected by the French Ministers with that of a restoration of treaties, for the infractions of which the indemnities were principally claimed. To obviate this embarrassment, which it had not been difficult to foresee, the American Ministers urged, in the spirit of their instructions, that those treaties having been violated by one party, and renounced by the other, a priority had attached in favor of the treaty with Great Britain, who had thereby acquired an exclusive right for the introduction of prizes;[7] wherefore that right could not be restored to France. The argument was pressed, both by notes and in conferences, as long as there remained a hope of it's utility, and until there appeared no alternative but to abandon indemnities, or as a mean of saving them, to renew, at least partially, the Treaty of Commerce. Whether, in fact, it could, or could not be renewed, consistent with good faith, then became a question for thorough investigation; in the course of which, the following considerations occurred.

1st.   It is not a breach of faith to form a Treaty with one nation inconsistent with an existing treaty with another, it being well-understood that the prior treaty prevails, and has the same operation as if the subsequent one were not formed; nor is it necessary or usual for a subsequent to make an express saving of the rights of a prior treaty, the law of nations having made that saving as complete and effectual, as it can be rendered. This rule of construction holds universally,

---

6. The journal and convention are printed in *Amer. State Papers, Foreign Relations*, II, 295–301. The convention is discussed in Alexander DeConde, *The Quasi-War: The Politics and Diplomacy of the Undeclared War with France, 1797–1801* (New York, 1966), 223–258, and Albert Hall Bowman, *The Struggle for Neutrality: Franco-American Diplomacy during the Federalist Era* (Knoxville, Tenn., 1974), 386–414.

The first copy of the convention arrived in Washington on Nov. 12, brought by William R. Davie. See Abigail Adams to Thomas B. Adams, Nov. 13, 1800, Adams Papers, Massachusetts Historical Society.

7. For a discussion of the final stages in the negotiations, see DeConde, *Quasi-War*, 247–253, and Bowman, *Struggle for Neutrality*, 403–413.

except when the subsequent treaty can have no operation but by violating the first; in which case, it will be taken for an agreement to come to a rupture with the power with whom the first was formed. 2nd.   Indeed by a clause in the 25th. Article of the British Treaty,[8] it is provided "that while the parties continue in amity, neither of them will in future make any treaty that shall be inconsistent with that or the preceding article,"—which articles contain among other things, the exclusive right of introducing prizes into the ports of each other. If however, the British be considered in the light of a prior treaty, as it must be to raise a doubt, all it's rights, as well those of a restrictive nature as others, would be saved, of course, and none of them would at any time, or in any degree, be affected by the subsequent stipulation. The subsequent stipulation, in the case supposed, altho' it should give in general terms the right of introducing prizes, would be understood with a limitation, that it was never to extend to a case, in which Great Britain should be the enemy.

3rd.   The instructions to the American Ministers authorised a renewal of the 17th. Article of the treaty of Commerce,[9] if it should be necessary, tho' with a special saving for two articles of the British Treaty. That special saving, however, cannot be material, as the settled rule of construction would, without it, make a saving still more comprehensive.

4th.   The renewal of the 17th. Article of the commercial treaty, is not conceived to be within the expression or design of the restraining clause of the British Treaty, "not in future to make any treaty that shall be inconsistent with &c." To recognize a pre-existing treaty which contains a stipulation inconsistent with &c., is not to make a new, or future treaty containing such stipulation. To recognize the former treaties, would be only to preserve, or restore the state of things existing when the British Treaty was formed, and not to introduce a new state of things, which was, doubtless, the event intended to be guarded against. It would be only to do what is usually done in the termination of misunderstandings. We are not to presume, and much less is it expressed that the United States and Great Britain meant to deprive themselves of the usual means of terminating national contests in which they might be involved. And the facility of terminating misunderstandings by restoring things to their former

8. Miller, ed., *Treaties*, II, 262.

9. See *Amer. State Papers, Foreign Relations*, II, 301–306, for a copy of the instructions to the envoys. Art. 17 prohibited privateering between France and the United States. Miller, ed., *Treaties*, II, 15–16.

condition, is not only so great, but so conformable to justice and so favorable to general tranquility, that the law of nations will not favour a construction which goes to deprive a contracting party of the benefit of it.

5th. The language in which pre-existing treaties are usually recognized at the close of a war, does not impart that the treaties have in fact ceased to exist, but rather that the causes which suspended their operation have ceased. And, in various instances such treaties are counted upon as becoming again operative, without any express provision to render them so.

6th. Nor is it conceived, that the treaties between the United States and France have undergone a more nullifying operation, than the condition of war necessarily imposes. Doubtless the Congressional act, authorising the reduction of French cruizers by force, was an authorization of war limited, indeed, in its extent, but not in nature. Clearly also, their subsequent act, declaring that the Treaties had ceased to be obligatory, however proper it might be for the removal of doubts, was but declaratory of the actual state of things. And certainly it was only from an exercise of the constitutional prerogative of declaring war, that either of them derived validity. So that the treaties in question, having had only the usual inoperation, might without a breach of faith, have the usual recognition.

7th. As far as the opinion of Great Britain goes, there would be no difficulty in recognizing a treaty, which gives to France an exclusive right to introduce prizes into the ports of the United States; because she, by a project of a treaty of peace, drawn up at her own Court in 1792, and offered by Lord Malmsbury to the French Plenipotentiaries, proposed to give to France such exclusive right in the British ports; that is, the project renewed the treaties of Paris of 1763 and of 1783—both of which renewed the commercial treaty of Utrecht of 1713, which contained such a stipulation.

The foregoing considerations induced the undersigned to be unanimously of the opinion, that any part of the former treaties might be renewed consistently with good faith.

They then offered a renewal with limitations of the 17th. Article of the commercial treaty, which without compromitting the interests of the United States would have given to France what her Ministers had particularly insisted on, as essential to her honor, and what they had given reason to expect would be deemed satisfactory. The overture however finally produced no other effect, than to enlarge the demand of the French Ministers, from a partial to a total renewal of the treaties; which brought the negociation a second time to a stand.

The American Ministers however, after a deliberation of some days, the progress *of events in Europe* continuing in the mean time to grow more unfavorable to their success, made an ulterior advance, going the whole length of what had been last insisted on. They offered an unlimited recognition of the former treaties, tho' accompanied with a provision to extinguish such priviledges claimed under them, as were detrimental to the United States, by a pecuniary equivalent, to be made out of the indemnities which should be awarded to American citizens. A compensation, which, tho' it might have cancelled but a small portion of the indemnities, was nevertheless a liberal one for priviledges, which the French Ministers had often admitted to be of little use to France, under the construction which the American Government had given to the treaties.

This offer, tho' it covered the avowed objects of the French Government, secured an engagement to pay indemnities, as well as the power to extinguish the obnoxious parts of the treaties. To avoid any engagement of this kind, the French Ministers now made an entire departure from the principles upon which the negociation had proceeded for some time, and resumed the simple unqualified ground of their overture of the 23d. Thermidor; declaring, that it was indispensable to the granting of indemnities, not only that the treaties should have an unqualified recognition, but that their future operation should not be varied in any particular, for any consideration, or compensation whatever. In short, they thought proper to add, what was quite unnecessary, that their *real object was to* avoid indemnities, and that it was not in the power of France to pay them.

No time was requisite for the American Ministers to intimate, that it had become useless to pursue the negociation any farther.

It accorded as little with their views as with their instructions, to subject their Country perpetually to the mischievous effects of those treaties, in order to obtain a promise of indemnity at a remote period —a promise which might as easily prove delusive, as it would reluctantly be made: especially, as under the guarantee of the Treaty of Alliance the United States might be immediately called upon for succours, which, if not furnished would of itself be a sufficient pretext to render abortive the hope of indemnity.

It only remained for the undersigned to quit France, leaving the United States involved in a contest, and according to appearances soon alone in a contest, which it might be as difficult for them to relinquish with honor, as to pursue with a prospect of advantage; or else to propose a temporary arrangement, reserving for a definitive adjustment points which could not then be satisfactorily settled, and providing in the mean time against a state of things, of which neither party could profit. They elected the latter; and the result has been the signature of a Convention.

Of property not yet definitively condemned, which the 4th. article respects, there are more than 40 ships and cargoes, and a number of them of great value, at present pending for decision before the council of prizes; and many others are doubtless in a condition to be brought there, if the claimants shall think fit.

Guards against future abuses are perhaps as well provided, as they can be by stipulations.

The article respecting convoys may be of use in the West Indies, till it shall be more in the power of the French Government than it is at present, to reduce the corsairs in that quarter to obedience.

As to the Article which places French privateers and prizes on the footing of those of the most favored nations, it was inserted as drawn by the French Ministers, without any discussion of the extent of its operation; the American Ministers having, in former stages of the negociation, repeatedly and uniformly declared, agreeably to the rule of construction settled by the law of nations, that no stipulation of that kind could have effect as against the British Treaty, unless the stipulation were derived from the former treaties, which it is here expressly agreed shall have no operation whatever. This article however, is less consequential, as it will soon be in the power of the United States, and doubtless also within their wisdom, to refuse to the privateers and prizes of any nation, an asylum, beyond what the rights of humanity require.

If with the simple plea of right, unaccompanied with the menaces of power, and unaided by events either in Europe or America, less is at present obtained than justice requires, or than the policy of France should have granted, the undersigned trust that the sincerity and patience of their efforts to obtain all that their Country had a right to demand, will not be drawn in question. We have the honor to be, Sir, With high respect, Your most obedient

OLIV: ELLSWORTH
W: R: DAVIE
W. V. MURRAY

To Rufus King

LS, RG 59, National Archives

[*October 4, 1800, Washington.* In dispatch no. 8, JM sends King £3,946 1s. 7d. to repay John and Francis Baring & Co. the sum borrowed for expenses incident to prize cases before the Courts of Admiralty and Appeals in England.[10]]

From John Adams

ALS, RG 59, National Archives

Dear Sir   Quincy, October 5, 1800
    Enclosed is a Memorial from a respectable Merchant in Boston Mr Babcock.[1] Mr Lewis has a similar request before you.
    Can We do any Thing in either Case or is it worth while to send another agent to negotiate with the Isle of France?

                                                                J ADAMS
Enclosed is the Permit signed for the Brig. Amazon to carry Passengers to France, sent me in yours of 26 Septr.

From John Adams

ALS, RG 59, National Archives

Dear Sir   Quincy, October 5, 1800
    Enclosed are some Packets of Newspapers &c recd from Mr Smith & a private Letter to you which I dared not open.[2]
    I am for sending half a dozen Frigates into the Mediterranean. With great Esteem &c

                                                                J. ADAMS

---

10. Oliver Wolcott transmitted the bill to repay Baring & Co. in Wolcott to JM, Oct. 3, 1800, Miscellaneous Letters Received, RG 59, National Archives.
    1. See the Petition of Adam Babcock to JM, Oct. 3, 1800, RG 59, National Archives. See a memorial from Jacob Lewis, Oct. 6, 1800, enclosed in Adams to JM, Oct. 10, 1800.
    2. Not found.

From John Adams

ALS, RG 59, National Archives

Dear Sir   Quincy, October 7, 1800

Enclosed are Papers recd from Governor Sargeant.[3] I pray you to keep them till I arrive. As they are private Communications to me, I would not wish them to be read by any but yourself. With great regard

J. ADAMS

From Rufus King

LS, RG 59, National Archives

No. 85. (duplicate)

Dr. Sir[4]   London, October 7, 1800

I have the satisfaction to inform you, that the Paris papers just arrived, under the article and sanction of official information, state that a treaty of Amity & Commerce between the U.S. of America and France was signed on the first instant. With perfect respect & Esteem, I have the honour to be, Dr Sir, yr. Obt. & faithful Sert.

RUFUS KING

From John Adams

ALS, RG 59, National Archives

Dear Sir   Quincy, October 9, 1800

Enclosed is a Letter from Mr Adam Babcock[5] a respectable Merchant of Boston whom I have known and esteemed for more than a

3. Not found.

4. The duplicate copy of this letter was received by the State Department on Jan. 1, 1801. On the address leaf is written "Charles Lee Esqu, Office Secy: of State, City of Washington, America," "per the ship Harriet, Captn. Orr., via Boston," and "Bristol Octr. 8th. 1800. Recd. under cover to & forwarded by Sir, Your most obed Servt. Elias VanderHorst." See also VanderHorst to JM, Oct. 11, 1800, RG 59, National Archives.

5. The letter from Babcock of Oct. 8, 1800, is enclosed in this letter in Miscellaneous Letters Received, RG 59, National Archives. Babcock wrote to recommend Andrew Spooner to negotiate a treaty with the government of the Isles of France and Bourbon, a market with which Babcock wished to commence trade.

quarter of a Century. Mr Spooner I also know and believe him to merit the Character given him by Mr Babcock. If it should be thought expedient to try a new Experiment at Negotiation with the Isle of France I dont believe We shall find a more proper Person to Conduct it as Agent than Mr Spooner. But I suppose nothing will be done definitively untill I see you at Washington. With great Esteem &c

J. ADAMS

From John Adams

ALS, RG 59, National Archives

Dear Sir   Quincy, October 10, 1800

Enclosed is a Letter or Memorial from Mr J. Lewis[6] late Consul at the Isle of France. I pray you to consider it in connection with that from Mr Babcock in favour of Mr Spooner. I know of no disqualification or demerit in Lewis. He has often called on me since his return, and I think him a considerate and well informed and well behaved Man.

The great difficulty will be to permit the Exportation and Importation of Merchandise. Nothing will be done I presume before my arrival at Washington. But the subject deserves the Consideration of the heads of departments. With great respect &c

J ADAMS

From Elbridge Gerry

Copy, Adams Papers, Massachusetts Historical Society

Sir   Cambridge, October 11, 1800

I have received your letters of the 15th & 25th of Sept, with the accounts enclosed in the former.[7]

---

6. The memorial from Jacob Lewis of Oct. 6, 1800, is enclosed in this letter in Consular Despatches, Port Louis, I, RG 59, National Archives. Lewis offered his services to negotiate with the government of the Isles of France and Bourbon. He had heard that that government had manifested a desire to treat with the United States, and he recommended some measures to effectuate peace between the two countries.

7. The letter of Sept. 25 has not been found.

On the 21st of July 1799, I had the honor of addressing to the President a letter, appealing from the statement of my account made by Mr Pickering.[8]

The salary, which I then claimed, being since confirmed by the just decision of the President, & the ballance due thereon, being as you state it, eighteen hundred & fifty five dollars & 48 cents, shall, agreably to your proposal, be drawn by a bill on yourself, as soon as I can dispose of it.

In regard to the charge by Mr Pickering of 579$ 94 for the passages of myself & servant, I stated to the President, that for 200 or 250 dollars, I could have been much better accomodated on board a packet—*that* the pretext of Mr Pickering for this extravagant charge, was grounded on two certificates, which he had procured from his messenger, purporting, "that the articles *mentioned* as *cabin stores* were purchased at my request" "that many were purchased by my special orders, & would not have been provided by Capt Geddes & himself: & *therefore* one half the amount should be charged to me." *That*, without animadverting on this non sequitur, neither the articles or their prices, which subjected me to this charge, were particularized. *That* Mr Humphreys was also inaccurate in his statement of facts respecting my request, which, as they stood in my mind, were related to the President. *That* finding at Havre neither he, or Capt Geddes could come over from Honfleur, I ordered a purchase to be made for compleating the list of stores, to the amount of about 200 dollars, an account of which has been communicated to the President. That had Mr Humphreys or Capt Geddes hinted to me that the articles procured for my passage to Europe, which I mentioned to the former, were not necessary for the passengers of the Sophia, or that to purchase the same, was not agreable to them; I should have provided stores for myself, Mr Humphreys, Capt Geddes, & my servant, which at the american rates, would have cost but 200, or 250 dollars, & would have exceeded by a third, the quantity requisite. *That* there were daily *seven* subsisted in the cabin, & cabin stores were likewise provided for two persons who did not take passage. *That* 1800 livres, equal to £75 sterling, were charged for grocery, a quantity sufficient for ten cabin passengers: & that I was charged for half of it, of 15 dozn. of claret, & of a hogshead of brandy, whilst my consumption

8. Gerry's letter to John Adams has not been found, but see JM to Gerry, Sept. 15, 1800, and Gerry to JM, Sept. 17, 1800. See also Timothy Pickering to Gerry, June 20, 1799, Pickering Papers, Massachusetts Historical Society.

of the wine did not exceed a dozen & an half & half the brandy would serve me twenty centuries. *That* notwithstanding "the articles were *mentioned* as cabin stores," many of them were increased for the steerage & ship passengers, & were so applyed: & none of them were appropriated to my use. These facts I had stated to the President, & it being impossible that the principle in regard to this particular, adopted by your predecessor, should be approved by me, I have agreably to your proposal, but with reluctance, again layed the subject before the President, & have further stated to him; *that* by the instructions of C. Geddes, he was to obey the orders of the Envoys or either of them, in France. *That* he & Mr Humphreys did accordingly apply to me from time to time for advice & directions on various subjects: *that* my order for stores had not in view my particular accomodation, but that also of the other cabin, steerage, & ship passengers: that my order comprized a number of articles, of which I made no use, but which, in the opinion of the best judges were indispensably necessary, in the excessive heat of the weather, to prevent putrid diseases, which, crouded as the Sophia was with passengers, were to be expected. *That* it was not possible for the cabin & even steerage passengers to have consumed above half a bushell of potatoes & onions *a day*, which was the quantity charged to me, & is but one among many instances of the unreasonableness & injustice of Mr Pickering's statement. Of these the President could not but be convinced, & has given it as his opinion, that 200 or 250 dollars are as many as ought to have been charged for the passages of myself & servant: & that on his arrival at Washington, he will have this matter, & that which relates to the value of guilder equitably adjusted. On this last subject I shall only observe, that Mr Pickering has charged the guilder at forty cents, whilst thirty nine cents were the rate established by Congress. See Volo 1 page 218 of the laws of the U.S.[9] This rule was in force twelve months after the last of my drafts, & altho it is in the act for the collection of duties, it is expressed in general terms, & was undoubtedly intended to apply to all cases of accounts: & if it was just in the former, it must be equally so, in the latter. Moreover, 40 cents was more than was obtained for the guilder at Paris, & altho an act of Congress, raised the guilder, twelve months after my drafts, to that amount, yet had that act lowered it to 38 cents, I must & ought to have been charged 39 cents.

9. Sec. 40 of an "Act to provide . . . for the collection of duties," of Aug. 1790, set the rate of exchange on the guilder at 39¢. The figure was increased to 40¢ effective June 30, 1799, by an act of Mar. 1799. 1 Stat. 167, 673.

If then Mr Pickering has disregarded the rule, he ought not to be supported in an illegal act: for this would be, to participate in it. If nevertheless all the publick ministers, or even those in the same embassy with myself, have acquiesced in this tax & shall not be hereafter reimbursed, right or wrong, I shall make no further objection to it.

When the two last points shall be finally adjusted by the President, please to order my account to be stated & transmitted to me, & it shall be immediately returned with my signature.

Whatever additional ballance shall appear to be due to me, I wish to receive it, if not inconvenient to yourself, by a postnote or order on the branch bank at Boston: it being difficult to negotiate orders on your city. I remain Sir very respectfully, your obedt sert

E GERRY

From Charles Lee

ADS, RG 59, National Archives

Washington, October 13, 1800

Having considered the petitions of Philip Desh and Abraham Shantz and the papers accompanying them the attorney General most respectfully reports it as his opinion, that on account of the ill state of health with which the petitioners are afflicted, they are proper objects of the Presidents mercy.[1]

CHARLES LEE

From William Smith, Jr.

ALS, RG 59, National Archives

[*October 13, 1800, Philadelphia.* Intending to sail to Aux Cayes, on the south side of Hispaniola, to collect debts due his friends and himself, Smith suggests the appointment of a consul there to aid in such business, and he offers himself for the position. He states that he has lived in St. Eustatius and St. Thomas prior to settling in Philadelphia. He asks for advice on whether to approach the president for the appointment. He also requests a passport.]

1. See John Adams to JM, calendared at Sept. 27, 1800.

From Stephen Girard

Letterbook Copy, Girard Papers, Girard College

[*October 14, 1800, Philadelphia.* Girard reports that his brig *Sally*, captured en route from the Batavian Republic by the British ship *Cleopatra*, has been taken to Halifax and condemned because of the claim that Girard is a French citizen. He encloses the notarized holograph opinion of Judge Brenton. Girard has entered an appeal, and he asks JM to direct Rufus King to assist in accelerating the case.[2]]

From David Humphreys

LS, RG 59, National Archives

[*October 14, 1800, Madrid.* In his dispatch no. 253,[3] Humphreys informs JM of the signing of the convention between France and the United States. He concludes with news of English battles, the epidemic in Cadiz, and the change of government in Vienna, which Humphreys thinks indicates an approaching peace.]

From William L. Smith

LS, RG 59, National Archives

[*October 15, 1800, Colares, near Lisbon.* In a letter marked "private," which was received by the State Department on Dec. 25, 1800, Smith relays news of affairs in Europe, particularly the extension of the armistice between France and Austria. If England agrees to a naval armistice, negotiations for a general peace will probably follow, otherwise Austria will probably negotiate a separate peace. Reports are that Malta has surrendered and that the

2. See JM to Girard, calendared at Oct. 24, JM to King, Oct. 24, and Girard to JM, Dec. 26 and 29, 1800. See also Girard to King, Nov. 4, 1800, Girard Collection, American Philosophical Society.

Girard (1750–1831), a Philadelphia merchant, was born in Bordeaux, France. He established the Girard Bank in 1812 and accumulated the largest fortune of any man in the United States up to that time. The judge may have been Edward Brabazon Brenton (1763–1845), who from 1799 to 1817 was deputy judge advocate to the forces in British North America. In 1810 he was appointed judge of the Court of Vice Admiralty in Nova Scotia.

3. The quadruplicate copy of this letter was received by the State Department on Dec. 26, 1800.

English have taken Cadiz, the latter depopulated by the plague. The plague is worse in Seville. A letter from Bordeaux suggests the American envoys in Paris are near completing their mission. He concludes with the news that "Berthier has left Madrid, & the dread of war between Port. & Spain is much abated."]

From Carlos Martínez de Yrujo

ALS, RG 59, National Archives

[*October 15, 1800, Philadelphia*. Yrujo encloses a copy of the sentence of the special district court for the New York district on the case of the *Sandwich*, which upheld his previous statements to JM.[4] The injuries done by Capt. Silas Talbot and his crew have brought harm not only to the Spanish government but also to the owners of the *Sandwich*. Yrujo requests that the owners be indemnified for the losses occasioned by the violence or ignorance of Talbot.]

From John Marsden Pintard

ALS, RG 59, National Archives

Sir   New York, October 16, 1800

The enclosed Protest[5] will explain to you the circumstances attending the capture and destruction of the Ship Columbus James Woods Master, of which I was owner. The papers and documents relative to this Business are daily expected here from the Havanas and when received I shall take the Liberty of forwarding them to you, In order that a claim may be made on the Spanish or French Governments for the value of the Ship and Cargo. If any claim is a just one I think the present comes under that description. I intended to have proceeded on to the seat of Government myself on this Business But the deranged State of my affairs in consequence of this capture obliges me to Remain for the present in this city and I am very fearfull may eventualy Ruin me. Another circumstance has however occurred that may make my Imediate presence there necessary. If so I must go on there, But such a jaunt would at this

4. The copy of the decree is filed following this letter in Notes from Foreign Legations, Spain, II, RG 59, National Archives. See also additional correspondence on the *Sandwich* case.

5. The protest has not been found. JM replied to this letter on Oct. 22, 1800.

moment be very Inconvenient to me. I therefore take the liberty of Requesting the favour of [*you*] to Inform me whether any and what Complaints have been lately made against me as Consul for the United States at Madeira. I am led to ask this f[*avour*] having seen a letter from you to my Brother in law Mr Samuel Bayard wherein you Inform him that it is probable a Vacancy may take place in the Madeira Consulate. Attempts were made last winter from a very Powerfull quarter to Remove me from that office and the papers and documents were laid before the President who thought proper to Continue me in my office.[6] I imediately Returned to Europe on my way to Madeira But on my arrival at Cadiz I found my Private affairs required my abscence from Madeira a few months Longer, lest therefore the duties of my office should suffer by my abscence. I prevailed on my Kindsman Lewis Searle Pintard Esqr. (a native of New York) to go out to Madeira and execute them for me. I called at Madeira myselfe on my way to this Country and Landed Mr Pintard there on the 16th of May last. Since which time I have heard from him and from many of my fellow citizens who have been there and am happy to Inform you that his conduct has Given general satisfaction to them. I hope therefore that If it should [*be*] found necessary to Remove me my Kindsman may be appointed my successor. He is a native American, Independant in his circumstances and his family and Connections well Known to the President and many of our Respectable characters. Concious of having Committed no fault that can justify a dismission from any office, I trust I shall be heard, and feel very confident that I can satisfy the President that the Complaints against me originated in and have been prosecuted with an unparralled malice by my enemies. I shall close this Letter with one Remark on the Conduct of Mr John Leonard who it appears by your letter to Mr Bayard is a Candidate for the Madeira appointment. He obtained a letter of Recommendation from Mr Bayard for a Consulate Intimating to him that he meant to apply for the one at St Lucas or Algesiras. He avails himselfe of this Letter to supplant the Brother in law of his Patron. How Mr Bayard could have Recommended him for any Publick office (Knowing his character) I am at a loss to account for. Mr Boudinot the director of the mint I beleive is accquainted with the character of Mr John Leonard and If he is

---

6. See Timothy Pickering to John Adams, Dec. 17, 1799, Pickering Papers, Massachusetts Historical Society. See also Adams to JM, Aug. 15, 1800, and additional correspondence on Pintard. JM's letter to Bayard has not been found.

contemplated to fill an office of trust under the Government of the United States I feel it my duty to referr you to Mr Boudinot for his character. I shall be in Philadelphia next week where I shall be obliged to you to address me a line in answer to this letter that I may if necessary proceed on to the seat of Government and have the Honor to be with very great Respect, Sir your most obedient and very Humble Servt

JOHN M PINTARD

From Israel Whelen

LS, RG 59, National Archives

[*October 16, 1800, Philadelphia*. Whelen is closing the accounts of the *Hero* according to JM's instructions. Ebenezer Stevens has informed him that John Murray & Son demand $3,543.31 from the United States. If that amount is to be paid, Whelen asks that $3,500.00 be remitted to him. Whelen has consulted with experienced merchants, Thomas Fitzsimmons and Robert Waln, who say that although some of the charges are high, it would be advisable to pay the sum awarded. He would have written earlier had he not been informed that JM was not in Washington.]

From Rufus King

LS, RG 59, National Archives

[*October 18, 1800, London*. In dispatch no. 86,[7] King reports that Parliament is called to meet on Nov. 11 to deal with political and economic problems. Relations between England and Denmark are not markedly improved after the signing of a convention. It is believed Austria will make a separate peace with France, and it is understood that talks between the French and the English are suspended, if not entirely broken off. The supply of corn in England is dangerously low, and prospects for an improved supply are not good.]

7. JM wrote on the verso that this dispatch was received on Dec. 24, 1800.

From Israel Whelen

ALS, RG 59, National Archives

[*October 18, 1800, Philadelphia.* Whelen refers to JM's letter of Sept. 25, in which JM requested that Thomas Thompson ship oars directly to Algiers. Whelen requests that JM supply a list of timber to be sent to Algiers to expedite lading. He urges haste in preparing items for the ship as the season for the ship's departure is fast advancing. Whelen also encloses a letter from Ebenezer Stevens[8] relative to a cargo for Tunis and requests JM's instructions in this case.]

To Commissioners of the District of Columbia

Letterbook Copy, RG 45, National Archives

[Washington], October 22, 1800

The President may be expected in a very few days and Mrs. Adams very soon after. They bring a number of male & female Servants. It will be impossible for them to obtain even temporary accomodations for so large a family should not the President's House be prepared for their reception.[9]

It appears then really important, that you should put as many Workmen as can work in it, on that House for one Week, that the apartments intended to be occupied, may be finished time enough to be cleaned and aired before the arrival of Mrs. Adams. In the present Scarcity of good Workmen, it is to be lamented, that any should have left the Presidents House. We are certain that the President himself would not be dissatisfied if the little houses in his Neighbourhood should remain this Winter and the intended removal of these houses we understand is the cause of the Workmen's leaving the work. Cannot you yield this point? We are willing to take upon ourselves the responsibility.

Pray suffer no more painting to be done in any Part of the house.

JOHN MARSHALL
BEN. STODDERT

8. The letter of Stevens to Whelen, Sept. 30, 1800, is filed following this letter in Miscellaneous Letters Received, RG 59, National Archives.

9. John Adams arrived on Nov. 1, and after spending his first night in the "President's house," he described it only as "habitable." John Adams to Abigail Adams, Nov. 2, 1800, Adams Papers, Massachusetts Historical Society.

From David Humphreys

LS, RG 59, National Archives

[*October 22, 1800, Madrid.* In his dispatch no. 254, Humphreys encloses letters relating to the case of the *Eliza* of Charleston.[1] The *Eliza* had been detained by the tribunal of commerce at St. Sebastian under the charge that Webster Brown, master, had a design of running away with and defrauding the legal owners of their property. Humphreys transmits the documents pertaining to the case so that it may be considered in the United States. Humphreys adds in a postscript that the American envoys have notified him that they signed the convention between the United States and France on Sept. 30.]

To John Marsden Pintard

Copy, RG 59, National Archives

Sir   Washington, October 22, 1800

I have just Received your letter of the 16th instant enclosing a protest on account of the Capture of the Columbus. This is one among many depredations committed by Spanish cruizers for which compensation will certainly be demanded by the Government of the United States. On this act your attendance at this place will be entirely unnecessary, as the same measure will be taken on the protest as would [*be*] adopted in your personal application. [*It*] is probable Commissioners may be appointed to adjust the claims of american citizens on the Spanish Government and it will I think be advisable for you to preserve the documents that the Privateer was Spanish and fitted out in a Spanish Port until it shall be Known what proceedings are to be had in such cases.

There have been serious complaints against you as Consul at Madeira, one of these was your abscence from that Port. Your removal was contemplated, but in Consequence of Mr Bayards letter to me all further procedings in your case were suspended.

No application for the office has been made by Mr Leonard nor

---

1. The six enclosures to this letter are filed following it in Consular Despatches, Cadiz, I, RG 59, National Archives. The duplicate copy of this letter was received by the State Department on Dec. 24, 1800.

have I ever seen or heard from him, in looking over the past recommendations for consulates I perceived a letter from Mr Bayard[2] in favour of Mr Leonard and in consequence of the respectability of the Recommendation I wrote to Mr Bayard concerning him.

The President will not act in the case til you have an opportunity of explaining fully any circumstance which may have been alledged against you.[3] I am Sir very Respectfully your Obt S.

(Signed) JOHN MARSHALL

From Commissioners of the
District of Columbia

Letterbook Copy, RG 42, National Archives

Gentlemen,   Washington, October 24, 1800
The few workmen who had quitted their work having returned the same day on which we had the honor of yours of the 22d, it seems to us unnecessary to take any further Measures respecting them. We shall however direct a communication to be made of the Contents of your letter, to such of these Workmen as are in the temporary Buildings, as have quitted the Works. We shall in the mean time increase the Hands by every means in our power, and shall have six additional Carpenters to Day at twelve OClock. We are, with sentiments &c

G. SCOTT
W. THORNTON

To Stephen Girard

ALS, Girard Papers, Girard College

[*October 24, 1800, Washington.* JM sends Girard copies of his letter to Rufus King of this same date, asking him to forward them to King along with his oath of citizenship if one was ever certified. He also asks Girard to send King a copy of Judge Brenton's opinion.]

2. Not found.
3. Pintard replied to this letter on Nov. 7, 1800.

To Rufus King

LS, RG 59, National Archives

No. 9.

Dear Sir   Washington, October 24, 1800

Mr. Girard, a merchant of Philadelphia, whose vessel, the Sally, was captured on her passage from Batavia, and condemned in Halifax, has appealed from the decision of the Judge of Vice Admiralty in America, and requests the interposition of this Department to aid the prosecution of his appeal.

You will much oblige me by giving to his case such attention as your situation will admit.

Mr. Girard appears to have been born in France, and to have removed to the United States in '74, where he has ever since resided and carried on trade, as a citizen of the United States.

I perceive no pretext for considering this gentleman as a frenchman, and cannot doubt the reversal of the sentence of the Court of Vice Admiralty in Halifax. I am, dear sir, with much respect & esteem, your obed. servt.

J MARSHALL

From Robert Liston

AL, RG 59, National Archives

Solitude, near Philadelphia, October 25, 1800

R. Liston presents his respects to General Marshall, Secretary of State.

You will see, Sir, by the enclosed papers, that a person of the name of Jameson, detained in prison at Montreal, is liable to be delivered upon demand by His Majesty's Government of Lower Canada, in conformity to the Treaty of 1794, he being charged with the crime of forgery committed within the jurisdiction of the United States.[4]

---

4. Thomas Jameson (b. *ca.* 1768) was accused of forgery in the state of New York and under art. 27 of the Jay Treaty was liable to be extradited from Canada to the United States. For the text of the article, see Miller, ed., *Treaties*, II, 263.

The documents are not enclosed with this letter, although copies are enclosed in JM to John Jay, Nov. 5, 1800. For more information on the Jameson case, see Jay to JM, Nov. 15, JM to Robert Shore Milnes, Nov. 28, and JM to Jay, Nov. 28, 1800.

The Magistrates of Montreal, regarding the matter in this point of view, gave notice of the man's detention to those of New York (through the medium of the British Consul General for the Eastern States) not doubting that a formal requisition would forthwith be made of his surrendry to justice, and confident at the same time that no objections would be made to a compliance with the terms of the Treaty on the part of the King's Governor of the Province.

Some difficulty or hesitation appears however to have taken place on the subject in the State of New York. No demand has been made that the offender be given up; and the Judges of the District of Montreal begin to think that they have not power to keep him longer in confinement.

The regular channel of communication on this occasion would perhaps have been between the Federal Administration of the United States and the provincial Government of Canada, rather than between Magistrates of an inferior order. Governor Jay appears to lean to this opinion; and if you, Sir, hold the same sentiments, I beg leave to suggest the expediency of laying the case before the President, and obtaining his resolution, with the least possible delay, that the essential purposes of publick justice may not be defeated by the defect of form. You may of course command any interposition of mine that may be deemed requisite.

To Caleb P. Wayne

ALS, Dreer Collection, Historical Society of Pennsylvania

Sir   Washington, October 25, 1800

I receivd while in Virginia your letter of the 3d. inst. which I have forwarded to Mr. Washington. Shoud he write to me on the subject you shall immediately receive any communication he may make. I am Sir very respectfully, Your Obedt. Servt.

J MARSHALL

From Rufus King

LS, RG 59, National Archives

[*October 26, 1800, London*. In dispatch no. 87, King acknowledges receipt of JM's letter of Aug. 16 and reports that he has relayed through Lord Grenville President Adams's congratulations to the king upon his "escape from the attempt to assassinate him." Inasmuch as news of the convention with France had just reached England, King thought the occasion of delivering Adams's message suitable "not only to renew the assurance of our friendship, but also to endeavour to discover the temper with which our Reconciliation with France is likely to be treated." Copies of King's letter to Grenville and of Grenville's reply are enclosed.]

From David Humphreys

ALS, RG 59, National Archives

[*October 28, 1800, Madrid*. Humphreys relates news of the plague in Spain and reports that a plan to assassinate Napoleon has been frustrated. Louis-Alexandre Berthier has been named to the post of minister of war. Humphreys encloses copies of Mariano Luis de Urquijo's letter on the plague and of his reply to Urquijo.]

To Benjamin Lincoln

LS, RG 59, National Archives

[*October 30, 1800, Washington*. JM sends a list of 52 Boston seamen who are being held on British warships because they have no proof of American citizenship. In a circular that was also sent to other collectors of the customs, JM asks Lincoln's help in locating friends or relatives who can supply the needed proof. All available means will be pursued to obtain the liberation of any man for whom evidence of citizenship is sent to the State Department.]

From Commissioners of the District of Columbia

Letterbook Copy, RG 42, National Archives

Gentlemen,   Washington, October 30, 1800
    As there are some large Accounts to discharge, on the score of paving, we should be much obliged to you to order the payment of the Balance of the paving Money. We are, Gentn, &c

G. Scott
W. Thornton
A. White[5]

To Richard Peters

Printed (facsimile), John F. Dillon, ed., *John Marshall: Life, Character and Judicial Services* . . . , I (Chicago, 1903), 97

Dear Sir   Washington, October 30, 1800
    I thank you for the book which accompanied your letter of the 24th. inst.[6]
    I beleive with you that much of the strength of jacobinism is attributable to the direct tax—a snare which has been long set for the federalists & in which they have at length permited themselves to be taken. Yet that can not be considerd as the sole cause of the prevalence of opposition. Many others concur in effecting the work.
    I do not however entirely despond. If the Legislature of Pennsylvania will elect by a concurrent vote our case is not absolutely desperate.[7]
    However the election may terminate good men ought still to continue their endeavors for the public happiness. I pray devoutly (which is no very common practice with me) that the future administration may do as little harm as the present & the past. Yours truely

J Marshall

---

5. Alexander White (1738–1804) was appointed commissioner in 1795 and served until 1802, when the board was abolished.
    6. Peters (1744–1828) was appointed a judge of the U.S. District Court of Pennsylvania in 1792. Justice James Iredell and Peters presided at the trial of John Fries, and in 1799 an account of that proceeding was published by Thomas Carpenter entitled *The Trials of John Fries and Others on Indictments for Treason* . . . (Philadelphia, 1799). Perhaps it was either this publication or Peters's book, *Agricultural Enquiries on Plaister of Paris* . . . (Philadelphia, 1797), that was transmitted with JM's letter.
    7. The question before the special session of the Pennsylvania legislature that con-

From Israel Whelen

LS, RG 59, National Archives

[*October 30, 1800, Philadelphia.* Whelen informs JM of the arrival of oars from Thomas Thompson and awaits orders on what to do with them.]

From Commissioners of the District of Columbia

Letterbook Copy, RG 42, National Archives

Gentlemen,   Washington, October 31, 1800

The Board have had frequent applications during this season to repair and make fit for use, the Bridges across Tyber Creek and James's Creek, now impracticable. Our funds are too low to admit our undertaking even these small, though necessary objects. We have directed Mr. Harbaugh to make a Survey of these Bridges, and he reports, that one hundred and fifty Dollars will make them perfectly practicable to Carriages. Small as this Sum is, we have it not to spare, but with your permission, will order the repairs to be done and paid for out of the Fund appropriated to the paving, if any Balance remains after the paving is completed; and should no Balance remain, then to be made out of our funds, when we have them.

There can be no doubt of the utility of these Bridges, and we wish much that they should be immediately repaired. With sentiments &c

G. SCOTT
W. THORNTON

---

vened on Nov. 5, 1800, was whether to choose presidential electors by joint or concurrent vote of both houses. A joint ballot would favor the Republicans, whereas a concurrent ballot might produce a deadlock that would result in the state losing its votes in the electoral college. A deadlock over which procedure to follow almost produced the results JM hoped for, but a compromise that slightly favored the Federalists was finally reached. See Jacob E. Cooke, *Tench Coxe and the Early Republic* (Chapel Hill, N.C., 1978), 387.

From Rufus King

LS, RG 59, National Archives

No. 88

Dear Sir,   London, October 31, 1800

The convention with France having been published at Paris, immediately found its way into the English newspapers, in which it appeared the day after Mr. Ellsworth's arrival in London: it's authenticity being confirmed by him, it became my duty to endeavour with as much diligence, and as extensively, as was in my power, *to*[8] *communicate* such sentiments and opinions *respecting it* as would be likely *to procure to it* a favourable consideration.

After conversing with the Lord Chancellor and some other of the ministers, *I found* an occasion to mention the subject *to the King* and tho' this was not altogether *regular I had* no reason to be dissatisfied with having *done so.*

After waiting several days, during *which I* might see and converse with the persons *about the court I* yesterday asked a conference with *Lord Grenville* which took place this morning. The conversation began *by my* observing that *I* wished to speak with *him* respecting *our reconciliation with France* in order that *I* might communicate *to my government which* would be desirous to understand the light in which *it was* considered *by the British government.*

This Beginning led to a free and apparently candid conversation respecting it which was followed *by Lord G* saying *to me that he* saw nothing *in the convention* inconsistent *with the treaty between them & us* or which afforded *them any* ground of complaint; nor did *he perceive in it anything* that might not have been expected, unless *it was the article* respecting *convoys which we were* certainly free to make, *but which* nevertheless just at the present juncture *had* somewhat *of a less friendly appearance than* might have been wished.[9] *I* expressed *my* satisfaction that *I* had not been mistaken in believing that *the british government* would find *nothing to object to in the convention* and remarked that the article of free Bottoms having made a part of the old Treaty it was natural enough that it should be inserted in the new one, and that

8. The words in italics were originally in code and were decoded by a State Department clerk.

9. For the British reaction to the convention, see Bradford Perkins, *The First Rapprochement: England and the United States, 1795–1805* (Berkeley, Calif., 1967), 126–127.

the Provision respecting Convoys seemed to be no more than a convenient consequence of that Article, by which the visit of the belligerent is not only restrained in it's object, but placed under special Regulations as to the manner in which it shall be made; and moreover *that convoys* would be indispensable to protect *our trade against french* Corsairs in the West Indies, which could not *at present be* controuled *by France.*

Lord Grenville had not manifested any marks of disappointment or discontent *concerning the convention* shewed no inclination to controvert what *I had just said* contenting *himself by* repeating, but without seeming to place much importance upon the observation, what *he* had before said with regard *to their* misunderstanding *with the northern powers.*

As the subject of convoys was before us I thought the occasion not an unfavorable one, concisely to suggest certain Reflections which had passed *in my mind* concerning it, and which are the foundation of the observations contained *in my No. 80.* After some general Remarks respecting the Rights of Neutrals and Belligerents *I* observed that it seemed *to me* practicable to devise Regulations by which the Trade of Neutrals might be secured by Convoys without affecting injuriously the right of search. It might for example be stipulated that no ship should be entitled to sail under convoy, who should not possess a certificate, in an agreed form, attesting her neutrality and the neutrality and innocence of her Cargo; the Consuls or other Agents of the Belligerents residing in the Neutral countries might assist in taking the Proofs upon which such Certificates should be granted; and it might moreover be settled that the visit of the Belligerent should be confined to the convoying Ship, the Commander of which on exhibiting the Certificates of the Ships under his Convoy should with them be entitled to proceed unmolested. Other Regulations might be devised for Places where the Agents of the Belligerent could not on account of the War assist in receiving the Proofs of neutrality.

Lord G without hesitation admitted the fairness of the Project, adding that it would be indifferent *to them* as belligerents whether the examination was made by *their* Agents before the sailing of the neutral Ship, or upon the Ocean by *their* naval Officers.

At the *close of the conference Lord G* spoke to *me* in favourable terms of Mr. Merry the Successor of Mr. Liston, saying that *he flattered himself that we shoud* find him an agreeable man. I mentioned to him that I expected soon to receive farther instructions respecting the Execution of the 6th. Article of our Treaty, and proposed that Mr. Merry should wait till they arrived to which he consented, tho' it was intended that Mr. Merry should have embarked for America in the course of a few days. With perfect Respect & Esteem, I have the honor to be, Dear Sir, Your obedt & faithful Servt

RUFUS KING

APPENDIX
Miscellaneous Papers
November 15, 1799–October 31, 1800

Because much of the correspondence that crossed the secretary of state's desk was largely routine, the editors have listed here only a number of the letters received by the State Department while John Marshall was in office. The letters included in this list are dispatches from consuls and ministers reporting the affairs of their jurisdiction. They are letters of protest from merchants whose vessels or cargoes have been impressed by enemy ships. Some of the letters are reports from bankers who administered United States accounts abroad. Many of these letters may have been handled exclusively by State Department clerks, and Marshall did not specifically write in reply to them.

The letters are listed chronologically by the date they were written. Included in the listing is the correspondent's name, his title, the date the letter was received, if given, and whether the letter was a copy, an autograph letter signed (ALS), or a signed copy (LS). Since many copies of the same letter were often sent to ensure the arrival of at least one of them, the particular letter that was received first is noted when known.

Most of these letters are in Record Group 59 in the National Archives. If a letter is not in this record group, its location is specifically stated following its description.

Since the slowness of ocean travel caused a lengthy time lapse between the dispatch and the receipt of letters, many letters came to Marshall's attention that were written to his predecessors in office. For this reason, the date the letter was received has been provided when available.

November 15, 1799, John Quincy Adams, U.S. minister, Germany
    (Berlin), received June 29, 1800, LS.
November 19, 1799, David Humphreys, U.S. minister, Spain (Madrid),
    received June 4, 1800, ALS (triplicate).
November 29, 1799, John Quincy Adams, U.S. minister, Germany
    (Berlin), received June 29, 1800, ALS.
January 12, 1800, William Vans Murray, U.S. minister, the Netherlands
    (The Hague), received May 1800, ALS.
January 14, 1800, John Quincy Adams, U.S. minister, Germany (Berlin),
    received June 29, 1800, LS (duplicate).
January 14, 1800, William Vans Murray, U.S. minister, the Netherlands
    (The Hague), received May 1800, ALS.
January 31, 1800, Frederick J. Wichelhausen, U.S. consul, Germany
    (Bremen), received July 3, 1800, ALS.

February 1, 1800, David Humphreys, U.S. minister, Spain (Madrid), received May 12, 1800, LS.

February 2, 1800, William Vans Murray, U.S. minister, the Netherlands (The Hague), ALS.

February 4, 1800, Willink, Van Staphorst & Hubbard, bankers, the Netherlands (Amsterdam), received July 23, 1800, LS.

February 6, 1800, William Vans Murray, U.S. minister, the Netherlands (The Hague), received May 1800, ALS.

February 10, 1800, Oliver Ellsworth and William R. Davie, U.S. envoys, France (Paris), LS.

February 13, 1800, William Vans Murray, U.S. minister, the Netherlands (The Hague), received July 20, 1800, ALS (triplicate).

February 15, 1800, Willink, Van Staphorst & Hubbard, bankers, the Netherlands (Amsterdam), received May 27, 1800, LS (triplicate).

March 1, 1800, Richard O'Brien, U.S. consul, Algiers, received December 24, 1800, ALS.

March 8, 1800, James Simpson, U.S. consul, Morocco (Tangier), received November 23, 1800, ALS.

March 10, 1800, William Vans Murray, U.S. minister, the Netherlands (The Hague), letterbook copy, Murray Papers, Pierpont Morgan Library.

March 10, 1800, Richard O'Brien, U.S. consul, Algiers, ALS.

March 11, 1800, Richard O'Brien, U.S. consul, Algiers, copy.

March 12, 1800, David Humphreys, U.S. minister, Spain (Madrid), received May 16, 1800, ALS.

March 12, 1800, Richard O'Brien, U.S. consul, Algiers, copy.

March 13, 1800, Rufus King, U.S. minister, England (London), received June 24, 1800, ALS (duplicate).

March 13, 1800, Moses Young, U.S. consul, Spain (Madrid), received July 10, 1800, copy (duplicate).

March 14, 1800, David Humphreys, U.S. minister, Spain (Madrid), received July 10, 1800, LS (quadruplicate).

March 15, 1800, Richard O'Brien, U.S. consul, Algiers, copy.

March 16, 1800, John Elmslie, U.S. consul, South Africa (Cape Town), received July 25, 1800, ALS.

March 17, 1800, Richard O'Brien, U.S. consul, Algiers, ALS.

March 18, 1800, Richard O'Brien, U.S. consul, Algiers, ALS.

March 20, 1800, Richard O'Brien, U.S. consul, Algiers, received December 29, 1800, ALS.

March 21, 1800, James L. Cathcart, U.S. consul, Tripoli, letterbook copy, Cathcart Papers, Library of Congress.

March 31, 1800, Stephen Cathalan, U.S. consul, France (Marseilles), received September 16, 1800, ALS.

April 1, 1800, David Lenox, U.S. agent, England (London), received July 23, 1800, copy (triplicate).

April 2, 1800, John Bulkeley & Son, merchants, Portugal (Lisbon), received June 6, 1800, copy.

April 3, 1800, William Vans Murray, U.S. minister, the Netherlands (The Hague), letterbook copy, Murray Papers, Pierpont Morgan Library.

April 3, 1800, Josef Yznardy, U.S. consul, Spain (Cadiz), ALS.

April 7, 1800, David Lenox, U.S. agent, England (London), copy (triplicate).

April 11, 1800, David Humphreys, U.S. minister, Spain (Madrid), received July 2, 1800, copy (duplicate).

April 14, 1800, William Eaton, U.S. consul, Tunis, ALS.

April 18, 1800, James L. Cathcart, U.S. consul, Tripoli, copy (duplicate).

April 19, 1800, Richard O'Brien, U.S. consul, Algiers, ALS.

April 19, 1800, Benjamin H. Phillips, U.S. consul, Curaçao, letterbook copy, RG 84.

April 20, 1800, William L. Smith, U.S. minister, Portugal (Lisbon), received June 28, 1800, ALS.

April 23, 1800, Rufus King, U.S. minister, England (London), received July 23, 1800, ALS (duplicate).

April 25, 1800, David Humphreys, U.S. minister, Spain (Madrid), received July 29, 1800, ALS.

April 25, 1800, Richard O'Brien, U.S. consul, Algiers, ALS.

April 26, 1800, William L. Smith, U.S. minister, Portugal (Lisbon), received July 28, 1800, ALS.

April 28, 1800, Josef Yznardy, U.S. consul, Spain (Cadiz), received July 12, 1800, copy.

May 1, 1800, Sylvanus Bourne, U.S. consul general, the Netherlands (Amsterdam), ALS.

May 1, 1800, Josef Yznardy, U.S. consul, Spain (Cadiz), received July 10, 1800, copy.

May 4, 1800, James Simpson, U.S. consul, Morocco (Tangier), received August 21, 1800, ALS.

May 5, 1800, John Bulkeley & Son, merchants, Portugal (Lisbon), received July 19, 1800, copy.

May 6, 1800, William L. Smith, U.S. minister, Portugal (Lisbon), received July 19, 1800, LS.

May 7, 1800, William Eaton, U.S. consul, Tunis, ALS.

May 7, 1800, William L. Smith, U.S. minister, Portugal (Lisbon), received July 23, 1800, LS.

May 8, 1800, Rufus King, U.S. minister, England (London), received August 9, 1800, LS.

May 8, 1800, Edward Stevens, U.S. consul general, Santo Domingo (Cape François), ALS.

May 9, 1800, David Humphreys, U.S. minister, Spain (Madrid),
    received July 22, 1800, ALS.
May 11, 1800, William Eaton, U.S. consul, Tunis, ALS.
May 12, 1800, James L. Cathcart, U.S. consul, Tripoli, ALS.
May 12, 1800, William Savage, U.S. agent, Jamaica (Kingston),
    received July 11, 1800, ALS.
May 14, 1800, Job Wall, U.S. consul, Guadeloupe (St. Bartholomew),
    ALS.
May 14, 1800, William Willis, U.S. consul, Spain (Barcelona), received
    July 2, 1800, LS.
May 15, 1800, James L. Cathcart, U.S. consul, Tripoli, ALS (triplicate).
May 16, 1800, Richard O'Brien, U.S. consul, Algiers, ALS.
May 20, 1800, John Bulkeley & Son, merchants, Portugal (Lisbon), copy.
May 20, 1800, David Humphreys, U.S. minister, Spain (Madrid), ALS.
May 24, 1800, John Quincy Adams, U.S. minister, Germany (Berlin),
    LS.
May 24, 1800, Edward Stevens, U.S. consul general, Santo Domingo
    (Cape François), received July 22, 1800, ALS.
May 27, 1800, James L. Cathcart, U.S. consul, Tripoli, ALS (triplicate).
May 28, 1800, Edward Stevens, U.S. consul general, Santo Domingo
    (Cape François), received June 20, 1800, ALS.
May 29, 1800, John Davis, merchant, Massachusetts (Dighton), LS,
    RG 76.
May 29, 1800, James Simpson, U.S. consul, Morocco (Tangier), ALS.
May 29, 1800, Josef Yznardy, U.S. consul, Spain (Cadiz), received
    August 7, 1800, LS.
May 30, 1800, James L. Cathcart, U.S. consul, Tripoli, letterbook copy,
    Cathcart Papers, Library of Congress.
June 1, 1800, William Eaton, U.S. consul, Tunis, ALS.
June 2, 1800, Rufus King, U.S. minister, England (London), received
    August 28, 1800, LS.
June 4, 1800, William L. Smith, U.S. minister, Portugal (Lisbon), ALS.
June 5, 1800, William Savage, U.S. agent, Jamaica (Kingston), copy
    (triplicate).
June 6, 1800, Job Wall, U.S. consul, Guadeloupe (St. Bartholomew),
    received July 17, 1800, ALS.
June 7, 1800, Thomas Appleton, U.S. consul, Italy (Leghorn), letterbook
    copy, RG 84.
June 7, 1800, James Simpson, U.S. consul, Morocco (Tangier), received
    September 3, 1800, ALS.
June 7, 1800, Ebenezer Stevens, purveyor, New York, received June 12,
    1800, LS.
June 9, 1800, Christopher Griffing, merchant, Connecticut (New
    London), ALS, RG 76.

June 11, 1800, John Quincy Adams, U.S. minister, Germany (Berlin), received September 14, 1800, ALS.

June 11, 1800, Rufus King, U.S. minister, England (London), ALS.

June 13, 1800, William Savage, U.S. agent, Jamaica (Kingston), ALS (triplicate).

June 16, 1800, William Eaton, U.S. consul, Tunis, ALS.

June 18, 1800, Frederick J. Wichelhausen, U.S. consul, Germany (Bremen), letterbook copy, RG 84.

June 21, 1800, Benjamin H. Phillips, U.S. consul, Curaçao, letterbook copy, RG 84.

June 23, 1800, William L. Smith, U.S. minister, Portugal (Lisbon), received August 20, 1800, ALS (duplicate).

June 24, 1800, John Quincy Adams, U.S. minister, Germany (Berlin), ALS.

June 24, 1800, Thomas Appleton, U.S. consul, Italy (Leghorn), letterbook copy, RG 84.

June 24, 1800, William Eaton, U.S. consul, Tunis, ALS.

June 27, 1800, David Humphreys, U.S. minister, Spain (Madrid), received August 26, 1800, LS (duplicate).

June 27, 1800, William L. Smith, U.S. minister, Portugal (Lisbon), ALS.

June 27, 1800, Frederick Wallaston, U.S. consul, Italy (Genoa), LS.

June 28, 1800, John Quincy Adams, U.S. minister, Germany (Berlin), LS.

June 28, 1800, William Eaton, U.S. consul, Tunis, ALS.

June 30, 1800, Willink, Van Staphorst & Hubbard, bankers, the Netherlands (Amsterdam), LS.

July 3, 1800, David Lenox, U.S. agent, England (London), received September 20, 1800, ALS.

July 4, 1800, William Eaton, U.S. consul, Tunis, LS.

July 4, 1800, Andrew Ellicott, surveyor, Pennsylvania (Philadelphia), ALS, RG 76.

July 5, 1800, John Quincy Adams, U.S. minister, Germany (Berlin), ALS.

July 5, 1800, Benjamin H. Phillips, U.S. consul, Curaçao, letterbook copy, RG 84.

July 7, 1800, Rufus King, U.S. minister, England (London), received September 14, 1800, ALS.

July 8, 1800, Richard O'Brien, U.S. consul, Algiers, received December 23, 1800, ALS.

July 9, 1800, William Vans Murray, U.S. envoy, France (Paris), ALS.

July 12, 1800, Ebenezer Stevens, purveyor, New York, LS.

July 13, 1800, William Cooper, U.S. representative, New York (Cooperstown), ALS.

July 14, 1800, William Savage, U.S. agent, Jamaica (Kingston), received September 3, 1800, copy.

July 14, 1800, James Simpson, U.S. consul, Morocco (Tangier), copy.

July 15, 1800, John Quincy Adams, U.S. minister, Germany (Berlin), received November 4, 1800, ALS.

July 16, 1800, Bird, Savage & Bird, bankers, Portugal (Lisbon), ALS.

July 17, 1800, Thomas Appleton, U.S. consul, Italy (Leghorn), letterbook copy, RG 84.

July 17, 1800, William Armstrong, merchant, New York, ALS, RG 76.

July 18, 1800, Rufus King, U.S. minister, England (London), received September 21, 1800, copy (duplicate).

July 18, 1800, William Savage, U.S. agent, Jamaica (Kingston), received October 2, 1800, ALS.

July 19, 1800, Richard O'Brien, U.S. consul, Algiers, copy.

July 21, 1800, William Eaton, U.S. consul, Tunis, ALS.

July 21, 1800, Samuel Hodgdon, intendant of military stores, Pennsylvania (Philadelphia), letterbook copy, RG 92.

July 21, 1800, Willink, Van Staphorst & Hubbard, bankers, the Netherlands (Amsterdam), LS (duplicate).

July 25, 1800, Sylvanus Bourne, U.S. consul general, the Netherlands (Amsterdam), draft, Duke University Library.

July 25, 1800, Thomas Welsh, Jr., secretary to U.S. minister, Germany (Berlin), received November 4, 1800, ALS.

July 26, 1800, Samuel Hodgdon, intendant of military stores, Pennsylvania (Philadelphia), letterbook copy, RG 92.

[July–August] 1800, Richard O'Brien, U.S. consul, Algiers, received December 23, 1800, ALS.

August 1, 1800, William Eaton, U.S. consul, Tunis, ALS.

August 2, 1800, Benjamin H. Phillips, U.S. consul, Curaçao, letterbook copy, RG 84.

August 2, 1800, Edward Stevens, U.S. consul general, Santo Domingo (Cape François), received September 18, 1800, ALS (duplicate).

August 6, 1800, Rufus King, U.S. minister, England (London), received September 30, 1800, ALS (duplicate).

August 8, 1800, Anthony Terry, vice-consul, Spain (Cadiz), LS.

August 9, 1800, Rogers & Owings, merchants, Maryland (Baltimore), ALS, RG 76.

August 10, 1800, Sylvanus Bourne, U.S. consul general, the Netherlands (Amsterdam), draft, Duke University Library.

August 12, 1800, Archibald Crary & Son, merchants, Rhode Island (Newport), received August 22, 1800, ALS, RG 76.

August 12, 1800, Gibbs & Channing, merchants, Rhode Island (Newport), received August 22, 1800, ALS, RG 76.

August 12, 1800, Rufus King, U.S. minister, England (London), received November 10, 1800, LS.

August 13, 1800, William L. Smith, U.S. minister, Portugal (Lisbon), received October 14, 1800, LS.

August 14, 1800, James L. Cathcart, U.S. consul, Tripoli, ALS
  (triplicate).

August 14, 1800, Edward Stevens, U.S. consul general, Santo Domingo
  (Cape François), LS (duplicate).

August 15, 1800, John Price, deputy collector, Maryland (Baltimore),
  ALS.

August 16, 1800, Richard O'Brien, U.S. consul, Algiers, ALS (triplicate).

August 16, 1800, William L. Smith, U.S. minister, Portugal (Lisbon),
  received *ca.* October 1, 1800, LS.

August 17, 1800, William L. Smith, U.S. minister, Portugal (Lisbon),
  received October 25, 1800, LS.

August 18, 1800, Robert Liston, British consul, Pennsylvania
  (Philadelphia), AL.

August 20, 1800, John Mitchell, merchant, France (Paris), ALS, RG 76.

August 21, 1800, Richard O'Brien, U.S. consul, Algiers, ALS.

August 21, 1800, William Savage, U.S. agent, Jamaica (Kingston),
  received October 3, 1800, ALS.

August 22, 1800, James L. Cathcart, U.S. consul, Tripoli, ALS.

August 23, 1800, William Savage, U.S. agent, Jamaica (Kingston), ALS.

August 23, 1800, Josef Yznardy, U.S. agent, Cuba (Havana), LS.

August 24, 1800, James McHenry, Maryland (Baltimore), draft.

August 25, 1800, Daniel Cotton, ship owner, New York, received
  August 29, 1800, ALS.

August 25, 1800, Edward Thornton, British secretary of legation,
  Washington, D.C., AL.

August 25, 1800, Frederick J. Wichelhausen, U.S. consul, Germany
  (Bremen), received October 30, 1800, ALS (duplicate).

August 26, 1800, Ebenezer Stevens, purveyor, New York, received
  August 29, 1800, LS.

August 28, 1800, Thomas Appleton, U.S. consul, Italy (Leghorn),
  letterbook copy, RG 84.

August 28, 1800, Sylvanus Bourne, U.S. consul general, the Netherlands
  (Amsterdam), ALS, Adams Papers, Massachusetts Historical
  Society.

August 30, 1800, David Matthew Clarkson, U.S. agent, St. Christopher,
  received October 3, 1800, ALS.

August 30, 1800, James Simpson, U.S. consul, Morocco (Tangier), ALS.

September 2, 1800, William Eaton, U.S. consul, Tunis, received
  November 11, 1800, ALS.

September 2, 1800, Rufus King, U.S. minister, England (London),
  received October 23, 1800, LS (duplicate).

September 3, 1800, Josef Yznardy, merchant, Maryland (Baltimore),
  received September 4, 1800, ALS.

September 5, 1800, James Simpson, U.S. consul, Morocco (Tangier),
  ALS.

September 10, 1800, Edward Stevens, U.S. consul general, Santo
     Domingo (Cape François), received October 10, 1800, ALS.
September 13, 1800, Thomas Appleton, U.S. consul, Italy (Leghorn),
     LS.
September 13, 1800, Richard O'Brien, U.S. consul, Algiers, ALS
     (duplicate).
September 16, 1800, Rufus King, U.S. minister, England (London),
     received November 10, 1800, copy (triplicate).
September 17, 1800, William L. Smith, U.S. minister, Portugal (Lisbon),
     LS.
September 18, 1800, David Humphreys, U.S. minister, Spain (Madrid),
     received December 23, 1800, LS.
September 20, 1800, Richard O'Brien, U.S. consul, Algiers, received
     April 2, 1801, ALS.
September 23, 1800, Andrew Ellicott, surveyor, Pennsylvania
     (Philadelphia), received September 25, 1800, ALS, RG 76.
September 23, 1800, Richard O'Brien, U.S. consul, Algiers, copy.
September 24, 1800, Head & Amory, merchants, Massachusetts (Boston),
     ALS, Adams Papers, Massachusetts Historical Society.
September 25, 1800, James L. Cathcart, U.S. consul, Tripoli, ALS.
September 30, 1800, Thomas Appleton, U.S. consul, Italy (Leghorn),
     letterbook copy, RG 84.
September 30, 1800, Sylvanus Bourne, U.S. consul general, the
     Netherlands (Amsterdam), copy.
October 1, 1800, Richard O'Brien, U.S. consul, Algiers, ADS.
October 1, 1800, David Lenox, U.S. agent, England (London), copy.
October 1, 1800, Richard O'Brien, U.S. consul, Algiers, ADS.
October 3, 1800, Adam Babcock, merchant, Massachusetts (Boston),
     ALS.
October 3, 1800, Richard O'Brien, U.S. consul, Algiers, ALS.
October 4, 1800, John Quincy Adams, U.S. minister, Germany (Berlin),
     received February 7, 1801, ALS.
October 6, 1800, William Eaton, U.S. consul, Tunis, ALS.
October 6, 1800, Job Wall, U.S. consul, Guadeloupe (St. Bartholomew),
     LS.
October 6, 1800, Frederick J. Wichelhausen, U.S. consul, Germany
     (Bremen), copy.
October 7, 1800, James L. Cathcart, U.S. consul, Tripoli, letterbook
     copy, Cathcart Papers, Library of Congress.
October 7, 1800, Robert Liston, British consul, New York, received
     October 14, 1800, AD.
October 8, 1800, Richard O'Brien, U.S. consul, Algiers, ALS.
October 10, 1800, Elias VanderHorst, U.S. consul, England (Bristol),
     ALS.

October 11, 1800, Thomas Appleton, U.S. consul, Italy (Leghorn), letterbook copy, RG 84.

October 11, 1800, Elias VanderHorst, U.S. consul, England (Bristol), ALS.

October 15, 1800, Thomas Appleton, U.S. consul, Italy (Leghorn), letterbook copy, RG 84.

October 17, 1800, Richard O'Brien, U.S. consul, Algiers, ALS.

October 18, 1800, James L. Cathcart, U.S. consul, Tripoli, ALS.

October 18, 1800, Benjamin H. Phillips, U.S. consul, Curaçao, letterbook copy, RG 84.

October 22, 1800, Richard O'Brien, U.S. consul, Algiers, ALS.

October 22, 1800, Elias VanderHorst, U.S. consul, England (Bristol), ALS.

October 24, 1800, Richard O'Brien, U.S. consul, Algiers, ALS.

October 25, 1800, Benjamin H. Phillips, U.S. consul, Curaçao, letterbook copy, RG 84.

October 26, 1800, Sylvanus Bourne, U.S. consul general, the Netherlands (Amsterdam), ALS.

October 26, 1800, William Eaton, U.S. consul, Tunis, received March 10, 1801, ALS.

October 29, 1800, Robert Ritchie, U.S. consul, Santo Domingo (Port Republican), copy.

October 31, 1800, Willink, Van Staphorst & Hubbard, bankers, the Netherlands (Amsterdam), received March 11, 1801, LS.

INDEX

Unlike earlier volumes, all index entries are combined into a single index in this volume. All names of individuals, all general subject entries, and all case names that appear in this volume are in the following index. As has been the usual practice, dates of individuals, if known, may be found at their first page reference; if in an earlier volume, the volume number and page reference will follow the name in parentheses.

A